A Learning Republic

How Learning Sustains Individuals
and Constitutional Self-Government

First Edition

ISBN: 979-8-9951005-0-8

Cover art concept by the author

Printed in the United States of America

This book is dedicated to those who desire only to be free individuals in a free society and to fulfill their potential through honest effort.

"To Work is to Pray

—Saint Benedict

"This boy is Ignorance.

This girl is Want.

Beware them both, and all of their degree, but most of all beware this boy,

for on his brow I see that written which is Doom,

unless the writing be erased."

— Charles Dickens, *A Christmas Carol* (1843)

Table of Contents

Introduction

A constitutional republic rests on a single, demanding premise: ordinary citizens, in whom the republic's sovereignty ultimately resides, must remain capable of disciplined judgment. Laws can restrain power. Institutions can distribute authority. But neither can substitute for the intellectual and moral capacities of the people who authorize them. Self-government endures only so long as citizens can evaluate claims, weigh evidence, revise beliefs, and act with foresight.

That capacity is not automatic. It must be formed, sustained, and renewed—generation after generation.

This is the work of a learning republic: a society that treats the cultivation of knowledge and judgment as essential civic infrastructure. In such a republic, learning is not confined to childhood, completed in adolescence, or reduced to credentials. Neither is civic participation time-limited to exclude later adulthood. Each is understood as a permanent obligation of citizenship and a precondition of liberty.

The insight is ancient yet urgent. From the founding forward, American political thought assumed that ignorance and freedom cannot coexist. Jefferson warned in 1816: "If a nation expects to be ignorant and free, in a state of civilization, it expects what never was and never will be." The experiment in self-government required more than elections and constitutions. It required citizens capable of understanding what they were choosing—and why.

The early republic was not tranquil. Trade routes were vulnerable. Empires contended. Systems of enslavement spanned continents. Religious and political conflicts crossed borders. Power was rarely restrained by consent alone. The innovation of 1776 was not the elimination of risk, but its relocation:

sovereignty distributed among citizens rather than concentrated in a throne or aristocracy. Pamphlets addressed the public mind. Arguments were printed, debated, weighed. Authority required persuasion.

This shift imposed a cognitive burden. A republic cannot rely on inherited hierarchy to stabilize disagreement. It must rely on disciplined judgment. Citizens must distinguish assertion from evidence, conviction from coercion, tradition from distortion. Moral teachers have long warned against confusing words with deeds—"By their fruits you will know them," Jesus cautioned. The principle is civic as much as spiritual: symbols endure, but intentions shift. The distortion is revealed not by the slogan, but by the fruit.

A learning republic requires citizens capable of making that distinction.

The world today differs technologically from 1776, but not fundamentally in its exposure to danger. Ideas now travel at digital speed—unfiltered, often unexamined. Children and adolescents encounter persuasive content long before they possess fully developed capacities for abstraction, impulse regulation, and long-range judgment. At the same time, the formation of civic habits has shifted. Where families, local associations, and apprenticeship once bore much of the responsibility for transmitting norms and shared understanding, formal schooling now carries a larger portion of that burden.

Modern political and commercial systems complicate the landscape further. Advanced analytics segment citizens into narrow demographic and psychological categories. Messaging is optimized not for shared deliberation but for targeted persuasion. The result is fragmentation: citizens encountering different streams of information, reinforced by different incentives, addressed as members of distinct political markets rather than participants in a common civic enterprise.

Such conditions do not make self-government impossible. They make it more demanding.

If a constitutional republic is to endure, it must take learning seriously—especially in the early years when foundational cognitive and moral structures are formed. It must also cultivate habits of integration rather than perpetual division. A society that sorts itself endlessly into factions risks weakening the shared reasoning on which sovereignty depends.

What earlier generations intuited has now become unavoidable. Knowledge expands more rapidly than any time-boxed curriculum or credential earned at a single moment can contain. Technological change alters work, communication, and civic life within a single decade. Information saturates daily existence, yet structured understanding grows more fragile. In such conditions, the failure to continue learning is not merely a personal setback; it becomes a civic vulnerability.

This book advances a straightforward claim: the long-term survival of a constitutional republic depends upon sustained, structured, lifelong learning among its citizens.

Part I traces how learning functioned in the early republic, how industrialization reshaped educational institutions, and how access widened while stratification persisted. Part II examines how learning actually occurs—drawing on lifespan developmental theory, dynamic memory research, and cognitive load theory. Part III turns from description to responsibility: protecting developmental windows, dismantling barriers, and fulfilling the civic duty of sustaining competence across adulthood.

This is not an argument against schools, nor a call to return to an imagined past. It is not an indictment of technology nor a defense of credentialism. It is not partisan. It rests on neither nostalgia for apprenticeship nor suspicion of modern institutions.

It is, instead, a call to align educational practice—formal and informal—with cognitive reality and civic necessity. And a reminder that learning does not end with schooling, nor with youth. Just as mass schooling linked education to childhood, industrialization linked productivity to a bounded working life. These administrative divisions brought efficiency and order. But they also fostered the illusion that learning and contribution have natural expiration dates. Absent disability, the capacity to learn, reason, mentor, and create persists across the lifespan. A constitutional republic cannot afford to treat later adulthood as intellectual dormancy.

Lifelong learning is not enrichment. It is the maintenance of sovereignty.

The tools available today—digital access, online platforms, data analytics, artificial intelligence—can expand opportunity beyond what Jefferson or Franklin could imagine. But tools do not guarantee wisdom. Information does not guarantee understanding. Access does not guarantee integration.

The deeper question is whether we will design systems that respect human development, reduce unnecessary cognitive burdens, and cultivate disciplined reasoning across the lifespan.

Independence was not secured once and for all by muskets or declarations. It must be renewed by every generation through learning and sustained vigilance. In a republic, sovereignty resides in the people. And sovereignty without understanding becomes unstable.

The founding itself illustrates this truth. The Constitution established a framework for ordered liberty while accommodating a grave contradiction. Compromises made for union permitted the continuation of human bondage within a nation that proclaimed universal equality. That contradiction erupted in civil war and left consequences that extended far beyond emancipation. The harm was not confined to a century; its effects have echoed across generations.

Among the most enduring legacies was the formal incorporation of racial categorization into the constitutional order. The Three-Fifths Compromise inscribed race into the architecture of governance. Though later amendments abolished slavery and repudiated its legal foundations, the habit of sorting citizens by inherited classification did not disappear from public life.

A republic committed to permeability—movement across economic and intellectual strata—must attend to both ends of the spectrum. It must resist permanent guardrails that shield inherited advantage from competition. It must also resist the quiet ossification of constraint that narrows opportunity before potential has matured.

Neither romanticism nor resentment will suffice. What is required is clarity about how learning unfolds, and a commitment to extending genuine opportunity for cognitive growth at every stage of life.

Regardless of your aptitudes or how you make a living—whether you earned your bona fides at Harvard or Hard Knocks—sustaining a craft, a livelihood, and a place in civic life increasingly requires continued learning in the face of changing technology and society. The arguments that follow are offered with every citizen of the republic in mind.

The work of renewal continues.

We the People of the United States,
in Order to form a more perfect Union
HOLY BIBLE

Part I: The History of Learning and Education in America

Chapter One: Learning Before Schooling

The Artisan Republic

You are walking down the cobbled streets of Philadelphia in the 1720s. The air smells faintly of wood smoke, horse sweat, and fresh ink from the city's presses. You step into a small tavern backroom lit by flickering candles, where a group of tradesmen and shopkeepers gather every Friday evening. They call it the Junto.

Here, Benjamin Franklin—only 21 at the time—sits not as a master but as a fellow learner. Around him are artisans, clerks, and printers, men who work long hours during the day but arrive at night hungry for conversation and improvement. Each member brings questions written out in advance, drawn from Franklin's list of prompts, such as: "Have you lately observed any defect in the laws of your country, of which it would be proper to move an amendment?" or "What beneficial project have you lately heard of, that it would be right to promote among us?" (Franklin, 1791, pp. 97–98).

For its members, the Junto is not just education but empowerment. These modest gatherings model civic learning: no one dominates, everyone contributes, and shared knowledge becomes a form of civic power. More than two centuries later, Franklin's Junto still stands as an early stirring of lifelong learning in America—practical, participatory, and tied directly to improving both the self and the common good.

The Founding — Ideals and Tensions

In the late eighteenth century, most nations were organized around hereditary authority. Kings ruled by succession. Parliaments, where they existed, were limited in scope or access. Social rank was largely fixed at birth. Education might elevate the exceptional individual, but it did not ordinarily confer civic authority on the many.

The American experiment was different. It extended political agency beyond aristocratic lineage and placed sovereignty in the hands of citizens. In a republic, sovereignty is not embodied in a throne; it is divided among the people. Each voter, juror, legislator, and participant in public life exercises a portion of authority once reserved for kings.

That distribution transformed learning from a private advantage into a public necessity. The obligation was not that every citizen becomes a scholar, but that each cultivates his or her capacities sufficiently to exercise judgment responsibly. When citizens deliberate together — bringing varied talents and experiences into lawful debate — the combined reasoning of the republic can surpass the wisdom of any single sovereign. The system presumes not perfection, but preparation.

Learning as a Civic Obligation in the American Experiment

If learning is inseparable from responsibility, then the question is not merely educational but civic. Societies do not educate in the abstract; they educate to sustain a way of life. In the American case, education has never been understood solely as a private good or a pathway to personal advancement, but as a public necessity tied to self-government. The habits of judgment, responsibility, and adaptation formed through learning were assumed to be essential not only for individual success but for the survival of the republic itself.

America has always cherished the ideal of education as a birthright of a free people, rooted in the conviction that a free people must also be a knowledgeable people. Thomas Jefferson argued that universal education was essential for preserving liberty, insisting that a nation could not be both ignorant and free. Benjamin Franklin, less a philosopher than a pragmatist, embodied the same spirit through civic invention. From the start, the American experiment was fueled by a belief that freedom must be matched with learning.

Across American history, each generation has had to learn how to live with new tools, new forms of work, and new social expectations. That pattern is now accelerating. Learning has never been confined to childhood or schooling. What is new, emerging gradually in the late eighteenth century and accelerating across the twentieth and twenty-first centuries, is the expectation that formal instruction, retraining, and skill development will accompany people throughout their lives. In such a world, education can no longer be treated as something finished in youth. It must become a lifelong practice, renewed again and again, if people are to preserve not only their livelihoods but also their capacity for freedom and self-government.

This section traces how that expectation emerged. It follows the American story from Franklin and Jefferson through the Civil War, industrialization, the G.I. Bill, and the digital age, with a particular focus on how technological change repeatedly reshaped what people needed to know and how they learned it.

Learning as a Birthright

From its earliest years, the United States tied education to self-government. The new republic rested on the radical conviction that a representative body of ordinary citizens, not an inherited aristocracy, would make the crucial decisions about laws, taxes, and war. That conviction immediately raised a question: how could a people govern themselves wisely if they were not broadly educated?

Thomas Jefferson (1816) argued that universal education was essential for preserving liberty, insisting that a nation could not be both ignorant and free. He proposed "A Bill for the More General Diffusion of Knowledge" to the Virginia legislature, calling for publicly funded primary schools in every county, open to all free children regardless of wealth. The bill failed, but the principle it advanced—that education was a public right and a civic necessity—shaped later debates about common schools and state universities.

Benjamin Franklin approached the same problem from a practical angle. Rather than theorizing about education, he built institutions for it. His famous Junto club in 1720s Philadelphia brought artisans, clerks, and tradesmen together weekly to read, debate, and propose civic improvements. Members refined one another's ideas and sometimes pooled resources to put them into action, laying the groundwork for projects such as the Library Company of Philadelphia. Franklin's Junto and later the American Philosophical Society were early laboratories of lifelong learning: voluntary associations in which adults pursued self-improvement and civic betterment side by side.

The timing was fortuitous. A new kind of nation, conceived by the people, with a government deriving its authority from the people, emerged just as the growth of human knowledge began to outpace the lifespan of a single generation. The Enlightenment had turned learning and discovery into a social process. Printing presses, pamphlets, and public societies accelerated the circulation and revision of ideas. What had once changed across centuries was now transforming within decades. In the twentieth century, Alfred North Whitehead would give this condition its most famous philosophical expression, arguing that the "cycle of the emergence of new knowledge and the obsolescence of earlier knowledge" had become shorter than a human life. But Franklin and Jefferson were already responding to this emerging reality by building a system of civic education into the fabric of the republic itself—libraries, lyceums, academies, and a call for public schools intended to help ordinary citizens keep pace with continual change. In America, lifelong learning was not an afterthought of modernity. It was part of the initial scaffolding of the American experiment: a means by which each generation could sustain and renew the republic.

The Deliberate Compromise — A Narrowing of Principle

Yet even as they built these civic institutions, many of the nation's leading founders understood that the principles they were articulating outpaced the social realities of their time. Nowhere was this clearer than in the contradiction between universal rights and slavery. No honest history of learning opportunities in America can ignore this contradiction and the impact it has had on so many of our citizens. Many enslaved people during that era managed to become literate despite laws in many slave states that made such teaching and learning punishable by death. Yet, as a result of this tragic history, our nation has been immeasurably blessed by the contributions of formerly enslaved citizens who, once given the freedom and opportunity to learn, established world-class institutions of learning, such as the Tuskegee Institution, and produced some indispensable contributors to our nation.

A significant antislavery current ran through the founding generation. Between 1777 and 1804, seven of the original thirteen states—Vermont, Pennsylvania, Massachusetts (through court rulings), New Hampshire, Connecticut, Rhode Island, and later New York and New Jersey—passed abolition or gradual emancipation laws. Franklin petitioned Congress in 1790 to end slavery; Alexander Hamilton, John Jay, John Adams, Gouverneur Morris (the author of the preamble to the U.S. Constitution), and others publicly denounced the institution as incompatible with republican liberty. Congress prohibited slavery in the Northwest Territory in 1787, signaling that at least part of the new republic would be built without it.

Even the principal founders who owned slaves nonetheless acknowledged that slavery contradicted the principles they had inscribed in the Declaration of Independence and the Constitution. Jefferson's famous reflection in *Notes on the State of Virginia*, "I tremble for my country when I reflect that God is just", captured the moral unease of a generation that knew it had not resolved the problem it had inherited. John Adams, who never owned slaves, wrote that he had held the practice in "abhorrence" his entire life and supported its "total extirpation." Gouverneur Morris called slavery a "nefarious institution" and "the curse of heaven on the States where it prevails."

But those aspirations collided with the political leverage of the Deep South. Delegates from South Carolina and Georgia made clear at the Constitutional Convention that they would reject the new federal union unless slavery received explicit protection. The resulting compromises—most notoriously the Three-Fifths Compromise—granted slaveholding states disproportionate representation in Congress by counting enslaved persons as "three-fifths of all other Persons" for apportionment. Because the federal government relied primarily on tariffs rather than direct taxes, Southern delegates understood that the political benefits of this enumeration would vastly outweigh any fiscal cost.

The Three-Fifths Compromise did more than distort representation. It built racial hierarchy into the very structure of national statistics. The first U.S. census in 1790, authorized by the Constitution, institutionalized a system of racial categories designed to count, control, and apportion power, not to promote learning or opportunity. Subsequent censuses refined and expanded these categories, but the underlying logic remained: Americans would be classified by inherited, immutable traits for purposes of political arithmetic.

The contradiction between the nation's founding principles and the institution of slavery shaped who was permitted to learn, what forms of learning were encouraged or suppressed, and how education developed across regions, particularly in the South. Slavery was not a peripheral injustice; it was a systemic moral failure that stood in direct opposition to the principles of liberty and equality the Founders publicly affirmed.

At the same time, understanding this contradiction requires understanding the stakes the Founders believed they faced. Writing in Common Sense, Thomas Paine warned that "now is the seed-time of continental union," and urged the colonies toward unity, but cautioned that even a small fracture at the founding could weaken the outcome over time—threatening the success of the union while leaving structural compromises whose consequences later generations would be compelled to confront. Paine's intent was not to defend moral compromise, but to underscore the fragility of the moment: without union, there would be no independence at all, and without independence, no future possibility of reform. James Madison made this logic explicit when he argued that constitutional government must be designed not for idealized citizens, but for fallible ones—and that its legitimacy depended on preserving the capacity of future generations to exercise better judgment than their predecessors. The Constitution, in this view, was not an endorsement of existing injustice, but a framework deliberately constructed to survive its correction.

The same political order that protected slavery also discouraged broad-based public schooling in the South. Statutes in Virginia, North Carolina, Georgia, South Carolina, and Missouri criminalized the education of enslaved people. Planters openly argued that educating laborers would upset the social hierarchy. Southern elites opposed not only the education of the enslaved, but also that of the non-slaveholding free population, arguing that educating the laboring classes would elevate them above their condition—making them unfit for the work they were expected to perform and, in turn, "destructive of their usefulness" (William Harper, *Memoir on Slavery* 1837).

This view was echoed by figures such as James Henry Hammond, who maintained that every society required a permanent laboring class "requiring but a low order of intellect and but little skill" (Mudsill Speech, 1858).

In the antebellum South, education was not treated as a universal good, but as a resource to be carefully managed. It was extended where it reinforced the social order and restricted where it might unsettle it. This pattern—of shaping access to knowledge in service of authority—has appeared in many different contexts across time, taking different forms but serving a similar function. The particulars vary—economic, political, or religious—but the underlying logic is consistent: when authority depends on limiting independent judgment, education is seldom left unconstrained.

Public support for common schools remained weak. Where the North gradually moved toward tax-supported education, many Southern leaders actively resisted it.

This divergence illustrates a central theme of this book. Technological and educational change are driven not only by inventions themselves but also by political and moral choices about whether to adopt them. In the North, mechanization and commercial expansion created new demands for literacy, numeracy, and technical knowledge; schooling expanded in response. In much of the South, a plantation economy built on coerced labor chose technological and educational stagnation to preserve a racial and political hierarchy. Both trajectories were shaped by technology, but in opposite ways: one by embracing it, the other by suppressing it.

The founders were flawed, but they were not blind. They drafted principles that condemned their own compromises, trusting that future generations would resolve what they could not. The ideals of natural rights, equality, and republican self-government were not celebrations of the world as it was; they were blueprints for the world as it ought to be. Later abolitionists, educators, and reformers would invoke those ideals repeatedly in expanding the circle of learning, dignity, and citizenship.

The Constitution secured union and stability. It also institutionalized a contradiction between declared principle and lived reality. That contradiction would shape the nation's political and educational development for generations.

Despite Paine's caution, the evil of slavery was thus admitted into the constitutional order not because the Founders believed it just, but because they believed, rightly or wrongly, that union was a precondition for any eventual reckoning. History would prove both the cost of that compromise and the capacity of the constitutional system to confront it. Within less than a century, Americans would shed blood on a scale unmatched in the nation's history to bring slavery to an end. The Civil War did not destroy the Constitution; it tested it. And despite that trial, the constitutional order survived, slavery was abolished, and the nation emerged with a clearer, if still incomplete, articulation of its moral commitments.

Many have described the constitutional compromise over slavery as the nation's "original sin." The phrase captures the gravity of the contradiction — a republic founded on liberty, tolerating human bondage within its legal framework. Yet the language of inevitability can mislead. The compromise was not an inherited stain but a deliberate political choice, made in pursuit of union. Its consequences were real, far-reaching, and costly. But they were not and are not destiny.

This is *not* the story of a condemned republic, trapped by its origins. It is the story of a learning republic — one that has erred, corrected, expanded, and continues the work of aligning its institutions with its principles.

The Artisan Republic: Learning Before the Rise of Mass Schooling

For most of human history, learning did not happen in classrooms. It happened in kitchens, in fields, in workshops, on ships, in courtrooms, and on battlefields. Children learned by watching, imitating, assisting, failing, and trying again. Knowledge was embedded in life. Skill was inseparable from responsibility. Instruction was rarely abstract; it was situated in necessity.

A boy apprenticed to a printer did not study "communication theory." He set type, inked plates, and distributed pamphlets. A girl learning to manage a household did not take a course in logistics. She calculated provisions, managed stores, negotiated purchases, and kept accounts. Learning was experiential, relational, and continuous.

In the early American republic, learning was neither confined to institutions nor sharply bounded by age. For most people, formal schooling was brief and limited in scope, often ending once basic literacy and numeracy were acquired. Historian Carl Kaestle notes that even in New England—where schooling rates were among the highest in the colonies and early states—extended formal education beyond early adolescence was uncommon. Lawrence Cremin similarly observed that schooling was irregular, locally variable, and deeply shaped by family circumstance and geography rather than by any standardized expectation of completion.

Colleges occupied an even narrower corner of American life. At the time of the first census in 1790, fewer than one percent of Americans attended college. Those who did were typically preparing for a small set of professions—most often the clergy, law, medicine, or public administration. As John Thelin documents, colleges were elite institutions serving a limited population, culturally visible but socially marginal to the daily lives of most citizens. For farmers, artisans, shopkeepers, sailors, and small proprietors, college education was neither accessible nor required for productive adulthood. Learning did not flow primarily through classrooms; it flowed through households, workshops, congregations, and civic life.

The dominant learning model of the early republic was therefore experiential and widely distributed. Children learned first within the family, absorbing skills through observation and participation long before they encountered formal instruction. Daily life itself was instructional: tending animals, maintaining tools, assisting with trade, managing household economies. As historian Joseph Kett has shown, apprenticeships extended this pattern into adolescence and early adulthood, binding learning directly to responsibility and contribution. Apprentices were not merely students; they were workers in training, accountable to masters, customers, and community standards. Steven Jacoby's work on apprenticeship systems underscores how knowledge was rarely abstracted from use. Skills mattered because they were tested immediately, refined through repetition, and evaluated by consequence.

Churches and civic institutions provided additional layers of learning. Sermons, public readings, town meetings, and voluntary associations functioned as informal schools of rhetoric, morality, and governance. Citizens learned how to argue, deliberate, organize, and judge not through coursework, but through participation. Kenneth Lockridge's studies of literacy suggest that reading and writing were sustained less by schooling alone than by religious practice, commercial necessity, and civic engagement. Learning was embedded in social roles rather than isolated as a preparatory phase.

Crucially, this system did not draw a sharp boundary between childhood learning and adult learning. Skill acquisition continued across the lifespan, shaped by changing responsibilities rather than age-based progression. An artisan refined technique over decades; a farmer adapted methods in response to land, weather, and markets; a merchant learned new forms of accounting and negotiation as trade networks expanded. Learning was cumulative, iterative, and continuous. One did not "finish" learning and then begin life; learning unfolded within life itself.

This pattern helps explain why early Americans did not generally speak of education as something separate from work or citizenship. The modern notion of schooling as a discrete, time-limited process—completed in youth and followed by occupational stability—had not yet fully emerged. Competence was demonstrated through performance, judgment, and reputation rather than credentials. Knowledge was valued insofar as it improved workmanship, sustained households, and supported civic participation.

In this sense, the early republic functioned as an artisan learning society rather than a schooled one. Learning was practiced rather than accumulated, embodied rather than abstracted, evaluated through consequence rather than certification. Only later, with the expansion of industrialization, urbanization, and state-administered schooling, would learning be progressively detached from work, age-graded, and institutionalized. The artisan republic reminds us that this separation was not inevitable. It was a historical development—and one whose consequences continue to shape how Americans understand learning today.

Apprenticeship as Education

In colonial America, apprenticeship was not a fallback option. It was the primary educational structure for most citizens. A young person bound to a master tradesman entered into a social and economic contract: years of labor in exchange for instruction, moral formation, and gradual responsibility.

Benjamin Franklin's early years in his brother's print shop illustrate this model. He learned literacy not merely as decoding words, but as persuasion, rhetoric, and civic influence. The workshop was his classroom; the public sphere was his examination.

Experiential learning carried several advantages:

- Knowledge was contextual.

- Feedback was immediate.

- Competence was visible.

- Responsibility scaled with mastery.

- Learning was tied to contribution.

There was no artificial separation between "school" and "real life." Life was the school.

Cultural Literacy in a Low-Velocity Society

Learning in the early American republic depended not only on how skills were acquired, but on the existence of a shared cultural framework that made communication, judgment, and disagreement possible. Cultural literacy—common language, moral narratives, historical reference points, and civic assumptions—was not taught systematically, yet it was widely acquired. This was possible because American society in the late eighteenth and early nineteenth centuries changed slowly, was locally cohesive, and was organized around overlapping institutions that reinforced the same ideas.

Families, churches, and civic life carried much of this burden. Children encountered the same stories, metaphors, and moral expectations repeatedly—at home, from the pulpit, in town meetings, and through public rituals. Bernard Bailyn, writing about colonial and early republican education, observed that learning was embedded in social life itself rather than confined to schools. The same biblical passages, classical references, and civic ideals appeared across settings, giving ideas durability through repetition rather than instruction.

This system did not require mass schooling to function. In most communities, a small number of highly literate figures—teachers, clergy, judges, physicians, and merchants—served as intellectual translators. Lawrence Cremin noted that their influence extended far beyond formal lessons. Through sermons, legal proceedings, correspondence, and public debate, they rendered broader intellectual traditions intelligible to ordinary citizens. Cultural knowledge diffused outward through conversation, imitation, and shared participation rather than through credentialed instruction.

Equally important was the pace of cultural change. The range of available texts was limited, print circulated slowly, and competing narratives were constrained by geography and technology. Walter Ong later described this as a world closer to orality than to modern textual saturation. Once acquired, cultural references remained stable across decades. A story learned in childhood remained intelligible in adulthood. Learning did not require constant updating to remain relevant, a condition Elizabeth Eisenstein later showed was fundamentally altered as industrial print expanded the number of texts, accelerated their circulation, and exposed readers to an ever-growing stream of competing interpretations.

Under these conditions, cultural literacy was not elitist because it was not scarce. It was ambient. People absorbed it simply by participating in community life. Disagreement was often fierce, but it took place within a shared vocabulary. As E. D. Hirsch would later argue, cultural literacy does not eliminate disagreement; it makes disagreement possible by ensuring that arguments refer to the same objects, histories, and assumptions.

This arrangement, however, was never universal. Enslaved people were deliberately excluded from formal literacy and civic participation, often by law. Yet, as W. E. B. Du Bois later observed, exclusion did not produce ignorance so much as *dual literacy*. Enslaved and later freed Black Americans learned to understand the dominant culture while maintaining parallel systems of meaning deliberately crafted to be intelligible primarily within their own communities. Cultural literacy, in this context, functioned both as a tool of power and as a form of survival.

Within the free population, however, shared cultural knowledge was broadly distributed and socially reinforced rather than credentialed. That balance began to erode as industrialization accelerated, populations grew more mobile, and communication technologies multiplied sources of information. Robert Putnam would later describe the downstream effects: weakening communal reinforcement and declining shared reference points. Cultural literacy could no longer be assumed. It had to be taught deliberately—or it would concentrate among those with privileged access to institutions and cultural capital.

This shift clarifies a central tension in modern education. Cultural literacy once emerged organically because society itself performed much of the work. As that social scaffolding weakened, schools inherited the responsibility—often without the coherence, authority, or shared agreement required to fulfill it. The problem is not that the importance of cultural literacy has changed. It is that its informal transmission can no longer be relied upon.

In this light, the absence of shared cultural literacy does not level the playing field. It produces a quieter, more corrosive form of elitism—one in which a relatively small group possesses the language, references, and interpretive frameworks needed to participate fully in public life, while others are left fluent only in their own subcultures. Cultural literacy, properly understood, is not a barrier to self-government. It is its precondition.

It must be said plainly, even at the outset, that this account of learning in early America does not describe a shared or uniform experience. Alongside the family-based, work-embedded learning of free households existed a far more severe condition: the deliberate suppression of learning under slavery. For enslaved people, access to literacy, skill transmission, and independent judgment was constrained not by accident, but by law and violence. Yet even under those constraints, learning did not vanish; it persisted through family, faith, work, memory, and quiet acts of resistance that would later fuel one of the most determined educational recoveries in American history. This book will return to that history in depth, because it shaped American learning at every stage that followed. For now, it is enough to recognize that from the beginning, learning in America unfolded along unequal paths—some cultivated, others constrained—yet never extinguished.

Clear Conceptual Separation: Learning ≠ Schooling

The institutions that dominated American higher education through the early Republic were overwhelmingly colonial and classical in origin, shaped by clerical training, moral philosophy, and European aristocratic norms rather than by the practical and technical skills a young, industrializing republic increasingly required (Thelin, 2011; Rudolph, 1962). Colleges such as Harvard (1636), Yale (1701), Princeton (1746), and Columbia (1754) were founded primarily to educate ministers, civic elites, and learned gentlemen rather than engineers, artisans, or industrial workers—a pattern reflected in the institutions established prior to 1830 (Geiger, 2015; see Appendix D). As a result, skilled trades, engineering knowledge, and technical competence were mainly transmitted outside the academy through apprenticeships, guild traditions, and on-the-job training systems that emphasized mastery through practice rather than formal credentials (Kett, 1982; Goldin & Katz, 2008). Reformers such as Seth Luther, Fanny Wright, and Robert Dale Owen criticized this disconnect in the 1820s and 1830s, arguing that American colleges remained bound to inherited European models and clerical authority while failing to serve the civic and industrial learning needs of the broader population (Wright, 1829; Owen, 1848; Luther, 1832). Their critique anticipated later nineteenth-century reforms—most notably the land-grant movement—that sought to realign higher education with the practical and productive life of the nation.

Stratification and Transition in the Early Republic

Even in the early republic, access to formal education was stratified. Elite grammar schools and academies prepared the sons of prominent families for university study, the ministry, law, and public leadership. Most other children relied upon household instruction, apprenticeship, or occasional subscription schools. There was no universal system of public schooling yet in place. Education was scarce, local, and often fee-based.

For free Black Americans in Northern cities, access to these institutions was inconsistent and frequently denied. In response, Black churches and civic associations established independent schools—such as the African Free School founded in New York in 1787—to provide literacy and moral instruction within their communities. In the Upper South, legal and social barriers further constrained educational opportunity for both free Black populations and the enslaved, especially as anxieties over insurrection grew in the early nineteenth century.

It is also important to recognize that slavery did not vanish from the North at once. New York enacted a Gradual Emancipation Act in 1799, freeing children born to enslaved mothers after that date, only after lengthy terms of indenture, and did not declare full emancipation until July 4, 1827 (New York Gradual Emancipation Act, 1799; New York Emancipation Act, 1817). New Jersey followed a similar path with its 1804 Gradual Abolition Act, and a small number of individuals remained legally enslaved there as late as the 1860 federal census. Complete abolition in New Jersey did not occur until the ratification of the Thirteenth Amendment in 1865 (New Jersey Gradual Abolition Act, 1804; U.S. Census, 1860; U.S. Const. amend. XIII).

The early republic, therefore, was neither uniformly free nor uniformly enslaved; it was in transition. Educational inequality during this period did not arise from a universal public system divided by statute, but from a landscape of limited institutions shaped by wealth, status, region, and race. Before the common school movement, inequality reflected scarcity and hierarchy rather than administrative uniformity.

Lifelong Learning and Civic Responsibility In the Early Republic

The early Republic rested on a simple but profound premise: learning and civic responsibility were inseparable from earned work. Free citizens—farmers, artisans, merchants—taught their children through daily life, apprenticeships, and family labor. This model assumed that productive effort grounded individuals in reality, tempered ambition, and sustained self-government.

Yet even in this formative period, two extremes threatened the balance. At one end, inherited wealth—whether from colonial land grants, merchant fortunes, or absentee estates—created a class of idle heirs who lived off rents, tenants, or speculation rather than personal labor. Northern merchant dynasties and Virginia gentry families alike passed down large holdings, fostering detachment and a sense of entitlement that some founders feared could erode republican virtue. At the other end, extreme poverty afflicted many free citizens: indentured servants' descendants, landless laborers in port cities, and frontier tenants on absentee-owned land often lived in chronic want, with little access to education or opportunity to build self-reliance.

Both extremes—unearned wealth and entrenched poverty—distorted the natural alignment of work, learning, and civic virtue. The Republic's founders understood that a stable polity required a broad middle ground of self-reliant, responsible citizens. Extreme concentrations of wealth or want, they feared, could fracture that foundation.

Across American history, investments in learning have consistently shaped the nation's economic strength and civic capacity. From early republican experiments in public education to later expansions through land-grant institutions, veterans' benefits, and community colleges, learning has functioned as a central mechanism through which opportunity and participation were extended. When access to education was restricted or unevenly distributed, the consequences were felt not only by individuals but by the republic as a whole. Understanding this historical relationship between learning, institutions, and civic life provides essential context for the chapters that follow.

Conclusion

This chapter explored the early American Republic as an "artisan republic," where learning was woven into the fabric of daily life through family instruction, apprenticeships, church teachings, and civic engagement. Benjamin Franklin's Junto exemplified this self-directed, collaborative approach, fostering practical knowledge and moral growth among tradesmen and citizens. The founding ideals—emphasizing self-reliance, virtue, and republican governance—envisioned education as a lifelong pursuit, inseparable from earned work and civic responsibility, far beyond formal schooling.

Yet these principles were compromised at the outset: the Constitution's accommodation of slavery, driven by the need for a viable union despite the moral and economic stakes, created profound inequalities in learning opportunities, constraining enslaved people to oral traditions and forced labor while distorting the republic's foundation. Even among free citizens, the era contained the beginnings of two corrosive extremes that threatened the balanced, self-reliant citizenry the founders sought: extreme inherited wealth, passed down through land grants, merchant fortunes, and absentee estates, which sometimes bred detachment and entitlement; and generational poverty, afflicting indentured servants' descendants, landless laborers, and frontier tenants, who faced limited access to education and opportunity. Both extremes—unearned wealth and persistent want—distorted the natural alignment of work, learning, and civic virtue, risking the broad middle ground of responsible citizens essential to self-government.

Despite these shadows, the era's model grounded individuals in reality, tempering extremes and sustaining the republic through productive effort. As the Republic matured, however, new forces loomed. The next chapter examines how industrialization disrupted this natural alignment of work and learning, ushering in common schools and age-bounded education while reshaping family dynamics and economic life—and how the corrosive effects of extreme inherited wealth and generational poverty continued to challenge the republic's foundation.

The chapter highlights the risks of extremes: inherited wealth fostering detachment and entitlement, and generational poverty limiting opportunity—both distorting the self-reliant middle ground essential to self-government. Despite these contradictions, the era's artisan model sustained the republic through embodied, responsible learning. As industrialization approached, however, this organic alignment of work, learning, and citizenship would face disruption, giving rise to common schools and new forms of stratification—developments explored in the next chapter.

Chapter Two: When Schooling Replaced Experiential Learning

Industrialization, the Common School, and the Growing Divide

You are walking through a mill town in eastern Massachusetts in 1830. The rhythmic clack of power looms echoes from brick factories along the river, their windows glowing late into the evening. Children of mill workers and shopkeepers hurry past, some still clutching slates or primers, others barefoot and weary from long hours tending machines or helping at home. In a modest schoolhouse nearby, a lone teacher struggles to manage students of every age, with little more than a few worn books

In Boston, two reformers are watching the same transformation from different angles.

and a chalkboard. The parents, now working twelve-hour days in factories, no longer have the time to teach their children the way their own parents did—through daily chores, family conversation, or apprenticeships in a trade.

Horace Mann, a young lawyer and state legislator in his mid-thirties, sits at his desk surrounded by reports and letters. Born in 1796 to a modest farming family in Franklin, Massachusetts, Mann had already seen the old ways fading. He had taught school briefly in his youth, studied law, and entered politics with a growing conviction: the scattered, poorly funded local schools were failing the children of a rapidly industrializing nation. Parents, pulled into wage labor, could no longer provide the hands-on education once common in homes and workshops. A new system was needed—free, tax-supported, open to all children, professionally staffed, and focused on common learning that would prepare them for citizenship and productive work in a changing economy. Mann's vision was structural and universal: the state must step in to ensure every child receives systematic instruction in literacy, morality, and republican values.

Across the city, Catharine Beecher, an educator and writer in her early thirties, was reaching a different conclusion. Born in 1800 into one of New England's most prominent intellectual families, she had seen the household's educational function eroding as mothers and fathers were drawn into paid labor or domestic burdens. But Beecher believed the solution lay not primarily in state institutions, but in women themselves. Women, she argued, possessed the moral sensibility, patience, and nurturing instinct best suited to character formation. She advocated for the professional training of female teachers who could extend the moral influence of the home into the schoolroom—preserving the intimate, domestic quality of early education even as the industrial economy pulled families apart. Her ideal was not a fully centralized public system, but a network of trained women who could carry forward the formative role once played by mothers in the household.

The death of her fiancé in a shipwreck in 1822 plunged her into grief and redirected her life toward public service. She founded the Hartford Female Seminary in 1823, one of the earliest institutions to offer young women a rigorous academic curriculum rather than the traditional "finishing school" training. Beecher believed that women were uniquely suited to moral and character education, and she argued that training female teachers was essential to meet the growing demand for instructors in the expanding common school system. In her writings, she urged women to embrace teaching as a patriotic and moral calling, extending the nurturing role of the home into the classroom.

Both Mann and Beecher recognized the same rupture: industrialization had separated work from home, and with it, much of the natural integration of learning and family life. Mann looked to the state and a universal institutional framework to compensate for the household's lost educational function. Beecher looked to women—trained, professionalized, and morally authoritative—to preserve the household's formative role in a new setting.

Neither Mann nor Beecher created the transformation sweeping New England in the early 1830s, nor could either have halted it. Each responded to forces already in motion— industrialization pulling parents into factories, rapid urbanization concentrating populations in mill towns and cities, and the widening gap between family life and the demands of a market-driven economy—by championing their respective visions for education's future. Mann believed universal, nonsectarian schooling would equip every child with literacy, moral habits, and republican values, enabling them to participate as informed and productive citizens capable of acquiring skills needed in the emerging industrial economy that industrialization had already set in motion. Beecher believed women possessed the natural sensibility and nurturing instinct to carry the formative power of the home into the schoolroom. Through works like *A Treatise on Domestic Economy* (1841) and *The Duty of American Women to Their Country* (1845), she urged the professional training of female teachers to extend domestic virtue into public education—keeping the intimate, character-shaping influence alive even as the household lost its productive role.

This chapter begins there—not with failure, but with adaptation—and asks what was gained, what was lost, and why those tradeoffs still shape learning opportunities today.

Industrialization

Between the founding generation and the 1830s, the structure of American life changed dramatically. At the time of independence, most Americans lived within an agrarian economy. Production and learning were interwoven. The household was not merely a site of consumption; it was a site of production. Farms produced food, textiles, tools, and trade goods. Artisans worked in shops attached to their homes. Children's labor was economically meaningful from an early age. A young person's path toward adulthood was visible and continuous: assistance became responsibility; responsibility became mastery.

In the founding era, economic production and family life were interdependent. The home was an economic unit. A farmer, shopkeeper, or artisan did not merely earn a living; he governed the rhythm of his labor. Work began at dawn or when necessary. It paused for weather, harvest cycles, religious observance, or family need. Children learned not in abstraction but in proximity. Literacy lessons might occur at the kitchen table between tasks. Arithmetic was practiced in accounts and measurements. Trade skills were demonstrated, imitated, corrected, and gradually entrusted.

The father—whether farmer or craftsman—was not only provider but instructor. Authority over work and authority over education were unified in the same person. This autonomy mattered. Because work was locally controlled, teaching could be woven into it. A boy assisting in the workshop learned not only technique but judgment. A daughter participating in household management learned calculation, negotiation, and responsibility. Instruction was not scheduled apart from production; it was embedded within it.

Industrialization disrupted the family-centered learning structures that had once integrated work, skill-building, and moral formation. As production centralized in mills and factories, the independent artisan increasingly became a wage earner. The employer, not the household head, sets the hours. The bell, not the family, marked the beginning and end of labor. Work became spatially separated from home and temporally rigid. Moreover, the factory economy concentrated extreme multi-generational wealth in the hands of a few owners and investors, often detached from the labor that produced it.

The Founders had foreseen this risk. Thomas Paine, in Common Sense (1776) and Rights of Man (1791), argued that true merit arises from personal effort and virtue, not from birth or inheritance. He warned that systems allowing wealth and power to pass unearned across generations would recreate the very aristocratic dependence the Revolution had sought to abolish. Thomas Jefferson worked to abolish feudal remnants brought over from England, such as 'primogeniture' and 'entail', which were designed to keep large estates intact across generations, thus creating and preserving hereditary wealth and aristocratic power. Adams believed that inherited wealth without labor created idleness and entitlement. In the industrial age, the concentration of extreme multi-generational wealth—often detached from the labor that produced it—revived those old concerns, challenging the republic's foundation in self-reliance and earned contribution.

With the shift from an artisanal to an industrial economy came a subtle but profound reversal: The father could no longer structure work around the needs of the family. The family now structured itself around the demands of work. This structural change had educational consequences. When the artisan owned his tools and controlled his time, he could bring a child alongside him gradually. When he became an employee, his labor was no longer divisible or adaptable. A child could not easily be integrated into a factory floor governed by machines and supervisors. Even when children did enter factories, they did so as laborers, not apprentices under paternal instruction.

The older model assumed continuity between childhood and adulthood. The newer model introduced separation. Work moved outward. Childhood remained inward. The space between them widened. Just as learning became increasingly confined to childhood and formal institutions, productive work was increasingly confined to a prescribed span of years—replacing the lifelong rhythm of contribution with a rigid sequence of employment followed by retirement.

By the 1820s and 1830s, that arrangement was under strain. The rise of textile mills in places like Lowell, Massachusetts, the expansion of canals and early railroads, and the growth of urban manufacturing began pulling productive labor out of the household and into centralized workplaces. What had once been done in kitchens and small shops moved into factories.

This was not merely a technological shift. It was a structural one. When spinning and weaving left the home and entered the mill, the rhythm of life changed. Work was no longer organized around seasons and daylight but around shifts and bells. The clock replaced the sun. Wages replaced barter. The employer replaced the household head as the organizer of productive time.

Children, who once contributed meaningfully within the household economy, increasingly faced a new question: where did they belong? Some entered factories. Others remained at home. But the seamless integration of childhood labor into adult productivity was fracturing.

The cotton gin transformed slavery from a regional institution into the economic engine of the South, dramatically increasing the value of enslaved labor and intensifying the desire to control it. Anti-literacy laws spread rapidly after 1831, following Nat Turner's rebellion, as Southern legislatures sought to prevent communication, organization, or escape. Learning for the enslaved became almost entirely oral and clandestine—passed through spirituals, stories, and covert trades—while formal schooling was criminalized.

At the same time, industrialization pulled Northern families from artisan workshops into factories. Adults, now wage laborers, were less available to teach children at home. The common school emerged as a partial solution—compulsory, standardized education for youth—replacing much of the natural, on-the-job learning of the early Republic.

These shifts magnified the two extremes. Enslaved people and early industrial workers faced grinding poverty and exploitation, fostering resentment and, in some cases, proto-radical responses (e.g., slave revolts, early labor organizing). Conversely, the cotton economy and Northern manufacturing fortunes created a growing class of idle heirs—planters who rarely labored and industrialists' children who inherited vast wealth. This detachment sometimes produced paternalistic reformism or outright radicalism: heirs, unmoored from earned work, could romanticize utopian schemes or fund causes that attacked the very system that enriched them.

The Republic's learning model—once rooted in earned responsibility—was being pulled apart. Extreme want crushed opportunity; extreme unearned wealth risked fostering ideologies divorced from practical reality. Both threatened the middle ground of self-reliant citizens that self-government requires.

Once work left the household, experiential learning left with it. Literacy could still be taught at home, but trade instruction increasingly required entry into industrial systems not designed for paternal oversight. The father's role as economic instructor diminished. His authority remained moral and familial, but his ability to integrate children into productive mastery narrowed.

The result was not merely economic dependency on wages. It was also a pedagogical dependency on institutions. The household necessarily surrendered part of its educational function along with its control over its schedule; if children could no longer learn primarily through participation in household production, then another structure would have to assume responsibility for early formation.

The Age of Jackson and the Democratic Tension

The Jacksonian era (roughly 1820s–1840s) celebrated the "common man." Property requirements for voting fell in many states. Political participation widened. Campaigning became mass spectacle. Newspapers proliferated. The electorate grew.

But widening political participation did not automatically produce widening economic stability or civic formation.

As market capitalism expanded, traditional forms of apprenticeship and household-based learning became less stable. Small master craftsmen found themselves competing with mechanized production. Skills that once required years of hands-on mastery could now be simplified or partially mechanized. The craft system that had anchored experiential learning was slowly eroding.

This is where figures like Seth Luther and Fanny Wright enter the conversation.

Seth Luther, a labor reformer, warned that mechanized production risked reducing workers to "appendages of machines." He feared the loss of skill, autonomy, and independence that had once characterized artisan labor. The "republican producer"—the self-governing craftsman—was giving way to the wage laborer dependent on industrial capital.

Fanny Wright, controversial and radical in her day, argued that education must expand to match the new industrial order. If economic structures were shifting, she said, then education must become more systematic, more accessible, and more deliberate. She saw clearly that the old household-based model could not carry the weight of a transforming society.

Both, in different ways, sensed the instability beneath the democratic rhetoric of the age. The political system was widening participation at the same moment the economic system was centralizing production. This tension mattered for education.

The franchise widened at the very moment when the primary site of civic formation was shifting. In the founding generation, children often absorbed civic norms within productive households where responsibility, contribution, and deliberation were daily practices. By the 1830s, as wage labor separated work from home and schooling assumed responsibility for literacy, civic formation increasingly occurred in classrooms rather than workshops or farms.

Common schools did not ignore moral instruction. Reformers intended them to cultivate virtue and discipline. Yet the nature of formation changed. Instead of learning citizenship through participation in economically meaningful roles, children encountered it through recitation, textbooks, and scheduled lessons. The republic expanded its electorate even as the lived apprenticeship of civic responsibility became less direct.

In the founding generation, civic formation often occurred within productive households. Fathers who governed farms or shops also governed the rhythm of family instruction. Children observed deliberation in practical matters—contracts, accounts, disputes, religious commitments. They learned literacy not only as a technical skill but as a tool for participation. Responsibility increased gradually. Civic norms were not merely described; they were modeled and expected.

Industrialization altered that arrangement. As work moved from household to factory, the father increasingly became an employee rather than an independent producer. The employer set the hours. The bell regulated the day. Work could no longer be adjusted easily to accommodate instruction. Children could not be integrated into factory production in the same apprenticeship manner that had once been possible in farms and artisan shops.

The household lost part of its pedagogical function. At the same time, reformers promoted the expansion of common schools to meet the needs of a growing republic. Literacy, numeracy, and moral instruction could now be delivered systematically to large numbers of children. Exposure to civic ideas became more universal.

Yet the nature of civic formation changed. The migration of civic formation from household to classroom introduced a subtle difficulty: its success became harder to measure. Literacy can be tested. Arithmetic can be examined. A child either reads the passage or does not; either solves the equation or fails to do so.

Civic understanding is different. A student may recite the structure of government, list constitutional amendments, or repeat moral maxims without internalizing them. In a household economy, civic norms were embedded in responsibility and observed in conduct. Disrespect for authority, indifference to duty, or failure of self-restraint appeared not on examinations but in daily behavior.

In the classroom, by contrast, civic learning became increasingly symbolic. Its assessment depended largely upon verbal affirmation rather than lived demonstration. This did not render civic education impossible. It did, however, make its success less immediately visible.

The common school could ensure exposure to civic ideas. It could not measure their adoption the way a family could when a child worked alongside parents in the household economy— where respect for authority, honesty in dealings, diligence in labor, and regard for obligation were visible in daily conduct long before any formal test or recitation could reveal them.

In the older model, civic formation was embedded in lived responsibility. A boy who cheated a customer in the family shop or shirked a chore was corrected immediately, not by abstract lecture but by the direct consequence of lost trust and diminished role. A daughter who mismanaged household accounts learned the cost of carelessness through the family's immediate circumstances. Civic norms—duty, fairness, self-restraint—were not merely described; they were demonstrated, observed, enforced, and internalized through participation in economically meaningful roles. Failure appeared in behavior, not on an examination sheet.

In the classroom, a student might recite the structure of government, enumerate the branches of power, or repeat maxims about virtue without the daily pressure of real-world accountability. The common school could deliver knowledge of civic principles; it could not, with the same immediacy, confirm that those principles had taken root in character and habit. The shift from observable conduct to verbal affirmation made adoption harder to verify—and, over time, easier to assume.

This change made the success of civic education less transparent and more reliant on faith in the system itself. The republic had gained universal exposure to civic ideas; it had lost the direct, familial mirror that once reflected whether those ideas were truly lived.

The Transformation of Home Life

In the founding era, the home was economically productive. Mothers, fathers, children, and apprentices all contributed to household output—whether spinning wool, tending fields, forging tools, baking bread, or keeping accounts. Education was inseparable from contribution. A child learned arithmetic by measuring grain, literacy by reading the family Bible or shop ledgers, responsibility by carrying water or minding younger siblings, and moral reasoning by observing parents negotiate with neighbors or resolve disputes. Work and learning were not sequenced into separate phases; they were interwoven in the daily rhythm of family life. The path to adulthood was visible and continuous: assistance became responsibility, responsibility became mastery.

By the 1830s, the ideology of "separate spheres" began to solidify (Welter, 1966). Men increasingly left the home each morning for wage labor in mills, factories, or commercial enterprises, returning only at night. Women were idealized as moral guardians of the domestic sphere—responsible for nurturing character, maintaining piety, and preserving the home as a haven from the harsh outside world. Children were gradually repositioned not as economic contributors but as dependents in preparation—first for schooling, then for future employment. This shift was subtle but profound.

When productive labor left the home, learning could no longer be embedded in it in the same way. If a twelve-year-old was no longer spinning wool beside her mother, forging nails with her father, or assisting in the family shop, then the experiential path toward competence narrowed. The seamless integration of skill-building, moral formation, and economic contribution fractured. Children no longer saw the full cycle of work—from planning and effort to reward and consequence—unfold before their eyes in the household. Instead, they were increasingly removed from production and placed in a preparatory holding pattern.

The gap between childhood and adulthood widened. Work became something that happened "out there" in the factory or office; childhood became something that happened "in here" under supervision. The household, once the primary site of both production and formation, lost much of its capacity to teach through doing. School began to fill that space—not as a perfect replacement, but as a necessary adaptation to a world in which parents could no longer organize their days around the gradual induction of children into adult roles.

The "separate spheres" construct was not merely logistical. It carried long-term consequences for how Americans came to understand learning, work, and civic responsibility. The republic had once relied on citizens whose virtue and competence were forged in the daily practice of productive life. As that practice moved outward and became time-bound, the foundations of self-government shifted—toward institutions that could, at best, simulate what the home had once provided naturally.

Deskilling in Industry and Its Educational Parallel

Industrialization introduced a new phenomenon: deskilling (Braverman, 1974). Tasks once performed by skilled artisans were broken into smaller, repeatable motions. A worker might operate a single machine component rather than oversee an entire production process. Knowledge that had once resided in the craftsman—judgment, improvisation, mastery—was transferred into the design of the machine or the production process itself.

This economic shift had a direct educational parallel: just as industrial production fragmented complex craft into discrete, standardized operations, schooling began fragmenting knowledge into discrete subjects, class periods, and standardized curricula. Learning was segmented, scheduled, and systematized. Both risked reducing the visible role of individual effort and judgment.

The Widening Gap

"He who proclaims it a religious duty to read the Bible denies me the right of learning to read the name of the God who made me."
—Frederick Douglass – 1845

In 1845, Frederick Douglass captured the stark moral contradiction of the era in a single, searing sentence: "He who proclaims it a religious duty to read the Bible denies me the right of learning to read the name of the God who made me." The words cut to the heart of a growing divide. While industrialization and the common-school movement brought expanded access to literacy and formal education for free children in the Northern states— where tax-supported systems spread, attendance rose, and literacy rates climbed—the same period saw intensified suppression in the slaveholding South. Laws prohibiting the teaching of enslaved individuals to read or write became widespread after Nat Turner's rebellion in 1831, turning literacy itself into a criminal act. The expansion of schooling was never universal. It was selective, sharply divided by region, race, and legal status.

This selectivity revealed a deeper paradox at the heart of the early 19th century. Political participation was expanding— property qualifications for voting fell in many states, campaigns became mass spectacles, newspapers proliferated, and the electorate grew dramatically. Yet at the very same moment, the very mechanisms that had once produced citizens capable of informed and well-reasoned participation were being eroded. Industrial production was centralized, pulling labor out of households and into factories. Household economies weakened as families lost control over their schedules and productive rhythms. Childhood lengthened as children were repositioned from contributors to dependents in preparation for future work. Schooling scaled to fill the gap, offering systematic instruction to increasing numbers of free children. Literacy was encouraged for some, while it was forbidden for others.

The expansion of suffrage came at the very time when the lived apprenticeship in civic responsibility—once embedded in productive household roles—was becoming less direct and less observable. In the founding generation, civic norms were absorbed through daily practice: responsibility, accountability, fairness, and self-restraint were demonstrated and corrected in real economic and familial contexts. As work moved outward and became time-bound, the intimate, experiential formation of those habits shifted to institutions that could, at best, teach civic ideas symbolically through recitation and curriculum. The republic was enfranchising more people even as the social structures that had once reliably produced capable, self-governing citizens were fracturing. The common school could broaden exposure to civic principles; it could not, with the same immediacy, confirm that those principles had taken root in character and conduct.

The Rise of Common Schools

The early American republic did not begin with a system of mass public schooling. Most children learned first at home or in small local schools, and many entered apprenticeships in adolescence. Education was decentralized, relational, and closely tied to productive work.

This model had strengths. It formed skilled artisans and capable household managers. It embedded learning within responsibility. But it was not designed for a rapidly industrializing nation of expanding cities, diverse populations, and widening political participation.

By the 1830s, the first sustained movement toward universal, tax-supported schooling was underway. Industrialization altered the structure of work. Urbanization disrupted traditional apprenticeships. Factories required punctuality, standardization, and basic literacy at scale. Immigration increased linguistic diversity. The young republic required citizens who could read laws, understand contracts, and participate in civic deliberation.

The mid-nineteenth century saw the ideal of schooling translated into large-scale institutions. Reformers such as Catharine Beecher, Horace Mann, and Henry Barnard argued that universal education was essential to moral uplift and civic stability (Cremin 1961; Tyack 1974). Mann's annual reports to the Massachusetts Board of Education championed free, nonsectarian "common schools" funded by public taxation, framing education as a public responsibility rather than a private charity (Mann 1848). Barnard promoted professional teacher training, standardized administration, and state-level supervision to ensure consistency and quality across districts (Barnard 1851). Beecher's Hartford Female Seminary advanced the idea that teaching was a moral vocation particularly suited to women, blending republican ideals with prevailing gender norms (Beecher 1846).

Common schools gradually expanded into graded systems with age-segmented classrooms, standardized textbooks, and prescribed curricula. Local districts consolidated; superintendents and school boards imposed uniform regulations; and emerging state offices of education collected data and disseminated what were increasingly described as "best practices" (Tyack 1974; Katz 1971). In this process, the organizational principles of the industrial age—efficiency, specialization, standardization, and hierarchical control—were deliberately applied to schooling, reshaping classrooms to resemble managed institutions rather than community ventures (Callahan 1962).

Over time, teaching shifted from a temporary civic contribution—often performed by men en route to careers in law, ministry, or commerce—to a lifelong occupation increasingly filled by women. As male wages rose in industry, business, and government administration, men left teaching for better-paid work. Women—often well-educated but barred from law, medicine, and many professional pathways—entered teaching in large numbers (Perlmann and Margo 2001). School boards discovered that women could be hired at significantly lower salaries, institutionalizing a gendered wage gap even as women became the backbone of the profession (Strober and Tyack 1980).

By the early twentieth century, teaching demanded mastery of complex subject matter, ethical discretion, and continual professional growth—expectations increasingly comparable to those of law and medicine—but without equivalent pay, authority, or public esteem (Labaree 2004). Teacher unionization emerged in part as a response to these structural inequities (Urban 1982).

Learning Under Constraint: Slavery and Dual Literacy

"If slavery is not wrong, nothing is wrong."

—Abraham Lincoln, April 16, 1864 (letter to Albert G. Hodges)

Readers may reasonably ask to what extent principal founders who themselves were large slaveholders—such as George Washington and Thomas Jefferson—were genuinely opposed to the constitutional compromise that permitted slavery's continuation within the new republic.

The historical record offers no evidence that either man mounted a determined effort to block the compromise. Washington presided over the Convention but did not publicly challenge its accommodation of slavery. Jefferson, serving abroad as Minister to France, expressed moral unease in private correspondence but proposed no politically viable plan for immediate abolition. Both appear to have accepted compromise as the price of union.

Their opposition, where it existed, was often framed in gradual or future-oriented terms. Jefferson advocated restricting slavery's expansion into western territories and supported ending the international slave trade. Washington later expressed support for gradual emancipation and arranged for the freeing of those he legally owned in his will. Yet neither advanced a comprehensive blueprint capable of resolving the contradiction in 1787.

Many founders seem to have assumed that slavery would diminish over time—perhaps as a result of economic shifts or moral progress. The economic expansion of cotton cultivation after the invention of the cotton gin in 1793 proved that assumption gravely optimistic.

The founding generation was not uniform on slavery. Of the fifty-six signers of the Declaration of Independence, roughly half owned enslaved people at some point in their lives. Of the delegates to the Constitutional Convention, a substantial minority were slaveholders, primarily from Southern states. Yet ownership did not map neatly onto opinion. Some slaveholders, including George Mason and Thomas Jefferson, left written criticisms of the institution, even while continuing to participate in it. Several non-slaveholding founders, such as John Adams and Alexander Hamilton, opposed slavery more consistently.

Few members of the founding generation publicly defended slavery as a moral good; most who addressed it described it as an inherited problem, deferred to future resolution.

The economic maturation of the plantation system shaped not only politics but also education. In the industrializing North, literacy increasingly aligned with economic participation and civic engagement. In the antebellum South, the incentives differed. Plantation agriculture required managerial literacy among elites, but it did not depend upon universal mass literacy for productivity.

As a result, the development of public schooling proceeded unevenly. Wealthier Southern families often secured private tutors or academies for their children. Planter households invested in classical education for sons destined for professional or political leadership. But tax-supported common school systems expanded more slowly than in Northern states, particularly in rural areas.

For the enslaved, literacy was frequently restricted by law. After events such as Nat Turner's rebellion in 1831, several Southern states strengthened prohibitions against teaching enslaved persons to read. Literacy, celebrated in Northern reform rhetoric as a civic necessity, was treated in the plantation system as a potential source of instability.

Among non-slaveholding white Southerners—who constituted roughly 75% of the white population according to the 1860 U.S. Census—educational access varied widely. Some regions developed modest public systems; others relied heavily on local subscription schools or informal instruction. The result was not universal illiteracy, but uneven institutional development that reinforced the feudal-like dominance of the slaveholding elite. Large planters controlled vast acreages of the best farmland, leaving limited high-quality land available for non-slaveholding whites. Many of these whites—estimated at 40–50% of the non-slaveholding population in plantation-heavy areas—were landless or near-landless, working as tenants, laborers on plantations, or in marginal upland regions. This left free whites as economic dependents in a system that prioritized planter interests over broad opportunity.

To be unmistakably clear: this does not imply that the suffering under this system was equal. Enslaved Black Americans endured systematic violence, family separation, forced labor, and the total denial of basic human rights—experiences of oppression far deeper and more brutal than those faced by non-slaveholding, landless whites. The point here is not to equate the two, but to show how the same concentrated landed power that enslaved millions also constrained and marginalized the majority of free whites, creating a society where opportunity and civic formation were deliberately limited for all but a small elite.

The Founders had explicitly rejected this kind of feudal-like arrangement. They saw hereditary wealth and concentrated land ownership as threats to republican equality and self-government. Thomas Jefferson called primogeniture and entail "feudal remnants" that created an artificial aristocracy detached from labor and virtue, and he worked to abolish them in Virginia. John Adams warned that extreme inherited wealth could corrupt republican institutions by elevating birth over merit. Their reforms aimed to keep the republic grounded in earned effort and broad-based opportunity, not in the kind of entrenched privilege that the antebellum South increasingly replicated.

The republic's founding compromise allowed this imbalance to take root; its correction would require generations of learning, struggle, and reform. Lincoln's judgment was moral, but it was also cognitive. If slavery was wrong, then the habits it cultivated—cruelty, moral blindness, and the refusal to learn—were wrong as well. Slavery did not merely deny freedom; it systematically reshaped how people learned, what they were permitted to know, and how knowledge itself functioned within society.

Seen this way, slavery was not only a denial of freedom but a systematic constraint on learning itself—one that produced sharply unequal literacies, distorted civic capacity, and left behind habits of thought that emancipation alone could not erase.

Slavery as a Limit on Human Development

Before turning fully to the American problem of dual literacy, slavery must be situated within a longer human history. Systems of human bondage long predate the modern era and appear across civilizations, taking varied forms depending on economic structure, religious tradition, and political power. As Thomas Sowell has observed, slavery was a universal institution for thousands of years, existing in every race and culture long before the Trans-Atlantic trade—Europeans enslaved other Europeans, Asians enslaved other Asians, Africans enslaved other Africans, and indigenous peoples of the Western Hemisphere enslaved their own (Sowell, 2005). What distinguishes different systems of slavery is not merely who was enslaved, but how thoroughly bondage extended into learning, family life, and the transmission of knowledge.

Early societies, as described in the Hebrew scriptures, acknowledged slavery as a social reality rather than an ideal. Biblical law regulated slavery without abolishing it, placing limits on duration, treatment, and hereditary status that distinguished debt servitude from permanent chattel bondage (Exodus 21; Leviticus 25; Deuteronomy 15). While these texts reflect moral tensions unresolved at the time, they consistently treat enslaved persons as moral agents—capable of religious instruction, family formation, and participation in communal life. Learning, though constrained by status, was not universally criminalized. Literacy, ritual knowledge, and ethical obligation remained meaningful even within conditions of unfreedom, a point noted by historians of the ancient Near East such as Raymond Westbrook and social historians of biblical law.

In ancient Greece and Rome, slavery was widespread and legally entrenched, yet similarly complex. Enslaved people performed agricultural labor, domestic service, skilled trades, and intellectual work. Roman households, in particular, often relied on enslaved tutors, accountants, physicians, and artisans; some of the empire's most educated labor was performed by enslaved Greeks (Finley, *Ancient Slavery and Modern Ideology*; Bradley, *Slavery and Society at Rome*). These systems were brutal and coercive, but they did not typically seek to eradicate learning itself. Enslaved people were often educated precisely because their knowledge increased their economic value, even as their freedom remained denied.

The early modern Mediterranean world presents a different pattern. From the sixteenth through the early nineteenth centuries, Islamic states along the Barbary Coast—particularly in Algiers, Tunis, and Tripoli—regularly captured and enslaved European Christians, including sailors and civilians from Britain, southern Europe, and, after independence, the United States. Thousands were held for ransom or forced labor, a practice extensively documented by historians such as Robert Davis (*Christian Slaves, Muslim Masters*) and reflected in early American foreign policy during the Barbary Wars. These same regions were deeply enmeshed in the trans-Saharan and Red Sea slave trades, supplying enslaved people from sub-Saharan Africa to markets across the Islamic world (Lovejoy, *Transformations in Slavery*). Slavery in these systems was not racial in origin, but it was absolute in power: human beings could be bought, sold, traded, or punished at the discretion of their owners.

Eastern Europe presents yet another instructive case. In Russia, serfdom bound millions of people to landowners until the mid-nineteenth century. Serfs could be sold with land, transferred, or conscripted at will; as late as the early 1800s, a serf might be exchanged for livestock or tools (Figes, *Natasha's Dance*; Moon, *The Russian Peasantry*). Nikita Khrushchev later recalled that his grandfather had been born into this condition—a reminder that serfdom persisted within living memory and ended only in 1861, in the aftermath of Russia's defeat in the Crimean War. Yet Russian serfs, while legally unfree, often retained access to family life, religious instruction, and practical skill transmission within village communities. Learning persisted where it could not be fully suppressed.

What distinguishes slavery in the modern Atlantic world—and particularly in the American South—is not its existence, but its design. Slavery became hereditary, racialized, and legally fortified in ways that aligned economic production, state power, and permanent social exclusion (Morgan, *American Slavery, American Freedom*; Berlin, *Many Thousands Gone*). Most critically, it became a system that deliberately suppressed learning.

By the late eighteenth and early nineteenth centuries, American slaveholding societies increasingly recognized literacy as a direct threat. Enslaved people who could read religious texts, legal documents, or political arguments were harder to control; those who could write could communicate, organize, and preserve memory beyond the reach of overseers.

47

In response, many states enacted explicit laws criminalizing the teaching of reading and writing to enslaved people—especially after uprisings such as the Stono Rebellion (1739) and Nat Turner's revolt (1831). These statutes, documented by historians such as Janet Cornelius and Heather Williams, reflected a clear understanding shared by slaveholders themselves: learning expands agency, and agency undermines absolute domination.

The result was a divided landscape of literacy: widespread and expanding in the free North, systematically restricted in the slave South. The common school could ensure exposure to civic ideas for many; for others, even the most basic tools of self-expression were denied. Slavery did not merely deny freedom; it systematically reshaped how people learned, what they were permitted to know, and how knowledge itself functioned within society.

Enforced Illiteracy and the Architecture of Control

From the earliest decades of the republic, enslaved people were denied access to literacy not incidentally, but deliberately. While basic learning for free children remained largely informal—embedded in family, work, church, and community—enslaved children were increasingly cut off even from these pathways. As slavery hardened into a racialized system of permanent bondage, Southern states began to codify learning prohibitions directly. Laws passed in the early nineteenth century criminalized teaching enslaved people to read or write, imposed fines and corporal punishment on instructors, and framed literacy itself as a threat to public order.

These laws reveal something essential: slaveholders understood that learning was power. Literacy enabled communication beyond immediate supervision, access to religious and political ideas, and the ability to imagine alternatives. To suppress learning was therefore not only to maintain labor control, but to narrow the future, to keep aspiration itself from forming.

Yet learning did not cease. It adapted.

Dual Literacy and the Burden of Fluency

Enslaved people developed what later scholars would recognize as a dual literacy: a constrained public bearing shaped by survival, alongside a private, often clandestine, world of meaning, memory, and interpretation. Spirituals, folktales, coded speech, and religious practice became carriers of historical knowledge, moral judgment, and shared identity—forms of learning that no authority could easily confiscate.

This asymmetry created a profound cognitive burden. Enslaved people were often required to understand the worldview, language, and expectations of those who held power over them, while simultaneously concealing their own thoughts, intentions, and interpretations. As W. E. B. Du Bois would later describe, this condition produced a divided consciousness—a constant act of translation between how one is seen and how one knows oneself to be. Though Du Bois wrote in the language of a later era, he was naming a learning environment forged under bondage: one that demanded extraordinary interpretive skill while punishing visible knowledge.

Frederick Douglass's own account makes this painfully clear. Literacy, once glimpsed, became both liberation and torment. Learning to read awakened moral clarity and historical awareness—but also intensified the pain of enslavement itself. Knowledge expanded faster than agency. The mind learned what the body was forbidden to enact. This is not learning as enrichment; it is learning under constraint.

The Damage Extends Outward

Crucially, this logic was not confined to wealthy planters. Poor whites—many of whom were economically exploited themselves—often became its most fervent defenders. As Douglass observed repeatedly, slavery degraded everyone it touched. When freedom is defined primarily as relative status rather than shared civic standing, it becomes brittle. If one group's sense of dignity depends on another remaining beneath them, progress by the latter is experienced as a threat rather than an achievement.

In this sense, slavery weakened the learning capacity of the slaveholding society itself. It normalized coercion over persuasion, hierarchy over judgment, and inherited status over earned competence. These are anti-learning habits. They dull curiosity, discourage adaptation, and replace inquiry with enforcement. Joe Carter's remark that "the slaveholder was the real slave" captures this irony with uncomfortable precision: a society that must suppress learning to preserve itself is already trapped.

Technology and Diverging Educational Paths

Throughout this book, terms such as black and white appear in discussions of American slavery and its aftermath. These terms are not employed as biological descriptors or cultural identities, but as historically contingent legal and administrative classifications imposed by the system of chattel slavery and later reproduced through state and federal data systems, including the census. Slavery in the United States operated by encoding labor status, rights, and social position into racial categories, transforming historically fluid identities into fixed markers of governance. Race, in this sense, was not a natural foundation of

American society, but a social construct that was operationalized as a technology of governance to sustain slavery.

This book does not seek to erase or minimize that history. It seeks instead to look forward—however cautiously and imperfectly—to a time when we have learned to stop categorizing one another by race so that we can begin to see through to the individual qualities now so often obscured when we stop at skin color. The persistent use of racial categories in official data collection, especially on the census, keeps those classifications alive and salient long after their original purpose has been repudiated. The data give rise to the categorization; the categorization gives rise to the expectation; the expectation shapes perception and opportunity. Until we cease collecting racial data in ways that require individuals to be sorted and reported as group members rather than as persons, the categories will continue to function as lenses that filter how we see one another—often before any individual evidence is considered.

The path to that future is not simple. It requires sustained, honest reckoning with the past, deliberate institutional redesign in the present, and the gradual cultivation of new habits of attention and judgment. Yet the hope remains: that a republic capable of learning from its own history might one day learn to see its citizens as they are—individuals bearing unique gifts, burdens, and potential—rather than as representatives of inherited administrative markers. Only then can we fully honor the principle that sovereignty resides in the people, each one counted not as a fraction or a category, but as a whole person.

The constitutional order endured its greatest trial and survived. Slavery was abolished, and the nation emerged with a clearer articulation of its moral commitments. That survival, however, must not be mistaken for completion. The failure of Reconstruction—exacerbated by President Lincoln's assassination and the abandonment of promised restitutions such as "forty acres and a mule"—allowed new forms of injustice to take root. Jim Crow laws, racial terror, and systematic exclusion would persist for generations, embedding inequality not only in institutions but in daily life. For many descendants of the enslaved, these injustices are not distant history; they are lived inheritance, present in memory, family narrative, and continuing disparities.

This book addresses that history neither to diminish the founding nor to excuse its failures, but to confront both honestly. A constitutional republic worthy of preservation is not one that denies its moral contradictions, but one that proves capable of learning from them. The American experiment is valuable not because it began perfectly, but because it created a framework within which injustice could eventually be named, contested, and, however incompletely, corrected. Understanding how learning, civic responsibility, and moral judgment evolve within that framework is essential if the republic is to continue that work rather than forget why it was undertaken in the first place.

Although the proponents of slavery were defeated through civil war, and the institution abolished through constitutional amendment, certain classificatory practices persisted, shaping data collection, public policy, and social analysis long after emancipation. The continued collection of racial categories in the decennial census reflects an administrative inheritance more than a present civic necessity. These classifications originated as tools of governance and accountability under slavery and were retained during Reconstruction for purposes of enforcement and administration, rather than being reconsidered or redesigned in light of slavery's abolition (Anderson, 1988; U.S. Census Bureau, 2002).

From the very beginning, the United States census has sorted people into racial boxes, a practice born in the Three-Fifths Compromise and carried forward by bureaucratic habit (Nobles, 2000; Anderson, 1988). Although the original political purpose for collecting racial data no longer exists, the practice persists—and with it, the tendency to interpret civic life through administratively defined categories. Today, these classifications shape funding formulas, research, and political strategy, but they also shape how children understand themselves. A five-year-old should arrive at kindergarten as a mind and a soul to be cultivated, not as a data point already labeled before they have had a chance to show their character, ability, or aspirations (Hochschild & Powell, 2008).

When societies organize public life around inherited labels, civic trust can weaken and political incentives often shift toward segmentation rather than shared purpose. Even when classifications are advanced with inclusive or remedial intentions, scholars have noted that they may also perpetuate the divisions they seek to address by stabilizing group-based narratives and expectations (Morning, 2011; Omi & Winant, 2014; Nobles, 2000). The consequence is not only social friction, but a republic made more susceptible to forces that exploit distrust and fragmentation.

Although racial categories were retained after abolition to support enforcement of civil rights, their continued use has drawn sustained criticism. Scholars argue that these classifications can reify historically imposed identities, influence expectations and outcomes, and perpetuate inequality by organizing policy and perception around group membership rather than individual civic standing (Anderson, 2015; Nobles, 2000; Sowell, 2004; Steele, 1997). Where possible, this study therefore prioritizes legal, economic, and institutional descriptions—such as *enslaved persons*, *non-slaveholding households*, and *landless free laborers*—to emphasize that racial categories were tools of administration rather than inherent features of the people to whom they were applied.

It is important to distinguish between the historical origins of racial categories and the ways those categories have been claimed, reinterpreted, and imbued with meaning by the people upon whom they were imposed. Formerly enslaved people were not complicit in the original construction of their racial identity in America. Racial categories were imposed through violence, law, and custom. Within those constraints, enslaved and formerly enslaved people asserted dignity, solidarity, and political voice by organizing together and turning identities once imposed upon them into sources of solidarity and action.

Acknowledging the legitimacy of those lived identities does not require treating the categories themselves as natural or permanent. The racial classifications that emerged under American slavery were designed as instruments of governance— to allocate labor, restrict rights, and stabilize hierarchy—and were then embedded in census practices and administrative data systems. This book argues that while such classifications once served specific historical functions, their continued circulation as default data categories risks perpetuating divisions that do not reflect biological reality or civic necessity. To interrogate the origins of racial data, therefore, is not to deny lived experience, but to ask whether tools created for domination should continue to organize how individuals in a self-governing society understands themselves.

Technological and Economic Divergence in the North and South

Before the Civil War, Northern agriculture entered a period of rapid mechanization. John Deere's steel plow, Cyrus McCormick's mechanical reaper, and new threshing and planting devices enabled one farmer to do the work of five or more. Railroads and canals linked Midwestern grain to expanding urban markets. By the 1850s, the North was becoming an industrial-agricultural economy built on innovation, wage labor, and continual reinvestment in machinery—developments that steadily increased demand for technical skill, literacy, and formal schooling.

Southern agriculture moved in the opposite direction. Apart from the cotton gin, the plantation system remained anchored in hand tools, mule power, and labor-intensive methods (Wright, 2006; Beckert, 2014). Enslaved labor was not merely an economic input but the foundation of a rigid social order that shaped Southern investment decisions and resisted technological change (Genovese, 1974; Johnson, 1999). Many planters believed that machines would be unreliable, difficult to supervise, or socially destabilizing in a system built on coercive labor discipline (Sellers, 1991; Majewski, 2000). James Henry Hammond articulated this logic explicitly in his 1858 "mudsill" speech, describing enslaved people as the indispensable laboring foundation upon which civilization rested. Others argued that enslaved workers—who reproduced, could be sold, and did not mechanically depreciate—were a sounder investment than machines that wore out or broke (Baptist, 2014; Fogel & Engerman, 1974).

This commitment to slave labor had cascading effects beyond technology, extending deeply into labor markets and education. By the 1840s and 1850s, slavery had sharply reduced demand for free labor legally classified as white, particularly among landless non-slaveholding households who had historically relied on agricultural and seasonal work (Merritt, 2014; Glossner, 2016).

Plantation slavery rendered many unskilled free laborers economically "superfluous," confining them to intermittent employment during planting and harvest seasons or excluding them from steady work altogether (Merritt, 2014). Slave competition also extended into trades and mechanical occupations, prompting petitions against the use of enslaved workers and contributing to chronic underemployment and wage suppression (Merritt, 2014). In regions dominated by plantation agriculture, landless households increasingly clustered near large slaveholders in hopes of finding work, even as their economic prospects deteriorated as the slave economy matured (Merritt, 2014).

Educational access mirrored these labor constraints. For the children of landless non-slaveholding families, schooling opportunities were extremely limited. Chronic poverty, geographic mobility, and the necessity of child labor meant that education, when available at all, was brief, irregular, and often inaccessible due to tuition fees, distance, or local resistance to public funding (Merritt, 2014).

Educational prospects were only marginally better for the additional 20–25 percent of Southern white households who owned small farms but did not hold enslaved people. These families were more likely to access subscription schools or short-term rural academies, yet attendance was seasonal and fragile, constrained by agricultural labor demands and the absence of a robust public education system (Merritt, 2014).

These educational limitations were not incidental. On the eve of the Civil War, approximately 25 percent of Southern white families owned enslaved people, down from roughly 35–

36 percent a decade earlier, reflecting increasing concentration of slave ownership among the wealthiest planters rather than any decline in slavery itself (Merritt, 2014). Rising slave prices during the cotton boom of the 1850s placed ownership beyond the reach of many small and middling farmers, while economic volatility pushed some marginal slaveholders back into non-slaveholder status. As slaveholding became more concentrated, planter elites—who exercised disproportionate influence over state legislatures—consistently resisted higher taxes to fund public education for the remaining 75 percent of the population, viewing such expenditures as unnecessary, inefficient, or socially destabilizing (Merritt, 2014; Genovese, 1974). Because public schooling required taxation of land and slave property, it directly threatened planter wealth and control. As a result, no Deep South state developed a comprehensive, uniformly accessible system of tax-supported public education prior to the Civil War.

It is also important to emphasize that "the South" was not a monolithic entity but a patchwork of sovereign states with distinct political economies and educational policies. Levels of landlessness, slave ownership, and school access varied substantially across states such as Virginia, North Carolina, South Carolina, Georgia, Mississippi, and Louisiana. Nevertheless, the overall pattern remains consistent: where slaveholding was most concentrated and planter political power strongest, public investment in education for non-slaveholding populations was weakest, and educational opportunity for both landless laborers and small farmers was most constrained (Merritt, 2014; Glossner, 2016).

At the same time, slavery reshaped the cultural meaning of labor itself. Manual and agricultural work became widely stigmatized as "slave work", eroding its perceived dignity among free laborers and weakening incentives to invest in skill acquisition or sustained training. Contemporary observers and later historians alike noted that the association of bodily labor with enslavement led many landless southerners to view work not as a pathway to independence or mastery, but as a marker of social inferiority (Merritt, 2014; Glossner, 2016). Elite southern ideology reinforced this degradation, portraying slavery as a system that exempted "respectable" citizens from toil while relegating landless non-slaveholding households to a marginal and often precarious social position (Glossner, 2016).

The result was not only a pattern of deliberate technological restraint and stagnation, but the emergence of a poorly educated majority population whose relationship to work had been structurally distorted. In suppressing innovation to preserve hierarchy, the antebellum South also suppressed demand for widespread literacy, technical training, and skill development. Where mechanization in the North compelled new forms of schooling and rewarded disciplined wage labor, resistance to technology in the South produced educational inertia and limited returns to effort or expertise. Over time, these conditions weakened the formation of habits associated with stable skill accumulation—regular schooling, long-term training, and predictable labor advancement—across large segments of the population. Both regions thus illustrate the same principle: educational needs and work norms are shaped not by cultural disposition alone, but by how societies organize labor, allocate opportunity, and relate to technology.

A learning republic rests on the conviction that no person is born to serve as the foundation upon which others stand. Human dignity and economic resilience depend on extending meaningful learning opportunities to every member of the citizenry. Societies that concentrate education and skill formation within a narrow elite while denying them to the majority may sustain hierarchy for a time, but they do so at the cost of adaptability and long-term stability. The historical record of the slaveholding South makes this clear. The collapse of that system did not merely end an unjust labor regime; it exposed the fragility of an economy and educational order built on the systematic suppression of learning. Later episodes in American history reinforce the same lesson. The challenges posed by the Soviet launch of Sputnik, for example, were met not by retreating into elite expertise alone, but by expanding educational access, scientific training, and opportunity across a much broader share of the population. To insist that education be broadly accessible is therefore not utopianism, but a conclusion grounded in lived experience and historical evidence—an expression of common sense forged in the aftermath of institutional failure.

Conclusion

This chapter examines the profound transformation of American learning during the antebellum era (1830–1865), as industrialization disrupted the artisan republic's experiential, household-embedded model and gave rise to institutionalized common schools. In mill towns like Lowell, Massachusetts, factories centralized production, separating work from home and eroding families' ability to integrate children into productive roles. Parents, now wage laborers, could no longer provide hands-on instruction through daily chores and apprenticeships, creating a rupture that reformers sought to address.

Horace Mann advocated state-funded, universal common schools to instill literacy, morality, and republican values, compensating for the household's lost educational function. Catharine Beecher emphasized women's role as professional teachers, extending domestic nurturing into classrooms via institutions like the Hartford Female Seminary. Both recognized industrialization's spatial and temporal shifts—work governed by bells rather than family rhythms—but proposed solutions blending institutional scale with moral formation.

The era introduced deskilling: complex crafts fragmented into repetitive tasks, mirroring schooling's segmentation into subjects, grades, and curricula. Civic education shifted from observable, responsibility-based household practice to symbolic classroom recitation, making virtue harder to verify. Childhood extended as a preparatory phase, widening the gap between youth and adulthood, while extremes of inherited wealth (detached elites) and generational poverty (exploited laborers) threatened self-reliant citizenship.

In the South, slavery intensified divergences. Post-1831 laws enforced illiteracy, viewing knowledge as a threat to control, yet enslaved people adapted through dual literacy— public compliance masking clandestine spirituals, folktales, and coded meanings. This cognitive burden, as Frederick Douglass described, awakened awareness but deepened torment, degrading all involved by normalizing coercion over inquiry. Technological stagnation preserved hierarchy, stifling Northern-style mechanization and broad schooling, while racial categories—rooted in governance tools like the census— persisted as administrative inheritances.

Overall, the chapter highlights gains in scaled education for free Northern children but losses in experiential depth and equity, exposing the republic's moral contradictions. As Civil War approached, these divides tested self-government's foundations, setting the stage for Reconstruction's educational reforms and ongoing struggles to align learning with technological change.

Chapter Three: A Chance to Bind the Wounds

The Work Begins

He had been denied literacy by law. That denial itself revealed its power.

As a child in bondage, Frederick Douglass understood what his enslavers already knew: literacy was not merely a skill; it was leverage. To read was to interpret. To write was to remember for posterity. To reason in public was to claim standing. So he learned in secret — by barter, by listening, by copying letters in the margins of discarded newspapers, by relentless determination at great personal risk.

The prohibition against his learning was not incidental. It was structural. A society that feared the literacy of the enslaved understood, perhaps more clearly than it wished to admit, that learning enlarges agency. If a man can read the law, he can question it. If he can read Scripture, he can interpret it. If he can write, he can testify.

By the time of the Civil War, Douglass had become a citizen-scholar, writer, and statesman. When the war ended, he stood not simply as a man released from bondage, but as a commanding voice in the struggle to define what freedom would mean.

Reconstruction would not be merely a political project. It would be an educational one. The central question was not only who was free, but who would be equipped — literate, skilled, and capable — to exercise freedom responsibly. Emancipation had ended slavery by decree. The Thirteenth Amendment to the Constitution had made it irrevocable. The Fourteenth

Frederick Douglass

Amendment guaranteed citizenship to those formerly enslaved. But the harder work was to expand learning and equip everyone for full civic and economic participation.

The nation had been given, at terrible cost, a chance to bind its wounds. Whether it would use learning to do so remained an open question.

This chapter traces that work: the surge toward literacy among the formerly enslaved; the contested rebuilding of civic life amid Reconstruction's hopes and reversals; the industrial transformations that continued to reshape schooling and skill formation; and the transformative post-World War II Servicemen's Readjustment Act of 1944—commonly known as the GI Bill—which dramatically expanded access to higher education and vocational training for millions of veterans. Across these eras runs a single thread: the intimate relationship between learning and capacity, between knowledge and the exercise of self-government. Emancipation opened the door to freedom, but only widespread, meaningful education could equip citizens to walk through it responsibly and sustain the republic's promise.

Reconstruction and the Struggle for Literacy

Seen in retrospect, the antebellum slave economy represents a near-perfect case study in how an economic system can undermine its own long-term educational and developmental foundations. By substituting coerced labor for skill formation, concentrating capital in human property rather than productive technology, and culturally devaluing manual and technical work, the plantation system systematically suppressed incentives for innovation, schooling, and human-capital investment. These choices did not merely constrain the lives of the enslaved; they also limited opportunities for non-slaveholding populations and inhibited the emergence of institutions capable of supporting a flexible, knowledge-based economy. When slavery collapsed, the South confronted emancipation without the educational infrastructure, diversified labor markets, or civic capacity necessary to absorb such a transformation. The enduring economic and educational consequences that followed were not historical accidents, but predictable outcomes of a system that had, for generations, treated learning and adaptation as threats rather than necessities.

History offers further evidence that this pattern is not unique. Wherever political systems have attempted to freeze a portion of the population into a permanent laboring class—whether through slavery, caste, or centralized economic control—education has consistently been treated as a threat rather than a public good (Genovese, 1974). In Marxist–Leninist regimes, for example, formally egalitarian rhetoric often concealed rigid hierarchies in which party cadres and administrative elites enjoyed privileged access to education while ordinary citizens faced tightly restricted opportunities (Fitzpatrick, 1979; Matthews, 1972; Djilas, 1957). Similar dynamics appear in colonial systems and authoritarian states, where learning among subordinated populations was deliberately constrained to prevent political or economic challenge (Dirks, 2001). In each case, suppressing education across large segments of society produced stagnation, resentment, and institutional fragility. This broader historical pattern provides essential context for understanding the educational struggles that followed emancipation in the American South.

The Civil War exposed and intensified America's educational divides. On one side, newly freed African Americans launched one of the most remarkable literacy movements in history. On the other, Southern elites struggled to accept even minimal schooling for the formerly enslaved and, in many cases, for poor whites as well.

During and immediately after the war, freed people and formerly enslaved communities across the South built schools in churches, cabins, and open fields—often before the Freedmen's Bureau organized its first classrooms (Anderson, 1988). Parents pooled modest resources to hire teachers; former soldiers taught evening classes; children taught younger siblings to read. Historians describe this as a "grassroots enlightenment," driven by an urgent conviction that literacy was essential to freedom (Foner, 1988).

Institutions such as Howard, Fisk, and Hampton were founded to train teachers and professionals for these communities. Booker T. Washington's Tuskegee Institute added a strong emphasis on practical skilled labor—agriculture, carpentry, masonry, printing, metalwork—alongside academic subjects (Washington, 1901). Students often constructed the very buildings they studied in, embodying the belief that labor directed toward self-improvement and community uplift is a form of civic virtue.

George Washington Carver's work at Tuskegee extended this vision into scientific innovation. Through research on crop rotation, soil regeneration, and practical rural economics, Carver offered a lifeline to impoverished Southern farmers struggling with depleted land and chronic debt (Holt 1943; Kremer 2011). His famous "movable school" wagon—an early form of mobile classroom—carried agricultural education directly into remote communities that formal schooling scarcely reached, translating laboratory knowledge into practical instruction for everyday use (Carver 1906; Hersey 2011). In doing so, Carver demonstrated how applied learning could restore both land and livelihoods, linking education not only to personal advancement but to community resilience and economic renewal.

These efforts pointed toward a learning republic in which formerly excluded citizens claimed education as a right and a tool of self-determination. Yet they unfolded within a broader political context that often resisted their implications. These postwar educational efforts also complicate some contemporary misunderstandings about the relationship between learning, identity, and cultural authenticity. In some contemporary educational contexts, Black students who pursue academic excellence have reported being accused by peers of cultural betrayal, a dynamic that scholars have linked to identity pressures rather than to any rejection of learning itself (Fordham & Ogbu, 1986; Fordham, 1996). Measured against the historical record, academic excellence is a self-directed hallmark of the Black cultural experience in America, not something imposed by the broader culture.

For formerly enslaved people, education was not a marker of assimilation or submission; it was an act of courage, resistance, and self-determination. Literacy had been criminalized under slavery, teachers had been beaten or driven out, and learning itself was treated as a threat to the social order. Yet in the face of those dangers, formerly enslaved communities across the South built schools with their own hands, pooled scarce resources to hire teachers, and placed extraordinary moral weight on education as the foundation of freedom and dignity (Anderson, 1988; Foner, 1988; Williams, 2005).

At the same time, large portions of the white Southern population—particularly poor whites—emerged from the Civil War with little tradition of public schooling and few institutional supports for learning. Antebellum plantation elites had discouraged broad education precisely because it threatened hierarchy, and those policies had constrained white and Black populations alike. In the decades immediately following emancipation, it was often Black communities—not white ones—that showed the greatest urgency and initiative in building schools, training teachers, and linking education to economic independence (Katz, 1987; Anderson, 1988; Ayers, 1992).

As is almost always the case, the successful development and use of educational opportunities by newly freed African Americans did not arise in a vacuum. The moral discipline, communal cohesion, and reverence for learning that fueled Reconstruction-era literacy efforts had been cultivated under bondage itself. Cultural historian and musicologist Joe Carter argues that African American spirituals offer a record of this inner life: they were not merely expressions of sorrow, but vehicles of theology, memory, and dignity. In Carter's interpretation, consistent with earlier scholarship (DuBois, W.E.B., 1903; Raboteau, 1978; Cone, 1972) spirituals sustained belief in moral order, encoded hope amid suffering, and in some cases carried layered meanings that facilitated resistance, escape, and communal solidarity. Far from reflecting intellectual deprivation, these songs reveal a people who learned, taught, and preserved meaning under conditions designed to extinguish it—preparing the ground for the extraordinary educational achievements that followed emancipation.

Seen in this light, academic striving within Black communities is not a departure from cultural tradition but one of its deepest continuities. The historical record suggests that the pursuit of learning—often under conditions of extraordinary adversity—was among the most defining features of Black civic life in the post–Civil War South. To dismiss academic excellence as cultural betrayal is to misunderstand and dishonor a legacy built by people who understood, perhaps more clearly than anyone, that education was the surest path from exclusion to full citizenship.

After Emancipation: The Self-Built Infrastructure of Learning

When slavery ended, the formerly enslaved pursued literacy with extraordinary urgency. Schools were built by freed communities themselves; adults learned alongside children; reading became a civic act. Booker T. Washington recalled that in the first years after emancipation, hope was widespread and violent crime was rare. Learning was understood not as status acquisition, but as a means of rebuilding lives and communities.

From an interview on the radio program "On Being" in 2003 we have the following story, told by Joe Carter, of an event shortly after emancipation:

Mr. Carter: One of the stories I seem to remember that she told, it was about — Emancipation Day had come. There was a group of former slaves, now, on an island off the coast of South Carolina. My parents were from South Carolina, all my family. And they were waiting for the emissary of the government to arrive in his little boat to tell them that they had received the deeds to their land, because the government had promised them not only freedom, but 40 acres and a mule. This was going to be a great, wonderful day. And the former slaves had gathered together on the island, waiting with bated breath. And finally, they saw the boat of the officer approaching. And they could tell, even from the distance, that his face was not happy and his countenance was somewhat sad. And they said there was a groan that just came from the crowd. And one of the older women from the crowd just stood up and began to make up a song on the spot. Do you want me to show you what that song is?

Ms. Tippett: Yeah, I do.

*Mr. Carter: I'll go to the piano. She sang, [singing] Nobody
knows the trouble I've seen
Nobody knows but Jesus
Nobody knows the trouble I've seen
Glory, hallelujah.
And then she spoke, looking to the people around her, she said,
Sometimes I'm up, sometimes I'm down. Oh, yes, Lord, sometimes
I'm almost level to the ground
Oh, yes, Lord.
Oh, nobody knows the trouble I've seen Nobody knows but Jesus
Nobody knows the trouble I've seen
Glory, hallelujah*

Yet emancipation did not dissolve the surrounding culture. As Reconstruction receded, Southern states erected new legal barriers—segregation, disenfranchisement, and economic exclusion—that constrained learning's civic payoff. When formerly enslaved people migrated north seeking relief, they encountered a different version of the same constraint. The North had opposed slavery, but it had never fully imagined social equality. Industrial cities offered wages and schools, but not belonging. Housing covenants, labor exclusion, and informal segregation delivered a consistent message: you may work here, but you may not belong here.

Over time, these continued indignities eroded the hope and forbearance that had come with emancipation. Learning could expand, but agency lagged. Literacy increased, but civic standing remained contested. Once again, awareness outpaced capacity.

Learning, Capacity, and Civic Repair

What slavery in America produced, then, was not simply a gap in schooling, but a deep distortion in how learning related to freedom. It created parallel learning lines—one enforced, one constrained—that widened through law, narrowed briefly through determined effort, and then collided with new institutional barriers. The result was not ignorance but fractured civic capacity.

This matters because learning is cumulative across generations. Habits of thought—whether curiosity is rewarded, whether knowledge is shared, whether progress is welcomed—persist long after formal systems change. Emancipation ended legal bondage, but it could not instantly restore the learning ecology that bondage had damaged.

A learning republic must therefore reckon honestly with constraint. Not to romanticize endurance, and not to excuse injustice, but to understand how learning survives, adapts, and sometimes fractures under pressure. Only then can learning be designed not merely to inform, but to repair—to reconnect literacy with agency, and knowledge with shared civic standing.

From the outset, this book treats learning not as a compartment of life, but as a continuous human activity—one that begins long before formal schooling and continues long after formal credentials are earned. Yet because early educational structures shape how individuals later understand learning, work, and responsibility, the architecture of formal education remains foundational. What happens in classrooms, workshops, and training halls echoes outward into careers, communities, and civic life. The question, then, is not merely how knowledge grows, but how people grow alongside it—and whether our institutions help or hinder that process.

Karl Popper suggested that the most basic philosophical concern shared by all thinking persons is cosmological: the problem of understanding the world, ourselves, and our knowledge as part of that world. For Popper, all science is rooted in this concern, and the growth of knowledge is best understood through the growth of scientific knowledge—knowledge that advances not by accumulation, but by conjecture, criticism, and correction. Ideas are proposed, tested against reality and against competing ideas, and refined or discarded. Intellectual progress, on this account, depends less on certainty than on openness to error. Importantly, Popper's account does not confine this process to formal laboratories or academic settings. Many of the most consequential advances—such as those associated with figures like Robert Fulton and Thomas Edison—emerged from applied, practice-centered work by men who were not credentialed by any university. Their innovations, grounded in experimentation, failure, and revision, not only transformed industry and infrastructure but later became foundational to scientific research itself, eventually absorbed into university curricula and credentialing systems. The growth of knowledge, in other words, has often flowed from practice to theory before returning to practice in a more formalized shape.

This understanding aligns closely with Alfred North Whitehead's observation that modern life is defined by the accelerating growth of human knowledge. Whitehead warned that education must adapt not merely to the expansion of information, but to the changing conditions under which knowledge is produced, transmitted, and applied. When institutions fail to evolve alongside the knowledge they steward, they risk becoming obstacles rather than conduits—repositories of credentials rather than engines of understanding.

Where Popper described the logic of knowledge growth, Thomas S. Kuhn examined its social structure. Kuhn argued that scientific research is conducted, at any given time, within a paradigm: a shared framework of assumptions, methods, exemplars, and standards that define legitimate inquiry. Paradigms function not only as intellectual scaffolding but as social structures, binding communities together through shared commitments. Much research, Kuhn observed, is devoted to solving puzzles the paradigm already assumes to be solvable, while anomalies are often set aside. Only when such anomalies accumulate beyond tolerance does a scientific revolution occur, replacing one paradigm with another.

Although Kuhn's analysis was directed at science, its implications extend naturally to education. Institutions that organize knowledge must continually absorb new domains of understanding, certify competence, and transmit authority. As knowledge expands, so too does the institutional role of universities—not only as sites of inquiry, but as credentialing bodies charged with signaling readiness, expertise, and trust. This expansion raises a deeper question: how should learning relate to lived responsibility?

The American response to that question can be traced, in part, to Benjamin Franklin, who rejected the separation of learning from practical engagement. For Franklin, education was inseparable from usefulness, character, and civic responsibility. Knowledge mattered because it enabled action; action mattered because it bound individuals to the consequences of their choices. Learning divorced from work, in Franklin's view, risked becoming ornamental—impressive in form, but inert in effect.

Similar concerns animated later thinkers, though they arrived at different conclusions. Reformers such as Seth Luther emphasized the dignity of labor and the educative power of meaningful work, while John Dewey argued that education is a continuous reconstruction of experience, best achieved when learning is integrated with real problems, social interaction, and purposeful activity. Even John Henry Newman, often cited in defense of liberal education, understood intellectual formation as the cultivation of judgment and character, not merely the accumulation of information.

Yet there has always been a serious and principled counterargument. Thinkers such as Allan Bloom contended that universities must remain insulated from practical demands in order to preserve the pursuit of truth. Bloom warned that subordinating education to utility—whether economic, political, or social—risks hollowing out intellectual seriousness. For him, the university's task was not to prepare students for specific forms of work, but to cultivate disciplined minds capable of confronting enduring questions. This position is neither trivial nor dismissible; it represents a coherent philosophical defense of knowledge pursued apart from immediate consequence.

This book takes that argument seriously—and then broadens the lens.

The central hypothesis advanced here is that learning fails whenever it is reduced to narrow knowledge acquisition divorced from responsibility, judgment, and character formation—whether that reduction occurs in universities or in workplaces. Formal education that isolates knowledge from meaningful practical experience and real responsibility risks producing individuals uncertain of agency, purpose, and consequence. Conversely, non-academic and career-technical training that focuses solely on technical competence risks producing individuals who are capable but insufficiently formed—efficient in execution, yet not fully trustworthy in judgment. Today, it can no longer be assumed that habits of character, civic responsibility, and ethical judgment have been fully formed prior to formal education or training. Accordingly, both universities and career-technical education systems, along with the workplaces in which learning continues, should aim to cultivate better persons, not merely more knowledgeable or technically proficient ones.

Historically, apprenticeship systems understood this intuitively. Progression from apprentice to journeyman required not only mastery of technique but the cultivation of reliability, judgment, and character. One did not merely learn how to perform a task; one learned how to be entrusted with it. In the medieval guilds—and later preserved symbolically in the traditions of the Freemasons—advancement signified moral as well as technical readiness. The tools of the trade served not only practical ends but also ethical ones, reinforcing standards of conduct, obligation, and trust. A journeyman was someone whose work could be relied upon, and whose judgment could be exercised without constant supervision.

Modern society continues to depend on this form of learning more than it often acknowledges, even as the language once used to describe it has faded from view. Intellectual work, policy analysis, and innovation all presuppose an infrastructure sustained by skilled hands—electricians, technicians, line workers, machinists, and maintainers of complex systems— whose absence would bring scholarship, commerce, and governance alike to a halt. Any account of education that fails to recognize this lineage misunderstands how learning has historically been tied to responsibility, and how the formation of trustworthy individuals has been as central to social stability as the transmission of knowledge itself. When credentialing systems—whether operating through universities or career-technical pathways—neglect the formation of character, civic responsibility, and trustworthiness, they do not merely fail learners; they place the stability of our society, and the health of our republic, at risk.

Because lifelong learning increasingly occurs in association with work, the habits and assumptions formed during early formal education matter profoundly. They shape how individuals later approach learning, responsibility, and adaptation in a changing world. The chapters that follow explore how these patterns emerged, how they hardened into institutions, and how they might be re-imagined—not to collapse education into training, nor to romanticize labor, but to recover learning as a formative, lifelong process through which individuals become not only knowledgeable, but capable of sustaining the world they inherit.

The Postwar Educational Order: Freedmen's Schools and Land-Grant Colleges

The Civil War also accelerated the restructuring of the national economy. Wartime demand spurred growth in railroads, iron and steel, textiles, and armaments. The federal government introduced new financial systems, including a national currency and the first income tax. By 1865, the North had taken decisive steps toward an integrated industrial economy dependent on literate, numerate workers capable of handling complex machinery and written instructions.

Two federal initiatives signaled how education was being reimagined in this new order. First, Congress created the Freedmen's Bureau in 1865 to assist formerly enslaved people in their transition to freedom. Working with northern missionary societies and Black communities, its education division helped establish thousands of schools across the South. These schools were often rudimentary and underfunded, but they embodied a radical claim: literacy and formal schooling were not privileges of race or property but tools of citizenship.

Second, the Morrill Land-Grant College Act of 1862 created a network of state colleges devoted to "agriculture and the mechanic arts." Funded through federal land grants, these institutions linked higher education directly to an industrializing economy, training engineers, agronomists, and applied scientists. A second Morrill Act in 1890 extended land-grant support to Black institutions, though under systems of legal segregation and unequal funding.

Together, Freedmen's schools and land-grant colleges reflected two faces of postwar educational policy: one focused on basic literacy and civic inclusion, the other on technical and professional expertise for an industrial economy.

In Northern and Western states, the Union war effort had highlighted the importance of literacy, numeracy, discipline, and logistical competence. Public support for tax-funded common schools grew. States expanded school oversight, taxation, and standardization. Immigration surged, and public schools became key institutions of civic assimilation and workforce preparation.

By the late nineteenth century, these forces converged into a new national model: increasingly centralized, bureaucratic, and professionalized schooling that would shape American life for the next century.

Unionization and Bureaucratic Constraints

Professional associations and unions such as the National Education Association—which gradually evolved into a quasi-union—and the American Federation of Teachers, founded in 1916, secured due-process protections, salary schedules, and workplace stability for a historically vulnerable workforce (Urban 1982; Murphy 1990). In many districts, collective bargaining brought predictable pay, benefits, and safeguards against arbitrary dismissal (Tyack 1974; Moe 2011).

At the same time, the structures created to defend teachers sometimes constrained innovation. Salary schedules typically rewarded years of service and formal credentials rather than classroom effectiveness or creative practice (Hanushek and Rivkin 2006; Podgursky and Springer 2007). Assignment and promotion were frequently governed by seniority rules, while contracts codified rigid time structures—fixed class periods, uniform school days, and detailed calendars—that limited schools' ability to adapt quickly to new technologies, emerging research on learning, or the distinct needs of communities (Tyack and Cuban 1995; Hess 2009).

These developments made sense in an era when the central challenge was to build, standardize, and stabilize mass schooling across a rapidly expanding nation. Over time, however, the institutional structures designed for that purpose became increasingly rigid. Teachers and other education professionals came to be responsible not only for instruction, but for responding to social change, technological shifts, and expanding public expectations, all while operating within systems largely shaped by late nineteenth- and early twentieth-century assumptions. The bureaucratic and contractual arrangements that once brought stability to the profession gradually limited its capacity to adapt, placing the burden of change on individual practitioners rather than on the institutions themselves (Labaree 2004; Hanushek and Rivkin 2006; Podgursky and Springer 2007; Mehta and Fine 2019).

Twentieth-Century Acceleration: Whitehead, the G.I. Bill, and Andragogy

By the early twentieth century, the accelerating pace of scientific and technological change had become impossible to ignore. Alfred North Whitehead gave this reality its classical philosophical formulation. In essays and addresses collected in *The Aims of Education* and *Business Adrift*, Whitehead argued that, for the first time in human history, the cycle of knowledge creation and obsolescence had become shorter than the human lifespan (Whitehead 1931). Under such conditions, education could no longer function as a one-time preparation confined to youth; it had to cultivate habits of continual learning, judgment, and adaptation capable of sustaining individuals across a lifetime of change.

As we have discussed, this insight did not originate with Whitehead. Figures such as Benjamin Franklin and Thomas Jefferson were designing for this reality long before it received a formal philosophical name. Their emphasis on civic learning, voluntary self-improvement, and the continual renewal of knowledge reflected an early recognition that a self-governing people must be educated not merely for a fixed body of information, but for an uncertain and evolving future.

The Great Depression and World War II tested this insight under extreme conditions. Wartime mobilization required rapid upskilling on an unprecedented scale: millions of Americans learned to operate complex machinery, navigate aircraft and ships, manage logistics, and master new communication technologies in compressed time frames (Mettler 2005; Hyman 1996). After the war, the Servicemen's Readjustment Act of 1944—the G.I. Bill—translated Whitehead's philosophical argument into public policy. By providing tuition, books, and living stipends, it enabled approximately 7.8 million veterans to pursue education and training through colleges, technical institutes, apprenticeships, and certification programs (Bound and Turner 2002; Mettler 2005). Higher education, once the preserve of a narrow elite, became a mass pathway for social mobility and national capacity building.

At the same time, educators began to ask a deeper question: how do adults learn differently from children? Malcolm Knowles, who studied at Harvard University in the late 1930s and early 1940s—when Whitehead's ideas were widely discussed in American intellectual circles—emerged as a central figure in articulating *andragogy*, the theory and practice of adult education (Knowles 1970; Merriam and Bierema 2014). Drawing on work with community programs, extension services, voluntary associations, and adult-education literature from the 1930s through the 1960s, Knowles argued that adults learn best when they are self-directed, when learning is problem-centered rather than subject-centered, and when prior experience is treated as a resource rather than a liability (Knowles 1980).

Taken together, Whitehead's philosophy, the educational expansion enabled by the G.I. Bill, and Knowles's theory of adult learning contributed to a new understanding of education in a free society. Learning was no longer viewed solely as preparation for work in youth, but as a lifelong process of growth, adaptation, and civic participation, essential to individual dignity and national resilience.

Lifelong Learning and Civic Responsibility

Across American history, investments in learning have consistently shaped the nation's economic strength and civic capacity. From early republican experiments in public education to later expansions through land-grant institutions, veterans' benefits, and community colleges, learning has functioned as a central mechanism through which opportunity and participation were extended. When access to education was restricted or unevenly distributed, the consequences were felt not only by individuals but by the republic as a whole. Understanding this historical relationship between learning, institutions, and civic life provides essential context for the chapters that follow.

The growth of college attendance in America has never been smooth or random. Instead, it follows a patterned response to rising technological complexity. Each major expansion aligns with a technological inflection point—industrialization, electrification and bureaucratic organization, digital computation, and now artificial intelligence (AI). As new technologies create novel forms of work and learning outside the academy, colleges eventually adapt by formalizing this knowledge into degree programs and credentialing systems. Over time, institutions of higher education move from observers of technological change to arbiters of legitimacy, determining which forms of knowledge are recognized, standardized, and credentialed.

For much of American history, low levels of formal college participation did not signal an absence of learning, but the presence of alternative learning institutions. Apprenticeships, workshops, laboratories, and workplaces functioned as the primary sites of skill transmission, judgment formation, and professional socialization. As universities expanded their role in credentialing technologically complex knowledge, they gradually absorbed functions once performed by work-integrated learning systems. This shift increased access to standardized credentials, but it also *altered the relationship between learning and work, substituting abstraction and scale for daily exposure to consequence, responsibility, and real-world constraint* (see Appendix E).

The relationship between technological innovation and higher education in America has evolved over time. In the early Republic and through much of the Industrial Revolution, many transformative technologies in emerged not from universities, but from skilled practitioners working outside formal academic systems. Innovators such as James Watt, George Stephenson, Thomas Edison, and later software pioneers learned through apprenticeship, experimentation, and sustained engagement with real-world problems. Their success illustrates a recurring truth: transformative learning often precedes formal theory and credentialing. Universities have historically entered the process later—systematizing, explaining, and certifying knowledge once its practical value is already proven. This pattern reminds us that learning is not owned by institutions, and that innovation has long flourished beyond the boundaries of formal education.

Thomas Edison's education unfolded not in classrooms but in telegraph offices, machine shops, and improvised laboratories. As a teenage telegraph operator, Edison learned electrical systems through work that carried immediate consequences: a faulty relay meant missed messages, a wiring error could cause fire, and unreliable equipment meant professional failure (Israel, 1998; Millard, 1990). By his early twenties, Edison had accumulated a depth of practical electrical knowledge that rivaled—and often exceeded—that of formally trained scientists of his era, not because of exceptional theoretical preparation, but because he lived continuously inside real technical problems that demanded solutions (Hughes, 1983; Carlson, 2000).

When Edison established his laboratory at Menlo Park in 1876, he created something unprecedented in American history: an organized system for industrial learning. Menlo Park was not a university. It offered no degrees, syllabi, or lectures. Instead, it functioned as a site of continuous experimentation—prototypes built, tested, failed, revised, and tested again. Learning occurred through immersion in work, and knowledge was validated not by publication alone but by whether devices functioned reliably under real operating conditions (Israel, 1998; Hughes, 1983).

From this environment emerged the phonograph, commercially viable incandescent lighting, electrical distribution systems, and the foundational architecture of modern power networks. These were not abstract theories awaiting application;

they were solutions forged under constraint, shaped by cost, durability, safety, and scale. Only later would universities systematize these domains—creating formal curricula in electrical engineering, materials science, and systems design to teach and credential knowledge already proven in practice (Calvert, 1967; Noble, 1977).

Edison himself grasped this order intuitively. "Genius is hard work, stick-to-itiveness, and common sense," Thomas Edison wrote to Samuel Insull in 1894. For Edison, this was not a moral exhortation about character, but an epistemological claim about how knowledge is produced. Learning occurred through sustained engagement with real problems; failure was not error to be avoided, but information to be accumulated; progress emerged through iterative trial rather than sudden insight. As Paul Israel documents, Edison consistently treated invention as a process of disciplined experimentation in which understanding was earned through work, persistence, and practical judgment rather than abstract speculation alone (Israel 1998).

This pattern extended beyond invention into infrastructure. In 1905, Edison helped found the Electric Bond and Share Company (EBASCO), later known as Ebasco Services Incorporated, to finance, build, and operate electrical systems at national scale. I began my professional career working for EBASCO. For Edison, the founding of EBASCO marked a transition from invention to infrastructure, and from individual mastery to organizational learning. The central challenges were no longer confined to devices or patents, but extended to system reliability, large-scale coordination, regulation, financing, and long-term operation. Electrical knowledge now had to be distributed across teams, standardized across regions, and sustained over decades.

This progression closely mirrors the critique later articulated by John Dewey, who warned that schooling detached from productive activity risks becoming abstract, brittle, and disconnected from consequence. Dewey argued that knowledge gains meaning only when it is tested through use—when ideas are embedded in action and subject to feedback from the real world (Dewey, 1916; 1938). Edison's enterprises embodied this principal decades earlier: learning occurred through participation in work where failure carried cost, success demanded revision, and understanding was inseparable from responsibility.

Once again, learning preceded formalization. Universities would follow by expanding programs in electrical engineering, power systems, and industrial management—codifying and credentialing bodies of knowledge that industries like Edison's had already made indispensable to modern life (Hughes, 1983; Noble, 1977; Nye, 1990). This sequence—practice first, theory later—was not unique to electricity, nor to the nineteenth century.

Two centuries earlier, the steam engine emerged from a similar interplay between practical problem-solving and partial scientific understanding. Long before thermodynamics existed as a formal discipline, European natural philosophers overturned an ancient assumption: that a vacuum could not exist. Experiments by Evangelista Torricelli demonstrated that air exerted measurable pressure and that an evacuated space could be created and sustained (Torricelli, 1644; Heilbron, 1979). These findings were reinforced by vacuum experiments across Europe, including public demonstrations in France and Germany that made atmospheric pressure both visible and undeniable (Shapin & Schaffer, 1985). What followed was not a mature scientific theory, but a practical realization: pressure differentials could be harnessed to do work.

That realization moved quickly from laboratory to workshop. Early steam engines—most notably those developed by Thomas Newcomen in the early eighteenth century—did not rely on high-pressure steam pushing pistons upward. Instead, they exploited vacuum. Steam was introduced into a cylinder and then condensed, creating a partial vacuum; atmospheric pressure then drove the piston downward (Newcomen, 1712; Hills, 1989). The engine functioned not because heat was theoretically understood, but because condensation and pressure had been rendered mechanically reliable. Later improvements by James Watt—especially the separate condenser—dramatically increased efficiency, again through iterative engagement with real machines rather than deductive theory (Watt, 1769; Dickinson & Jenkins, 1927).

From these machines came the science. The effort to understand why engines wasted heat eventually gave rise to thermodynamics, not the reverse. Sadi Carnot's analysis of heat engines was explicitly motivated by the practical limits of steam power already in widespread use (Carnot, 1824). Later formalizations by Clausius and Kelvin systematized principles that industry had already revealed through trial and failure (Cardwell, 1971). The sequence is unmistakable: invention precedes explanation; work precedes theory. As with Edison's laboratories, the steam engine reminds us that *learning is not owned by institutions.* It migrates to wherever responsibility, consequence, and curiosity converge—a defining hallmark of a learning republic.

The steam engine ultimately teaches a broader lesson than technological sequence alone. Humanity will continue to advance science and technology; curiosity, ingenuity, and problem-solving are universal human traits. What changes over time is where this work is done and how societies choose to support it. Leadership in discovery has never been permanent, nor should it be understood as a zero-sum contest by default.

A learning republic, properly understood, is not an empire of intellect competing reflexively for dominance. It is a society that demonstrates what becomes possible when learning opportunities are broadly available to all who are willing to seize them—where, as Thomas Edison repeatedly demonstrated, hard work, perseverance, and responsibility are treated as civic virtues rather than exceptional traits. When education remains in active conversation with real problems and real consequences, when theory and practice continually inform one another, and when early learning equips citizens to adapt across a lifetime, innovation follows naturally. Other nations may—and should—do the same. If many societies commit themselves to learning, there is ample room for cooperation, exchange, and shared prosperity.

History, however, offers no guarantee that all nations will pursue knowledge in ways compatible with republican self-government. When rival states embrace ideologies hostile to liberty, civic equality, or human dignity—and when those ideologies pose genuine threats to a free society's survival—the question is no longer one of mutual flourishing alone. In such circumstances, maintaining scientific, technological, and institutional superiority becomes a matter of national self-preservation.

The goal, then, is not permanent dominance for its own sake, but durable capacity: the ability to defend free institutions, sustain innovation, and adapt faster than forces that would undermine them. A learning republic leads not by seeking superiority in every circumstance, but by pursuing partnerships while ensuring that when superiority is required—intellectually, technologically, or institutionally—it can be achieved without abandoning its principles. In doing so, it shows a path forward that others may freely choose to follow, and that free societies must be prepared to defend.

Technological Anxiety and the Long Arc of Work

Moments of major technological change are almost always accompanied by fear. When the steam engine spread through Britain and America, critics warned that machines would displace labor and render large segments of the population economically obsolete. Similar anxieties resurfaced with electrification, mass production, computing, and now artificial intelligence. The worry is perennial: that innovation will exhaust the supply of meaningful work.

History tells a different story.

At the dawn of the twentieth century, the American workforce was still overwhelmingly engaged in forms of employment that depended on work-integrated learning—apprenticeship, practice, and experiential judgement—rather than on formal academic credentialing. In 1900, roughly 38–41 percent of U.S. workers were employed in agriculture, another substantial share in manufacturing and manual trades, and many others in clerical or domestic service. About 4–6 percent of the workforce fell into what contemporaries classified as professional occupations, a category that included engineers, scientists, physicians, educators, and other technical specialists. Work was often physically demanding and economically precarious (U.S. Census Bureau, 1900; Kuznets, 1966; Goldin & Katz, 2008).

Over the course of the twentieth century, technological progress did not eliminate work—it transformed it. Mechanization reduced the need for agricultural labor, industrial automation reshaped manufacturing, and new technologies created entirely new domains of employment. By the turn of the twenty-first century, the occupational structure of the United States had inverted. Approximately 40–45 percent of the workforce was employed in professional, technical, and managerial roles, with higher educational requirements, greater autonomy, and substantially better working conditions than those available to earlier generations (Autor, Levy, & Murnane, 2003; Goldin & Katz, 2008; U.S. Bureau of Labor Statistics, 2000). Far from disappearing, work multiplied— becoming more specialized, more knowledge-intensive, and more closely tied to formal learning and training.

The pattern is consistent across technological revolutions. Innovation displaces *tasks*, not *purpose*. It eliminates forms of labor that trap human effort in repetitive, low-skill activity, while generating demand for new kinds of work that require judgment, design, coordination, and problem-solving. These transitions are disruptive, and they place real burdens on workers caught between old skills and new demands. But attempts to suppress innovation in order to preserve existing jobs misunderstand the source of economic vitality. The long-term engine of expanding opportunity has never been technological restraint; it has been the capacity of societies to equip their citizens to move into the work that new technologies make possible.

Seen in this light, learning and innovation are not threats to employment but its precondition. Societies that respond to technological change by expanding education, reskilling pathways, and access to new forms of expertise tend to experience rising productivity and more varied forms of meaningful work. Those that attempt to freeze economic structures in place may delay change briefly, but they do so at the cost of stagnation. A learning republic does not promise that every job will remain the same. It promises something more durable: that as the nature of work evolves, citizens will not be left behind by it

From Practice to Credential: How Universities Respond to Learning Demand

Universities in the early days of the Republic were primarily classical and clerical institutions, playing little direct role in technological invention. Only in the late nineteenth and twentieth centuries, with the rise of the research university and federal support for scientific inquiry, did higher education become a consistent incubator of new technologies. Even then, while universities increasingly originated foundational knowledge, the learning demands created by widespread technological adoption continued to arise first in practice. Higher education's enduring role has been less to lead mass learning than to consolidate, formalize, and credential knowledge once its social and economic importance is already established.

Contemporary technology entrepreneurs such as Elon Musk illustrate a modern variation of an older pattern. While Musk possesses formal education in physics and economics, his most consequential learning occurred outside the university, through immersion in complex engineering problems, sustained self-study, and iterative work with expert teams. In domains ranging from aerospace to electric vehicles, mastery was achieved not through credentials, but through practice under real constraints. Universities would later expand programs aligned with these industries, formalizing and credentialing knowledge that had already been proven in the field. Musk's career underscores a recurring truth: while higher education contributes foundational knowledge, transformative learning often occurs where responsibility, risk, and consequence converge.

These patterns point to an often-overlooked implication for education itself. If transformative learning consistently emerges where responsibility, risk, and consequence are real, then environments that combine study with meaningful work deserve closer attention—not as compromises, but as powerful learning contexts. When learners are accountable to colleagues, customers, patients, or systems that respond to their decisions, knowledge is no longer abstract. It becomes consequential. Historically, apprenticeships, early engineering practice, and modern technological innovation all relied on this fusion of learning and responsibility. The challenge for a modern learning republic is not to choose between education and work, but to design learning environments in which each informs and disciplines the other.

From the founding of the republic to the dawn of artificial intelligence, American patterns of learning have followed a consistent, if often misunderstood, rule: when technology becomes more complex, learning expands; when technological demands remain stable, the forms of learning required to function in daily life change little. This expansion of learning, however, has not always—or even primarily—taken place within colleges and universities. For much of American history, learning responded to technological change through apprenticeships, workplace training, self-study, and civic participation, with higher education playing only a limited and specialized role.

In 1790, fewer than one percent of young adults attended college. This statistic does not indicate a lack of learning, but rather the narrow purpose colleges served at the time. Higher education was largely confined to the preparation of clergy, lawyers, and a small governing elite. Most Americans acquired the skills they needed—farming, craftsmanship, navigation, commerce, and mechanical repair—through family transmission, apprenticeships, and experience. The technological environment of the early republic, shaped by print culture, local markets, and manual production, placed relatively modest demands on formal schooling. Literacy and numeracy were widely valuable, but advanced academic instruction was rarely necessary for productive or civic life.

For several decades, college enrollment remained low not because Americans were uninterested in learning, but because colleges were not yet aligned with the dominant learning needs of the society. This began to change with the Market Revolution and the early Industrial Age. Between roughly 1820 and 1880, canals, railroads, mechanized agriculture, telegraphy, and an expanding clerical economy transformed how work was organized and coordinated. These changes introduced new demands for calculation, record-keeping, technical understanding, and administrative oversight. Learning expanded rapidly across the population, largely through on-the-job experience and emerging professional practices. Only gradually did colleges begin to absorb some of this knowledge into formal curricula. As they did, college enrollment rose modestly, reaching roughly five percent by 1900—not as the source of learning itself, but as one institutional response to a broader expansion of learning already underway.

The long-run relationship between college enrollment, field specialization, and population reach is documented in detail in Appendices F and G. Appendix F traces enrollment by field group from 1790 to 1940, when colleges remained small but highly concentrated in classical curricula. Appendix G extends the analysis from 1950 to 2020, capturing the postwar expansion of higher education and the growing population penetration of technical, professional, and applied fields. Together, these tables illustrate how universities gradually absorbed learning demands that initially emerged outside the academy, rather than originating them.

Viewed over time, the composition of college study changed far more dramatically than college participation itself. In 1790 and 1870, classical fields dominated college enrollment—but college itself touched only a tiny fraction of Americans. As a result, classical education shaped elites rather than the population at large. The term "classical" is used descriptively, not evaluatively, to denote the historically dominant curriculum of early American colleges rather than to imply superiority or obsolescence. As total enrollment expanded after 1900, the share of students in classical fields declined, yet the absolute proportion of Americans exposed to those disciplines still rose. Meanwhile, technical, professional, and applied fields grew both in share and in population reach, reflecting universities' gradual absorption of learning demands generated by technological complexity.

When viewed over the full arc of American higher education, the shift in enrollment patterns is unmistakable. In the late nineteenth century, colleges were dominated by classical fields—Latin, Greek, philosophy, rhetoric, moral instruction, and law—reflecting their origins as clerical and elite institutions largely disconnected from the technical demands of an industrializing society. These curricula changed little from those available in the early Republic and served a narrow population preparing for the ministry, law, or public administration.

As new technologies transformed work, governance, and economic organization, colleges did not expand simply by enrolling more students into this inherited curriculum. They expanded by incorporating new domains of knowledge—engineering, applied science, agriculture, business, health, and professional practice—many of which had developed first through apprenticeships, industrial practice, military training, and on-the-job learning outside the academy. The growth of higher education was therefore driven by curricular diversification aligned with technological complexity, not by the replication of classical instruction at scale.

At the same time, the absolute number—and eventually the percentage—of Americans studying classical fields did rise, from well under one percent of the population in the early nineteenth century to roughly twelve percent by the early twenty-first. This increase, however, reflects changes in access and institutional reach, not renewed occupational demand for classical education. The proliferation of colleges and universities, improved transportation networks, declining reliance on subsistence agriculture, compulsory primary education, expanded secondary schooling, and later the introduction of public universities and federal aid dramatically widened the pool of individuals able to attend college at all. As higher education became geographically accessible, financially attainable, and socially normalized, classical fields persisted as one among many options within an enlarged system.

In this sense, the relative decline of classical fields as a share of total enrollment is not evidence of cultural retreat or intellectual abandonment. It is evidence of institutional adaptation. Universities grew by absorbing new forms of technologically and professionally relevant knowledge while continuing to carry forward elements of their original curriculum. Classical study survived not because it scaled to meet modern technical demands, but because expanding institutions could afford to preserve it alongside newer fields. Higher education expanded by responding to technological complexity—while classical education expanded primarily because access to higher education itself expanded.

Then, between 1900 and 1940, a second wave of technological change—electrification, the telephone, the automobile, office machines, and radio—transformed nearly every industry and every city. These systems introduced new requirements for calculation, coordination, maintenance, and management. Engineers, accountants, radio technicians, chemists, and administrators became essential to daily economic life. Much of this learning initially occurred through technical institutes, corporate training programs, military instruction, and on-the-job experience. Colleges and universities, however, increasingly became one pathway—though not the only one—through which this emerging knowledge could be systematized and credentialed. College enrollment rose accordingly, climbing from roughly 5 percent of young adults in 1900 to nearly 15 percent by 1940.

Yet degree completion lagged far behind participation. This persistent delay—what we might call the *technology–institution gap*—is visible throughout the historical record. When new technologies raise the skill demands of work, learning expands quickly across society through multiple channels. Formal institutions respond more slowly, constrained by funding models, admissions practices, curriculum design, and credentialing norms. Only after these structures adjust—often decades later—do graduation rates begin to rise. World War II and the GI Bill dramatically accelerated this alignment by expanding public universities, standardizing credentials, and subsidizing access. By 1980, college enrollment had exceeded 35 percent, while degree attainment was finally approaching 20 percent.

The Digital Revolution of the 1990s and 2000s repeated this pattern with even greater intensity. As personal computing, the internet, and cloud-based systems reshaped nearly every occupation, learning demands surged far beyond what existing institutions could immediately absorb. Coding, networking, digital design, and data analysis were often learned first through self-study, workplace immersion, bootcamps, and informal communities. Enrollment in higher education nonetheless climbed above 50 percent as colleges gradually incorporated these domains into formal programs. In the early twenty-first century, the rise of artificial intelligence and advanced automation has again raised the skill bar. Participation in higher education now approaches 60 percent, with degree attainment nearing 40 percent—reflecting not the exhaustion of learning demand, but the ongoing effort of institutions to catch up to it.

Conclusion

This chapter positions Reconstruction as a pivotal educational project for the American republic, linking learning to civic repair after slavery's distortions. Opening with Frederick Douglass's clandestine pursuit of literacy—symbolizing knowledge as agency amid structural suppression—it examines emancipation's promise and challenges. The Thirteenth and Fourteenth Amendments ended bondage and granted citizenship, but true freedom required equipping formerly enslaved people with skills for participation.

Postwar, freed communities drove a "grassroots enlightenment," building schools in makeshift spaces before the Freedmen's Bureau intervened. Institutions like Howard, Fisk, Hampton, and Tuskegee (under Booker T. Washington) blended academics with practical trades, fostering self-improvement and virtue. George Washington Carver's innovations in agriculture and "movable schools" extended education to rural areas, promoting community renewal. This urgency countered antebellum devaluation of learning, highlighting Black academic striving as a cultural continuity of resistance—rooted in spirituals' encoded wisdom—not betrayal.

Yet Southern elites resisted, limiting schooling for Blacks and poor whites, perpetuating divides. Northern migration offered opportunities but met exclusion, eroding hope as awareness outpaced agency. The chapter contrasts slavery's suppression with broader historical patterns in authoritarian systems, where education threatens hierarchy.

Philosophically, it draws on Karl Popper's conjecture-based knowledge growth, Alfred North Whitehead's adaptation to accelerating information, Thomas S. Kuhn's paradigms, and Benjamin Franklin's integration of learning with responsibility—advocating environments fusing theory and practice.

Chapter Four: The Night the Sky Moved

From Strategic Science to Networked Knowledge and Rapid Cultural Change

In October of 1957, the night sky over Peoria was still dark enough to see the stars.

The house stood four blocks up from the Illinois River. From the back door, a quiet side street sloped gently toward the river. If you walked a few yards into that lane and looked past the rooftops, you could see the water. The city was modest in size and not yet washed in permanent light. Storefronts closed at dusk. Streetlamps cast narrow amber circles that dissolved quickly into shadow. If a porch light was switched off, the sky returned. Windows were open. Air conditioning was rare. A radio, placed near the sill, carried the evening broadcast outward through the screen. The announcer's voice drifted into the yard.

The Soviets had launched something into orbit.

Families stepped outside because the newspaper had printed predicted pass times. Fathers shaded their eyes. Mothers stood quietly in the cooling air. Children pointed at the wrong stars first.

Then someone would say, "There." A small, steady point of light moved across the sky — unblinking, deliberate, indifferent. It crossed from horizon to horizon in several measured minutes.

It was Sputnik 1.

The slope toward the river did not change. The current below continued its patient course. Bradley University, only a short distance away, remained quiet behind its brick facades. Yet above that hillside neighborhood — which memory has never released — the first signal of a new era crossed the sky.

In the early mornings, a grandfather might take a small boy down toward the river with a fishing pole. Mist lifting from the water. Barges moving slowly. The world at ground level felt inherited and stable. But overhead — unseen in daylight — something now circled the Earth. The shock was not explosive. It was structural. If the sky could be entered, it could be measured. If it could be measured, it could be mastered. And if it could be mastered, then knowledge, industry, and courage would determine the balance of power.

Within months, Congress would pass the National Defense Education Act. Science and mathematics would be reframed as matters of national security. Universities would become engines of research and innovation. Learning as a civic responsibility became an even greater part of our strategic infrastructure.

In cities today, such a light might vanish into glare. The horizon hums with LEDs, and we look down into illuminated screens more often than up into darkness. But in 1957, from a quiet side street near the river, with porch lights switched off and a radio speaking softly through an open window, the sky was still legible.

From Overconfidence to Orbit

According to Robert A. Divine, in his 1993 book "The Sputnik Challenge", Democratic senators such as Henry M. (Scoop) Jackson and Stuart Symington had been critical for several years, leading up to that day in 1957, that President Eisenhower's administration did not allocate enough money for national defense. This would have included America's satellite program and the construction of what was to be America's first satellite, Vanguard, which, at the time of the Sputnik launch, was projected to be ready by early 1958. Vanguard, a six-inch-diameter satellite weighing only 3.5 pounds, was tiny compared to Sputnik's 22-inch diameter and 184-pound weight. That weight and size made the successful launch into orbit of Sputnik even more ominous to the American defense and scientific community Nevertheless, the American scientific community was congratulatory to the Soviet scientific community. While members of the Eisenhower administration dismissed Sputnik as a sideshow with no real scientific or military significance, journalists were calling the surprise success of Sputnik a crisis of confidence, comparing its significance to the splitting of the atom and labeling it a national emergency as great as Pearl Harbor. Finally, the democratic opposition, led by former President Harry Truman and Senator Adlai Stevenson, called for an all-out American mobilization to meet this threat and the challenge to our preeminence. Interestingly, the American satellite program may have been slowed by official concerns and debates over the legality of flying satellites in orbits that would take them over other nations' airspace. The Soviets forged ahead on the assumption that, because of the Earth's rotation, no nation could claim any part of the space outside of the Earth's atmosphere.

The Stoic philosopher and Roman Senator Seneca observed that hardship teaches discipline while prosperity dulls it. The pre-Sputnik decade suggests the latter; the mobilization that followed illustrates the former. Adversity clarified. It consolidated will. It narrowed priorities. It converted latent capacity into visible achievement. The lesson is not that prosperity is weakness. It is that prosperity diffuses urgency.

The years following the Second World War were marked by expansion, not urgency. American industry surged. Suburbs spread outward. Universities filled with veterans under the G.I. Bill. The nation's scientific triumphs during the war — radar, logistics, atomic power — seemed to confirm a durable superiority. Confidence was not irrational; it was earned. But confidence can relax vigilance.

It was only natural that the generation who endured Prohibition, a decade-long depression with unemployment approaching twenty-five percent, and years of total mobilization in a global war would want something different for their children. They had stood in speakeasys and breadlines. They had rationed. They had written letters across oceans. They had watched the world burn and helped rebuild it.

When prosperity finally arrived — suburban homes, steady employment, expanding universities, the baby boom — it felt earned. Parents who had lived through scarcity and sacrifice understandably wished for ease and stability for the next generation.

It is not difficult to imagine how the message might have been conveyed, even unintentionally: We endured so that you would not have to. We fought so that you could live securely. We suffered so that you could be safe. And for a time, it appeared to be true. The war was won. The economy grew. The United States stood preeminent. The sense of being permanently "out of the woods" was not delusion; it was relief.

But relief can soften vigilance. By the mid-1950s, the nation was not apathetic. It was confident. It did not believe it needed to prove itself again. Rockets were being developed, but as weapons, not as symbols. Orbit was conceivable, but not urgent. Leadership seemed secure.

Then a small sphere began to circle the Earth. The shock of Sputnik 1 was not from a technological deficiency. It was a psychological recalibration. The assumption of permanent security dissolved. We are never out of the woods. The generation that had known deprivation and war suddenly confronted a new form of vulnerability. One that required science, education, and disciplined investment rather than battlefield mobilization. Adversity returned in a different form, and urgency followed.

In the years leading up to 1957, the United States did not lack scientists, engineers, or rockets. It lacked urgency. Victory in the Second World War had been decisive. The atomic bomb, radar, long-range bombers, and industrial mass production had convinced Americans that technological superiority was not merely current — it was structural. The nation's geography still provided two oceans of distance. Its economy expanded. Suburbs grew. Televisions flickered in living rooms. The middle class widened under the provisions of the G.I. Bill. Confidence felt rational. We were justifiably proud.

American rocket development continued through the 1950s, but it was framed primarily as weaponry. Ballistic missiles were extensions of the deterrence strategy. The emphasis was on delivery systems, not orbital spectacle. Space itself was considered a scientific frontier, not yet a theater for geopolitical signaling.

The Soviet Union saw the matter differently. For Moscow, being first mattered. First satellite. First man in orbit. First woman. First spacewalk. First lunar probe. Firsts were strategic theater, proof of ideological vitality, and industrial competence. Where American planners saw rockets as instruments of defense, Soviet planners saw orbit as transportation and demonstration. A satellite circling the Earth would not merely collect data; it would communicate superiority.

The shock was not that America had no rockets. It was that someone else had moved first — and had done so publicly. A small sphere that beeped for twenty-one days revealed not technological weakness, but strategic overconfidence. The sky was no longer a sanctuary. If a satellite could orbit, a weapon could as well. Pride does not prevent capability. But it can delay urgency.

Mobilization Under Threat

When Sputnik 1 crossed the sky in October 1957, the shock was not that America lacked engineers. It was that America had assumed its leadership required no contest. The small satellite did little more than orbit and transmit a radio pulse, yet its significance was immense. Divine (1993) wrote that President

Eisenhower met with the Scientific Advisory Committee (SAC) that had been formed by President Truman in 1951. His question to them: Is the Soviet Union ahead of us scientifically? The committee chair, I.I. Rabi, responded that although America was still ahead in science and technology, the current trend would soon put the Soviets ahead because the Soviets were placing a greater emphasis on scientific literacy in their schools. Despite Eisenhower's initial skepticism that the Soviet system was educating only a handful of elites, he soon began searching for ways to encourage Americans to turn the Sputnik challenge into a sustained effort of scientific advancement.

The response was swift and concentrated. Although the Vanguard satellite launch is eclipsed in our national consciousness by the later success of Telstar, America proceeded to launch Vanguard in March 1958 as the second artificial satellite to orbit the Earth. Whereas Sputnik was launched with a set of batteries that allowed it to send data for only 21 days, Vanguard had a solar power system that allowed it to send data for over six years. Vanguard allowed us to study the shape of the Earth's gravitational field, and its six antennas allowed for precise measurements. Although Sputnik 1 has long since left orbit and burned up on reentry into Earth's atmosphere, as of this writing, Vanguard I, mocked as the "Grapefruit Satellite" by Premier Kruschev, is still in orbit. Within a year, NASA was formed, and federal investment in science education surged. Within five years, America placed Telstar, a successful communications satellite, into orbit around the Earth that could relay radio and television broadcasts around the world. In 1962, Telstar 1 relayed the first live transatlantic television broadcast. Unlike Sputnik, which proved the sky could be entered, Telstar proved it could be used. Sputnik had been a symbol. Telstar was a system. Although the Eisenhower administration did not buy into the belief that the soviets were pulling ahead of us scientifically, the real fear was that if their rockets could deliver such a bulky and heavy payload into space, they might be on the verge of perfecting an intercontinental ballistic missile (ICBM), which would be not only the world's first ICBM but one capable of delivering a nuclear warhead to the United States.

Within twelve years, the United States placed a man on the moon. Between the Sputnik challenge and the moon landing, American research universities, defense laboratories, and industrial contractors aligned in a level of coordinated effort rarely seen in peacetime. When President Kennedy announced the lunar goal in 1961, the objective was clear: demonstrate unequivocal technological leadership. Apollo was not an incremental exploration. It was a concentrated mobilization. At its peak, the program consumed roughly four percent of the federal budget. Engineers, contractors, universities, and federal agencies aligned around a single, visible objective. The Saturn V rocket was not merely engineering; it was orchestration. In 1969, the United States achieved the moon landing. The sprint had succeeded.

It was the mobilization not only of budgets and laboratories, but of imagination. A prosperous country had rediscovered urgency. A confident nation had found discipline. The Saturday morning launch was not merely a program schedule; it was civic alignment made visible. That alignment would culminate in Apollo. And then it would dissipate. For a time. We will discuss Artemis later.

If Telstar signaled that orbit could carry voices, the Mercury program made orbit personal. On certain mornings in the early 1960s, families gathered around televisions for launches. The broadcast did not feel like a spectacle; it felt like participation.

Countdown clocks ticked. Commentators spoke in careful tones. Engineers' voices crackled over open microphones.

When Alan Shepard lifted off in 1961, the nation watched not only a rocket but a representative. His mission was brief — a suborbital flight — but it marked a turning point. America was no longer merely reacting. It was ascending.

Children memorized names the way earlier generations had memorized baseball lineups. The original NASA Mercury astronauts — the "Mercury Seven" — became fixtures of the national imagination:

- Alan Shepard
- John Glenn
- Gus Grissom
- Scott Carpenter
- Wally Schirra
- Gordon Cooper
- Deke Slayton

To a young boy, they were not abstractions. They were known by name. Gus Grissom — even the name itself sounded forged for flight. The intimacy of those broadcasts mattered. The nation did not simply fund science; we witnessed it and took pride in it. We learned the language of boosters, capsules, and recovery ships. Technical vocabulary entered living rooms.

This was mobilization under threat, but also mobilization through attention. The space program was not hidden behind classified walls. It was televised. It was narrated. It was absorbed. And in that absorption, a generation internalized urgency.

The moon landing was not a weekday interruption or a classroom television rolled into place. It was Sunday evening,

July 20, 1969. Families had finished dinner. Church services were done. In one Midwestern living room, at a Sunday school gathering, children who had been playing moments earlier gathered around a television set as the Lunar Module descended. The room was not silent in the way a launch broadcast had been silent years earlier. There was the noise of children. Adults shifting in chairs. Someone adjusts the antenna. Then the voice: "Houston, Tranquility Base here. The Eagle has landed."

In that moment, a program that had begun as a response to Sputnik 1 achieved its visible objective. Twelve years earlier, a sphere had beeped overhead. Now, a human voice spoke from the surface of the moon. The mobilization had culminated.

Because it was aired live on television on Sunday evening —not behind closed doors, not limited to specialists — the achievement belonged to everyone. It entered living rooms, fellowship halls, and church basements. A republic under pressure had aligned its attention and its resources long enough to accomplish something extraordinary.

The Fifty-Five Year Question

So, we arrive at the present. If we placed men on the moon in 1969, why are we speaking, more than half a century later, about returning cautiously? The answer is not lost knowledge. It is altered incentives.

Much like Sputnik, Apollo had been designed as a proof-of-concept and a geopolitical first. Once the objective was achieved, the urgency dissolved. The Cold War did not end, but the symbolic contest for the moon had. Repeating lunar landings offered diminishing geopolitical returns. Public attention shifted. Budget tolerance contracted. The nation reallocated its focus.

The post-Apollo decades did not represent technological decline. They represented redirection. Investment flowed into:

- Satellite communications
- Navigation systems
- Weather monitoring
- Integrated circuits
- Computing
- The early ARPANET
- Eventually, the internet

The center of gravity moved from physical demonstration to informational dominance. Instead of planting flags, the United States built networks. Apollo was justified by existential competition. Today's lunar initiatives must be justified by long-term exploration, commercial viability, scientific research, and international cooperation. Those motivations require coordination rather than fear. A sprint fueled by rivalry is easier to initiate than a marathon sustained by prosperity. The deeper question for a learning republic is whether we can generate disciplined, long-term alignment without an existential threat. Adversity clarifies. Prosperity diffuses.

The nation that once concentrated its effort to win a race now operates within a distributed, networked system of public-private partnerships, global supply chains, and competing domestic priorities. It has not forgotten how to reach the moon. It has reconsidered why. The difference between 1969 and today is not competence. It is consensus.

When the United States went to the Moon in the 1960s, it went the way a nation goes to war — with concentration, urgency, and an end date already implied. The Apollo program was not designed to create a place where people would live. It was designed to demonstrate that a free society — where the people are sovereign, and government acts in their service — could mobilize knowledge and solve a problem faster than a centralized system in which authority rests in the state, and citizens serve its purposes.

Half a century later, the United States has begun again, but in a different spirit. The Artemis program does not aim to repeat Apollo. Instead of one mission carrying everything, it assembles a system. The Space Launch System lifting crews in the Orion spacecraft, meeting other vehicles, transferring to landers, and returning through a developing network that will eventually include staging stations and reusable transports. The architecture resembles trade more than conquest: ships depart, arrive, depart again. The goal is not a moment but a sustainable effort.

Accelerated Cultural Change

In the fall of 1963, our country school still felt older than the decade. Four teachers covered eight grades. Farm boys carried pocketknives, not for fighting but to cut the twine from a bale of hay to feed the livestock before boarding the bus for school. They sometimes witnessed and discussed calves born before dawn. Eighth-grade girls brought records by artists such as Ricky Nelson, Elvis Presley, and Jerry Lee Lewis to play when the principal, who doubled as our teacher, stepped out of the room. Our classroom that year was a mix of fourth and eighth-grade students, so the ages ranged from nine to fourteen years.

Then November came. I remember learning of President Kennedy's assassination, as a nine-year-old, while on the playground during recess. The air felt different that afternoon. The playground grew silent. As if someone had lowered the volume of the world. In the weeks after President Kennedy's assassination, the country moved carefully. Christmas felt muted. Public language softened. Adults lowered their voices.

Then, in February 1964, four young Englishmen stepped off a plane in New York. When the Beatles appeared on The Ed Sullivan Show, only seventy-three days after the JFK assassination, the screaming and tears at their concerts were regarded as teenage hysteria. It may have been something deeper. A nation that had absorbed months of grief suddenly found permission to exhale. The energy felt disproportionate because it carried more than rhythm. It carried release.

Everything changed. We, nine-year-old boys who had argued over marbles and swapped comic books, began discussing music. The eighth-grade girls' records changed. By spring, it was the Beatles and Herman's Hermits spinning on the classroom turntable.

Following on the heels of the Beatles were numerous British musical groups, many of whom had been playing American black rhythm and blues music. They arrived in America and played this music to audiences who had never heard it before. America had already experienced an earlier tremor in 1956, when Elvis Presley carried rhythm and blues into mainstream white audiences. Working with the songwriting team of Jerry Leiber and Mike Stoller, Presley helped transmit a musical vocabulary rooted in Black Southern tradition. "Hound Dog," written by Leiber and Stoller for Big Mama Thornton, had already traveled one cultural path before reaching Elvis's stage. Soon, Elvis's manager, Colonel Tom Parker, who controlled who had direct access to the singer, ultimately restricted the collaboration between Presley and the songwriters Leiber and Stoller, and redirected Presley's career toward Hollywood films and commercially driven projects.

By the early 1960s, popular music in much of mainstream America had returned to lighter themes — cars, beaches, adolescent romance. When British bands revived and amplified American blues and rhythm traditions, they reintroduced that earlier charge with intensified force. What had flickered in 1956 now surged. Music had long served as generational glue. The swing era had done so during World War II. What distinguished the 1960s was not that youth shared songs, but that amplified music became a boundary marker. In a newly networked culture, sound increasingly differentiated youth identity from institutional authority.

Ian MacDonald, in Revolution in the Head, noted that The Beatles' success was not just musical but *cultural*, aligning with emerging youth identity and generational self-awareness in 1960s America. The zebra crossing in front of Abby Road Studios is a cultural icon. My long-suffering wife and I, both in our 70s, walked more than an hour across the West End of London last year just to see it.

The mobilization that placed men on the moon relied on disciplined engineering, but it also relied on clarity of objective. The goal was visible, the outcome measurable, and the consequences immediate. In the same decade, however, technocratic confidence migrated into a different arena. Under Robert McNamara, a former president of Ford Motor Company and one of the "best and brightest" of his generation, war became a problem of systems analysis. Quantitative metrics — sorties flown, targets destroyed, body counts tallied — became indicators of progress. In The Best and the Brightest, David Halberstam described cabinet meetings in which intellectual dominance often mattered as much as deliberation. Debate could become performance. Precision could substitute for wisdom. Decades later, Robert McNamara would write in In Retrospect that the failure lay not in lack of intelligence or dedication, but in misjudgment — in misreading history, culture, and the limits of military power. Systems and metrics had obscured deeper realities.

With the new communications satellites in place, for the first time in American history, sustained combat operations were reported nightly into domestic living rooms. Correspondents stood amid smoke and debris. Footage of firefights, evacuations, and casualty counts accompanied the evening news. The conflict in Vietnam did not arrive weeks later in print. It arrived each night, compressed into minutes, sequenced between commercial breaks. The same infrastructure that had allowed Americans to watch rockets ascend now allowed them to watch a war in near real-time. It was a very personal war because if it didn't directly affect your family, it affected a family that you knew. War was no longer abstract. It was visible, and visibility affects interpretation. While policy discussions in Washington increasingly relied on metrics and projections, the public encountered imagery. Sortie counts and body counts were summarized numerically in briefings. But the nightly news did not display spreadsheets. It displayed faces. In a networked environment, image and number do not weigh equally.

The Vietnam War was a critical force in transforming American culture, especially for young people. The widespread use of television brought brutal images of the conflict into homes, fueling public dissent and youth activism. Their music amplified the dissent. The war introduced a wide cross-section of young Americans to drugs.

Long before the Vietnam War, the mountains where Myanmar, Laos, and Thailand meet — later called the Golden Triangle — were already tied into global narcotics commerce. The region's terrain made large-scale agriculture difficult but favored poppy cultivation, and opium had been grown there since at least the 16th–17th centuries.

In early Southeast Asian societies, opium was not primarily criminal. It functioned as medicine, trade commodity, and taxable good. When European colonial empires consolidated control in the 19th century, they did not suppress the drug; they systematized it. The French colonial administration in Indochina operated an official monopoly that generated state revenue, and even revolutionary movements later financed their governments through opium taxation.

After World War II the colonial system fractured. Nationalist wars, insurgencies, and border instability reshaped the uplands into semi-autonomous zones where central authority was weak. The decisive turning point came in 1949 when defeated Chinese Nationalist (Kuomintang) forces fled into Burma and took control of the mountain regions. They expanded cultivation and protected trafficking networks in exchange for arms and survival.

By the mid-1950s, production surged dramatically, in some areas increasing ten- to twenty-fold, because opium was the only reliable commodity that traders would purchase in insecure war zones. Thus, the narcotic trade had become a currency of stateless warfare. The drug's spread among American troops in Vietnam reached epidemic proportions. Lee N. Robins, in her study of drug use among American soldiers in Vietnam, reported that heroin use was as high as 34% of the troops. However, she found that when the troops returned home, very few continued the use of the drug. The drug problem was apparently attached to the environment, and not the person.

Although addiction rates collapsed upon the return home of the soldiers, cultural transmission of the drug culture still occurred. Many of us had classmates who had returned from Vietnam, and their stories of drug use were intriguing.

As the war in Vietnam escalated, student deferments linked higher education to military policy in an unprecedented way. Continued enrollment provided temporary protection from conscription, and college attendance expanded rapidly during these years. Much of that growth reflected the longer postwar expansion of opportunity, yet the deferment structure added a new layer of incentive. Academic standing now carries consequences beyond scholarship alone. The intersection of education and national service introduced pressures that subtly altered institutional dynamics, including debates over grading standards and evaluation practices.

As cultural dissent expanded in the mid-1960s, it would be naïve to assume that America's geopolitical adversaries ignored it. Intelligence services of every superpower seek opportunities to amplify division within competitors. Soviet propaganda during the Cold War frequently highlighted racial injustice and antiwar sentiment in the United States, not because it created those grievances, but because they existed.

Yet exploitation can only take advantage of divisions and doubts. The unrest on American campuses was rooted primarily in domestic realities — the draft, rising casualty counts in Vietnam, and a growing generational skepticism toward institutions. Foreign actors may have magnified the noise, but the signal originated at home. Fragmentation rarely requires invention. It requires amplification. The assassination of President Kennedy unsettled emotional security. The escalation in Vietnam strained trust in leadership. The draft personalized foreign policy for millions of young men. Televised war footage compressed the distance between battlefield and living room.

Cultural acceleration intensified the generational divide. The same networks that had unified attention around Mercury launches now amplified protest songs and campus unrest. None of this required foreign invention. It required only amplification. Cold War adversaries were neither blind nor passive. Soviet propaganda outlets routinely highlighted racial injustice, antiwar demonstrations, and domestic dissent in the United States. Intelligence services of every superpower study fault lines in competitors. But exploitation follows fracture. It does not create it from nothing. The deeper lesson is structural: once a society's information networks expand, every crack, every division among people, becomes more visible — and more scalable.

Thus, Apollo 11's landing in July 1969 was viewed by a very different nation than the one that celebrated the success of Telstar. We were a country strained by war, protest, and generational conflict. For millions, it was the culmination of a disciplined national effort. For others, it symbolized misdirected priority. In the early 1970s, songwriter John Stewart captured the critique in a haunting lyric about a girl in Calcutta who "watched a man named Armstrong walk upon the moon." The contrast was deliberate: technological magnificence against persistent human suffering.

The argument was not frivolous. It was moral. Why invest so heavily in lunar exploration while poverty endured on Earth? Yet the question contained an assumption that investment in exploration and investment in human welfare were mutually exclusive. The space program did not merely plant flags. It accelerated materials science, telecommunications, computing, and manufacturing. It employed hundreds of thousands of Americans. It expanded engineering education. It stimulated industries that would shape global development for decades, including in countries far from Cape Canaveral.

Apollo was not charity withheld. It was capability and opportunity expanded. But capability, when viewed through different moral lenses, does not look the same. That divergence marked a turning point. The moon landing no longer unified interpretation. It revealed an interpretive fracture.

Seeds of Division Were Sown Even Before Telstar's Triumphant Broadcast

In October 1960, during the razor-thin presidential race between Richard Nixon and John F. Kennedy, Martin Luther King Jr. was arrested in Atlanta for participating in a sit-in at a segregated department store. Sentenced to hard labor at a brutal Georgia prison for a probation violation from a minor traffic offense, King's life was in genuine peril—lynchings and violence against Black prisoners remained common, and he was not yet a national figure whose death would spark widespread outrage. The King family appealed to both candidates for intervention.

Nixon, who had championed the 1957 Civil Rights Act and earned honorary membership in the NAACP in the 1940s for his early advocacy, chose not to act publicly. He viewed the matter as a state issue and weighed the electoral risks in the South, believing he needed to win the presidency first to enact lasting change without political constraint. Despite their prior friendship and Nixon's frequent advice-seeking calls, King later reflected on Nixon's silence with disappointment: "It was as if Nixon had never heard of me."

Kennedy, however, made a compassionate call to Coretta Scott King and had his brother Robert pressure Georgia officials, securing King's release the next day. One well-timed act—Kennedy's call—reshaped public memory and shifted loyalties.

The irony is striking. Nixon had been one of the strongest congressional advocates for civil rights legislation in the 1950s, leading the push for the 1957 Voting Rights Act against fierce opposition from Southern Democrats. As a California congressman in the 1940s, he had been awarded honorary membership in the NAACP for his early advocacy against discrimination, including anti-lynching legislation and fair employment practices. Kennedy, by contrast, had voted for the weakened version of the 1957 Voting Rights bill after opposing stronger enforcement provisions. Yet in this visible moment, Kennedy's gesture carried the day in public perception, while Nixon's restraint—driven by long-term strategy—cost him dearly in the narrative.

Yet the deeper lesson is this: a republic depends on leaders who understand that true stewardship—especially when entrusted with the leadership of the party of Lincoln—means rising above the temptation to win at all costs and choosing instead to do what is right when the moment is visible, and the stakes are clear. History remembers not just who won, but who dared to act justly in the face of risk. More broadly, the episode reveals how powerful a single moment in time can be. One well-timed gesture—Kennedy's call—reshaped perceptions, shifted loyalties, and set in motion a realignment whose consequences still echo in American politics. History is not always moved by grand strategies or long-term records; sometimes it turns on a single act, amplified by timing, symbolism, and public memory. In a learning republic, the challenge is to recognize those moments, understand their weight, and learn from them. This same principle applies to education in America. When leaders prioritize short-term optics over the long-term civic need for broad, practical access to learning—whether through vocational pathways, community colleges, or the college of hard knocks—the republic pays a price in diminished opportunity and shared purpose.

The incident upended perceptions of the parties. For generations, Republicans had championed civil rights—from Lincoln's Emancipation to Eisenhower's enforcement of school desegregation in Little Rock—while Democrats, dominated by Southern segregationists like LBJ in his early career, blocked anti-lynching laws and voting rights measures. But Kennedy's single, well-timed intervention flipped the script in Black communities, boosting his share of the African American vote to 68–70% (up from Eisenhower's 39% in 1956) and providing the margin in key states like Illinois and Michigan. This accelerated a realignment: Black voters, already shifting Democratic for New Deal economics, now saw the party as a civil rights ally, while Republicans began courting disaffected white Southerners. By 1964, with Barry Goldwater's opposition to the Civil Rights Act, the pivot was complete—Black support for Democrats hit 94% under LBJ.

This realignment fractured the national consensus that had fueled the space race. The shift was structural: as Black voters moved decisively toward Democrats in response to civil rights gestures and policy differences, Republicans increasingly courted white Southern voters alienated by the same changes. Neil Maher writes in *Apollo in the Age of Aquarius* (2017) that the early 1960s optimism surrounding American space efforts—symbolized by Telstar's transatlantic broadcasts in 1962—gave way to a polarized politics in which civil rights battles, amplified by Vietnam and cultural upheaval, redefined party identities and eroded cross-partisan trust. Roger D. Launius, former NASA Chief Historian, documents in his analysis of polling data that public support for Project Apollo never reached majority enthusiasm in the 1960s and declined sharply as Vietnam and domestic crises dominated attention, making large national projects harder to sustain in a divided republic. Teasel Muir-Harmony similarly shows in *Operation Moonglow* (2020) that the bipartisan geopolitical unity behind Apollo was fragile and tied to the early 1960s moment; by the late 1960s, the civil rights realignment and Vietnam shifted national focus, fracturing the consensus that had once rallied resources and imagination around space exploration.

Yet it also taught a deeper lesson: adversity, like Sputnik, can clarify priorities—but only if we learn from history without partisan blinders. Nixon's hesitation in 1960, despite his strong civil rights record, underscores this irony: his belief that winning was essential for lasting impact led to a decision that ultimately contributed to the GOP's loss of Black voters and the deepening partisan divide. More broadly, the episode reveals how powerful a single moment in time can be. One well-timed gesture—Kennedy's call—reshaped perceptions, shifted loyalties, and set in motion a realignment whose consequences still echo in American politics. History is not always moved by grand strategies or long-term records; sometimes it turns on a single act, amplified by timing, symbolism, and public memory.

Valuing All Paths: Nixon's Defense of Career and Technical Learning

Amid the campus unrest and enrollment surges of the Vietnam era, one voice consistently reminded the nation that learning is not synonymous with schooling—and that scholarly pursuits are not inherently superior to mastering a trade or craft. Vice President and later President Richard Nixon repeatedly articulated this belief, drawing on the republic's early traditions of home-based and apprenticeship learning.

Nixon argued that "too often vocational education is foolishly stigmatized as being less desirable than academic preparation," and that the system must allow students to combine "the most valuable features of both vocational and academic education." He championed career education—a comprehensive initiative to ensure every student left high school with a marketable skill or clear path—stating in his 1972 State of the Union address that it grew from his conviction that schools should build "self-reliance and self-sufficiency" for a "productive and fulfilling life."

This stance echoed the early Republic's reliance on apprenticeships and family-guided learning, before industrialization necessitated common schools. Nixon recognized that not everyone is suited for—or benefits from—a four-year college degree. He pushed for expanded vocational programs, research grants, and policies that honored diverse capabilities: engineers and artisans, scholars and skilled tradespeople. "We need everyone," he implied—America's strength lay in cultivating all forms of human potential, not in funneling youth toward a single model of success.

Yet the Vietnam-era draft inverted these priorities. Deferments drove inflated enrollments, often mismatched with student interests or aptitudes, while grade inflation protected deferments rather than measuring genuine learning. Universities became draft havens rather than places of disciplined inquiry. The resulting distortions—credentialism, skills gaps in trades—underscored Nixon's warning: when we devalue practical learning, we weaken the republic itself.

Cold War Science, Credentialism, and the Technical Capability Crisis

The postwar decades brought both expansion and distortion. In response to the launch of Sputnik in 1957, American policymakers poured resources into advanced mathematics, physics, and engineering, strengthening the scientific infrastructure needed for Cold War competition (Rudolph 2002; Geiger 1997). At the same time, the four-year academic degree increasingly became the cultural gold standard of success. Vocational and technical education—though crucial to the functioning of the economy—often carried lower prestige and received comparatively less institutional attention (Labaree 1997).

By the late twentieth century, deindustrialization, automation, and globalization were reshaping the labor market. Many well-paid manufacturing jobs disappeared, relocated, or were transformed by new technologies (Autor, Levy, and Murnane 2003; Goldin and Katz 2008). In theory, higher education would prepare workers for new roles; in practice, the proliferation of degrees sometimes widened the gap between credentials and demonstrable technical capability. Career and technical education (CTE) programs were neglected, apprenticeships declined, and civics instruction waned (Symonds, Schwartz, and Ferguson 2011). A growing share of young people were steered toward college even when the fit was poor, while skilled trades faced persistent shortages (Carnevale, Smith, and Strohl 2010).

Before addressing pathways, it is necessary to confront the role of signaling. In education and labor markets alike, credentials function not only as evidence of skill acquisition but as social signals—communicating status, presumed competence, and future potential to employers, institutions, and peers. As Michael Spence demonstrated in his foundational work on job-market signaling, such signals often operate independently of the actual capabilities they are meant to represent (Spence 1973). Over time, the four-year college degree came to signal general intelligence, perseverance, and social legitimacy, while career and technical credentials—regardless of their rigor or economic value—were widely interpreted as signals of limitation or diminished promise (Labaree 1997; Carnevale, Smith, and Strohl 2010). These perceptions shaped behavior upstream: students, parents, counselors, and schools responded rationally to the prevailing signal structure, steering young people toward college even when the fit was poor and away from technical pathways even when aptitude and interest were strong.

Research on STEM attrition and credential inflation suggests that part of the emerging technical capability crisis stems not from a lack of intelligence or effort among students, but from uneven signaling across academic disciplines. Engineering, physics, and other mathematically intensive fields impose externally constrained standards—governed by physical laws, cumulative skill hierarchies, and unambiguous correctness—that quickly expose gaps in preparation (Seymour and Hewitt 1997; Chen 2013). Many non-STEM programs, by contrast, vary widely in methodological rigor, cumulative technical demand, and performance thresholds. When standards differ so sharply, students encountering early resistance in technically demanding fields may switch majors for reasons unrelated to interest, motivation, or long-term potential (Stinebrickner and Stinebrickner 2014).

This distortion is compounded by a narrow conception of intelligence. Research on multiple intelligences, most prominently associated with Howard Gardner, challenges the assumption that human capability can be reduced to a single academic dimension (Gardner 1983). Individuals may excel in logical-mathematical reasoning, spatial and mechanical intuition, interpersonal judgment, linguistic expression, or embodied problem-solving—often in combinations that resist simple ranking. A society that equates intelligence primarily with abstract academic performance risks misreading talent. We are all capable of doing something that others—just as gifted in their own domains of excellence—cannot easily do. When educational systems privilege one narrow form of excellence and treat others as secondary, they misallocate human potential rather than cultivate it (Sternberg 1997; Gardner 1999).

Modern technological societies require vastly more engineers, physicists, and applied technologists than philosophers or historians—not because one form of knowledge is intrinsically more valuable than another, but because the material infrastructure of contemporary life depends upon technical competence at scale (National Academies 2017). Yet engineering and physics curricula have too often been structured to treat early failure as disqualification rather than as a stage of mastery. Research shows that many capable students exit technical fields not because they lack ability, but because early setbacks are interpreted—by institutions or by students themselves—as permanent judgments rather than signals for targeted support and iterative learning (Seymour and Hewitt 1997; Ohland et al. 2008). A learning republic does not lower standards for technical competence; it designs pathways that allow capable individuals time, feedback, and structured support to meet those standards. Forgiving early failure is not indulgence—it is talent conservation.

Dan Sturtevant and others describe the cumulative result as a technical capability crisis: a widening mismatch between the skills a technologically sophisticated economy requires and the skills existing educational institutions reliably produce (Sturtevant 2019; National Academies 2017). The problem is not simply the number of degrees conferred, but the alignment between what people are trained to do and what contemporary society actually needs.

The consequences of this misalignment are increasingly visible from the employer side of the economy. Jim Farley, chief executive of Ford Motor Company, has repeatedly argued in public interviews that the United States faces a profound shortage of skilled technical workers—not only engineers, but technicians, electricians, toolmakers, and advanced manufacturing specialists essential to modern industrial production (Farley 2022; Farley 2023). Farley has emphasized that many of these roles require deep technical competence, continual upskilling, and systems-level understanding, yet do not require a traditional four-year academic degree. In his view, the problem is not a lack of work ethic or intelligence among young people, but an educational signaling system that systematically undervalues career and technical education while oversubscribing college pathways that are poorly aligned with industrial needs.

Farley's critique echoes the broader signaling failure described earlier. When a bachelor's degree functions as the default marker of ability, students who might thrive in applied technical fields are diverted away from pathways that would better match their talents, while employers struggle to staff roles critical to productivity, innovation, and national competitiveness (Spence 1973; National Academies 2017). Farley has argued that rebuilding robust apprenticeship pipelines and modern CTE programs is not an act of nostalgia, but a prerequisite for competing in an era of electric vehicles, advanced manufacturing, and digitally integrated supply chains (Farley 2023).

Seen in this light, the technical capability crisis is not confined to education policy debates; it is experienced daily by firms attempting to operate technologically sophisticated systems with an insufficiently prepared workforce. The disconnect Farley describes reinforces a central claim of a learning republic: talent exists across the population, but institutions misroute it. When capable individuals are steered away from technical mastery because of status signaling rather than aptitude, both workers and society incur long-term costs.

The Digital Age: Technology as Instrument and Environment

The internet has made knowledge available at a scale that Thomas Jefferson or Alfred North Whitehead could scarcely have imagined. In the mid-1990s, Bill Clinton quipped that when he took office only high-energy physicists had heard of the World Wide Web; four years later, even his cat had its own page (Clinton 2000). Today, billions of people carry smartphones more powerful than the computers that guided the Apollo missions, compressing unprecedented computational capability into everyday life (NASA 2019; McGee 2020).

Digital platforms have transformed how learning is delivered. Universities—including large nonprofit institutions—now offer entire degree programs online, enabling working adults to study in the evenings after work or while caring for families (Allen and Seaman 2017). Platforms such as Coursera, edX, and Udemy provide modular courses in subjects ranging from cloud computing to photography, often taught by industry practitioners as well as university faculty (Hollands and Tirthali 2014). Community colleges and public libraries increasingly host hybrid programs that blend online instruction with local support, expanding access while preserving human connection (American Library Association 2019).

Inherited Structures and Civic Measurement

The institutional arrangements established during the founding and expansion of the American republic did not disappear as circumstances changed; they persisted, often repurposed for new administrative goals. Categories and systems originally designed to support governance, taxation, and political representation continued to shape how educational opportunity was organized and measured. Over time, these inherited structures interacted with evolving social, economic, and technological conditions in ways that would later complicate access to learning and civic participation—a set of challenges examined in detail in subsequent chapters.

Dewey, Tocqueville, and the Apprenticeship Tradition

Long before contemporary debates about higher education and workforce alignment, American thinkers recognized that learning divorced from productive work carries civic risk.

Alexis de Tocqueville observed that American society was sustained not primarily by abstract political theory, but by habits formed through participation in everyday economic and civic life. Work, for Tocqueville, was not merely a means of survival; it was a school of moderation. Commercial and professional activity forced Americans to negotiate differences, accept limits, and cooperate with others whose beliefs they did not share. These habits tempered ideological excess by anchoring citizens in practical reality.

John Dewey, often misunderstood as a proponent of schooling detached from material concerns, argued the opposite. For Dewey, education was most effective when it was continuous with lived experience, especially productive activity. He warned that learning confined to symbolic or rhetorical exercises risked becoming detached from consequence. Knowledge, in Dewey's formulation, was not validated by coherence alone, but by its ability to guide intelligent action in the world.

The apprenticeship tradition—which predates both modern universities and modern societies—embodied this principle. In this sense, contemporary forms of work-integrated learning represent not a departure from educational tradition, but a return to a long-standing model in which learning, responsibility, and civic formation developed together. Apprentices learned not only technical skill, but judgment, restraint, and responsibility through participation in real work under real constraints. Error had consequences. Success required cooperation. Mastery was demonstrated through performance, not proclamation.

The integration of learning with meaningful work has long served as a quiet stabilizer in self-governing societies. Thinkers such as Tocqueville and Dewey understood that education divorced from consequence risks becoming unmoored from judgment, while apprenticeship traditions demonstrated how responsibility disciplines learning through practice. Residential academic environments, for all their strengths, concentrate identity formation in ways that can intensify shared affiliation without always being disciplined by external responsibility, particularly when young learners are insulated from economic and civic accountability. By contrast, work-integrated learning—through apprenticeships, cooperative education, or professional practice—anchors ideas in reality, requiring learners to negotiate difference, accept limitation, and bear responsibility for outcomes. Pathways that combine study with meaningful work do more than prepare people for employment; they cultivate citizens capable of sustaining disagreement without fracture and conviction without absolutism.

Conclusion

This chapter explores the mid-20th-century pivot from postwar confidence to renewed educational urgency, triggered by Sputnik 1's 1957 orbit—a symbol of Soviet technological prowess that shattered American assumptions of unchallenged superiority. Opening with a vivid scene of families gazing skyward in Peoria, Illinois, it contrasts pre-Sputnik complacency (e.g., underfunded satellite programs like Vanguard) with the swift mobilization that followed: formation of NASA, the National Defense Education Act (1958) emphasizing STEM, and massive investments in research universities and defense labs. Critics like Senators Jackson and Symington, alongside public outcry equating the launch to Pearl Harbor, reframed science as national security, accelerating innovations from Telstar's transatlantic broadcasts to the Apollo moon landing (1969).

The narrative traces broader technological waves: post-WWII GI Bill expansions democratizing higher education; electrification and automation demanding new skills learned via apprenticeships and on-the-job training before universities formalized them; and the digital revolution (1990s–2000s) surging demands for coding and data analysis through self-study and bootcamps. Enrollment patterns (detailed in Appendices F–G) reveal institutions lagging behind complexity—classical fields persisting for elites while applied domains grew with access. North-South divergences reaffirm technology's driver: Northern mechanization spurred dense learning ecosystems, while Southern stagnation confirmed innovation's role in educational evolution.

Philosophically, it draws on Seneca's hardship-discipline link, Alfred North Whitehead's shortening knowledge cycles, and John Dewey's integration of learning with experience, warning against divorcing education from consequence. Figures like Elon Musk exemplify transformative mastery via immersion, not credentials alone. As AI raises the skill bar, the chapter argues for lifelong, work-embedded pathways to sustain adaptability and self-government.

This era's mobilizations—from Sputnik's sprint to digital adaptations—highlight learning's strategic infrastructure, setting the stage for Section Two's examination of human learning mechanisms and their civic implications.

Jefferson's call for universal education established a foundational principle: a self-governing republic depends on an informed citizenry. Over time, the nation steadily broadened its understanding of who properly participates in constitutional self-government—a trajectory the author affirms without reservation. Every community of American citizens should be included both in learning opportunities and in the representative process.

Yet history shows that as such participation expanded, educational preparation did not always advance in step. Education was widely understood as essential to self-government, but access to it remained uneven and incomplete. This mismatch produced a recurring structural tension within the republic: political inclusion was sometimes extended before the learning infrastructure necessary for informed participation had been firmly established.

A durable republic requires more than formal recognition alone. New participants must first be acknowledged as rightful members of the civic body, but that recognition must then be matched by sustained investments in learning opportunities that prepare citizens for civic responsibility. When participation expands faster than educational systems adapt, the burden placed on individuals often exceeds the preparation they have been given, weakening not only personal agency but the representative process.

This pattern—welcoming new participants into civic life more rapidly than institutions were prepared to support them—has recurred during periods of social and technological change.

It arose not because newcomers lacked commitment or capacity, but because general educational systems expanded unevenly while fewer resources were devoted to deliberating civic learning structures designed to transmit the republic's foundational principles, lawful norms, and expectations of civic conduct—principles without which participation cannot be sustained.

What John Dewey helps us see is that a free society is not merely a system of voting or formal rights, but a way of living together. In *Democracy and Education*, Dewey described a free, self-governing society as "a mode of associated living, of conjoint communicated experience" (Dewey, 1916). Participation, in this sense, is not exhausted by casting a ballot. It requires shared understanding, mutual intelligibility, and the habits of cooperation that make self-government possible.

From this perspective, the challenge faced during periods of rapid social change—whether the arrival of large immigrant populations in the late nineteenth century or the expansion of suffrage in the twentieth—was not that new participants were unfit for self-government. On the contrary, many arrived with strong motivation to belong, contribute, and participate. The structural problem lay elsewhere: the learning systems required to translate commitment into effective civic participation lagged behind the expansion of civic inclusion (Dewey, 1916; Dewey, 1927).

Dewey would have rejected the idea that a free society is sustained by exclusion. But he was equally clear that self government cannot function without education. Education, he argued, is the means by which a self-governing society "renews itself" across generations (Dewey, 1916, p. 87). When individuals are brought into civic life without access to shared language, institutional knowledge, or opportunities for informed participation, the burden placed on them exceeds the preparation they have been given. The result is not empowerment, but strain—on individuals and on civic institutions alike (Dewey, 1927).

Seen through this lens, the experiences of immigrants in the late nineteenth and early twentieth centuries illustrate not a failure of republican principle, but a failure of sequencing. Civic inclusion expanded faster than the educational infrastructure needed to support it. Community-based responses—settlement houses, labor schools, civic leagues, and adult education programs—emerged precisely to close that gap. They functioned as spaces where learning, work, and civic identity developed together rather than in isolation (Addams, 1902; Dewey, 1937).

This pattern reinforces a central claim of this book. A durable self-governing society requires more than the extension of formal rights. It requires deliberate investment in learning environments that allow new participants to acquire not only skills, but shared civic understanding. When education precedes and accompanies participation, civic responsibility deepens. When participation is expanded without corresponding learning opportunities, civic life becomes more fragile—not because new participants lack capacity, but because the institutions meant to prepare them have not kept pace (Dewey, 1916; Dewey, 1938).

By the late nineteenth century, American society was undergoing a profound transformation. Industrialization, urbanization, and mass immigration altered the conditions of work and civic life within a single generation. In response, new forms of education emerged outside traditional schools. Settlement houses, labor schools, civic leagues, and adult education programs sought to translate civic inclusion into effective participation by linking learning directly to lived experience. These institutions reflected a recognition that education could not be confined to childhood, nor to formal schooling alone.

Yet even these innovations were shaped by an older assumption: that education could prepare individuals for relatively stable roles in work and society. That assumption began to fracture as scientific and technological change accelerated. In 1929, Alfred North Whitehead captured the rupture when he observed that the cycle of knowledge had become shorter than a human lifespan. What once could be learned in youth and relied upon for a lifetime now risked becoming obsolete within decades. Education, he argued, would have to become continuous or fail.

The mid-twentieth century confirmed Whitehead's insight. The G.I. Bill demonstrated that large-scale adult education could reshape a nation's economic and civic capacity, and that adults brought distinctive experience, motivation, and responsibility to learning. It also marked a decisive shift: education was no longer merely preparation for life, but a recurring necessity across it.

Taken together, these developments mark a transition from universal education to lifelong learning. What began as a republican safeguard—education sufficient to sustain self-government—has become an ongoing requirement in a society where work, knowledge, and civic demands continually change. The historical record shows that when learning opportunities expand alongside participation, civic responsibility deepens; when they lag behind, strain accumulates.

Building on ideas that trace back at least to the Jacksonian era, John Dewey argued in *Experience and Education* (1938) that learning is not a matter of passive transmission but a continuous reconstruction of experience. Education, in this view, is not preparation for some future condition of life, but an active process through which individuals develop judgment by engaging with real problems, social relationships, and practical activity. Dewey insisted that knowledge gains meaning only when it is connected to lived experience, requiring education to integrate work, cooperation, and problem-solving rather than treating them as external or secondary to academic instruction.

Contemporary conditions make explicit what earlier generations understood implicitly: a republic capable of self-government must be a learning society across the full span of life. As Christopher Dede and John Richards argue in *The 60-Year Curriculum (2020)*, education can no longer be confined to youth or treated as preparation for a stable future that no longer exists. In a world where knowledge, technology, and economic structures evolve faster than individual careers, learning must be continuous, embedded in meaningful work, and broadly accessible if citizens are to remain independent rather than dependent, adaptive rather than brittle. This is not merely an economic imperative. A constitutional republic survives only insofar as its citizens retain the capacity to revise judgment, acquire new competencies, and participate responsibly in civic life over time. Lifelong learning, properly understood, is not an innovation of the digital age but the modern expression of an old republican truth: self-government requires a people who can continue to learn.

Section One has traced how American institutions gradually confronted this reality. The chapters that follow turn from history to mechanism. They examine how human learning unfolds across the lifespan, the constraints under which it operates, and the conditions under which learning systems support—or undermine—the civic capacities upon which a constitutional republic depends.

SNHU

Part II: The Science of Learning and Memory across the Lifespan

Chapter Five: Learning Across the Lifespan

How Prior Learning and Neurological Maturation Shape the Capacity to Learn

In the middle of the twentieth century, psychology believed it already knew the shape of a human life. Childhood was a period of growth. Adulthood was a plateau. Old age was decline. Learning followed the same arc: rapid acquisition early, consolidation in youth, and inevitable erosion thereafter.

Paul Baltes began his career based on that assumption. Like his contemporaries, he was trained to study development by comparing the young to the old and treating the differences as loss. But as longitudinal data accumulated, something refused to fit.

Older adults did not simply perform worse. In some domains, they performed *differently*—sometimes more slowly, but often more selectively, more strategically, and with greater contextual judgment.

The anomaly deepened when Baltes examined adulthood itself. Capacities did not peak and then vanish. They traded places. Reaction speed softened while pattern recognition strengthened. Novel problem-solving appeared to decline while expertise deepened. This apparent decline may reflect not only changes in cognitive processing but also reduced exposure to novelty and the brain's adaptive reallocation of resources toward tasks more aligned with accumulated experience. Even in childhood, gains arrived paired with losses: as language emerged, access to earlier sensory memories faded; as impulse control grew, spontaneity narrowed.

For much of the twentieth century, developmental psychology told a simple story. Human beings grew during childhood, stabilized in adulthood, and declined with age. Learning was assumed to belong to the early years; later life was framed largely in terms of loss.

Paul Baltes came to believe that this story was not merely incomplete—it was misleading.

Across decades of research, Baltes argued that human development unfolds across the entire lifespan, not as a straight line of progress or decay, but as a dynamic process of adaptation. At every age, individuals gain certain capacities while losing others. Growth and decline, he insisted, are not opposites separated by time; they coexist throughout life. What changes is not whether development occurs, but how it must be managed.

What Psychology had often framed as loss was, in many cases, the consequence of an unrecognized gain. Changes in learning behavior observed in later adulthood are frequently not signs of diminished capacity, but the visible effects of cognitive reorganization and accumulated experience.

With age, individuals tend to develop greater discernment—a refined ability to distinguish between what is consequential and what is trivial. This discernment functions as a filter, reducing engagement with tasks whose outcomes are unlikely to justify the required effort. At the same time, adults acquire increasing levels of *crystallized intelligence*: a deep reservoir of knowledge, patterns, and conceptual frameworks built through years of learning and experience.

Taken together, these gains can produce learning behaviors that, to a younger observer, may appear as loss—reduced interest in a wide range of learning tasks, greater selectivity, or less time spent pursuing new domains. Crystallized intelligence enables older learners to integrate new information more efficiently by anchoring it to existing knowledge structures, while selectivity reflects a strategic judgment about relevance rather than a diminished willingness or ability to learn. What appears as disengagement is often the rational prioritization of learning in light of experience, purpose, and limited time.

Baltes' realization of this view of the lifespan quietly overturned a century of assumption. Learning did not belong to youth alone. Growth and loss were not sequential stages separated by age. They were simultaneous features of human development at every point in life. From this insight emerged a powerful framework. To function effectively under real-world constraints, individuals engage in selection, focusing on goals that matter most; optimization, investing effort to strengthen chosen capacities; and compensation, devising new strategies when abilities inevitably diminish. Learning, from this perspective, is not the accumulation of knowledge in youth followed by its gradual erosion. It is a lifelong process of recalibration—an ongoing negotiation between aspiration, limitation, and context.

Baltes' work quietly overturned the assumption that adult learners are simply late, deficient, or lagging. Adults, he showed, are doing exactly what development requires: adapting learning strategies to changing cognitive, social, and physical conditions. The question is not whether adults can learn, but whether learning environments are designed to recognize how learning actually works across a life.

This reframing has profound implications. If development continues across the lifespan, then confining education to childhood and adolescence produces a structural misalignment between how humans develop and how societies organize learning. If learning is adaptive rather than linear, then pauses, detours, and compensatory strategies are not failures but features of mature cognition. And if loss is an inevitable companion of growth, then systems that demand uninterrupted accumulation will systematically exclude those most in need of learning opportunities.

Taken together, lifespan development research suggests that learning opportunities must be matched not only to what individuals need to know, but to how cognition, motivation, and priorities evolve over time. When learning environments are rigidly standardized or confined to narrow stages of life, effort increases, engagement erodes, and learning becomes unnecessarily fragile. What follows is not simply a call for more education later in life, but for learning opportunities that can adapt to changing developmental needs, contexts, and constraints as they arise.

A lifespan perspective therefore points away from keeping citizens perpetually enrolled in institutions and toward learning opportunities that are well designed, accessible, and aligned with human cognition and the learner's developmental phase and evolving dispositions. Under such conditions, learning begins to function less as an episodic obligation and more as a natural part of life—much as literacy eventually did after writing moved beyond the confines of stone tablets.

Only after understanding learning as a lifelong process can we properly interpret the experiences of real people navigating education amid work, family, illness, and other responsibilities. With this framework in place, the composite learners introduced in this chapter can be seen not as exceptions, but as representative cases—individuals responding rationally to the developmental constraints of adult life.

Lifespan Theory Overview

Human development is not a simple upward trajectory with continuous gains, but a dynamic arc with curves and setbacks, and both gains and losses at every phase. Lifespan psychology, led by scholars such as Paul Baltes, emphasizes three principles: growth, maintenance, and regulation of loss. Development continues into late life, even if the balance shifts toward adapting to decline. Erik Erikson's psychosocial stages remind us that identity, intimacy, productivity, and integrity are each developmental tasks tied to learning. Together, these perspectives stress that learning must be lifelong because development is lifelong.

Research converges from multiple directions on how learning changes across the lifespan. Psychologist Raymond Cattell first distinguished between two broad forms of intelligence: fluid intelligence, which supports rapid reasoning, working memory, and novel problem-solving, and crystallized intelligence, which reflects accumulated knowledge and experience. Longitudinal behavioral studies, most notably those conducted by Timothy Salthouse, show that fluid intelligence typically peaks in early adulthood and then declines gradually as processing speed and working-memory efficiency change. Crystallized intelligence, by contrast, continues to build across decades and often remains stable well into later life. Together, these patterns help explain why learning feels different at different ages, even when overall capability remains high.

Cognitive neuroscience helps explain why this shift occurs. Neuroimaging studies show that fluid intelligence depends heavily on late-maturing frontal and parietal control networks—systems optimized for speed, flexibility, and novelty, but also metabolically demanding and increasingly costly to sustain with age. Crystallized intelligence, by contrast, reflects the gradual consolidation of knowledge within distributed cortical networks shaped by long-term experience. As the brain ages, it relies

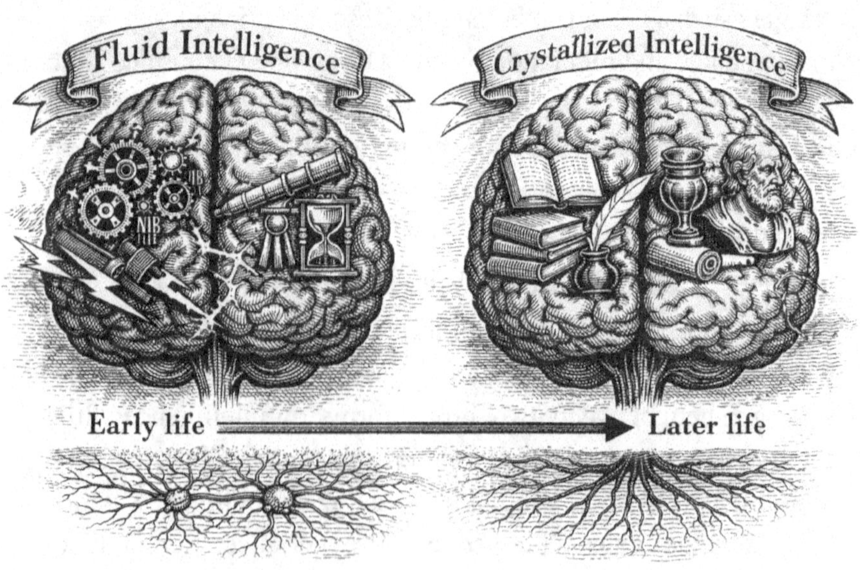

more heavily on these knowledge-based systems—not because intelligence diminishes, but because experience-based strategies are often more stable, efficient, and adaptive than rapid, resource-intensive reasoning.

From the learner's own perspective, this transition is rarely experienced as a loss of intelligence. Instead, adults increasingly draw on pattern recognition, judgment, and accumulated understanding. Learning becomes more selective, deliberate, and purposeful, guided by what matters most and by connections forged over time rather than by sheer speed or breadth. What appears externally as slowing often reflects an internal reweighting of cognitive resources toward strategies that better fit the realities of adult life.

Importantly, this reorganization is not fixed or purely passive. Longitudinal neuroimaging studies indicate that adults who remain engaged in sustained, novel learning show slower decline and more adaptive reorganization in the same fronto-parietal networks associated with fluid intelligence. While age-related changes in processing speed and working memory persist, continued engagement with new and demanding material appears to preserve functional capacity by maintaining neural efficiency and supporting compensatory recruitment rather than by halting biological aging itself (Park et al., 2014; Nyberg et al., 2012; Lövdén et al., 2010).

Early Childhood: Senses, Language, and Memory in Bloom

Theodore (Age 5) — The Preverbal Cusp

Theodore is five years old, standing on the edge of memory's great transition. His world is alive with words—over a

thousand of them—yet many of his earliest impressions still linger in forms he cannot describe or name (Simcock & Hayne, 2002). The smell of crayons, the creak of his classroom chair, the rhythm of his teacher's voice lodge deep inside him. He is just learning to weave these sensations into stories he can tell. The past two or three years are becoming accessible to him as narrative, while earlier experiences fade into silence, recoverable only when a stray scent or sound pulls them back.

Each day, Theodore effortlessly accomplishes learning feats that no formal instruction could replicate. He speaks in full sentences without ever having been taught grammar rules. He recognizes faces instantly, distinguishing friend from stranger in a crowded room. He knows when a smile signals approval and when a frown signals caution. He absorbs the unspoken routines of classroom life—when to sit, when to line up, when laughter is welcome and when silence is expected— without anyone explicitly explaining these rules. These are not achievements of reasoning or conscious strategy; they are the products of learning systems that operate automatically, rapidly, and with minimal cognitive effort.

This is the delicate cusp where sensory traces give way to verbal memory—a window into how learning itself is shaped by the brain's development. His prefrontal cortex—the brain's "control center" for planning and inhibition—is still developing, leaving him impulsive and highly suggestible, both wondrously open to learning and strikingly vulnerable (Nelson & Luciana, 2008; Bauer, 2015). Neuroscience research tells us that Theodore's brain will not fully mature until the final stages of adolescence—sometimes as late as 22 years of age (Giedd et al., 1999; Casey et al., 2008).

Before Theodore was able to speak and understand language, his memories were encoded largely through sensory inputs—sight, sound, smell, touch, taste (Bauer, 2015). Long before he could name a dog, he knew how to approach one cautiously. Before he could explain affection, he could recognize comfort in a caregiver's voice. At five, he is beginning to weave his life into stories he can tell— what psychologists call autobiographical memory, which emerges in tandem with language (Fivush & Nelson, 2004).

Developmental memory studies show that preverbal memories depend heavily on sensory and perceptual encoding systems rather than linguistic ones. They can be vivid and powerful, yet difficult to access once language becomes dominant (Simcock & Hayne, 2002; Bauer, 2015). Young children cannot reminisce in the adult sense or deliberately summon these early memories; instead, they often return only when the child encounters something familiar—the scent of a parent's shirt, the lullaby sung at bedtime, the feel of a favorite blanket. These cues do not prompt explanation; they prompt recognition.

As Theodore's vocabulary expands, retrieval systems reorganize around linguistic cues, rendering nonverbal memories increasingly inaccessible (Fivush & Nelson, 2004; Bauer, 2007). As a result, these early-life, sensory-encoded memories tend to surface only under matching sensory conditions—through smells, sounds, spatial cues, or affective states—or indirectly during dreaming, when associative networks are activated outside the constraints of conscious, language-driven retrieval (Tulving, 1983; Rubin, 2006; Stickgold & Walker, 2013). These early sensory-encoded traces do not disappear; they remain latent within the mind's architecture, capable of resurfacing at any point across the lifespan—sometimes as a puzzling feeling of familiarity when similar sensory conditions are encountered, and sometimes when the systems that normally govern attention, recall, and regulation are strained—a dynamic we will return to when we examine cognitive load and stress later in this book.

For Theodore, that means his memory world is vivid but fragile. A smell of crayons or the sound of his teacher's voice may carry more weight than he could ever put into words, precisely because he does not yet have the words. As he grows and language takes root, those impressions will be reshaped into stories he can tell and share. The gift of language will make his memories easier to organize and recall—but it will also place many of those earliest sensory memories forever out of reach, recoverable only in flashes triggered by a smell, a sound, or a taste years later.

What makes this stage remarkable is not what Theodore struggles to do, but what he accomplishes effortlessly. He learns by immersion, by exposure, by participation. His mind is exquisitely tuned to extract patterns from the world without overloading conscious thought. This is the quiet power of biologically primary learning: it allows the child to master the foundations of human life—language, social understanding, emotional attunement—before formal instruction ever begins.

Biologically Primary Learning, Memory, and Cognitive Load in Early Childhood

Several complementary research traditions help explain why early childhood learning feels effortless in some domains and fragile or constrained in others—and why instruction must align with the brain's developmental architecture.

David Geary provides the foundational distinction between biologically primary and biologically secondary knowledge (Geary, 2002; Geary, 2007). Biologically primary knowledge includes capacities such as spoken language, face recognition, social reasoning, and basic intuitive quantity sense. These forms of learning emerge reliably across cultures without formal instruction because they are supported by evolved neural systems. By contrast, biologically secondary knowledge—reading, writing, formal mathematics, and scientific reasoning—consists of culturally invented skills that must be explicitly taught and carefully scaffolded.

John Sweller's Cognitive Load Theory explains the mechanism underlying this distinction (Sweller, 1988; Sweller, Ayres, & Kalyuga, 2011). Working memory is sharply limited in both capacity and duration, especially in young children. Biologically primary learning places minimal demands on working memory because much of the processing is automated by specialized neural circuits. Biologically secondary learning, however, depends heavily on working memory until schemas are gradually constructed and automated. Instruction succeeds or fails largely on whether it respects these limits.

Developmental memory researchers Gabrielle Simcock and Harlene Hayne provide critical empirical evidence for how early learning is shaped by language and encoding format. In a seminal series of studies, Simcock and Hayne (2002) demonstrated that children can retain memories of events that occurred before they had the language to describe them—but those memories are often inaccessible to later verbal recall. The limitation is not storage, but retrieval: memories encoded in nonverbal, sensory formats cannot easily be accessed once recall becomes language dependent.

Their work introduced the concept of language-dependent recall, showing that as children acquire language, memory retrieval systems reorganize around linguistic cues. Experiences that cannot be verbally encoded become increasingly difficult to retrieve intentionally, even though they may still influence behavior when triggered by sensory stimuli such as smell or sound (Simcock & Hayne, 2002). This finding helps explain why early childhood memories feel vivid yet elusive—and why early learning is deeply shaped by perceptual and emotional context.

Their paper, *"Breaking the Barrier? Children Fail to Translate Their Preverbal Memories Into Language"* (Simcock & Hayne, 2002), became a cornerstone in understanding childhood amnesia—the reason adults seldom recall experiences from before age 3. In follow-up work (Simcock & Hayne, 2003; Jack, Simcock & Hayne, 2011), they show that even six years later, fragments of those preverbal memories can persist, surfacing as actions or feelings long before they can be spoken. The research resonates with contemporary studies on the neurobiology of memory formation, suggesting that the hippocampal-language interface matures only gradually, limiting verbal recall of early events (Bauer, 2007; Nelson & Fivush, 2004).

Patricia Bauer and Robyn Fivush extend this work by showing how the emergence of language transforms memory into autobiographical narrative—memories that can be deliberately recalled, structured, and shared with others (Fivush & Nelson,

2004; Bauer, 2015). Language does not merely label experience; it reorganizes cognition by providing a scaffold for temporal sequencing, causality, and self-concept.

Taken together, these theorists point to a unified conclusion: early childhood learning is optimized when it aligns with biologically primary systems and minimizes unnecessary cognitive load. While biologically secondary skills cannot become innate, instruction can partially align them with primary pathways through repetition, social embedding, and gradual automation. The goal is not early abstraction, but schema formation—building durable mental structures that later learning can efficiently build upon.

For Theodore, this means that learning environments rich in language, sensory engagement, and social interaction are not just developmentally appropriate—they are cognitively essential. When early instruction respects the limits, strengths, and vulnerabilities of the developing mind, it lays the groundwork for learning that can endure across a lifetime.

Adolescence: Body, Brain, and Identity in Turmoil

Marcus (Age 16) — The Adolescent Brain

Marcus, at sixteen, stands at the threshold of foresight. His brain has matured to the point where he can project the consequences of his actions—a capacity that slows his instinctive reactions compared to childhood but adds depth to his judgment. Yet his prefrontal cortex will not be fully wired until his early twenties, leaving him in a liminal zone: more capable of long-term reasoning than Theodore, but still highly sensitive to reward, novelty, and peer influence (Giedd et al., 1999; Sowell et al., 2001; Gogtay et al., 2004; Casey et al., 2008).

For Marcus, this new capacity is both empowering and unsettling. He notices himself hesitating in ways he never did as a child. When he played football at twelve, his reactions were lightning-fast, unburdened by second thoughts. Now he sometimes pauses just long enough to miss the perfect pass—his brain running a quick cost-benefit analysis before his body moves. It frustrates him, yet it signals growth: he is learning to connect present actions with future outcomes. The gradual synchronization of prefrontal cortex and limbic system—the neural circuits for judgment and emotion—underlies the adolescent's uneven self-regulation (Luna et al., 2010; Casey et al., 2019).

At the same time, Marcus lives in an environment that constantly tugs him toward impulsivity. His phone buzzes with notifications; video games reward split-second reflexes; social media offers instant gratification. Dopamine systems peak in adolescence, making risk-taking exhilarating and distraction nearly irresistible (Steinberg, 2014; Somerville & Casey, 2010). Research on social feedback and reward cues shows that adolescents are particularly sensitive under peer observation (Chein et al., 2011; Sherman et al., 2016). His challenge is not simply to learn algebra or history, but to master the balance between an older brain system that craves immediate reward and a newer one still learning how to plan, delay, and anticipate.

In this tension lies both the risk and the promise of adolescence: the risk of being swept along by impulse and distraction, and the promise of growing into a deliberate adult capable of shaping his own future.

Identity, Neurodevelopment, and the Adolescent Brain

Erik Erikson framed adolescence not merely as a biological phase but as a psychosocial moratorium—a necessary pause between childhood dependence and adult responsibility. In *Childhood and Society* (1950), he identified the central developmental crisis of this stage as identity versus role confusion, arguing that adolescence is defined by the urgent task of forging a coherent sense of self across time.

For Erikson, adolescence was not about rebellion for its own sake, but about integration. The young person must reconcile inherited traits, past experiences, and future aspirations into an identity that can be carried forward into adult responsibility. In *Identity: Youth and Crisis* (1968), Erikson emphasized that this process unfolds within "cultural mirrors"—family, school, peer groups, institutions, and the nation itself. Identity, in his view, is not invented in isolation; it is negotiated in relationship to the surrounding social order.

What Erikson could not yet see—but intuited with remarkable accuracy—was the biological substrate underlying this psychosocial struggle. His description of adolescence as a period of heightened sensitivity, experimentation, and instability closely parallels what modern neuroscience would later reveal about the developing brain.

The Architecture of Cortical Maturation

Beginning in the 1990s, neuroimaging studies led by Jay Giedd at the National Institute of Mental Health transformed scientific understanding of adolescence. Using longitudinal MRI data, Giedd and colleagues demonstrated that the human brain undergoes extensive structural reorganization during adolescence, particularly in the prefrontal cortex, the region associated with planning, impulse control, and long-term decision-making (Giedd et al., 1999).

Rather than developing linearly, cortical maturation follows a back-to-front trajectory: sensory and motor regions mature first, while prefrontal systems are among the last to fully integrate—often not reaching adult-level connectivity until the early twenties (Sowell et al., 2001; Gogtay et al., 2004). This finding provided a neurophysiological explanation for the behavioral patterns Erikson described decades earlier: adolescents can reason abstractly yet struggle to consistently regulate behavior under emotional or social pressure.

The adolescent brain, in other words, is not deficient—but unfinished.

Building on this foundation, B. J. Casey and her collaborators articulated what has become known as the dual-systems model of adolescent development. Their research shows that limbic and reward-related systems—particularly those involving dopamine signaling—mature earlier than prefrontal control systems, creating a temporary imbalance between motivation and regulation (Casey et al., 2008; Somerville & Casey, 2010).

This imbalance helps explain why adolescents like Marcus can understand risks intellectually yet still engage in impulsive behavior, especially in emotionally charged or peer-saturated contexts. Functional MRI studies demonstrate that adolescents show heightened neural responses to reward cues and social feedback, particularly when peers are present (Chein et al., 2011; Sherman et al., 2016). Under these conditions, cognitive control systems are more easily overridden—not because adolescents lack knowledge, but because regulatory circuits are still stabilizing.

Casey's later work emphasizes that this period of neural plasticity is not merely a vulnerability, but an opportunity. The same sensitivity that amplifies risk-taking also supports learning, adaptation, and social attunement—capacities essential for adult competence (Casey et al., 2019).

Risk, Reward, and Social Context

Psychologist Laurence Steinberg extended these findings by demonstrating how adolescent decision-making shifts dramatically depending on social context. In controlled experiments, Steinberg showed that adolescents take far greater risks when peers are watching, even when they fully understand the potential consequences (Steinberg, 2014).

This work underscored a critical point for education and civic preparation: adolescent behavior cannot be understood—or guided—without accounting for the interaction between brain development and environment. Identity formation, impulse control, and moral reasoning are not abstract capacities; they are shaped in real time by social signals, emotional stakes, and perceived belonging.

Synthesis: Identity Meets Neurobiology

Taken together, these theorists reveal adolescence as a convergence point between identity formation and neurobiological reorganization. Erikson named the developmental task; neuroscience has mapped its constraints.

Adolescents are capable of remarkable insight, creativity, and learning. Yet their cognitive systems operate under conditions of heightened reward sensitivity, incomplete regulatory control, and intense social influence. Learning at this stage is therefore not merely informational—it is formative. It shapes habits of judgment, self-concept, and responsibility that will persist long after neural maturation is complete.

For educators and institutions, the implication is clear: adolescence demands learning environments that respect both the strengths and vulnerabilities of the developing brain. Expectations must challenge without overwhelming, structure without infantilizing, and guide without coercing. When identity development is supported rather than exploited, adolescence becomes not a period to endure, but a foundation on which adult agency can be built.

Design Implications: Education, Media, and Civic Readiness in Adolescence

The convergence of identity formation and ongoing neurobiological maturation carries direct implications for how learning environments should be designed during adolescence. As developmental psychologist Laurence Steinberg has shown, adolescents possess emerging capacities for abstraction, moral reasoning, and long-term planning, yet these capacities operate within neural systems that remain highly sensitive to reward, novelty, and social evaluation. This imbalance reflects the uneven maturation of brain systems responsible for motivation and self-regulation (Casey et al., 2008; Steinberg, 2014). Instructional environments that emphasize unstructured autonomy, constant stimulation, or emotionally charged content can therefore place excessive demands on regulatory systems that are still under construction, increasing vulnerability to cognitive overload and impulsive judgment (Steinberg, 2014; Sweller, 2011).

Effective adolescent education therefore requires intentional scaffolding. Structure, clear expectations, and opportunities for guided decision-making help externalize regulatory functions that the brain has not yet fully internalized (Luna et al., 2010). When learning tasks are sequenced to gradually increase cognitive and emotional demands, adolescents can practice judgment under conditions that promote growth rather than reactivity.

This principle extends beyond classrooms into media and civic exposure. Adolescents are increasingly immersed in digital environments that reward speed, outrage, and social signaling. Research shows that under peer observation—whether physical or virtual—adolescents are more likely to prioritize immediate social rewards over deliberative reasoning (Chein et al., 2011; Sherman et al., 2016). Without counterbalancing experiences that cultivate reflection, dialogue, and delayed gratification, these environments can distort the development of civic judgment.

Civic readiness, then, is not achieved by information alone. It depends on learning contexts that respect the adolescent brain's developmental profile—challenging young people to think critically while protecting them from cognitive overload and premature moral absolutism. Education at this stage must aim not simply to inform, but to cultivate habits of discernment and self-regulation that can mature alongside the brain itself, gradually shifting control from external structure to internal judgment (Luna et al., 2010; Zimmerman, 2002).

Young Adulthood: Peak Agility Under Heavy Demands

Sophia (Age 28) — Peak Agility, Heavy Demands

Sophia is twenty-eight, standing in the whirlwind of young adulthood. By day she works long shifts as a registered nurse in a busy hospital ward; by night she completes coursework toward becoming a nurse practitioner. Her phone buzzes with clinical alerts, her laptop holds online modules and discussion boards, and her patients' faces linger in her thoughts long after she leaves the hospital.

Neurologically, Sophia has reached full structural maturity. Her prefrontal cortex—the region responsible for planning, foresight, impulse control, and integration of emotion with judgment—is fully developed (Sarah-Jayne Blakemore, 2008; Arain et al., 2013). The long process of synaptic pruning and myelination that began in childhood is now complete, enabling adult-level self-regulation and complex decision-making.

Cognitively, Sophia is near the peak of fluid intelligence—the ability to reason quickly, solve novel problems, and adapt to un-

familiar situations (Raymond Cattell & John Horn, 1967; Timothy Salthouse, 2010). Neuroimaging studies suggest that during this stage, the brain often operates with maximal efficiency: complex tasks can be executed using fewer neural resources than in adolescence or later adulthood (Rypma & D'Esposito, 2000; Cabeza et al., 2002; Park & Reuter-Lorenz, 2009).

Yet this efficiency is also a vulnerability. Because Sophia can process *so* much, she is routinely asked to process *too* much. Electronic health records, monitoring systems, continuing education requirements, rotating schedules, and constant digital interruptions all compete for her attention. Research on multitasking and sustained cognitive demand shows that even highly capable adults experience erosion of working memory, increased error rates, and diminished well-being when cognitive load remains chronically high (Mark et al., 2016; Uncapher et al., 2017).

Sophia can handle more than Theodore or Marcus—but her brain is not invincible.

Her stage of life is both a high point and a crucible. The habits she forms now—what she practices repeatedly, what she ignores, what she chooses to master—will echo for decades. In many ways, Sophia embodies the urgency of lifelong learning: at precisely the moment the brain is strongest, the world asks the most of it.

If adolescence is marked by imbalance between motivation and regulation, young adulthood represents a period of neural consolidation and maximal efficiency. By the late twenties, prefrontal networks supporting planning, impulse control, and goal maintenance have largely completed structural maturation (Arain et al., 2013; Casey et al., 2008). Functional imaging studies indicate that adults in this stage often solve complex problems using fewer neural resources than either adolescents or older adults—a phenomenon described as peak neural efficiency (Rypma & D'Esposito, 2000; Park & Reuter-Lorenz, 2009).

For learners like Sophia, this maturation enables sustained attention, complex integration of information, and effective self-regulation under pressure. At the same time, the very efficiency of these systems introduces a new vulnerability: cognitive overload. Because young adults can process large volumes of information, modern environments often demand that they do so continuously. Multitasking, persistent digital interruptions, and high-stakes professional responsibilities place sustained load on working memory and executive control systems (Sweller et al., 2019; Mark et al., 2016).

Neurophysiological research suggests that under chronic load, even mature executive systems degrade in performance. Working memory capacity narrows, error rates increase, and emotional regulation becomes less stable (Uncapher et al., 2017). Unlike adolescents, young adults may not exhibit impulsivity, but they are susceptible to exhaustion, burnout, and attentional fragmentation.

The implication for lifelong learning is critical: success at this stage depends less on adding demands and more on intelligent design. Learning environments for young adults must respect not only cognitive strengths, but also limits—supporting automation, schema development, and transfer rather than constant novelty. Sophia's stage demonstrates that maturity does not eliminate vulnerability; it simply changes its form.

Peak Fluid Intelligence and the Burden of Selectivity

The experience Sophia inhabits—high cognitive capacity paired with sustained pressure—is well documented in the literature on adult cognition, learning, and development.

The foundation lies in the distinction between fluid and crystallized intelligence, first articulated by Raymond Cattell and later refined by John Horn. In their seminal work *Age Differences in Fluid and Crystallized Intelligence* (1967), Cattell and Horn demonstrated that fluid intelligence—reasoning speed, working memory, and novel problem-solving—peaks in early adulthood, while crystallized intelligence—accumulated knowledge, schemas, and domain expertise—continues to grow across the lifespan. Sophia stands near the apex of fluid capacity, but her filters for relevance and efficiency are still under construction.

Longitudinal and cross-sectional research by Timothy Salthouse further clarifies this dynamic. In *Theoretical Perspectives on Cognitive Aging* (1991) and later syntheses (2004, 2010), Salthouse showed that performance depends not only on intelligence per se, but on processing speed and working-memory capacity—both of which impose constraints on performance even in early adulthood. Young adults can manage extraordinary complexity—but only when task demands are structured to respect those limits. When demands accumulate without relief, performance erodes gradually through fatigue, distraction, and error rather than sudden failure.

Research across cognitive psychology and organizational science shows that sustained cognitive overload rarely produces abrupt failure. Instead, performance erodes gradually through fatigue, distraction, and increasing error (Baumeister et al., 1998; Lorist et al., 2005; Hockey, 2011). Over time, this erosion reshapes self-perception: individuals become less willing to take on new tasks, more selective in their engagement, and increasingly likely to interpret their own disengagement as loss of interest rather than as a rational response to unrelieved demand (Maslach & Leiter, 1997; Demerouti et al., 2001). When this pattern persists, self-attributions of disinterest or limited capacity can consolidate into enduring beliefs about one's abilities and preferences, narrowing future learning choices and reinforcing trait-like patterns of avoidance and disengagement (Bem, 1972; Bandura, 1997; Roberts et al., 2006).

This erosion is central to cognitive load theory, developed by John Sweller. In *Cognitive Load During Problem Solving* (1988) and *Cognitive Load Theory* (2011), Sweller demonstrated that learning is constrained by working memory and that poorly designed instructional or work environments impose extraneous cognitive load—mental effort that consumes capacity without contributing to understanding. For learners like Sophia, extraneous load is not confined to classrooms; it is embedded in digital interfaces, documentation systems, interruptions, and parallel task demands that fragment attention throughout the day.

The adult-learning literature emphasizes that this stage is nevertheless uniquely suited to integration of experience and learning. David Kolb's *Experiential Learning* (1984) argued that adult learning proceeds through cycles of concrete experience, reflective observation, abstract conceptualization, and active experimentation. Sophia's clinical practice is not ancillary to her education—it is the substrate that gives theoretical knowledge coherence. Learning detached from consequence remains brittle; learning embedded in responsibility becomes durable.

Developmental psychologists have also highlighted the structural instability of this period. Jeffrey Arnett, in *Emerging Adulthood* (2000; 2015), described young adulthood as a distinct developmental phase characterized by identity exploration, instability, and delayed consolidation of adult roles. Individuals are treated as fully responsible long before their professional identities and coping strategies have crystallized. The result is a prolonged period of high demand paired with incomplete scaffolding.

Taken together, these bodies of work converge on a single conclusion: young adulthood is not simply a period of peak capability, but a period of maximum exposure. The brain is powerful, but the margin for overload is narrow. When learning systems align with this reality—by integrating work, reducing extraneous load, and honoring prior experience—growth accelerates. When they ignore it, even the most capable learners experience strain.

Sophia's experience is therefore not anomalous. It is emblematic of a broader structural truth: Lifelong learning succeeds not by demanding more from learners at moments of peak capacity, but by designing learning environments that respect the limits, strengths, and vulnerabilities of the mind at each stage of life.

Midlife: Crystallized Strength and Selective Attention

William (Age 51) — Midlife Neural Efficiency

William is fifty-one, and his mind no longer feels like it did at thirty—but it feels better trained. He notices the change most clearly when learning something new. The raw speed that once carried him through unfamiliar material has softened. Multitasking drains him more quickly than it once did, and prolonged exposure to novelty taxes his working memory (Salthouse, 2004; Verhaeghen & Salthouse, 1997). He moves more deliberately now, recognizing that constant skimming and rapid task switching extract a price.

In exchange, he has gained far more than he has given up. William's crystallized intelligence—the accumulated knowledge, mental models, and schemas built across decades—has never been stronger (Horn & Cattell, 1967; Ackerman, 1996). He excels at recognizing patterns, contextualizing problems, and filtering signal from noise. Where younger learners must hold many elements in working memory at once, William often sees the structure of a problem almost immediately. Experience has compressed complexity.

After a long day managing a regional team, William opens his laptop to continue an online course in data analytics. The syntax does not flow as effortlessly as it does for his younger classmates. They type faster, experiment more freely, and recover more quickly from small errors. But William brings something they do not: judgment shaped by consequence. He has lived inside systems long enough to know where data lies, where incentives distort outcomes, and where elegant solutions fail in practice.

He does not race to finish each assignment. Instead, he pauses to ask better questions. *Why does this pattern matter? What decision would it inform? What would break if this assumption were wrong?* His learning is slower, but it is deeper; anchored in context rather than novelty.

Neuroscience confirms what William experiences intuitively. Processing speed and working memory show reliable age-related decline beginning in mid-adulthood, but semantic knowledge, vocabulary, and expertise remain stable or continue to grow well into the fifties and beyond (Salthouse, 2009; Park et al., 2002). The midlife brain becomes less efficient at rapid switching, but more efficient at choosing what deserves attention.

William no longer tries to learn everything. He learns *selectively*. And that selectivity is not a weakness—it is the defining cognitive strength of midlife.

Expertise, Selectivity, and the Midlife Mind

K. Warner Schaie fundamentally reshaped how psychologists understand adult intelligence. Rejecting the assumption that intelligence simply peaks in youth and declines thereafter, Schaie recognized that much of the evidence for decline came from flawed cross-sectional comparisons. Younger and older adults were being compared as if they were the same person at different ages, ignoring the powerful influence of cohort, education, and technological context.

To correct this, Schaie launched the Seattle Longitudinal Study in 1956, following multiple cohorts across decades (Schaie, 1994). The findings were decisive: many cognitive abilities—particularly verbal comprehension, reasoning, and spatial skills—remain stable or improve into midlife. What declines earlier and more consistently is processing speed, not understanding.

This distinction matters profoundly for learning design. Midlife learners are not less capable; they are differently capable. Their cognition favors integration over acquisition, judgment over speed. Later work with Sherry Willis demonstrated that adult cognition remains plastic: targeted training can produce durable gains even in later adulthood (Willis & Schaie, 2006).

Schaie reframed midlife not as the beginning of decline, but as a period of reorganization.

Fluid and Crystallized Intelligence

The conceptual backbone of William's experience lies in the distinction between fluid and crystallized intelligence, first articulated by Raymond Cattell and elaborated by John Horn. Fluid intelligence supports rapid problem-solving, mental flexibility, working memory, and the ability to reason in unfamiliar situations, while crystallized intelligence reflects the accumulation of knowledge, mental models, and strategies built through years of experience and practice (Cattell, 1963; Horn & Cattell, 1967). Importantly, these two forms of intelligence follow different developmental trajectories across the lifespan rather than rising and falling together (Horn, 1982; Salthouse, 2010).

Fluid intelligence is not a qualitatively superior form of intelligence, nor does it represent a more advanced cognitive state. Rather, it is preferentially recruited in situations that are genuinely novel. Contexts in which few relevant schemas exist and problems must be reasoned through from first principles. As individuals accumulate experience, however, fewer situations remain truly novel. As Roger Schank observed in his work in cognitive psychology, learning proceeds by acquiring a sufficient repertoire of schemas—stored cases, scripts, and expectations—such that new experiences can be interpreted as variations on what is already known. When this threshold is reached, new information increasingly connects to existing knowledge structures, mitigating novelty and reducing reliance on resource-intensive fluid processing. Learning then proceeds primarily through the refinement and extension of prior understanding rather than through raw problem-solving.

Midlife often marks a transition point in this balance. Measures of processing speed and working memory show gradual decline beginning in early adulthood, while crystallized intelligence continues to strengthen across midlife and beyond (Salthouse, 2010; Hartshorne & Germine, 2015). This shift does not reflect diminished intellectual capacity, but a reorganization of cognitive resources. Raw speed gives way to judgment. Breadth gives way to depth. Learning becomes less about absorbing large volumes of unfamiliar information and more about situating new ideas within an already rich conceptual framework.

This transition helps explain a familiar pattern in professional life. Midlife adults may find tasks that demand constant novelty, rapid task-switching, or shallow skimming more taxing than they once were. At the same time, they often outperform younger colleagues in complex, ill-defined problems that require prioritization, pattern recognition, and the application of experience across contexts—domains where expertise and domain knowledge play a decisive role (Ericsson et al., 2006; Baltes et al., 1999). What appears externally as slowing is often internally experienced as selectivity: an increasingly refined sense of which problems are worth pursuing, which details matter, and which paths are likely to lead somewhere meaningful.

Expertise emerges from this interplay. As crystallized intelligence deepens, it allows midlife learners to rely less frequently on fluid reasoning while achieving equal or greater effectiveness through well-organized knowledge and efficient strategies. Neurocognitive research suggests that this shift reflects not loss, but adaptation: the brain increasingly favors stable, knowledge-based networks that support reliable performance under realistic constraints (Reuter-Lorenz & Park, 2009; Nyberg et al., 2012). In this way, midlife cognition illustrates a central principle of the lifespan perspective:

intelligence does not peak and decline along a single dimension but reorganizes—shifting from exploration toward informed judgment as experience accrues.

Processing Speed, Working Memory, and Constraint

Neuropsychologist Timothy Salthouse provided the physiological clarity underlying these behavioral patterns. His work demonstrated that declines in adult cognition are driven primarily by reductions in processing speed and working-memory capacity—not by loss of knowledge or reasoning ability (Salthouse, 2004; 2009).

Crucially, Salthouse showed that these constraints explain *how* cognition changes, not *whether* learning continues. When tasks overload working memory or demand constant task-switching, midlife learners struggle. When instruction aligns with existing schemas and allows time for integration, they excel.

This insight dovetails directly with cognitive load theory: midlife learning succeeds when extraneous load is reduced, germane load is supported, and instruction respects the learner's accumulated mental architecture.

Selective Optimization with Compensation

Paul and Margret Baltes' Selective Optimization with Compensation (SOC) model provides the unifying framework for midlife cognition (Baltes & Baltes, 1990). As individuals age, they adapt by:

- Selecting goals aligned with their strengths and values
- Optimizing resources to pursue those goals effectively
- Compensating for losses through strategy, tools, or collaboration

Midlife learners like William embody this model intuitively.

They narrow focus, deepen expertise, and compensate for reduced speed through planning and experience. Learning becomes strategic rather than expansive—less about breadth, more about depth.

Together, these theorists converge on a single conclusion: midlife cognition is not diminished cognition. It is cognition architected by long-term experience; shaped by decades of practice, feedback, and consequence.

The midlife brain reflects a more highly structured cognitive architecture, in which discernment and meaning increasingly guide attention and judgment, even as the raw speed characteristic of youth gradually recedes. Midlife cognitive slowing reflects not just loss, but reorganization: processing becomes less exhaustive and more selective as accumulated experience reshapes how attention, memory, and judgment are deployed. Learning environments that ignore this reality—by demanding constant multitasking, rapid turnover, or unfiltered information—undermine adult learners. Environments that respect it unlock extraordinary capacity.

This reorganization does not represent an endpoint in cognitive development, but a transition in how experience is increasingly filtered, prioritized, and integrated. And it points forward to the next stage of the lifespan, where selectivity deepens further—not as constraint, but as wisdom. Moreover, it points forward to the next stage of the lifespan, where selectivity deepens further—not as constraint, but as wisdom.

Later Life: Selectivity, Plasticity, and Meaning

Ellen (Age 72) — Later Life Wisdom and Selectivity

Ellen, at seventy-two, navigates yet another landscape. Processing speed and working memory show natural decline, and

the hippocampus—critical for forming new episodic memories—is less efficient than it was in youth (Salthouse, 2009; Nyberg et al., 2012). Yet research shows the brain remains plastic even in later life, capable of growth and adaptation when stimulated (Park & Reuter-Lorenz, 2009; Lövdén et al., 2010; Erickson et al., 2011).

Ellen's strength lies in selectivity. She chooses what is meaningful, invests in what aligns with values, and draws on vast reserves of crystallized intelligence accumulated over decades (Baltes & Staudinger, 2000; Li et al., 2004). Older adults often score higher on measures of emotional regulation and life satisfaction, evidence that perspective can be refined rather than diminished (Carstensen et al., 2011; Gross et al., 1997).

At seventy-two, Ellen enters a different kind of classroom. Retired from a long career in electrical engineering, she now devotes her time to a faith-based learning center where study, service, and reflection converge. She participates in community outreach, reading with children, guiding discussion, and drawing on decades of experience to frame ideas in ways that resonate across generations.

Her learning is deliberate and selective. She prepares carefully, reflects deeply, and accepts that it may take longer to master a new digital tool or adapt to unfamiliar methods. Yet selectivity has become a strength rather than a limitation. She no longer feels compelled to learn everything or keep pace with every new development. Instead, she chooses what aligns with her values and commitments. This focus allows her to see patterns and connections that younger learners often miss, transforming experience into insight and learning into contribution.

Older adults may experience a decline in fluid intelligence, but they retain—and often refine—the ability to see meaning, prioritize, and distill complexity into insight (Reuter-Lorenz & Park, 2014; Staudinger & Glück, 2011). For Ellen, learning is not about keeping up; it is about staying alive to the world— mentally sharp, socially connected, and civically engaged. She embodies the promise of lifelong learning: it is never too late to grow, and growth itself is a form of freedom.

Lifespan Adaptation, Neural Reorganization, and the Biology of Wisdom

Paul and Margret Baltes fundamentally reshaped how aging is understood by rejecting the notion that development ends in adulthood. Their lifespan developmental theory framed human growth as lifelong, multidirectional, and adaptive, shaped by both gains and losses across time (Baltes, 1987; Baltes, Lindenberger, & Staudinger, 2006). Central to this framework was the model of Selective Optimization with Compensation (SOC), which described successful aging not as resistance to decline, but as strategic adaptation: individuals selectively focus on goals aligned with values, optimize remaining strengths, and compensate for losses through new strategies, tools, or social supports (Baltes & Baltes, 1990).

Crucially, later neurophysiological research has shown that this adaptive selectivity is not merely a psychological coping strategy—it is reflected in the brain's changing architecture. Timothy Salthouse's work demonstrated that age-related decline is domain-specific, affecting processing speed and working memory earlier and more reliably than semantic knowledge, vocabulary, or expertise (Salthouse, 1996; 2009). Rather than signaling global deterioration, these changes reflect a narrowing of cognitive throughput alongside preservation of high-value knowledge systems.

Building on this, Denise Park and Patricia Reuter-Lorenz advanced the Scaffolding Theory of Aging and Cognition (STAC), proposing that the aging brain actively recruits alternative neural networks to maintain performance (Park & Reuter-Lorenz, 2009; Reuter-Lorenz & Park, 2014). Functional neuroimaging studies show that older adults often display broader, more bilateral activation patterns, compensating for localized inefficiencies by drawing on distributed networks. This scaffolding supports goal-directed cognition even as raw speed declines.

Research by Lars Nyberg and colleagues further clarified the neurobiological basis of later-life memory change. While the hippocampus becomes less efficient in forming new episodic memories, older adults increasingly rely on semantic memory systems and prefrontal networks that support integration, abstraction, and meaning making (Nyberg et al., 2012). Memory does not simply weaken; it changes its operating mode, favoring relevance and coherence over exhaustive detail.

Importantly, plasticity persists well into later life. Longitudinal studies led by Kirk Erickson demonstrated that physical activity and cognitively engaging environments can induce measurable increases in hippocampal volume and improvements in memory even in older adults (Erickson et al., 2011). Similarly, Lövdén and colleagues showed that sustained cognitive challenge can slow or partially reverse age-related decline, underscoring that the aging brain remains responsive to environmental demands (Lövdén et al., 2010).

Together, these neurophysiological findings converge with the Baltes' theoretical framework: later-life cognition is not defined by loss alone, but by adaptive reallocation, or neuroplasticity. The mind becomes more selective, more meaning-driven, and more strategically efficient. Wisdom, in this view, is not sentiment or nostalgia—it is an emergent property of a brain that has learned what to prioritize, what to ignore, and how to deploy its resources in service of what matters most (Baltes & Staudinger, 2000; Staudinger & Glück, 2011).

Later life is often described in terms of what has slowed or narrowed. But selectivity is not withdrawal; it is concentration. As fluid processing speed diminishes, crystallized intelligence— knowledge organized through decades of experience—becomes more coherent, more contextual, and more usable. What appears from the outside as reduced throughput is, from within, a shift toward meaningful engagement.

When Ellen engages with a group of children in her community, she is transmitting lived context. Her presence collapses temporal distance and facilitates in the children a sense of continuity with the world before their time. Through her voice, the younger listeners acquire a mental bridge to an earlier era—one they could not receive from a guide of their own generation, however well-trained.

This is not nostalgia; it is civic work. Societies that neglect the role of older adults as interpreters of history and experience lose access to a form of intelligence that cannot be digitized or accelerated. In later life, learning continues not primarily through accumulation, but through refinement—and teaching becomes a reciprocal act, sustaining purpose for the teacher while anchoring understanding for the learner.

In a Learning Republic, this exchange is not incidental. It is essential. Lifelong learning is not only about staying current; it is about remaining connected—across generations, across time, and across shared civic memory.

The Cognitive Neuroscience of Aging

As people move into their 60s, 70s, and beyond, many aspects of thinking do change. A large body of research in cognitive neuroscience—using brain-imaging tools like fMRI, MEG, and EEG—shows that certain abilities, especially selective attention (the capacity to focus on what matters while tuning out distractions), appear to weaken with age (Leenders et al., 2018; Mok et al., 2019; Rogers et al., 2018).

One clear example comes from studies that watch the brain in real time during attention tasks. In one experiment, researchers showed older adults (average age 68) pictures of faces and houses and asked them to focus on just one category while ignoring the other (Mok et al., 2019). Using fMRI, they saw which brain areas lit up when participants successfully paid attention to the "right" pictures. The older adults in this study were healthy, well-educated, and carefully screened— no neurological issues, normal vision and hearing, and high mental status scores. Their performance was strong, and the brain patterns looked similar to those of younger people when they were attending correctly. But the researchers noted an important caveat: this group was unusually fit and educated. When scientists study healthier, higher-functioning older adults, age-related declines in attention are often less pronounced—or sometimes not detectable at all.

Other studies using different tools tell a more consistent story of change. In one MEG experiment, older adults (median age 66) showed far less of the brain's natural "suppression signal" (alpha waves) when trying to ignore irrelevant information compared with younger adults (Leenders et al., 2018). Behaviorally, the younger group was also more accurate. A similar EEG study found that older adults (median age 75) struggled more with selective listening—picking out important words in one ear while ignoring a competing stream in the other—and their brain waves didn't show the same clear difference between "paying attention" and "missing the mark" that younger people did (Rogers et al., 2018). In short, the neural machinery that helps us filter out distractions appears to run less efficiently in many older adults.

That doesn't mean the aging brain simply loses ground everywhere. Some researchers have found that older adults can actually bind together more pieces of information—even seemingly irrelevant ones—than younger adults can (Campbell & Hasher, 2018). In one clever experiment, participants saw pictures with distracting text overlaid on them. Later, they had to remember which pictures had the "wrong" text. Older adults were significantly better at noticing those mismatches. What looks like "leakage" of irrelevant detail into memory may actually be an asset: the older brain tends to notice broader patterns and connections that younger brains sometimes filter out too aggressively.

Motivation and reward also play a role. Several studies suggest that older adults remain sensitive to potential gains but show reduced brain activation when anticipating losses or punishment (Swirsky & Spaniol, 2019). This can make them more cautious or less responsive to negative feedback during learning tasks—something teachers and trainers should keep in mind when designing feedback for older learners. The same research indicates that while some aspects of cognitive control (ignoring distractions, switching tasks) may decline, the ability to choose meaningful goals and direct effort toward them often remains strong.

Taken together, the neuroscience paints a realistic but hopeful picture: aging brings real changes in attention, filtering, and some kinds of cognitive control, but these changes vary widely depending on health, education, and lifestyle. Highly educated, healthy older adults often perform closer to their younger selves than averages suggest. And some apparent "weaknesses" (like remembering more incidental detail) can be strengths in situations that reward pattern recognition and wisdom.

The takeaway for a learning republic is straightforward: we should design education and training that respects these changes rather than pretending they don't exist. That means pacing instruction thoughtfully, providing clear goals and positive incentives, minimizing unnecessary distractions, and giving older learners time and support to process feedback. When we do, we don't just help individuals keep learning—we keep the whole society's collective wisdom alive and growing.

Lifespan Theory in Practice: Motivation, Selectivity, and Commitment

Lifespan theory does not merely describe cognitive change; it describes motivational reorganization. Across adulthood, individuals do not simply accumulate knowledge. They recalibrate their investments. Time horizon compresses. Effort becomes more selective. Activities are pursued not because they are available, but because they are meaningful.

If this theoretical architecture is correct, educational participation in later adulthood should reflect it.

The doctoral research underlying this book began with a practical question: How can we reduce the cognitive and temporal burden adult learners face when navigating large, undifferentiated course catalogs?

Traditional course catalogs do not require learners to review every available course, nor is such exhaustive review typically expected. In practice, prospective students scan selectively, narrowing options quickly in order to reduce time and effort. Yet an optimal choice—one that aligns closely with a learner's interests, goals, and developmental priorities—can only be made with awareness of the full range of possibilities. When the available options number in the dozens or hundreds, a comprehensive review becomes impractical. Learners must compare descriptions across pages, hold multiple alternatives in working memory while evaluating fit, and remember previously encountered learning outcomes as new ones appear. The process is time-intensive and cognitively demanding. Even when learners externalize information onto paper, the time investment increases. Decision fatigue may set in long before the landscape of opportunity has been adequately surveyed.

We designed a recommender system to address this structural limitation. By organizing learning outcomes across the entire catalog into searchable domains and presenting them in a unified framework, the system allowed learners to review the full spectrum of what could be learned—quickly, systematically, and without the burden of sequential page-by-page comparison.

Rather than narrowing prematurely, learners could begin with outcomes and allow aligned courses to surface accordingly.

The study therefore explored whether replacing a monolithic catalog with a guided recommender system would reduce this structural friction. The intervention involved parsing the full course catalog into a relational database, extracting stated learning outcomes using natural language processing techniques that identified Bloom's taxonomy verbs, and linking those outcomes to their respective courses. Instead of requiring learners to sift through course descriptions sequentially, the system presented learning outcomes organized by knowledge domain—business and finance, history, psychology, civics, and others. Learners selected desired outcomes, and the system generated course recommendations aligned with those selections.

The detailed cognitive and methodological analysis of this system appears in Chapter 7. Here, the focus is developmental: Why was this question particularly relevant for older adult learners, and how did their patterns of participation reflect lifespan theory?

Older adults were selected deliberately. Lifespan research suggests that participation in later adulthood is governed by selective investment. Educational engagement is weighed against time, effort, and competing commitments. Learning is chosen when its perceived value exceeds its perceived cost.

The study was therefore designed with developmental hypotheses in mind. Initial onboarding was structured as a face-to-face orientation session. This was not merely procedural convenience. It was grounded in socioemotional selectivity theory. Social interaction was expected to amplify commitment by increasing perceived benefit and reducing uncertainty. The design assumed that relational context would strengthen persistence.

Then a global pandemic intervened.

In-person sessions were cancelled. Orientation shifted abruptly to independent, virtual initiation. The anticipated social environment disappeared. The initial complexity of engagement increased. Participants were required to navigate unfamiliar systems remotely during a period of broader uncertainty.

More than half withdrew prior to full participation.

From a narrow experimental standpoint, this represented attrition. From a lifespan standpoint, it represented confirmation.

The study was designed over several months under the assumption that both experimental and control groups would begin with structured, face-to-face orientation sessions. These sessions were developmentally intentional. In-person training was expected to establish relational trust, reduce uncertainty, and provide guided initiation into the learning environment.

When the COVID-19 lockdown made face-to-face gathering impossible, that structure collapsed almost overnight. Months of preparation premised on direct interaction could not be executed. Both groups were required to shift to remote initiation without the anticipated in-person support.

In response, substitute materials were developed rapidly. Written help files were produced, and separate electronic bulletin boards were created for the experimental and control groups to host distinct training materials. What had been designed as guided, interactive onboarding became text-based and self-directed. Participants were now required not only to commit to virtual learning, but to navigate layered instructions independently before engagement could begin.

This alteration increased the complexity of initiation. The relational reassurance of in-person guidance was absent. The volume of preparatory information expanded. The structure of entry became less intuitive and more effortful.

More than half of enrolled participants withdrew prior to active participation.

From a procedural standpoint, this represented attrition. From a lifespan standpoint, it revealed patterned selectivity under conditions of heightened initiation complexity and diminished relational reward.

Lifespan theory predicts that when perceived investment rises and anticipated return declines, selective withdrawal follows. Older adults allocate effort strategically. When an opportunity appears to require disproportionate time, attention, or uncertainty relative to its expected benefit, disengagement may represent adaptive prioritization rather than diminished capability.

Subsequent participant feedback reinforced this interpretation. For many, the primary appeal of enrollment had been social engagement. Intellectual interest remained, but the relational dimension had anchored commitment. When that dimension was removed, the motivational equation shifted.

This outcome does not indicate diminished capacity. It reflects adaptive selectivity. In later adulthood, learning must justify itself.

A learning republic that seeks lifelong participation must therefore understand not only cognitive architecture, but motivational architecture. Access alone is insufficient. Availability alone does not sustain engagement. Educational structures must align perceived value with developmental priorities.

The study's cognitive and methodological implications will be examined in Chapter 7. Here, its significance lies in demonstrating that lifespan theory predicts not only patterns of cognitive change, but patterns of participation itself. Although the reduction in sample size limited statistical power, the disruption provided an unexpected opportunity to observe lifespan selectivity under real-world conditions. From a developmental perspective, participant withdrawal and persistence patterns aligned closely with theoretical predictions regarding perceived investment, relational motivation, and adaptive prioritization.

The Lifespan Arc: Schemas, Scripts, and the Architecture of Meaning

Taken together, Theodore, Marcus, Sophia, William, and Ellen embody the arc of human learning: from sensory traces in early childhood, to the dawning foresight of adolescence, to the exploration and overload risk of early adulthood, to the seasoned judgment of midlife, and finally to the selectivity and crystallized wisdom of later life. Their lives illustrate a central truth: learning is never neutral. It is shaped by the stage of life in which it occurs. A child absorbs differently than an adolescent; an adult learns differently than a retiree. Each stage brings distinctive strengths to cultivate and vulnerabilities to respect.

Across these stages, one theme binds the arc together: the mind organizes experience into patterns. From the earliest play schemas of childhood ("bedtime means pajamas and story"), to adolescent identity scripts ("who I am among my peers"), to professional expertise in adulthood ("how this system behaves when stressed"), the brain's core strategy remains remarkably consistent. It transforms experience into structured expectation. Each new encounter either reinforces existing schemas or forces their revision.

In this sense, lifelong learning is not simply the accumulation of information. It is the continual reorganization of mental architecture—revising schemas, refining judgment, and reallocating attention. Over time, learning moves from sensation to story, from impulse to foresight, from speed to wisdom, and from breadth to meaning. What changes across the lifespan is not the presence of learning, but the way cognition manages complexity under evolving biological, social, and motivational constraints.

This perspective clarifies why education cannot be designed for an abstract or timeless "student." Learning environments succeed only when they align with how cognition actually functions at different stages of life. Theodore needs sensory grounding and trustworthy scaffolding. Marcus needs identity support and protection from reward-driven distraction. Sophia needs load management and durable routines. William needs connection to prior knowledge and respect for depth. Ellen needs pace, meaning, and the freedom to choose. The same lesson that liberates one learner can overwhelm another—not because of differences in intelligence or motivation, but because the cognitive demands interact differently with the learner's developmental profile.

Seen through this lens, development is never a simple story of gain followed by decline. Across the lifespan, gains and losses coexist. In early childhood, the growth of language expands expressive capacity while rendering many preverbal memories less accessible. In adolescence, the emergence of foresight introduces judgment at the cost of reflexive speed. In young adulthood, peak cognitive agility is paired with heightened vulnerability to overload. In midlife, processing speed declines while expertise, pattern recognition, and contextual judgment often reach their height. In later life, episodic recall may slow even as selectivity, emotional regulation, and meaning making strengthen. At every stage, learning remains adaptive, reshaping itself in response to changing conditions rather than simply diminishing.

Together, these patterns reveal a central claim of the lifespan perspective: mature cognition is not defined by accumulation alone, but by the strategic reorganization of attention, memory, and effort. What appears externally as slowing often reflects internal selectivity. What appears as disengagement may be a rational response to cognitive load, competing responsibilities, and altered time horizons. Adult learners are not deficient versions of younger ones; they are individuals responding intelligently to the realities of work, family, health, and responsibility.

Across a single lifetime, the human brain rewrites itself countless times. From early sensory immersion, through the turbulence of identity formation, into the integration of expertise and finally toward reflective judgment, learning remains a continuous process of adaptation. It is best understood not as steady accumulation, but as the ongoing reconfiguration of schemas, scripts, and priorities through which experience is interpreted and meaning is made.

Importantly, the age-related shift from fluid to crystallized intelligence does not imply that the brain loses its capacity for novel learning. Neuroplasticity persists across the lifespan, but it expresses itself differently with age. When older adults engage in sustained, unfamiliar learning—such as mastering a new technology, language, or conceptual domain—fluid intelligence–like processes are recruited again. However, neuroimaging research shows that this recruitment does not

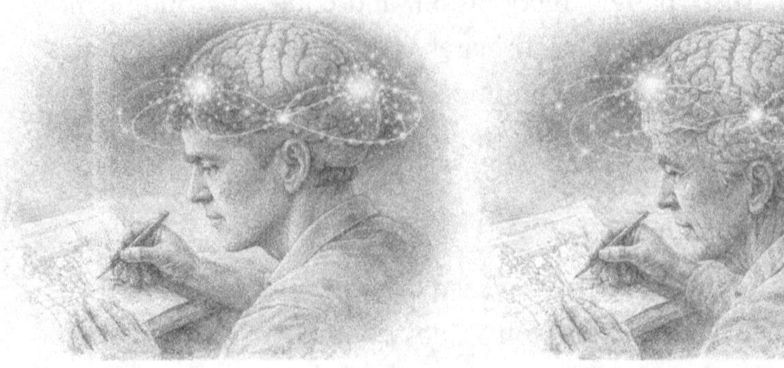

simply reactivate the same neural circuits relied upon in youth. Instead, the aging brain adapts by engaging alternative or more distributed networks, compensating for structural changes in regions that once supported rapid, resource-intensive reasoning. Learning in later life therefore reflects not a return to youthful processing, but a reorganization of cognitive labor—one that draws on experience-based scaffolding to support novelty under changed biological conditions (Park & Reuter-Lorenz, 2009; Cabeza et al., 2002; Nyberg et al., 2012).

This understanding sets the stage for the chapters that follow. If learning succeeds or fails not because of intelligence or effort alone, but because of how cognitive demands interact with limited mental resources, then design matters profoundly. The next chapter examines one of the defining challenges of the modern world: pervasive cognitive overload. Drawing on cognitive load theory, it explores how working memory—remarkably powerful yet strictly limited—struggles in environments saturated with information, choice, and interruption, and why instructional design often determines whether learning deepens into insight or collapses under excess.

Conclusion

Chapter Five challenges the long-standing assumption that learning is primarily a function of childhood followed by stabilization and inevitable decline. Drawing on lifespan development theory, the chapter argues instead that human development is lifelong, multidirectional, and adaptive. At every age, individuals gain certain capacities while losing others; growth and loss are not sequential phases separated by decades, but processes that coexist across the entire lifespan. What changes is not whether development occurs, but how learning must be managed under shifting cognitive, biological, and social constraints.

Viewed across the lifespan, learning is best understood as the continual reorganization of mental architecture rather than the accumulation of information. Early learning is rooted in sensory experience; adolescence is shaped by identity formation and emotional volatility; young adulthood brings peak capacity alongside overload risk; midlife favors integration and judgment; later life emphasizes selectivity and meaning. Each stage brings distinctive strengths to cultivate and vulnerabilities to respect. Recognizing this arc is essential for understanding why cognitive load, rather than intelligence or motivation alone, often determines whether learning succeeds or fails.

Chapter Six: Dynamic Memory in Human and Machine Learning

How Experience is Organized into Structured Knowledge

It is 1982 at Yale University. Cognitive psychology professor Roger Schank sits in a cluttered office, the walls plastered with hand-drawn diagrams—arrows looping between boxes labeled *memory, expectation, experience*. Books spill from shelves. Papers lie stacked in loose, meaningful disorder.

A graduate student asks, almost casually, "Professor, how is it that when we walk into a restaurant, we already know what to expect—being seated, getting menus, ordering, eating, paying—without having to consciously recall each step every time?"

Schank leans back in his chair and smiles. "Because," he says, "we don't store every event. We store schemas—mental blueprints of typical experiences—and scripts that guide our actions."

With that, Schank and his students begin to sketch what would become one of the most influential models of human memory. Knowledge, they argue, is not organized as isolated facts or abstract rules, but as structured, experience-based patterns—what Schank and Abelson would formally describe as scripts (Schank & Abelson, 1977). These scripts allow us to move fluidly through the world, anticipating what comes next without conscious deliberation.

The power of the idea lies in its economy. Scripts reduce cognitive effort. They allow prediction without calculation, action without rehearsal. They explain how people navigate novelty by relying on familiarity—how we adapt new situations to old experiences rather than reasoning from first principles each time.

As Schank and his collaborators continued their work, efforts to model human reasoning did not abandon this framework but pushed it forward. Schank's theory of schemas, scripts, and memory organization packets was refined into case-based reasoning, a computational approach that treated reasoning itself as the retrieval and adaptation of prior experience rather than the application of abstract rules.

Case-based reasoning also offered a practical advantage that rule-based systems struggled to provide: explainability. Because a case-based system arrives at a decision by retrieving and adapting prior cases, its reasoning can be articulated in familiar, human terms—*this situation resembles earlier situations, and here is how those were resolved.* In contrast, rule-based systems often produce conclusions through long chains of abstract conditionals whose internal logic may be formally correct yet opaque even to their designers.

This alignment with human reasoning was not incidental. Building on his earlier work on schemas, scripts, and memory organization packets (MOP), Roger Schank treated explanation as a core requirement rather than a post hoc feature. By grounding computation in remembered experience, case-based reasoning made it possible for end users to understand *why* a system reached a particular decision, not merely *what* decision it produced.

As a consequence, designers and engineers could more readily inspect, question, and refine their systems. Errors could be traced to inappropriate cases, missing experiences, or faulty analogies rather than buried in layers of brittle rules. In this sense, case-based reasoning did more than model human learning—it reduced the distance between human understanding and machine reasoning, lowering the risk of hidden logic flaws and increasing confidence in system behavior.

What began as an attempt to explain why a restaurant feels familiar would go on to shape how machines learn from experience. And in that arc—from human memory to artificial reasoning—lies a central insight for this chapter: learning, whether human or artificial, succeeds not by eliminating difficulty, but by organizing experience so that recovery, reuse, and adaptation are possible under conditions of change.

This chapter explores the dynamic nature of human memory, drawing on foundational cognitive models and their intersections with lifespan development theory. Memory is not a static repository but a reconstructive, adaptive system that evolves across the lifespan, enabling individuals to organize experiences into schemas, retrieve contextual details, and adapt to new challenges. As articulated in lifespan theory (Baltes, 1987), memory processes undergo gains and losses throughout life, with plasticity allowing compensation for age-related declines. These dynamics are particularly relevant for lifelong learning, where cognitive reserve—built through education and experience—can mitigate aging's impact on episodic and working memory. Building on cognitive architectures like Baddeley's multicomponent working memory model, Schank's schemas and scripts, and Tulving's episodic memory, we examine empirical, neurological, and phenomenological evidence from aging research. This narrative underscores how memory sustains individual adaptation and self-government in a learning republic, where knowledge obsolescence demands continuous renewal (Whitehead, 1931; Densen, 2011).

The Dynamic Foundations of Memory: Models and Mechanisms

In the mid-1960s, Richard Atkinson and Richard Shiffrin proposed what became one of the most influential frameworks in cognitive psychology: the multi-store model of memory (Atkinson & Shiffrin, 1968). Often called the "modal model" because it synthesized so much of the era's research, it envisioned memory as three distinct stores arranged in a linear sequence.

Information first enters sensory memory—a very brief, high-capacity register that holds raw perceptual input (visual icons for about 0.5 seconds, auditory echoes for 3–4 seconds). Most of this fades almost immediately unless attention selects a small portion for further processing. Selected information then flows into short-term memory (later called working memory), a limited-capacity store that holds about seven items (plus or minus two) for roughly 15–30 seconds without rehearsal. Rehearsal—repeating information verbally or mentally—extends its duration, while decay or interference causes loss. Finally, through rehearsal and meaningful encoding, information transfers to long-term memory, a theoretically unlimited, relatively permanent store that holds facts, skills, and experiences for minutes to a lifetime.

The model was elegant in its simplicity. It explained classic phenomena: why we forget phone numbers if we don't repeat them (short-term decay), why rehearsal helps transfer to long-term storage (repetition strengthens encoding), and why interference from similar items disrupts recall (competition in the short-term store). Atkinson and Shiffrin also emphasized control processes—attention, rehearsal strategies, retrieval cues—that allow individuals to move information between stores actively.

Yet the single-box view of short-term memory soon showed its limits. Experiments revealed dissociations that a unitary store could not easily explain: verbal and visual tasks interfere less with each other than two verbal tasks do; articulatory suppression (saying "the" repeatedly) disrupts verbal recall but not spatial imagery; patients with phonological loop deficits (e.g., conduction aphasia) still manage visuospatial tasks. These findings suggested that short-term memory is not one undifferentiated buffer but a collection of specialized subsystems.

Enter Alan Baddeley and Graham Hitch. In 1974, they proposed a multicomponent model that retained Atkinson–Shiffrin's three-store structure but replaced the monolithic short-term store with a dynamic, modular system: a central executive coordinating two subordinate systems (phonological loop and visuospatial sketchpad), later joined by an episodic buffer. Baddeley's framework preserved the idea of limited capacity and rehearsal but gave it anatomical and functional granularity—exactly what was needed to explain dual-task performance, modality-specific interference, and lifespan changes in cognitive aging.

The Atkinson–Shiffrin model remains a foundational milestone. It shifted psychology from behaviorism to information-processing metaphors, providing the first clear architecture for how sensory input becomes durable knowledge. But its single-box short-term store proved too rigid for the complexities of real cognition. Baddeley's multicomponent refinement—and the dynamic, reconstructive extensions that followed—better captured how memory actually works in the wild, both in human minds and in the machine systems that increasingly emulate them.

Memory's dynamism lies in its ability to encode, store, retrieve, and reconstruct experiences in response to changing demands. At the core is working memory (WM), a limited-capacity system for temporary storage and manipulation of information essential for learning and problem-solving. Alan Baddeley's multicomponent model (Baddeley & Hitch, 1974; Baddeley, 2000) posits WM as a system comprising a central executive (for attention control), phonological loop (verbal rehearsal), visuospatial sketchpad (visual/spatial manipulation), and episodic buffer (integrating multimodal info with long-term memory). This model highlights memory's flexibility: WM is not a single buffer but a coordinated network that adapts to task demands, with temporal limits (e.g., info decays without rehearsal; Peterson & Peterson, 1959) and spatial constraints (e.g., 7 ± 2 chunks; Miller, 1956).

Alan Baddeley's multicomponent model of working memory, first proposed with Graham Hitch in 1974 and refined over decades, revolutionized our understanding of how the mind handles information in real time. Far from a single, passive buffer, Baddeley envisioned working memory as a flexible, modular system: a central executive directing attention and coordinating subprocesses, a phonological loop for verbal rehearsal and sound-based information, a visuospatial sketchpad for manipulating images and spatial data, and later (2000) an episodic buffer that integrates these streams with long-term memory and other modalities. This model emphasized dynamism: working memory is not static storage but an active workspace where limited resources are allocated, rehearsed, and bound into coherent experiences.

What makes Baddeley's framework particularly resonant today is its uncanny parallels in machine learning architectures. Just as human working memory evolved to handle the demands of survival and adaptation, AI systems have been designed to mimic these modular, attention-driven processes to manage the explosion of data and computation in modern learning tasks. Schank's dynamic memory theory focused on long-term organization, but Baddeley provided the short-term "engine" that makes retrieval and adaptation feasible under constraints. Machine learning engineers, often implicitly, have borrowed these ideas to build models that process, integrate, and adapt information in ways that echo the human mind's multicomponent efficiency. Below, we explore these parallels component by component, drawing on neurological insights from human cognition and their computational counterparts in AI.

The Central Executive: Attention as the Director

In Baddeley's model, the central executive acts as the control center—allocating attention, prioritizing tasks, and coordinating the subordinate systems (loops and sketchpad). It's akin to a supervisor juggling multiple inputs without overwhelming the workspace, suppressing distractions and shifting focus as needed. Neurologically, this maps to prefrontal cortex activity, where executive functions like inhibition and task-switching occur (fMRI studies show heightened activation during dual-task scenarios; Shallice & Burgess, 1991).

In machine learning, this executive function is mirrored in attention mechanisms, most famously in transformers (Vaswani et al., 2017). Self-attention allows a model to weigh the importance of different elements in an input sequence—much like the central executive prioritizes relevant chunks in working memory. For example, when processing a sentence, the model computes attention scores to focus on key words (e.g., subject-verb relations), suppressing noise. This parallels human selective attention: older adults, with reduced prefrontal efficiency, struggle with inhibition (Leenders et al., 2018), just as early neural nets without attention suffered from vanishing gradients in long sequences.

Modern extensions like multi-head attention in GPT models divide processing into parallel "heads," each specializing in different aspects (e.g., syntactic vs. semantic relations)—echoing Baddeley's modular subsystems. In retrieval-augmented systems, the "executive" role expands: attention heads decide which retrieved cases (from a vector store) to integrate, adapting dynamically to query demands. This computational parallel not only scales human-like focus but also compensates for AI's own limits, such as finite context windows, by offloading less relevant data.

The Phonological Loop: Rehearsal for Sequential Data

The phonological loop handles verbal and auditory information through rehearsal: an articulatory control process (inner speech) and a phonological store (short-term sound buffer). It explains phenomena like the word-length effect—longer words decay faster without subvocal repetition (Baddeley et al., 1975). Neurologically, it's linked to left-hemisphere language areas (Broca's for rehearsal, temporoparietal for storage), with aging reducing loop efficiency, leading to poorer verbal recall (Leenders et al., 2018).

AI replicates this with recurrent neural networks (RNNs) and long short-term memory (LSTM) units (Hochreiter & Schmidhuber, 1997). RNNs maintain a "hidden state" that carries information sequentially, simulating rehearsal: each timestep updates the state based on new input and prior "memory." LSTMs add gates (forget, input, output) to control what to retain or discard, preventing information decay over long sequences— directly analogous to the loop's decay prevention via rehearsal. In natural language processing, LSTMs handle speech recognition or text generation by "rehearsing" phonetic patterns, much as the loop maintains verbal chunks.

In modern transformers, positional encodings and recurrent variants (e.g., RWKV or Linear Transformers) echo the loop's sequential nature, allowing models to "rehearse" long dialogues or narratives without full recomputation. For lifelong learning apps, this means AI tutors can maintain conversational context, adapting responses to user history—compensating for human WM decline in older learners by "looping" key phrases back into prompts.

The Visuospatial Sketchpad: Manipulating Visual and Spatial Worlds

The sketchpad processes visual and spatial information, allowing mental rotation or navigation imagery. It's capacity-limited (3–4 objects; Luck & Vogel, 1997) and neurologically tied to right-hemisphere parietal regions, with aging impairing spatial manipulation (Mok et al., 2019).

In AI, convolutional neural networks (CNNs) parallel this: layers of filters convolve over images, extracting features (edges, shapes) and manipulating spatial hierarchies (LeCun et al., 1989). Pooling operations compress visual data like the sketchpad's chunking, while vision transformers (ViTs) use attention to "sketch" spatial relationships. In generative models like Stable Diffusion, latent space manipulation allows "mental rotation" of concepts—e.g., adapting a retrieved image case to new viewpoints.

This parallel enables AI to extend human visuospatial memory: augmented reality apps for older adults (Cicconi & Marchese, 2019) overlay navigational aids, compensating for hippocampal decline in spatial tasks.

The Episodic Buffer: Integration and the Road to Hybrid Systems

Added in 2000, the episodic buffer binds multimodal info into coherent episodes, linking WM to long-term stores (Baddeley, 2000). It explains chunking across senses and ties to Tulving's episodic memory.

AI equivalents are memory-augmented networks (e.g., Neural Turing Machines), which add external memory for binding sequences into "episodes." RAG systems act as episodic buffers: retrieving contextual "chunks" from knowledge bases to ground generation, mimicking human episodic reinstatement.

Overall Implications: Baddeley's modularity inspires hybrid AI: attention (executive), recurrence (loop), convolution (sketchpad), and external memory (buffer) create systems that process dynamically, like humans. In a learning republic, these parallels enable AI to extend memory plasticity—e.g., RAG tutors retrieving personalized cases for older learners—while respecting human limits. Yet, without ethical design, they risk disembodied overload, a theme for the next chapter.

Complementing Baddeley, Roger Schank's work on schemas and scripts (Schank & Abelson, 1977; Schank, 1999) frames memory as structured patterns derived from experience. Schemas are mental blueprints for typical scenarios (e.g., a "restaurant script" guiding expectations from seating to payment), reducing cognitive effort by allowing prediction and adaptation. Dynamic memory theory (Schank, 1999) extends this, proposing memory as reconstructive: schemas evolve through "memory organization packets" (MOPs), reorganizing experiences for reuse. Empirical studies support this: Graesser (1982) showed schemas guide inferences but distort incongruent details; Rubínová et al. (2021) found repeated exposure to narratives builds schemas, improving recall but highlighting deviations.

The Multi-Component Working Memory Model

Cambridge, 1973. Psychologist Alan Baddeley is frustrated. The classic Atkinson–Shiffrin model treats short-term memory as a single box—input, store, output—but his experiments suggest otherwise. When people listen to words and watch visual patterns at the same time, their performance does not degrade as much as expected. It's as if the brain runs two channels in parallel.

Working with Graham Hitch, Baddeley proposes a radical model: working memory is not a single buffer but a system—a central executive directing two subsystems: the phonological loop for verbal information and the visuospatial sketchpad for images and spatial reasoning (Baddeley & Hitch, 1974). Later, he adds the episodic buffer, integrating these with long-term memory (Baddeley, 2000). This model still anchors nearly every learning theory in use. It explains why learners benefit when audio narration complements graphics, but not when

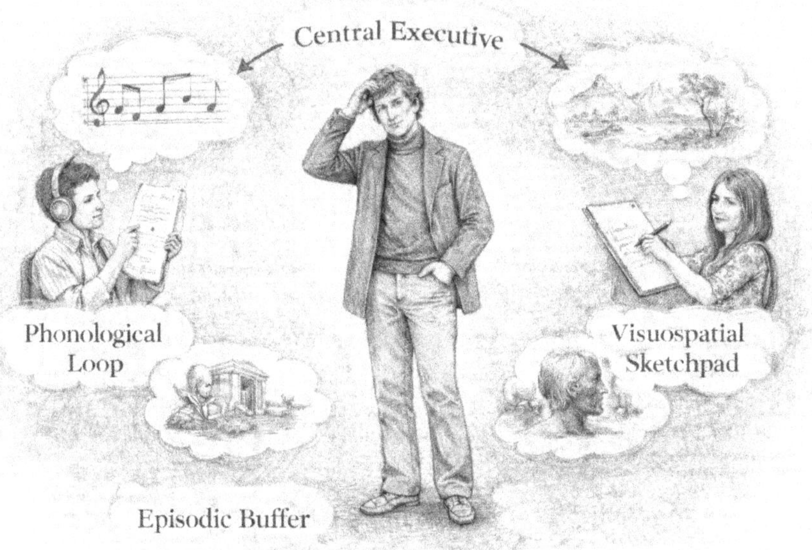

Baddeley's Working Memory Model

both present identical text. It also underpins dual-channel processing, later expanded by Clark & Paivio (1991) and Mayer (2019).

Endel Tulving's episodic memory (Tulving, 1972, 1983) adds a personal, temporal dimension, distinguishing it from semantic memory (factual knowledge). Episodic memory enables "mental time travel"—reliving past events with contextual details (what, where, when) and autonoetic consciousness (self-aware reliving). This reconstructive process links to lifespan continuity, allowing individuals to draw on autobiographical episodes for identity and adaptation. Neurological evidence ties episodic memory to the hippocampus and prefrontal cortex: fMRI shows activation during retrieval (Gelbard-Sagiv et al., 2008), with schemas facilitating reinstatement (Fenerci et al., 2024).

These models intersect: Baddeley's episodic buffer bridges WM and episodic long-term storage (Baddeley, 2000), while schemas scaffold episodic recall (Masís-Obando et al., 2022, mPFC activation). Dynamic neural models like Dynamic

Neural Resource (DyNR; Tomić et al., 2024) further emphasize temporal evolution, where memory fidelity shifts due to noise and signal accumulation.

The central executive allocates attention, suppresses distractions, and shifts focus—functions tied to prefrontal cortex activity (Shallice & Burgess, 1991). The phonological loop maintains verbal material through subvocal rehearsal (inner speech) and a passive store for sound traces, explaining the word-length effect and articulatory suppression (Baddeley et al., 1975). The visuospatial sketchpad handles mental imagery and spatial manipulation, with capacity limits of 3–4 objects (Luck & Vogel, 1997). The episodic buffer acts as an integrative workspace, binding verbal, visual, and long-term elements into temporary representations.

Endel Tulving's episodic memory (Tulving, 1972, 1983) adds a personal, temporal dimension, distinguishing it from semantic memory (factual knowledge). Episodic memory enables "mental time travel"—reliving past events with contextual details (what, where, when) and autonoetic consciousness (self-aware reliving). This reconstructive process links to lifespan continuity, allowing individuals to draw on autobiographical episodes for identity and adaptation. Neurological evidence ties episodic memory to the hippocampus and prefrontal cortex: fMRI shows activation during retrieval (Gelbard-Sagiv et al., 2008), with schemas facilitating reinstatement (Fenerci et al., 2024).

These models intersect: Baddeley's episodic buffer bridges WM and episodic long-term storage (Baddeley, 2000), while schemas scaffold episodic recall (Masís-Obando et al., 2022, mPFC activation). Dynamic neural models like Dynamic

Neural Resource (DyNR; Tomić et al., 2024) further emphasize temporal evolution, where memory fidelity shifts due to noise and signal accumulation.

The central executive allocates attention, suppresses distractions, and shifts focus—functions tied to prefrontal cortex activity (Shallice & Burgess, 1991). The phonological loop maintains verbal material through subvocal rehearsal (inner speech) and a passive store for sound traces, explaining the word-length effect and articulatory suppression (Baddeley et al., 1975). The visuospatial sketchpad handles mental imagery and spatial manipulation, with capacity limits of 3–4 objects (Luck & Vogel, 1997). The episodic buffer acts as an integrative workspace, binding verbal, visual, and long-term elements into temporary representations.

This model explains dual-task dissociations: verbal suppression disrupts word recall but spares spatial imagery; patients with phonological loop deficits (e.g., conduction aphasia) still navigate visuospatial tasks. It also accounts for lifespan changes: aging reduces central executive efficiency (inhibition, task-switching), phonological loop speed, and buffer binding capacity (Leenders et al., 2018; Mok et al., 2019), while older adults compensate by offloading to long-term schemas and crystallized knowledge—precisely what Baltes's SOC framework predicts.

Baddeley's multicomponent model remains the dominant framework for understanding how limited-capacity processing supports complex cognition. It underpins multimedia learning principles: narration plus animation leverages separate channels, while on-screen text plus narration overloads the visual channel. Most importantly for this chapter, the episodic buffer provides the interface where short-term manipulation meets long-term structures—schemas, scripts, and episodic traces—allowing dynamic memory to operate in real time.

From Human to Machine: AI Parallels to Baddeley's Model

The modular, attention-driven architecture Baddeley proposed for human working memory finds striking parallels in modern machine learning systems—especially those that must process, integrate, and adapt information under tight computational constraints.

The central executive—the control center that allocates attention, prioritizes tasks, and suppresses distractions—finds its closest counterpart in attention mechanisms, most famously in transformers (Vaswani et al., 2017). Self-attention allows a model to weigh the importance of different elements in an input sequence—much like the executive prioritizes relevant chunks in working memory. For example, when processing a sentence, the model computes attention scores to focus on key words (e.g., subject-verb relations), suppressing noise from less relevant tokens. This mirrors human selective attention: older adults, with reduced prefrontal efficiency, struggle with inhibition (Leenders et al., 2018), just as early neural nets without attention suffered from vanishing gradients in long sequences.

Modern extensions like multi-head attention in GPT models divide processing into parallel "heads," each specializing in different aspects (e.g., syntactic vs. semantic relations)—echoing Baddeley's modular subsystems (phonological loop for verbal, sketchpad for visual/spatial). Each head attends to a different subspace, allowing the model to capture multiple patterns simultaneously, much as the human executive coordinates separate verbal and visuospatial streams.

In retrieval-augmented systems, the executive role expands: attention heads decide which retrieved cases (from a vector store) to integrate, adapting dynamically to query demands. This computational parallel not only scales human-like focus but also compensates for AI's own limits—finite context windows, quadratic attention costs—by offloading less relevant data and concentrating processing on high-priority "chunks."

The phonological loop (verbal rehearsal) finds echoes in recurrent neural networks (RNNs) and long short-term memory (LSTM) units. RNNs maintain a "hidden state" that carries information sequentially, simulating rehearsal: each timestep updates the state based on new input and prior memory. LSTMs add gates (forget, input, output) to control what to retain or discard, preventing information decay over long sequences—directly analogous to the loop's decay prevention via rehearsal. In natural language processing, LSTMs handle speech recognition or text generation by "rehearsing" phonetic or syntactic patterns.

The visuospatial sketchpad is mirrored in convolutional neural networks (CNNs) and vision transformers (ViTs). CNNs convolve filters over images to extract spatial hierarchies (edges → shapes → objects), while pooling compresses visual data like the sketchpad's chunking. Vision transformers use attention to "sketch" spatial relationships, allowing models to manipulate mental imagery equivalents (e.g., adapting retrieved images to new viewpoints in generative systems).

The episodic buffer—binding multimodal info into coherent episodes—finds its closest parallel in memory-augmented networks (e.g., Neural Turing Machines, Differentiable Neural

Computers) and retrieval-augmented generation (RAG) pipelines. The buffer integrates verbal, visual, and long-term elements; RAG retrieves contextual "chunks" from external stores and binds them to the query before generation, mimicking episodic reinstatement.

These parallels are not coincidental. AI engineers, consciously or not, have rediscovered Baddeley's insight: complex processing under constraints requires modularity, attention control, rehearsal mechanisms, and integration buffers. In a learning republic, this convergence enables AI to extend human memory plasticity—e.g., RAG tutors retrieving personalized cases for older learners, compensating for reduced WM capacity—while reminding us that design must respect the same limits that shape human minds. That respect is the subject of the next chapter.

Schank's Legacy

Among the first to turn Schank's theoretical vision into a working system was Janet Kolodner, then a doctoral student at Yale. Her program CYRUS (1980–1983) modeled the memory of former U.S. Secretary of State Cyrus Vance, storing diplomatic events as structured episodes indexed by thematic knowledge packets. When asked about a state dinner in Moscow, CYRUS retrieved a similar dinner in Beijing, adapted details (location, participants, protocol), and generated a plausible response—even when no exact match existed.

Kolodner's contribution was more than technical. She demonstrated that reasoning could be memory-driven rather than rule-chained, and that machines could "remind" themselves of past cases in much the same way humans do. Years later, she carried the same insight into education, developing Learning by

Design™, a project-based middle-school science curriculum in which students iteratively design artifacts (vehicles, ecosystems) and reflect on failures by reusing and adapting prior class cases. The parallel is striking: just as CYRUS adapted diplomatic precedents, LBD students adapt prior design experiences to solve new problems. Kolodner's career thus traces a direct line from Schank's dynamic memory theory to both early AI and constructivist classroom practice—showing that the same reconstructive principles that make human learning efficient can also guide machine intelligence and human-centered pedagogy.

Janet Kolodner's student David Leake took CBR in a particularly introspective direction. At Indiana University, Leake developed theories and systems that allow reasoners to monitor their own failures, generate explanations for why a retrieved case did not work, and choose targeted learning strategies to repair and strengthen memory (Leake, 1996; Leake & Ram, 1995). His work on explanation-driven case adaptation and goal-driven learning made CBR more robust and self-reflective—qualities that resonate in modern AI systems that must debug and improve themselves over time.

This intellectual thread runs directly to the present. Leake's student Thomas P. Reichherzer, now at the University of West Florida, further developed explanation-driven adaptation, introspective learning, and CBR applications in tutoring and knowledge acquisition (Reichherzer & Leake, 2006). Reichherzer advised the present author's master's and doctoral dissertations and co-authored papers exploring how memory-based reasoning can inform adaptive educational systems, including work on structural case-based reasoning for activity recognition in smart home environments (Satterfield et al., 2012). That direct connection underscores a persistent truth:

the reconstructive, adaptive principles Schank first articulated continue to shape both machine intelligence and human-centered learning design—from early case-based systems to today's retrieval-augmented models and eLearning tools that extend human memory plasticity across the lifespan.

Memory Across the Lifespan: Gains, Losses, and Plasticity

Lifespan theory (Baltes, 1987) frames memory changes as multidirectional and multidimensional, with gains (e.g., crystallized knowledge) and losses (e.g., fluid abilities) co-occurring. Plasticity—neural and behavioral adaptation—compensates, as alternate brain regions offset declines (Baltes, 1987; Maguire et al., 2006, hippocampal enlargement in cab drivers). Biocultural co-constructivism highlights how biology, culture, and choices shape memory: Early education builds cognitive reserve, delaying dementia (Lövdén et al., 2020; Davies et al., 2018).

Cognitive aging research reveals episodic memory's vulnerability: Declines in selective attention, WM capacity, and processing speed emerge after 65 (Salthouse, 2019; Spreng & Turner, 2019; Veríssimo et al., 2022). fMRI studies (Mok et al., 2019) map selective attention to frontoparietal networks, with reduced activation in older adults (Leenders et al., 2018, MEG alpha waves). EEG evoked potentials (Chad Rogers et al., 2018) show diminished selectivity in auditory tasks, with weaker ERPs (e.g., P300) for relevant stimuli.

Tulving's episodic framework illuminates these shifts: Aging impairs contextual binding (Old & Naveh-Benjamin, 2008), reducing autonoetic reliving. Yet, semanticization—

episodic memories becoming factual over time—preserves core knowledge (Irish, 2020). Phenomenologically, older adults report vivid positive low-arousal memories (Mickley & Kensinger, 2009), aligning with socioemotional selectivity theory (SST; Carstensen et al., 1999): Limited time horizons prioritize emotionally meaningful recall.

Empirical evidence: Cross-sectional/longitudinal studies (Salthouse, 2019) show linear fluid declines, but quasi-longitudinal methods (Schaie & Willis, 2010) reveal sustained abilities into middle age. Interventions like music learning (Jünemann et al., 2020) or language acquisition (Pfenninger & Polz, 2018) boost hippocampal volume, enhancing episodic recall. Neurological meta-analyses (Emch et al., 2019) confirm frontoparietal involvement, with dopamine modulation (Köhncke et al., 2018) sustaining systems via exercise.

Selective optimization with compensation (SOC; Baltes & Baltes, 1990) applies: Older adults optimize schemas for familiar tasks, compensating for WM limits. SST predicts selectivity: Focus on positive, generative activities (Obhi et al., 2021; Narushima et al., 2018) preserves episodic richness for well-being.

Neurological and Phenomenological Insights into Aging Memory

Neurologically, episodic memory relies on medial temporal lobe (hippocampus for binding) and prefrontal cortex (retrieval control). Aging reduces hippocampal volume (Lister & Barnes, 2009), impairing pattern completion (Trelle et al., 2020): fMRI shows weaker reinstatement of event details. Frontoparietal deficits (Emch et al., 2019) explain WM declines, with subcortical updating slowed (Trutti et al., 2025). Dopamine loss (Fan et al., 2021) exacerbates, but plasticity (e.g., vigorous exercise increasing receptors; Köhncke et al., 2018) counters.

Phenomenologically, memory feels reconstructive: Epistemic feelings of "pastness" (Perrin et al., 2020) evoke autonoesis, but aging flattens vividness for neutral events (Fancourt & Steptoe, 2019). Collective memory (Bogotá, 2025) sustains identity via shared schemas, while hyper-binding (Campbell & Hasher, 2018) aids co-variance detection, a gain amid losses.

Empirical studies: Altieri et al. (2020) link cognitive reserve (education, leisure) to lower apathy; Wang et al. (2020) correlate dispositional hope with cortical volume, emphasizing early foundations.

From Human to Machine: Schank's Bridge to AI

The intellectual lineage from Schank to Kolodner to Leake to Reichherzer has carried case-based reasoning forward across nearly five decades, each generation refining the core insight: learning—human or artificial—thrives when past experience is retrieved, adapted, explained, and retained dynamically. That same reconstructive principle, once implemented in small laboratory systems like CYRUS, now operates at planetary scale in today's large language models.

Modern machine learning has rediscovered and massively scaled Schank's memory-driven approach, though often without explicit acknowledgment of its origins. The key mechanism is retrieval: instead of generating responses solely from parametric knowledge encoded in weights, contemporary systems first retrieve relevant context from an external memory store, then condition generation on that retrieved material. This mirrors the retrieve-reuse-revise-retain cycle of CBR, but with statistical rather than symbolic indexing.

At the heart of this shift are vector embeddings and similarity search. Text—queries, documents, passages—is transformed into dense vectors in high-dimensional space (typically 768 to 4096 dimensions) using models such as BERT, Sentence-BERT, or more recent encoders. Semantic similarity is then measured via cosine distance or dot product: a query vector is compared against a pre-computed database of vectors, and the nearest neighbors are retrieved as context. This is case retrieval at internet scale—Schank's reminding process, but executed in milliseconds across billions of tokens.

Retrieval-Augmented Generation (RAG) takes this retrieval step and integrates it directly into the generation pipeline. A user query is embedded, relevant documents or passages are fetched from a vector store (often using approximate nearest-neighbor search for speed), and the retrieved content is concatenated with the query before being passed to the language model. The model then generates an answer grounded in the retrieved context, dramatically reducing hallucination and improving factual accuracy. The parallel to CBR is unmistakable: retrieval activates relevant "cases" (documents), reuse maps them to the current problem (query), and generation adapts the content to produce a tailored response. Recent variants even incorporate explicit revision steps—reranking retrieved items, fusing multiple sources, or refining the query itself—echoing CBR's revise phase.

Memory-augmented neural networks push the analogy further. Early systems like the Neural Turing Machine (Graves et al., 2014) and Differentiable Neural Computer (Graves et al., 2016) gave transformers an explicit, differentiable external memory matrix with read/write heads controlled by attention. Modern descendants—Memformer, Neural Episodic Control, End-to-End Memory Networks, and transformer variants with long-context memory—enable one-shot learning, continual adaptation, and reasoning over extended histories without catastrophic forgetting.

The key parallel remains: both humans and machines use pattern-based retrieval to reduce computation under constraints. Human working memory holds roughly seven chunks; retrieving a schema compresses dozens of details into one reusable unit. Transformers face finite context windows and quadratic attention costs; retrieval offloads the burden, allowing the model to focus on adaptation rather than regeneration. Yet the analogy is incomplete: human memory is episodic, embodied, and emotionally colored; AI retrieval is statistical and disembodied. Humans adapt through conscious reflection and social feedback; current LLMs adapt through gradient updates or prompt engineering.

Roger Schank never saw memory as a mere filing cabinet. In his view, the mind does not passively store facts to be retrieved on demand; it actively reconstructs experience, drawing on patterns of past situations to anticipate, explain, and solve new ones. The restaurant vignette illustrates this elegantly: we do not recall every meal we have ever eaten; we recall a generalized structure—a script—that tells us what comes next and why. When something deviates (a waiter brings the check before dessert), the mind notices the anomaly and updates its script library. This reconstructive, adaptive quality is what makes human memory dynamic rather than static.

Schank's ambition went beyond describing human cognition. He wanted to build machines that reason the same way. In the late 1970s and 1980s, artificial intelligence was dominated by rule-based expert systems: programs that encoded domain knowledge as if-then rules and chained logical inferences to reach conclusions. Schank found this brittle. Rules break when the world deviates from the expected; they require exhaustive enumeration of every possible scenario. Humans, by contrast, rarely reason from first principles. They remind themselves of similar past experiences and adapt what worked before. Why not equip computers with the same capability?

This question gave rise to case-based reasoning (CBR), Schank's most enduring contribution to AI. CBR treats reasoning as an act of memory: when confronted with a new problem, the system retrieves a similar past case from its memory store, adapts the solution to fit the current context, applies it, and—if successful—retains the outcome as a new case for future use. The process is often summarized in four steps (Aamodt & Plaza, 1994):

- **Retrieve**: Identify the most similar past case (or cases) based on surface and structural features.

- **Reuse**: Map the retrieved solution to the new problem, adapting where necessary (e.g., substituting variables, repairing broken steps).

- **Revise**: Evaluate the adapted solution in the current context; repair failures if the outcome is unsatisfactory.

- **Retain**: Store the successful resolution as a new case, updating indices so future retrieval can find it more accurately.

Two early systems embodied this vision. CYRUS (1979–1983), developed by Janet Kolodner under Schank's supervision at Yale, answered questions about the travels and diplomatic activities of former U.S. Secretary of State Cyrus Vance. It stored events as structured episodes, indexed by thematic knowledge packets (MOPs), and retrieved similar past events to infer answers when direct matches were missing. If asked about a state dinner in Moscow, CYRUS might retrieve a similar dinner in Beijing, adapt details (location, participants), and generate a plausible response.

PROTOS (1980s, University of Texas, Bruce Porter and Ray Bareiss) took CBR into concept learning and classification. It acquired new concepts by comparing them to stored exemplars, asking an expert for explanations when mismatches occurred, and refining its indices. PROTOS learned to classify diseases by storing diagnostic cases and adapting them to new symptoms, demonstrating that memory-based learning could scale to real-world domains without exhaustive rules.

These systems were not mere proofs of concept. They showed that machines could learn incrementally, handle novelty through analogy, and improve over time—precisely the qualities Schank argued were essential for robust intelligence. CBR's appeal lay in its psychological plausibility: humans reason by analogy far more than by formal deduction, and early CBR systems captured that intuition in code.

Fast-forward four decades, and the echoes are unmistakable in modern machine learning.

The rise of vector embeddings and similarity search in transformer-based models is a direct descendant of CBR's retrieval step. Large language models (LLMs) convert text into dense vectors in high-dimensional space (typically 768–4096 dimensions), where semantic similarity is measured by cosine distance or dot product. A query vector is compared against a database of document or passage vectors; the nearest neighbors are retrieved as context. This is, in essence, Schank's reminding process implemented at scale: the model "remembers" past text by finding patterns most similar to the current input.

Retrieval-Augmented Generation (RAG) takes this further, directly mirroring CBR's retrieve-reuse cycle. In a standard RAG pipeline:

- A query is embedded and used to retrieve relevant documents or passages from an external knowledge base.

- The retrieved content is concatenated with the query and fed to the LLM.

- The model generates an answer grounded in the retrieved context, reducing hallucination.

This is strikingly analogous to schema activation: the retriever activates relevant "cases" (documents), and the generator adapts them to the current problem (query). Recent variants even incorporate adaptation steps—reranking retrieved items, fusing multiple sources, or refining the query itself—paralleling CBR's revise phase.

Memory-augmented neural networks push the analogy deeper. The Neural Turing Machine (NTM, Graves et al., 2014) and its successor, the Differentiable Neural Computer (DNC, Graves et al., 2016), gave neural networks an explicit, differentiable external memory matrix with read/write heads controlled by attention mechanisms. These systems learn to store and retrieve information dynamically, much as Schank's MOPs organize episodic knowledge. Modern descendants—such as Memformer, Neural Episodic Control, and End-to-End Memory Networks—extend this idea, enabling one-shot learning, long-context reasoning, and continual adaptation without catastrophic forgetting.

The key parallel is striking: both humans and machines use pattern-based retrieval to reduce computation under constraints. Human working memory is limited to roughly seven chunks; retrieving a schema or script compresses dozens of details into one reusable unit. AI faces similar pressure: transformers have finite context windows, and inference is computationally expensive. Retrieval of similar cases (via embeddings or RAG) offloads the burden, allowing the model to focus on adaptation rather than regenerating knowledge from scratch.

Yet the analogy is not perfect. Human memory is episodic, embodied, and emotionally colored; AI retrieval is statistical and disembodied. Humans adapt through conscious reflection and social feedback; current LLMs adapt through gradient updates or prompt engineering. Schank's vision was that machines should learn incrementally from experience, retain what works, and repair what fails—precisely what CBR promised. Modern AI has scaled retrieval to billions of tokens, but it still struggles with true long-term adaptation, explainability, and avoidance of brittleness.

In a learning republic, this bridge matters profoundly. If machines can organize and adapt experience as humans do, they become partners in lifelong learning—retrieving relevant knowledge, reminding us of forgotten patterns, and extending our cognitive reach. But only if we design them to respect the same constraints that shape human minds. That design challenge is the subject of the next chapter.

Conclusion

Dynamic memory, from Baddeley's WM to Tulving's episodic reliving and Schank's schemas, evolves across life per Baltes' (1987) gains/losses. Aging impairs fluid aspects but preserves crystallized via reserve and plasticity. Neurological evidence (fMRI declines) and phenomcnological vividness (positive bias) highlight adaptation. For lifelong learning, designs must mitigate load, fostering a republic where memory sustains self-government amid change. Future chapters explore developmental protections for these processes.

Chapter Seven: Cognitive Load and the Architecture of Learning

The Limits of the Mind

It is the mid-1950s, and George A. Miller is watching his subjects fail.

They fail politely, earnestly, and predictably. Seated in quiet laboratory rooms, they listen to sequences of tones, or strings of digits, or lists of words. They concentrate. They rehearse. They try harder. And then—at roughly the same point every time—their performance collapses.

Seven items. Sometimes six. Sometimes eight. Rarely more.

Miller is not studying laziness, distraction, or intelligence. His participants are bright, motivated, and cooperative. Nor is he studying learning in the everyday sense. He is probing

something more elemental: the capacity of the human mind to hold information in awareness at all.

Across task after task, the same boundary appears. Whether the material consists of numbers, letters, pitches, or spatial positions, conscious processing seems to hit a wall. Add one more element, and accuracy drops sharply. Subtract one, and performance recovers. The pattern is so stable that it becomes impossible to ignore.

In 1956, Miller gives the phenomenon a name—*"The Magical Number Seven, Plus or Minus Two"*—half amused, half astonished by how stubborn the limit proves to be (Miller, 1956). The title understates the significance of what he has uncovered. This is not a quirk of memory technique or task design. It is a structural constraint.

The mind, it turns out, does not scale gracefully with effort.

What Miller begins to see is that human cognition operates within a narrow workspace—a mental stage on which only a few actors can perform at once. When that stage is uncrowded, reasoning flows. When it is overloaded, even simple tasks unravel. People lose track of steps, confuse sequences, abandon problems midstream—not because they lack ability, but because the architecture of consciousness itself has been exceeded.

There is an important twist. Miller notices that the limit applies not to raw information, but to *chunks*—units of meaning. A chess master can hold an entire board position in mind as a single structured pattern, while a novice sees only scattered pieces. The limit is not fixed content, but organization. Learning, therefore, is not about stuffing more into the mind. It is about restructuring information so that more can fit.

This insight quietly detonates long-standing assumptions about education and intelligence. If conscious processing is sharply limited, then instructional failure cannot always be blamed on poor motivation or weak aptitude. Sometimes the problem is design. Too much information arrives too quickly. Too many elements must be coordinated at once. The learner's mind is asked to do what it cannot.

Miller himself does not set out to reform education. He is trying to understand cognition. But his discovery will ripple outward—into psychology, neuroscience, instructional design, human-factors engineering, aviation safety, medical training, and eventually into every domain where complex learning matters.

What begins as a puzzle about memory becomes a foundational truth about learning:

The mind has bandwidth. And when we exceed it, learning does not merely slow—it breaks.

That truth will shape everything that follows.

Managing the Mind's Bandwidth

In the previous chapter we touched on cognitive load, the constraints of working memory, and biologically primary learning as opposed to biologically secondary learning. In this current chapter we will discuss cognitive load theory in detail. Working memory is what we refer to when we use the term "Consciousness" (Cooper, 1998). Recall that biologically primary knowledge includes capacities such as spoken language, face recognition, social reasoning, and basic intuitive quantity sense that are necessary for human survival. Geary (2008) argued that because biologically primary knowledge is essential for human survival, humans are endowed with both the capacity and the motivation to acquire it. These forms of learning "emerge reliably across cultures under ordinary developmental conditions. As a result, they require little deliberate conscious effort and are not constrained in the same way by the bandwidth limits of working memory. By contrast, biologically secondary knowledge—reading, writing, formal mathematics, and scientific reasoning—consists of culturally invented skills that must be explicitly taught in successive stages as the mind becomes ready to assimilate the information. Any discussion in this book we speak of cognitive load and the constraints of working memory, we are only discussing the biologically secondary learning.

Before turning to the theorists, it is worth clarifying the problem they were circling. Human cognition did not develop from classrooms, textbooks, or abstract symbol manipulation. It developed from participation in lived environments: speaking, navigating social relationships, interpreting cause and effect, and pursuing goals under real constraints. The tension between this experiential architecture and the demands of formal instruction is the through-line connecting Miller's memory limits, Baddeley's working-memory model, Schank's scripts, and Sweller's cognitive load theory. What began as laboratory puzzles about memory capacity ultimately converged on a deeper insight: learning succeeds or fails depending on how well instruction aligns biologically secondary knowledge with the mind's biologically primary systems.

Working memory is a small, fragile space in the mind where *conscious life* happens—where we hold what we are reading, what we are comparing, what we are deciding, and what we are trying not to forget. Cognitive load theory begins with a simple claim: learning rises or collapses depending on what can fit inside that space at one time. Sweller and colleagues describe working memory as the cognitive structure in which conscious processing occurs (Sweller, van Merriënboer, & Paas, 1998).

When the workspace of consciousness—what cognitive scientists typically call working memory—is relatively uncluttered, learners can reason, connect ideas, and construct new understanding (Miller, 1956; Baddeley, 1992; Cooper, 1998). When that workspace becomes crowded—by excessive complexity, poorly sequenced information, distraction, or anxiety—often as a result of weak instructional design, learning does not merely slow down. It degrades. Learners lose the thread of an argument, mis-sequence steps in a procedure, and abandon tasks that matter to them—not from laziness or lack of motivation, but from cognitive overload (Sweller, 1988; Sweller, Ayres, & Kalyuga, 2011; Paas & Van Merriënboer, 2020).

This difference in design explains why the same individual can feel capable—even fluent—in one learning environment and incapable in another, despite working within the same knowledge domain. The limiting factor is not always intelligence or effort. Often it is architecture: the bandwidth of working memory, the structure of long-term memory, and the degree to which instruction respects those constraints—or wastes them (Chandler & Sweller, 1991; Kirschner, Sweller, & Clark, 2006).

The early cognitive scientists did not begin with classrooms. They began with puzzles: why people can hold only a small number of elements "in mind" at once (Miller, 1956), why those elements decay rapidly without rehearsal (Peterson & Peterson, 1959), why experts recall meaningful patterns rather than surface details (de Groot, 1966; Chase & Simon, 1973), and why novices become overwhelmed by problem-solving steps that experts barely notice (Sweller, 1988). From these puzzles emerged a framework that would eventually matter everywhere learning occurs—schools, workplaces, cockpit checklists, medical training, and the modern digital world, where data and learning content are abundant, but usable information is scarce—and attention, consequently, is even scarcer (Sweller et al., 2019; Paas & Van Merriënboer, 2020).

Learning Environment as Total Milieu

When we speak of a "learning environment," we often default to classrooms, curricula, or instructional design. But this is a narrow view—one appropriate primarily to biologically secondary learning, which depends on formal instruction and deliberate effort (Geary, 2008; Sweller, Ayres, & Kalyuga, 2019). From a developmental and cognitive perspective, a learning environment is not merely where instruction occurs; it is the entire milieu in which an individual lives and acts.

From infancy onward, the human organism is immersed in a continuous learning environment composed of social relationships, material conditions, cultural norms, physiological states, and affordances for action (Bronfenbrenner, 1979; Gibson, 1979). Long before a child encounters formal schooling, they are learning—how to interpret signals, how to respond to novelty, how to regulate attention, how to persist or withdraw, how to explore or avoid. These early learning processes are overwhelmingly biologically primary: they emerge through interaction with the environment rather than explicit instruction, and they rely on perception, imitation, emotion, and action rather than conscious deliberation (Geary, 2008; Tomasello, 2019).

Developmental neuroscience further suggests that learning begins even before birth. Fetuses can recognize and retain auditory patterns, including maternal speech rhythms, indicating that early neural organization is shaped by environmental input well before conscious awareness is possible (DeCasper & Spence, 1986; Moon, Cooper, & Fifer, 1993; Partanen et al., 2013). These early adaptations do not involve abstract reasoning, but they establish expectations about predictability, effort, and meaning that later learning must work within.

Crucially, within this total environment, the child does not merely absorb information. The child learns how to learn.

Early Choice Patterns and the Architecture of Learning

In early life, most cognitive tasks are not experienced as "assignments" but as situations. A stimulus appears; the organism responds. Some responses are exploratory, effortful, and agentic. Others are avoidant, passive, or deferential. Over time, these responses consolidate into habitual patterns of engagement (Piaget, 1952; Bandura, 1986).

A child who repeatedly experiences challenge as manageable—because caregivers scaffold effort, environments reward persistence, and stress remains tolerable—learns that cognitive effort is something to enter into (Bandura, 1997; Dweck, 2006; Gopnik et al., 1999; Shonkoff & Phillips, 2000). Another child, equally capable in raw cognitive terms, may learn that challenge is overwhelming, punitive, or futile, and may adapt by disengaging. Research on learned helplessness demonstrates that such patterns can emerge even in individuals with intact cognitive ability when effort fails to reliably produce meaningful outcomes (Seligman, 1975; Abramson, Seligman, & Teasdale, 1978).

Importantly, neither child is consciously deciding to become an "active" or "passive" learner. Both are adapting rationally to what their environments make sensible. These adaptations matter because biologically secondary learning—reading, mathematics, abstract reasoning, technical skill—requires deliberate, effortful engagement of working memory (Sweller, 1988; Baddeley, 2000). Whether an individual later approaches such tasks with curiosity, anxiety, persistence, or avoidance is therefore not primarily a function of intelligence, but of learned response patterns shaped long before formal instruction begins (Duckworth et al., 2007; Dweck, 2006).

Lifelong Learning as the Accumulation of Choices

As individuals mature, learning environments become more explicit—and more optional. Unlike biologically primary learning, which unfolds automatically, biologically secondary learning increasingly depends on choice: whether to engage, persist, reflect, revisit, and integrate (Geary, 2008; Sweller et al., 2019).

Over the lifespan, these choices compound. Individuals who repeatedly choose environments that stretch their schemas— through work, study, dialogue, or responsibility—gradually reorganize their cognitive architecture. They build richer schemas, reduce working-memory load in familiar domains, and appear "more intelligent" in contexts aligned with their experience (Chase & Simon, 1973; Ericsson, Krampe, & Tesch-Römer, 1993). Others, facing the same formal opportunities, may decline them—not from incapacity, but from habits of disengagement learned earlier.

From this perspective, apparent intellectual capacity is not a fixed trait revealed by testing, but an emergent property of:

- early biologically primary learning experiences (Geary, 2008; Tomasello, 2019),

- the affordances and constraints of one's environment (Bronfenbrenner, 1979; Gibson, 1979), and

- the cumulative pattern of choices an individual makes when learning opportunities appear (Bandura, 1986; Duckworth et al., 2007).

The Moral and Civic Implication

This view carries a profound implication for a learning republic.

If intelligence is shaped not only by instruction but by environment, then societies bear responsibility not merely for schools, but for the conditions under which learning-oriented choices become reasonable, sustainable, and rewarding. Families, workplaces, civic and faith-based institutions, technologies, and cultural norms all participate in forming the learning environment across a lifetime (Heckman, 2006; OECD, 2018).

A society that treats learning as episodic and institutional will misread human potential. A society that recognizes the entire milieu as a learning environment can design conditions in which more citizens choose engagement over withdrawal, growth over stagnation, and agency over passivity.

That, ultimately, is what distinguishes a republic that merely offers education from one that truly cultivates learners.

The Total Learning Environment and the Recoverability of Learning

From the very beginning of life, learning does not occur in discrete episodes or formal settings. It unfolds within a total environment—physiological, familial, social, material, and cultural—long before the child ever encounters schooling. Even before birth, the human brain is already organizing experience. Research in developmental neuroscience shows that fetuses can discriminate sounds, recognize maternal voices, and retain auditory patterns, suggesting that foundational learning processes begin in utero, particularly for biologically primary capacities such as language rhythm and emotional regulation (DeCasper & Spence, 1986; Moon, Cooper, & Fifer, 1993; Partanen et al., 2013). While this early learning does not involve abstract reasoning, it establishes the neural expectations through which later experience will be interpreted.

Research in developmental neuroscience shows that fetuses can discriminate sounds, recognize maternal voices, and retain auditory patterns, suggesting that foundational learning processes begin in utero, particularly for biologically primary capacities such as language rhythm and emotional regulation (DeCasper & Spence, 1986; Moon et al., 1993; Partanen et al., 2013). Although this early learning does not involve abstract reasoning or symbolic knowledge, it nonetheless constitutes learning in a schema-theoretic sense: the incorporation of stable expectations and preferences into the earliest organizing structures of long-term memory. These expectations—regarding prosody, affective tone, and sensory continuity—shape how later experience is perceived and regulated, functioning as probabilistic priors rather than fixed traits.

Crucially, such early formed schemas influence but do not determine later learning trajectories. Longitudinal and intervention studies consistently show that individuals who enter childhood with maladaptive learning expectations—such as avoidance of cognitively demanding tasks or heightened sensitivity to failure—can, under supportive instructional and social conditions, develop robust learning strategies and achieve high levels of academic and professional competence. This capacity for recovery reflects continuity rather than contradiction in human learning systems: the same biologically primary mechanisms that encode early expectations through prenatal and neonatal experience—such as sensitivity to rhythm, affective tone, and sensory continuity—remain plastic and responsive to later experience. Neural and behavioral research demonstrates that executive functions central to learning regulation, including inhibitory control and cognitive flexibility, can be strengthened through targeted intervention well into childhood and beyond (Diamond & Lee, 2011), consistent with broader evidence of experience-dependent brain plasticity across the lifespan (Kolb, Gibb, & Robinson, 2003). Within educational settings, changes in instructional structure, feedback timing, and cognitive load management enable learners to reorganize earlier-formed schemas into more efficient and resilient knowledge structures (Sweller, Ayres, & Kalyuga, 2011), demonstrating that early expectations—however formed—are revisable rather than destiny-bound.

Across development, the brain retains substantial plasticity, with experience capable of reorganizing neural structures and functional pathways well beyond early childhood (Kolb, Gibb, & Robinson, 2003). This plasticity extends to executive functions—such as inhibitory control, working-memory regulation, and cognitive flexibility—which play a central role in learning persistence and self-regulation and have been shown to improve through targeted experience and instructional intervention (Diamond & Lee, 2011). In educational contexts, recovery occurs through schema modification: instructional designs that manage cognitive load and provide structured support enable learners to reorganize maladaptive expectations—such as task avoidance or overload sensitivity—into more efficient and resilient knowledge structures (Sweller, Ayres, & Kalyuga, 2011). Together, these findings support what may be termed the Principle of Recoverable Learning: the claim that early learning conditions shape initial expectations, but that effective learning systems are defined by their capacity to support reorganization, adaptation, and renewed progress across the lifespan.

After birth, these expectations are shaped continuously by the child's surroundings. Family interaction, stress exposure, language richness, nutrition, sleep, safety, and the predictability of cause-and-effect all contribute to how cognitive effort is experienced. Over time, individuals learn—implicitly— whether effort leads to understanding or confusion, agency or frustration, reward or threat. Research on learned helplessness demonstrates that repeated exposure to environments in which effort fails to produce meaningful outcomes can condition passivity and avoidance, even in capable individuals (Seligman, 1975; Abramson, Seligman, & Teasdale, 1978). Conversely, environments that reliably connect effort with progress cultivate persistence, curiosity, and adaptive risk-taking.

Crucially, these patterns are learned—but they are not immutable. Cognitive science, neuroscience, and adult learning research converge on a hopeful conclusion: the human brain remains plastic across the lifespan. Neuroplasticity persists well into adulthood, allowing individuals to reorganize neural pathways in response to sustained cognitive challenge, especially when learning is meaningful and appropriately structured (Kandel, 2001; Lövdén et al., 2010). Aging brains compensate through scaffolding—recruiting alternative neural networks to support performance—demonstrating not decline alone, but adaptation (Park & Reuter-Lorenz, 2009).

Importantly, the implications of early and prenatal learning do not suggest that individual educational institutions can—or should—be held responsible for compensating for neonatal and early-life conditions that shape learners' initial expectations and habits. Schools encounter learners long after these foundational schemas have formed. Addressing their effects therefore requires a broader societal response: one that recognizes early developmental environments as a shared civic concern rather than an individual institutional failure. As Dr. Paul Gibson and others have argued, community-level engagement—supported and coordinated by federal policy—offers the only scalable means of strengthening early developmental conditions while preserving the educational mission of schools.

Cognitive Load Theory clarifies why this recovery is possible. When learning environments reduce extraneous load and support schema formation, learners experience early success, which reshapes emotional responses to effort itself (Sweller, Ayres, & Kalyuga, 2019). Effort ceases to feel punishing and begins to feel productive. Over time, this alters motivation—not through exhortation, but through experience. Similarly, research on metacognition shows that adults who learn how learning works—how to pace effort, manage attention, and select effective strategies—become better learners regardless of their early educational history (Flavell, 1979; Dunlosky et al., 2013).

This is the deeper promise of a learning republic. While early learning environments matter enormously, they do not permanently determine an individual's intellectual trajectory. Adults who come to understand their own cognitive architecture—who learn that difficulty is not deficiency, that overload is not failure, and that effort must be designed rather than endured—can re-enter learning on new terms. They may not recover lost time, but they can recover agency. In doing so, they demonstrate that learning is not a childhood privilege or a fixed endowment, but a lifelong civic capacity—one that can be renewed whenever individuals are given the tools to learn how to learn.

The Principle of Recoverable Learning

Learning environments should be designed so that cognitive overload is temporary, recoverable, and informative—not terminal.

Early environments teach individuals whether cognitive effort is something from which one can recover. When effort reliably leads to insight, rest, consolidation, and renewed capacity, learners come to trust the learning process itself. When effort leads instead to confusion, shame, or exhaustion with no resolution, learners learn a different lesson: disengagement is safer than persistence.

Cognitive Load Theory clarifies why this distinction matters. Working memory is not only limited—it is fragile under sustained overload. When overload becomes chronic, learners experience decision fatigue, reduced motivation, and a narrowing of attention. But when overload is bounded and followed by recovery, consolidation can occur. Schemas strengthen. Tasks that once strained working memory become automated. What was effortful becomes fluent.

The Principle of Recoverable Learning reframes difficulty not as a flaw, but as a design variable. Challenge is necessary; overload is sometimes unavoidable. What matters is whether learners are given time, structure, and support to recover—to reorganize information into schemas that reduce working-memory load. Recall that the numerical constraint on how many pieces of information can be held in working memory simultaneously does not imply a limitation on the size or complexity of any single piece. A "chunk" may consist of an entire theoretical framework—or even everything one understands about one's own culture and culture in general—just as readily as it may consist of a single digit in a telephone number.

In this sense, recovery is not rest alone but integration: what once consumed multiple fragile elements in consciousness can, over time, be consolidated into a new or existing schema in long-term memory. When recovery is built into the learning environment, learners return not merely refreshed, but cognitively restructured—able to carry more with less strain.

This principle also explains why learning remains possible—even transformative—well into adulthood. Early environments may shape default responses to challenge, but they do not close the door. Adults who come to understand the architecture of learning can deliberately seek environments that respect cognitive limits, reduce extraneous load, and reward sustained effort. In doing so, they can retrain their relationship with difficulty itself.

This principle carries a broader civic implication. In a learning republic, learning opportunities for adults cannot be supplied primarily through mandate or institutional compulsion; they must arise chiefly from the self-directed initiative of citizens themselves. Formal institutions can scaffold, support, and extend learning, but they cannot substitute for the internal decision to engage. A republic depends not on passive recipients of instruction, but on a population willing to assume responsibility for its own understanding—of history, technology, policy, and consequence.

Self-government presupposes self-education. Citizens who cannot, or will not, direct their own learning eventually cede judgment to others who will. Over time, this transfer of cognitive responsibility erodes the very conditions of republican governance. The danger is not ignorance alone, but dependency: when individuals abandon the work of learning, they surrender the capacity to evaluate claims, resist manipulation, and participate meaningfully in decision-making. A learning republic endures only so long as a majority of its citizens remain active learners—

capable of teaching one another, correcting one another, and governing themselves.

Later chapters will return to this principle in different guises: in discussions of stress and decision fatigue, in workplace learning, in digital environments that tax attention, and in the design of institutions capable of supporting lifelong adaptation. Across all of them, the same insight holds: a learning republic does not eliminate difficulty—it ensures that difficulty is survivable, meaningful, and ultimately empowering.

Conscious Effort, Reflection, and Offline Processing

If the learning environment is the total milieu in which an individual lives, then cognitive load becomes the decisive bottleneck only once learning requires deliberate, conscious processing. In biologically primary learning—such as early language acquisition, social attunement, motor coordination, and emotional regulation—learning unfolds largely outside the constraints of working memory. These capacities emerge through interaction, imitation, and perception, without sustained conscious effort or instruction.

Biologically secondary learning is different. Reading, mathematics, formal reasoning, technical skills, and abstract knowledge must pass through working memory—the narrow workspace of conscious effort, reasoning, and decision-making. No matter how rich, supportive, or well-intentioned a learning environment may be, biologically secondary learning succeeds or fails at this bottleneck. When working memory is overloaded, learning degrades; when it is protected, learning can proceed.

This distinction matters because early learning environments do more than transmit primary skills. They shape how individuals later respond when learning *does* require effort. Long before children encounter formal instruction, they are learning whether challenge is tolerable, whether effort leads to resolution, and whether cognitive strain is something from which one can recover. These lessons, learned in biologically primary ways, profoundly influence how individuals engage biologically secondary learning across the lifespan.

Cognitive load theory makes a clear and essential claim: biologically secondary learning requires deliberate, conscious effort, and that effort occurs within the narrow bandwidth of working memory (Sweller, 1988; Sweller et al., 2019). Yet this does not imply that learning halts when conscious attention is withdrawn. Rather, once effortful engagement has introduced new information into the cognitive system—however incompletely organized—learning can continue through processes that operate outside immediate awareness. Long before the architecture of working memory was understood, John Dewey described this phenomenon as *reflection*: a phase following active experience in which meaning is reorganized, connections are clarified, and insight emerges not through further exertion, but through thoughtful distance (Dewey, 1933).

Contemporary cognitive science now provides a mechanistic account of this process. Research on *incubation effects* shows that stepping away from an unsolved problem can increase the likelihood of insight, particularly after periods of high cognitive demand (Sio & Ormerod, 2009). Neuroimaging studies indicate that during rest or mind-wandering, the brain's default mode network remains active, supporting memory consolidation, associative recombination, and the integration of prior knowledge (Raichle et al., 2001; Christoff et al., 2009). Additional evidence from learning and memory research demonstrates that consolidation processes—especially those occurring during rest and sleep—strengthen newly formed schemas without requiring sustained working-memory engagement (McClelland et al., 1995; Walker & Stickgold, 2006).

Crucially, these offline processes do not bypass cognitive load constraints; they depend upon them. Conscious effort in working memory supplies the raw material—initial representations, partial schemas, unresolved structures—upon which offline processing can operate. Reflection reorganizes what effort introduces; it does not replace it. When cognitive load overwhelms working memory, there is little coherent material to consolidate. When effort and release are deliberately balanced, however, learning unfolds across time rather than collapsing under strain. In this way, Dewey's reflective cycle and cognitive load theory converge on a single insight: durable learning is not continuous exertion, but a rhythm—one that alternates between focused attention and restorative reorganization.

From Primary Acquisition to Designed learning

While biologically primary knowledge emerges through developmentally established learning mechanisms operating largely outside conscious instruction, the transition to biologically secondary knowledge marks a decisive shift: learning now depends not on automatic acquisition, but on instructional design that must contend explicitly with the limits—and history—of human working memory. Every learning task involving the acquisition of biologically secondary knowledge—knowledge that is not acquired automatically through normal human development but must be taught—operates under a simple but unforgiving constraint: human working memory is limited. More specifically, Human working memory is limited in width rather than depth: it can actively process only a small number of novel, unintegrated elements at one time, but each element may represent a highly complex schema stored in long-term memory. In this sense, the constraint on working memory applies to the *number* of elements held in consciousness, not to the internal complexity of those elements once they have been organized through learning. This does not mean that complexity comes without cost: the construction of such schemas is itself cognitively demanding and often fragile during early formation—a point that becomes central once we examine the different forms of cognitive load in detail.

When learning fails under these conditions, it is rarely because individuals lack intelligence. Nor is it adequately explained by an absence of motivation. What often appears to observers as "low motivation" is more accurately understood as a learned pattern of cognitive avoidance, formed through repeated exposure to overload, failure, or poorly structured instruction early in life. Such avoidance is adaptive rather than pathological—it conserves limited cognitive resources—but it becomes maladaptive in formal learning environments. Effective instructional design must therefore recognize this reality and take responsibility not only for managing cognitive load, but for supporting recovery from avoidance, gradually rebuilding the learner's willingness to engage sustained cognitive effort through structure, pacing, and success-contingent feedback.

For learners who experience a persistent conflict between an intrinsic desire to learn and a learned need to protect self-worth or conserve limited executive resources, avoidance does not occur without cost. Research indicates that such individuals often experience heightened anticipatory anxiety and stress responses *prior* to task engagement, reflecting expectations of cognitive overload or evaluative threat rather than indifference to learning itself (Eysenck, Derakshan, Santos, & Calvo, 2007; Putwain,

Connors, Woods, & Nicholson, 2013). When effort is perceived as a risk to identity or competence, learners may disengage as a means of self-worth protection, even while continuing to value learning and achievement (Covington, 1992; Dweck, 2006). Over time, this unresolved approach–avoidance conflict is associated with chronic emotional strain, including shame, rumination, and emotional exhaustion, as well as behavioral patterns such as compulsive procrastination, perfectionism, and task displacement—responses that can appear pathological but are more accurately understood as adaptive reactions to prior experiences of failure, overload, or loss of agency (Steel, 2007; Maier & Seligman, 2016). Importantly, these patterns are frequently accompanied by physiological stress responses and somatic symptoms, underscoring that cognitive avoidance is not merely motivational but regulatory in nature (Lupien, McEwen, Gunnar, & Heim, 2009). What is often labeled disengagement thus reflects not a lack of desire to learn, but a system caught between competing imperatives of growth and self-protection.

Problem Solving vs. Schema Consolidation in Cognitive Load Theory

To understand why disengagement can be productive, it is essential to distinguish between problem solving and schema consolidation— two processes often conflated in everyday accounts of learning, but sharply differentiated within cognitive load theory.

Problem solving is a real-time, working-memory–bound activity. It occurs within working memory and is tightly constrained by its limited capacity and duration (Miller, 1956; Peterson & Peterson, 1959). When learners are novices, problem solving frequently relies on means–ends analysis, which imposes high intrinsic cognitive load while contributing little to durable schema acquisition (Sweller, 1988). Under these conditions, sustained conscious effort can saturate working memory without producing progress. It is therefore common for solutions to emerge only after learners disengage consciously and step away, allowing partially formed representations to reorganize outside the narrow constraints of active problem solving. This dynamic helps explain why excessive unguided problem solving is often inefficient—or even counterproductive—for learning.

Schema consolidation, by contrast, is largely an offline process. Once information has been introduced and partially organized through conscious effort, learning continues through integration into existing memory structures—what Roger Schank famously described as the incorporation of new experience into scripts, cases, and explanatory frameworks that give knowledge meaning and usability (Schank & Abelson, 1977; Schank, 1982; Schank, 1999). In Schank's account, learning is not the storage of facts but the reorganization of experience: new information is assimilated by modifying, extending, or indexing existing stories that guide future reasoning and action.

This consolidation process depends less on working memory bandwidth and more on time, repetition, and reactivation. Evidence from cognitive neuroscience converges with Schank's theory, showing that memory consolidation continues during periods of rest and sleep, strengthening neural representations and reorganizing knowledge without conscious awareness (McClelland, McNaughton, & O'Reilly, 1995; Walker & Stickgold, 2006; Diekelmann & Born, 2010). Rather than competing with cognitive load theory, this work clarifies its boundary: working memory governs conscious problem solving, while schema consolidation reshapes long-term knowledge structures beyond the workspace of awareness.

Seen together, Schank's script-based theory of learning and modern consolidation research explain why insight often arrives after effort has paused. The mind continues to work—not by juggling elements in consciousness, but by quietly reorganizing experience into more powerful and accessible forms.

Biologically primary learning aligns closely with Schank's experience-based memory model. These forms of learning do not depend on deliberate explanation or sustained working-memory effort. Instead, they operate through the automatic formation of scripts and stories derived from lived experience. Language, social understanding, and basic causal reasoning are acquired not as abstract rules, but as patterns of participation—indexed by goals, emotion, and consequence.

Schank's theory helps explain why biologically primary learning is resilient, durable, and universally acquired: it is stored in the mind's most natural representational format—experience organized as scripts and stories. Such learning emerges through participation in meaningful activity and is indexed by goals, emotion, and consequence rather than by formal symbols.

Biologically secondary learning, by contrast, depends on abstract symbol systems rather than lived experience. Reading, writing, mathematics, and formal scientific reasoning are not acquired automatically through participation in everyday life. They must be consciously constructed, deliberately rehearsed, and effortfully integrated into existing scripts and schemas held in long-term memory. In Schank's terms, secondary knowledge must be *fitted* into experiential structures that were not designed to support it natively, a process that places sustained demands on working memory and attention.

This distinction clarifies why biologically secondary learning is fragile, uneven, and highly sensitive to instructional design.

When abstract knowledge is poorly connected to meaningful experience, it remains inert. When instruction succeeds in anchoring symbols to scripts—through example, story, simulation, or practice—secondary learning becomes more durable by borrowing the architecture of primary learning itself.

Cognitive load theory fully accommodates this distinction. Germane cognitive load—the effort devoted to schema construction—begins in working memory but does not end there. The role of instruction, therefore, is not to maximize conscious effort indefinitely, but to *optimize the handoff* from effortful processing to consolidation. When learning environments demand constant problem solving without recovery, they exhaust working memory and impair consolidation. When they alternate effort with reflection, spacing, and rest, they respect the architecture of the mind.

This distinction clarifies why insight often arrives *after* stepping away. The solution does not appear because the learner kept working unconsciously on the problem in the same way; it appears because the cognitive system was allowed to reorganize information outside the narrow constraints of working memory. What feels like sudden insight is often the delayed outcome of earlier, effortful engagement.

In *Dynamic Memory Revisited* (1999), Roger Schank issued a direct challenge to conventional schooling, arguing that formal education too often teaches abstract facts and procedures detached from the experiences that would make them usable. Drawing on decades of work in artificial intelligence, cognitive psychology, and case-based reasoning, Schank contended that human memory is organized around goals, stories, and lived situations—not decontextualized symbols—and that instruction ignoring this architecture produces knowledge that is brittle, inert, and difficult to apply (Schank, 1999).

Schank's critique has aged remarkably well. Subsequent research across cognitive science, instructional design, and neuroscience consistently confirms his central claim: learning divorced from experience is fragile, inert, and costly to maintain in working memory. While schools continue to rely heavily on symbol-first instruction, research shows that biologically secondary learning becomes more durable, transferable, and less cognitively taxing when it is anchored in scripts, cases, and goal-directed activity. Cognitive load theory, case-based reasoning, and neuroscience now converge on the same conclusion Schank articulated decades ago: learning succeeds when abstract knowledge is fitted into the mind's experiential architecture rather than imposed upon it.

Decision Fatigue and the Illusion of Working Harder

Failure to respect this rhythm leads to decision fatigue—the gradual erosion of judgment following repeated acts of effortful choice (Baumeister et al., 1998; Persson et al., 2019). In learning contexts, decision fatigue manifests as shallow processing, premature conclusions, avoidance, or disengagement. Learners may blame motivation or ability, when the true constraint is architectural.

Dewey anticipated this danger in *How We Think* (1933). Reflection, he argued, is not passive idleness but a necessary phase in which experience is digested and meaning is formed. Cognitive load theory now provides the structural explanation Dewey lacked: reflection reduces extraneous load, restores working memory capacity, and enables schema consolidation. Together, they reveal why effective learning environments are not those that demand constant attention, but those that are deliberately paced.

Dewey and Sweller describe the same learning reality from different vantage points. Dewey identified *reflection* as the critical phase in which experience is reorganized into knowledge, warning that uninterrupted exertion dulls thought rather than sharpening it. Sweller later supplied the cognitive architecture underlying Dewey's intuition: working memory is narrow, fragile, and easily exhausted.

Where Dewey spoke of reflective pauses, Sweller speaks of load management. Where Dewey warned against forcing attention beyond its limits, Sweller demonstrated those limits empirically. Dewey's philosophy explains why learning requires rhythm; Sweller's theory explains how that rhythm is enforced by the mind itself.

Stress, Overload, and the Limits of Continuous Problem Solving

Cognitive load theory was never intended to describe learning as a continuous act of conscious exertion. On the contrary, it warns that sustained problem solving under high load carries predictable costs. When intrinsic, extraneous, and germane cognitive load together exceed working memory capacity, performance deteriorates, errors increase, and learning stalls (Sweller et al., 1998; Sweller et al., 2019). Over time, prolonged engagement under high load can lead to working memory resource depletion, decision fatigue, and reduced self-regulation (Chen et al., 2018; Persson et al., 2019).

Stress intensifies this effect. Cognitive science research shows that stress consumes working memory resources directly—through intrusive thoughts, emotional regulation demands, and heightened vigilance—effectively acting as an additional form of extraneous cognitive load (Eysenck et al., 2007; Plass

& Kalyuga, 2019). Under stress, learners may *feel* as though they are working harder while accomplishing less, because conscious problem-solving capacity has been partially diverted to managing affect rather than structure. This helps explain a familiar experience: the harder one pushes through fatigue and stress; the less insight emerges.

Here, stepping away from a task is not avoidance; it is regulation. When learners disengage from effortful problem solving—by walking, resting, or shifting attention—the working memory bottleneck relaxes. This reduces extraneous load and allows cognitive resources to recover, restoring the conditions under which learning can resume productively. In this sense, strategic disengagement is not a break *from* learning but a prerequisite *for* its continuation.

Attentional Control Theory (ACT; Eysenck et al., 2007) suggests that anxiety shifts control away from goal-directed attention and toward stimulus-driven attention (threat vigilance), reducing efficiency on tasks that depend on executive control and working memory. In some cases, the "threat vigilance" described by ACT may be directed inward rather than outward, as attention is consumed by efforts to regulate distressing self-evaluations. This inward vigilance diverts executive resources away from goal-directed learning and toward emotional self-management.

Effortful emotion regulation is not cognitively free. Suppressing distress, managing guilt or shame, and monitoring self-evaluative thoughts all require executive control, drawing upon the same limited working-memory resources needed for comprehension and learning (Gross, 1998; Richards & Gross, 2000; Schmeichel, 2007). Research on anxiety and attentional control demonstrates that threat—

whether external or internal—shifts resources away from goal-directed processing toward vigilance and regulation, reducing working-memory efficiency (Eysenck et al., 2007). Neuroimaging studies confirm this competition at the neural level, showing overlapping prefrontal systems supporting both emotion regulation and working memory (Ochsner & Gross, 2005). From a cognitive load perspective, these processes function as extraneous load, shrinking the effective capacity of consciousness available for biologically secondary learning (Plass & Kalyuga, 2019).

The Impact of Anxiety on Learning

Anxiety impairs learning through two distinct but complementary pathways, depending on the type of knowledge involved. Biologically secondary learning—reading, mathematics, formal reasoning—depends directly on working memory and executive control, and anxiety degrades it by shrinking the effective capacity of consciousness available for symbol manipulation and schema construction (Eysenck et al., 2007; Plass & Kalyuga, 2019). Biologically primary learning, by contrast, does not rely on sustained working memory and therefore is not diminished in the same architectural sense. Instead, anxiety interferes indirectly by narrowing attention, suppressing exploration, and biasing experience toward threat and avoidance (Easterbrook, 1959; Gray, 1982). Under chronic stress, primary learning continues, but it is reshaped: curiosity declines, social engagement contracts, and experience is encoded into rigid, defensive scripts rather than flexible, adaptive ones (Schwabe & Wolf, 2013; Panksepp, 1998). Thus, anxiety impoverishes learning twice—by collapsing the workspace of conscious processing and by distorting the experiential substrate on which learning depends.

Such resurfacing of pre-verbal memory is especially common during periods of heightened stress, when the brain shifts away from deliberate, prefrontal control and relies more heavily on older, emotionally and sensorily encoded memory systems—often reactivating early-life traces during sleep and dreaming (Payne & Kensinger, 2010; van der Helm et al., 2011; Stickgold & Walker, 2013).

This dual effect of anxiety is not confined to laboratory settings. Phenomenological accounts from educators working in high-poverty schools provide vivid confirmation of how chronic stress reshapes both learning and teaching. In *Thanking Teachers Working in High-Poverty Schools (2023)*, Paul Gibson documents classrooms in which students arrive already cognitively taxed by instability, insecurity, and vigilance, while teachers simultaneously carry a persistent moral strain—anxiety and guilt arising from the awareness that their students' needs exceed what time, authority, and available resources allow them to address. From a cognitive perspective, these experiences function as extraneous load for both learners and instructors: attention is divided, working memory is partially consumed by regulation of distress, and reflective bandwidth is diminished. Gibson's accounts illuminate how the cognitive architecture described here is experienced under sustained stress, where anxiety reshapes engagement long before any instructional design choice is made.

Experimentation and Results

In a previous chapter we examined patterns of participation through lifespan theory, focusing on motivational selectivity and perceived investment. The present chapter turns to a different question: What cognitive demands are imposed by the structure of course selection systems, and can those demands be measurably reduced through architectural redesign?

Cognitive load theory begins from a simple but consequential premise: working memory is limited. When instructional or navigational structures impose unnecessary demands on that limited capacity, performance, efficiency, and persistence suffer. Of particular concern is extraneous cognitive load—the load generated not by the inherent complexity of the task itself, but by the way information is presented.

Traditional course catalogs require learners to engage in sequential comparison. They must review descriptions, retain prior options in working memory while examining new ones, and integrate dispersed information into coherent judgments. This structure imposes extraneous demands unrelated to the learner's substantive goal: identifying a course aligned with desired learning outcomes.

The doctoral study underlying this book was designed as a controlled test of whether restructuring the architecture of course selection could reduce perceived extraneous cognitive load.

Participants were randomly assigned to one of two groups: experimental and control.

Experimental Group: Recommender System

The experimental group used a course recommender system. Rather than reviewing course descriptions sequentially, participants began by selecting desired learning outcomes organized by knowledge domain (e.g., business and finance, history, psychology, civics). Upon submission of selected outcomes, the system generated course recommendations aligned with those choices.

This architecture was intentionally designed to:

- Reduce the need for sequential page-by-page comparison

- Minimize working memory burden during option evaluation

- Externalize comparison logic within the system

- Support outcome-first rather than description-first navigation

The design hypothesis was that this structure would reduce perceived extraneous cognitive load during course selection.

Control Group: Structured Catalog Application

The control group did not continue using the traditional catalog interface. Instead, they used a newly developed application that presented courses grouped by knowledge domain and allowed direct selection of courses within those categories.

The decision to build a separate application for the control group was methodologically intentional. Introducing a recommender system to the experimental group necessarily introduced new technology. If the control group had continued using the familiar catalog interface, differences in perceived cognitive load could have been attributed to novelty effects rather than architectural differences.

By providing both groups with new applications, the study controlled for the cognitive demands associated with learning unfamiliar technology. Both groups were required to adapt to a new interface. However, only the experimental group's interface was designed explicitly to reduce extraneous load through outcome-based filtering and system-generated recommendations.

The control interface may have offered modest navigational improvement over a monolithic catalog by organizing courses by knowledge area, but it did not fundamentally alter the sequential comparison structure. It therefore served as an appropriate comparison condition: novel technology without intentional cognitive load reduction.

Cognitive Load Hypothesis

The primary cognitive load hypothesis was:

Participants in the experimental group would report significantly lower perceived extraneous cognitive load during course selection than participants in the control group.

This hypothesis rested on core principles of cognitive load theory:

1. Working memory has limited capacity.

2. Sequential comparison tasks impose retention and integration demands.

3. Reducing unnecessary search and comparison processes reduces extraneous load.

4. System-supported filtering externalizes cognitive operations that would otherwise burden working memory.

If the recommender architecture successfully reduced comparison burden and information retention demands, participants should experience lower perceived mental effort relative to the control condition.

Measurement of Perceived Cognitive Load

Perceived cognitive load was measured using an adapted instrument based on work developed by Fred Paas, one of the leading contributors to cognitive load theory. Paas's mental effort rating scale has been widely used in instructional research to measure subjective cognitive load.

With Dr. Paas's permission—graciously granted upon request—the instrument was adapted to fit the context of course selection and navigational decision-making. Participants rated the mental effort associated with completing the task, allowing comparison across conditions.

While subjective measures do not directly quantify working memory load, they are well established within cognitive load research as reliable indicators of perceived mental effort, particularly when comparing instructional conditions.

Methodological Note on Pandemic Disruption

As discussed in relation to Lifespan theory, the COVID-19 lockdown disrupted in-person orientation and increased onboarding complexity for both groups. From a cognitive load perspective, this disruption introduced additional extraneous demands unrelated to the core selection task. Participants were required to interpret written help materials and navigate electronic bulletin boards in place of guided training.

Although this environmental shift reduced sample size and constrained statistical power, it also introduced a real-world escalation of extraneous load. The system's ability—or inability—to mitigate that burden under heightened conditions provides an additional lens through which results can be interpreted.

Results

Data were analyzed to evaluate differences in perceived extraneous cognitive load between the experimental (recommender system) and control (structured catalog application) groups.

Due to the COVID-related disruption described in Chapter 5, participant attrition reduced the final sample size substantially, limiting statistical power. As a result, statistical findings must be interpreted cautiously, with attention to effect magnitude and directional consistency rather than reliance solely on p-values.

Perceived Cognitive Load

Participants completed an adapted mental effort rating instrument based on the work of Paas. Mean perceived cognitive load scores were calculated for each group.

Consistent with the primary hypothesis, the experimental group reported lower average perceived cognitive load than the control group. Although the difference did not reach conventional levels of statistical significance—likely due to reduced sample size—the direction of the effect aligned with predictions derived from cognitive load theory.

Effect size estimates suggested a meaningful reduction in perceived mental effort associated with the recommender system relative to the structured catalog interface. The magnitude of the difference indicates that architectural restructuring of course selection may reduce extraneous demands imposed during navigational decision-making.

Interpretation Under Reduced Statistical Power

Given the constrained sample size, absence of statistical significance cannot be interpreted as absence of effect. Instead, the pattern of results—directionally consistent with theoretical prediction and supported by effect size estimates—provides provisional evidence that system-supported filtering may reduce extraneous cognitive load during course selection.

Future research with larger samples and controlled onboarding conditions would be necessary to confirm the magnitude of this effect under stable environmental circumstances.

In this respect, the findings combined quantitative comparison with qualitative insight into real-world engagement behavior. Beyond numerical differences in reported mental effort, patterns of withdrawal, participant communications, and informal reflections revealed recurring themes: the importance of anticipated social interaction, sensitivity to initiation complexity, and reassessment of time commitment under uncertain conditions. While not derived from formal qualitative methodology, these observations provided contextual evidence consistent with theoretical predictions regarding selectivity and perceived investment.

Cognitive Architecture and the Design of a Learning Republic

Cognitive load theory reminds us that limitations in working memory are not personal weaknesses; they are universal constraints. Educational systems that impose unnecessary extraneous demands do not merely inconvenience learners. They tax finite cognitive resources.

The course catalog is often treated as neutral infrastructure—an administrative listing of offerings. Yet as this study suggests, its structure carries cognitive consequences. When learners must perform sequential comparisons across dispersed descriptions, retain multiple options in working memory, and integrate information under time pressure, cognitive effort is expended on navigation rather than learning itself.

Architectural design matters.

The recommender system tested in this study did not reduce the intrinsic complexity of learning. It did not simplify course content. Instead, it sought to reduce extraneous burden at the point of entry—allowing learners to focus their cognitive resources on substantive engagement rather than structural navigation.

When scaled beyond a single institution, this insight carries broader implications. A learning republic depends upon citizens capable of continual intellectual growth. If participation in education is hindered by avoidable structural friction, cognitive taxation accumulates. Over time, such friction disproportionately discourages those whose time and attention are already limited.

Reducing extraneous cognitive load is therefore not merely an instructional preference. It is a structural responsibility.

Systems that externalize comparison processes, organize information around meaningful outcomes, and reduce unnecessary search demands respect the architecture of human cognition. They align institutional design with cognitive reality.

In combination with the developmental insights discussed in Chapter 5, the implications become clearer: lifelong learning depends upon both motivational alignment and cognitive alignment. Institutions must design for both.

The study presented here offers modest empirical support for this proposition. Even under disrupted conditions, architectural differences in course selection systems were associated with differences in perceived mental effort. While further research is required to refine these findings, the principle remains: educational infrastructure shapes cognitive experience.

A learning republic must therefore attend not only to what is taught, but to how entry into learning is structured. When structural friction is reduced, participation becomes more sustainable. When cognitive burden is managed wisely, citizens are freed to devote their finite working memory to understanding rather than navigation.

Conclusion

This chapter established the cognitive architecture that governs all biologically secondary learning. Beginning with George Miller's discovery of limited cognitive bandwidth, it showed that conscious processing occurs within a narrow workspace—working memory—whose constraints cannot be overcome by effort alone. The chapter distinguished biologically primary learning, which emerges through ordinary participation in the world and operates largely outside this bottleneck, from biologically secondary learning, which depends on deliberate instruction and must pass through working memory's limited capacity. Because individuals develop within a total learning milieu long before formal schooling begins, early environments shape habitual responses to challenge—whether effort is approached, avoided, or endured. From this foundation, the chapter introduced the Principle of Recoverable Learning: effective learning environments do not eliminate difficulty, but design difficulty so that overload is temporary, informative, and followed by consolidation. Drawing on research in reflection, incubation, and memory consolidation, the chapter argued that durable learning is rhythmic rather than continuous—alternating focused effort with offline reorganization. It concluded by showing how stress and anxiety function as extraneous cognitive load, consuming executive resources and reshaping experience in ways that degrade learning even when motivation remains intact. The next chapter turns from cognitive architecture to environment design, tracing how these principles have been expressed, violated, and transformed as learning moved from physical settings to digital systems.

PART III: THE INDIVIDUAL AND INSTITUTIONAL CIVIC RESPONSIBILITIES

Chapter Eight: Protecting Developmental Windows

Abilities, Vulnerabilities, and the Stewardship of Development

In the early 2000s, developmental psychologists Gabrielle Simcock and Harlene Hayne were studying memory in very young children. They discovered something quietly unsettling: infants and toddlers could remember far more than anyone had assumed. The problem was not storage—it was access.

In one experiment, children were shown a simple but novel event: an unusual toy manipulated in an unfamiliar sequence. Months later, when asked to recall what they had seen, the youngest children often appeared to remember nothing at all. Their silence looked like forgetting. But when the researchers

altered the retrieval cue—providing language that matched the child's developmental stage at the time of the original experience—the memories resurfaced. The event had been encoded. It simply could not yet be retrieved in the absence of the right linguistic scaffolding.

The implication was profound. Experiences were being stored without the verbal framework needed to access them later. Learning had occurred, but it remained locked away until language development caught up. What appeared as forgetting was, in fact, a developmental mismatch between encoding and recall.

This quiet discovery points to a larger principle: development does not simply accumulate knowledge over time. It opens and closes windows of accessibility. Miss the window—or overwhelm it—and the learning does not vanish, but it becomes harder to reach. Learning is not only about exposure. It is about timing.

Developmental Timing and Cognitive Stages

Jean Piaget understood this intuitively nearly a century earlier. In his Geneva laboratory in 1929, he watched children pour water from tall glasses into short ones. When asked which glass held more, preoperational children pointed to the taller one—until, one day, they didn't. Their reasoning had not simply grown by accumulation; it had reorganized. Each cognitive stage (sensorimotor, preoperational, concrete operational, formal operational) represented a qualitative shift in how the child constructed reality. Push a concept too early—before the logical scaffolding is ready—and it is like pouring water into an unformed vessel.

Erik Erikson, lecturing at Harvard in 1959, sketched a different but complementary map. On the blackboard, he drew eight psychosocial stages, each defined by a central tension: trust vs. mistrust, autonomy vs. shame, industry vs. inferiority, identity vs. role confusion. For adolescents, he explained, the task is forging a coherent identity amid rapid physical, emotional, and social change. Without adequate guidance, youth can become "diffused selves," chasing external validation rather than internal integration.

Lawrence Steinberg brought biological precision to these insights. In 2014, at Temple University, he leaned into an fMRI monitor and watched teenage brains light up like fireworks in response to social rewards. The prefrontal cortex—the neural seat of judgment, impulse control, and long-term planning—lagged behind the emotional circuitry of the limbic system. Adolescents were biologically primed for risk and novelty but lacked the full capacity to anticipate consequences. This mismatch, Steinberg argued, should shape education policy and digital exposure: protect the young brain from environments that exploit immature neural circuits.

Together, these perspectives—Piaget's cognitive stages, Erikson's psychosocial tensions, Steinberg's neurodevelopmental asynchrony—remind us that when learning occurs matters as much as what is learned. Cognitive readiness, emotional maturity, and neural architecture form a symphony. One easily thrown off-key by premature exposure or overstimulation.

The early years—birth to roughly age seven—represent a critical window for neural wiring. Synaptic density peaks, language scaffolds meaning, and the brain learns what to trust and what to filter. But this same openness also makes young children uniquely vulnerable. Their brains absorb everything, not yet equipped with the inhibitory control to sort signal from noise. Maryanne Wolf warns that each new medium rewires the brain's circuitry. When exposure begins before metacognition has emerged, that circuitry can harden in ways that privilege reaction over reflection. The stakes are not merely academic—they are developmental.

Developmental Windows

In a learning republic, stewardship begins with the individual. Human development unfolds in windows of opportunity and vulnerability, each stage requiring protection and guidance to foster capable, resilient citizens. This chapter explores those windows through the lives of five individuals, drawing on developmental science to reveal how timing shapes learning—and how a society that honors biology can sustain both personal growth and civic capacity.

Early Childhood

Consider Theodore, age five. His greatest asset is plasticity; his greatest risk is unfiltered exposure. When a caregiver reads aloud, pauses to explain, or encourages prediction, the brain knits together sensory, linguistic, and emotional pathways. These bridges, once built, become lifelong highways for learning. But when a child is left alone with flashing screens and algorithmic toys, the brain receives strong impressions but weak understanding. Simcock and Hayne showed that preverbal memories fade without language to anchor them. Patricia Kuhl found that infants learn phonemes from live social speech but not from equivalent video input. Excessive screen time before age five predicts poorer language and attention outcomes that persist into school years. What looks like abundance is, for the very young, often overload.

Theodore, at five years old, is immersed in a developmental window of extraordinary opportunity and profound vulnerability—a phase where his brain is a sponge for experiences, yet one that requires careful stewardship to avoid lasting distortions. This period aligns with what Jean Piaget described in his foundational work as the preoperational stage, roughly spanning ages two to seven (Piaget, 1952). Here, Theodore's thinking is egocentric and intuitive; he uses symbols, language, and imagination to represent the world, but lacks fully logical cause-and-effect reasoning. He might, for instance, believe that the sun follows him because he moves, or that inanimate objects have intentions, reflecting a magical quality to his cognition that makes everyday discoveries vivid and engaging.

Emotionally, Theodore navigates Erik Erikson's stage of initiative versus guilt, outlined in Erikson's 1959 lectures and writings, where the central tension involves asserting independence through exploration and play. Success in this phase builds a sense of purpose and confidence; with supportive guidance, Theodore can take risks in safe ways, like building forts or inventing stories, fostering creativity and self-efficacy. But criticism or overrestriction can instill guilt, inhibiting his natural drive to initiate and learn from trial and error.

Neurologically, Theodore's brain is at peak plasticity, with synaptic density surging as connections form rapidly in response to stimuli. This openness allows him to absorb language, social cues, and basic concepts at an astonishing rate, but it also heightens risks from mismatched or overwhelming input. As Gabrielle Simcock and Harlene Hayne demonstrated in their 2002 and 2003 studies on early memory, young children like Theodore can encode experiences vividly, but retrieval depends on matching the developmental tools available at the time—such as emerging language skills. Without verbal anchors, memories may remain inaccessible, turning potential learning into locked-away impressions. Patricia Kuhl's 2011 research further illustrates this: infants and toddlers learn phonemes and social patterns best through live, interactive speech, where caregivers respond contingently; passive exposure, like from videos, fails to wire those circuits as effectively.

The opportunities in this window are immense: Interactive, scaffolded activities—such as a caregiver reading aloud, pausing to explain, or encouraging prediction—knit together sensory, linguistic, and emotional pathways, building lifelong foundations for empathy, curiosity, and problem-solving. These bridges, once formed, become highways for future learning, enhancing his ability to make sense of the world.

Yet the risks are equally significant. Overstimulation from unfiltered environments—flashing screens, algorithmic toys, or constant audio loops—can create strong sensory impressions without fostering deep understanding. Dimitri Christakis and colleagues, in their 2018 study, documented that excessive screen time before age five predicts poorer language development and attention control, effects that linger into school years. For children in high-poverty environments, these risks compound with even more immediate threats to development, as Paul Gibson describes in his book *Thanking Teachers Working in High-Poverty Schools* (2021). Drawing from firsthand accounts of educators in under-resourced districts, Gibson recounts how five-year-olds like Theodore might arrive at school having had no sleep the night before, perhaps because of overcrowded living conditions or family instability; they may be unfed, their empty stomachs growling through morning lessons; or they might have witnessed traumatic events, such as a parent's arrest or the entire family sleeping in a car due to eviction. In these scenarios, the child's brain—already primed for high absorptivity but low discernment—struggles to prioritize learning tasks amid survival signals. Hunger impairs concentration and memory consolidation, sleep deprivation disrupts neural pruning and emotional regulation, and chronic stress elevates cortisol levels, potentially shrinking the hippocampus and hindering long-term learning (as shown in studies by Megan Gunnar and colleagues, 2010). For these children, the developmental window narrows not just from biological timing but from environmental assault, making it harder to form those essential synaptic bridges.

Nutrition plays a pivotal role in this window, as the brain and body require specific nutrients for optimal growth. During early childhood, essential fatty acids, iron, zinc, and vitamins like A, B, and D support neural myelination, synapse formation, and cognitive functions such as attention and memory (Cusick & Georgieff, 2016; Roberts et al., 2022). Deficiencies can lead to delayed motor skills, reduced IQ, and behavioral issues. In extreme poverty, food insecurity—often resulting in inadequate caloric intake or nutrient-poor diets—exacerbates these risks, increasing the likelihood of stunting, anemia, and impaired executive function (Chilton, 2007; Jensen et al., 2017). Children from low-income households may lack access to fresh fruits, vegetables, and proteins, leading to micronutrient gaps that hinder brain development and school readiness (UNICEF, 2024; APA, 2023).

Even in families with sufficient means, poor parental choices can pose similar threats. Allowing children to eat whatever they want—often leading to diets high in processed foods, sugars, and fats—instead of enforcing healthy, balanced meals at the family table can result in overnutrition or micronutrient imbalances.

Such habits are linked to obesity, hyperactivity, and cognitive deficits; for instance, high sugar intake correlates with attention issues and emotional instability, while diets low in whole foods deprive the brain of omega-3s and antioxidants needed for neural health (Mahmood et al., 2021; Chen et al., 2024). Without disciplined routines like family meals, children miss out on modeled healthy eating and social-emotional learning, potentially fostering impulsive behaviors or nutritional gaps that mirror those in poverty-stricken homes (O'Brien & MacIntyre, 2023). In both cases, the absence of consistent, nutrient-rich nourishment undermines the brain's ability to capitalize on this plastic phase, turning a window of opportunity into one of missed potential.

What fires together wires together, as neuroscientists often say; premature or mismatched demands can overload Theodore's developing circuits, leading to fragmented attention or weaker foundational skills. In high-poverty contexts, schools can serve as a counterbalance, with teachers providing not just instruction but basic stability—meals, routines, and emotional support—that reopen the window for growth. Stewardship here means aligning experiences with biology: prioritizing relational, purposeful interactions over passive input. For Theodore, this window is not just about accumulation—it's about building a resilient architecture for a lifetime of learning. Miss it, and the costs echo forward; honor it, and the rewards compound across his development.

Adolescence

Adolescence brings a different kind of turbulence. The brain undergoes massive synaptic pruning, carving out efficient pathways while discarding unused ones—a process that peaks in early adolescence and continues into the early twenties (Giedd et al., 1999; Blakemore & Mills, 2014). Gray matter volume declines as unnecessary synaptic connections are eliminated, while white matter thickens through myelination, speeding neural transmission and enhancing efficiency (Sowell et al., 2004; Paus, 2005). Hormonal surges—particularly increases in testosterone and estrogen—flood emotional circuits, especially the amygdala and ventral striatum, heightening sensitivity to reward and social approval (Casey, Getz, & Galván, 2008; Blakemore, Burnett, & Dahl, 2010). Yet the prefrontal cortex—responsible for foresight, impulse control, and long-term planning—continues to mature well into the mid-twenties (Steinberg, 2014; Gogtay et al., 2004). This prolonged maturation creates a neurobiological asynchrony: the limbic system, which drives emotion and reward-seeking, reaches functional maturity earlier than the prefrontal regions that regulate it (Somerville et al., 2010; Casey et al., 2011). Adolescents are cognitively capable of abstract reasoning— able to debate justice, identity, or moral dilemmas—but remain neurobiologically asynchronous. They can grasp complex ideas in theory, yet struggle to regulate impulses in the moment when emotional arousal or peer influence is high (Steinberg, 2008; Luna, Padmanabhan, & O'Hearn, 2010).

This asynchrony is not a flaw; it is a developmental feature that primes adolescents for risk-taking, novelty-seeking, and social learning—qualities that historically aided survival and adaptation. But in modern environments saturated with instant digital rewards and minimal built-in structure, the same biology can amplify distraction, poor judgment, and emotional volatility if left unsupported. The prefrontal cortex's gradual maturation gives Marcus the emerging capacity to foresee consequences, yet for nearly a decade after age sixteen, his emotional circuitry will often outpace his regulatory "brakes." This window is therefore one of immense potential—when guided support channels intensity into mastery, creativity, and purpose—but also one of real vulnerability, where mismatched demands can entrench habits of impulsivity or disengagement that echo long after the turbulence subsides.

Marcus, age sixteen, stands at this crossroads. In class, the teacher talks about careers. He imagines himself as a pilot, a musician, a streamer—all in one breath. The world feels infinite, each possibility burning bright. Inside his head, a quiet revolution unfolds. Dopamine circuits in the ventral striatum and nucleus accumbens surge with every ping, every like, every new idea, driving an intense craving for novelty and immediate reward (Casey, Getz, & Galván, 2008; Blakemore, Burnett, & Dahl, 2010). At the same time, cortisol spikes at the slightest hint of criticism or social threat, flooding the amygdala and heightening emotional reactivity (Dahl & Gunnar, 2009). This is the hallmark of the adolescent brain: the limbic system, which governs emotion and reward, reaches functional maturity earlier than the prefrontal cortex, the region responsible for impulse control, foresight, and long-term planning (Somerville et al., 2010; Casey et al., 2011). The result is a powerful but unsteady engine—capable of extraordinary passion, creativity, and idealism, yet prone to distraction, risk-taking, and poor judgment when the brakes are not yet fully installed.

Research has mapped this asynchrony in detail. Longitudinal MRI studies led by Jay Giedd and colleagues at the National Institute of Mental Health (Giedd et al., 1999; Gogtay et al., 2004) showed that gray matter peaks in early adolescence and then undergoes extensive pruning, while white matter continues to myelinate well into the twenties, gradually strengthening connections between emotional and regulatory regions. Laurence Steinberg's dual-systems model (Steinberg, 2008; 2014) formalizes the insight: the socioemotional system (reward sensitivity, peer influence) matures earlier than the cognitive-control system (prefrontal regulation), creating a window of heightened vulnerability to external stimuli and internal impulses. This biological mismatch explains why Marcus can intellectually grasp the long-term consequences of his choices yet still act on the pull of the moment—whether it's staying up until 3 a.m. scrolling or skipping homework to game with friends.

The same neural sensitivity that makes him impulsive also primes him for passion and creativity—if the environment provides structure and respect. When adults offer clear boundaries, meaningful mentorship, and opportunities to channel intensity into mastery—whether through music, sports, debate, or hands-on projects—the adolescent brain's extraordinary adaptability can forge resilience, purpose, and innovation (Blakemore & Mills, 2014; Steinberg, 2020). Without that support, the same circuits can reinforce habits of distraction, avoidance, or poor judgment that carry forward long after the turbulence subsides.

Marcus's world hums with possibility and peril. What he needs most is not suppression of his energy, but wise, timely guidance that honors both the fire and the emerging brake within him.

Marcus navigates a developmental window defined by profound transformation—a phase of heightened exploration, identity formation, and emerging independence, yet one fraught with risks from biological asynchrony and external pressures. This period corresponds to Jean Piaget's formal operational stage, which typically begins around age eleven or twelve and continues into young adulthood (Piaget, 1952). Here,

Marcus gains the capacity for abstract reasoning, hypothetical thinking, and systematic problem-solving; he can ponder "what if" scenarios, debate ethical dilemmas, or envision future paths, moving beyond the concrete logic of childhood to more sophisticated intellectual engagement. This shift opens doors to deeper learning, creativity, and civic awareness, allowing him to grapple with complex ideas in school, relationships, or society.

Emotionally, Marcus is deep in Erik Erikson's stage of identity versus role confusion, as articulated in Erikson's 1959 framework, where the core task is forging a coherent sense of self amid competing roles—as student, friend, family member, or emerging citizen. Success here fosters a strong identity and fidelity to values; with supportive relationships and opportunities for experimentation, Marcus can build resilience, purpose, and social competence. But confusion or external imposition can lead to role diffusion, where he might adopt superficial identities from peers or media without authentic integration.

Neurologically, Marcus's brain is undergoing significant remodeling, with the prefrontal cortex—crucial for executive functions like impulse control, decision-making, and foreseeing consequences—only recently gaining sufficient maturity to moderate risks, though it won't fully develop until around age 25 (Steinberg, 2014; Casey et al., 2008). Gray matter pruning refines neural efficiency, while white matter myelination speeds connections, but the limbic system (governing emotions and rewards) outpaces the prefrontal brake, creating a "gas pedal without full brakes" dynamic (Somerville et al., 2010). This asynchrony primes Marcus for novelty-seeking and social rewards, enhancing learning through experiences like team projects or debates, but also heightening vulnerability to impulsivity under stress or peer influence.

The opportunities in this window are vast: With his prefrontal cortex coming online, Marcus can channel intensity into mastery—through internships, extracurriculars, or mentorships that blend academic and real-world skills—fostering innovation and long-term planning. Interactive, guided activities, such as community service or structured debates, strengthen neural pathways for empathy, critical thinking, and civic responsibility, capitalizing on his brain's hyperlearning phase (Blakemore & Mills, 2014).

Yet the risks loom large, amplified by environmental factors. Overstimulation from digital environments—endless social media scrolls or gaming—can exploit this asynchrony, leading to fragmented attention or heightened anxiety, as O'Brien and MacIntyre documented in their 2023 examination of media's impact on adolescent cognition.

High-poverty environments pose severe risks to adolescent development and school persistence, often amplifying the foundational traumas seen in younger children like those described in Paul Gibson's *Thanking Teachers Working in High-Poverty Schools* (2021). While Gibson's accounts focus on elementary-age students—detailing how five-year-olds arrive at school exhausted from sleepless nights in unstable housing, hungry from skipped meals, or shell-shocked from witnessing parental arrests or family evictions—these stressors do not dissipate as children age. Instead, they compound, contributing to a cascade of academic, emotional, and behavioral challenges that increase the likelihood of disengagement or dropout by age 16. Data consistently shows that early poverty-related adversities predict poor outcomes in adolescence, with many affected youth exiting school prematurely.

Research on adolescents in high-poverty settings highlights similar daily hardships, often exacerbated by greater independence and exposure to community violence. For instance, a 2022 report from the U.S. Department of Education's National Center for Education Statistics (NCES) analyzed data from the High School Longitudinal Study of 2009, finding that 15–20% of low-income high school students (ages 14–18) reported chronic food insecurity, which correlates with lower attendance, reduced cognitive performance, and higher dropout rates. These teens, much like Gibson's younger subjects, may start their day without breakfast, leading to fatigue, irritability, and impaired focus during classes—issues that intensify in adolescence when academic demands require sustained attention and executive function.

Sleep deprivation is another persistent thread, with studies showing that high-poverty adolescents face disrupted rest due to overcrowded or unsafe housing, family obligations (e.g., caring for siblings while parents work nights), or environmental noise. A 2019 study published in *JAMA Pediatrics* examined over 1,800 teens from low-income urban areas and found that 25–30% experienced chronic sleep insufficiency (less than 7 hours per night), linked to housing instability like evictions or car-sleeping—mirroring Gibson's anecdotes but for older children. This lack of sleep impairs prefrontal cortex function, which is still maturing until around age 25 (Steinberg, 2014), making it harder for someone like Marcus to regulate emotions, plan ahead, or engage in learning tasks. The result? Higher rates of behavioral issues, absenteeism, and academic failure.

Trauma from events like parental arrests or family instability is particularly acute for adolescents, who may internalize these experiences more deeply due to their emerging sense of identity. The CDC's Adverse Childhood Experiences (ACEs) study, updated in 2023 data from the Behavioral Risk Factor Surveillance

System, indicates that teens with high ACE scores (including household incarceration or homelessness) are 2–4 times more likely to report depression, anxiety, or substance use, which disrupt school attendance and performance. A 2021 report from the Annie E. Casey Foundation on youth in poverty found that 40% of low-income adolescents had experienced at least one major housing disruption (e.g., eviction or sleeping in cars), correlating with a 25–30% higher dropout risk by age 18. For Marcus, witnessing a parent's arrest at night could trigger hypervigilance or distrust of authority, making school feel unsafe or irrelevant.

These cumulative stressors often lead to disengagement, with many such children not remaining in school by age 16. NCES data from 2022 shows that the high school dropout rate for low-income students is 8–10% (vs. 4% nationally), with chronic absenteeism (missing 15+ days per year) affecting 25–35% of poverty-impacted teens—often starting from unaddressed elementary issues like those Gibson describes. Teachers in high-poverty secondary schools report similar challenges to Gibson's elementary educators: students arriving hungry, sleep-deprived, or traumatized, but with added layers like gang involvement or part-time jobs to support families (as noted in a 2020 Urban Institute study on urban adolescent poverty). Interventions like school-based mental health services, free meals, and flexible scheduling can help retention, but systemic poverty often overwhelms these efforts, leading to early exits for work, parenthood, or disillusionment.

In sum, while Gibson's book spotlights elementary struggles, the literature confirms these persist and evolve for adolescents, heightening dropout risks and underscoring the need for holistic support to keep teens like Marcus engaged through graduation.

Nutrition remains critical here, as the adolescent brain demands fuel for its rewiring—omega-3 fatty acids, iron, and antioxidants support myelination and cognitive sharpness (Roberts et al., 2022). Extreme poverty heightens risks through malnutrition or inconsistent meals, leading to deficits in attention, executive function, and emotional regulation (Cusick & Georgieff, 2016; Jensen et al., 2017). Even in affluent homes, poor parental choices—like permitting unrestricted junk food or skipping family meals—can create similar issues; diets high in sugars and processed foods correlate with hyperactivity, reduced focus, and obesity-related cognitive impairments (Mahmood et al., 2021; Chen et al., 2024). Without disciplined routines, teens miss modeled healthy habits and social bonding, potentially exacerbating impulsivity in this already volatile phase.

Mismatched demands during adolescence can entrench habits of distraction or poor judgment, while aligned support builds resilience. For a sixteen-year-old like Marcus—whose prefrontal cortex is only partially mature and whose emotional circuitry still outpaces self-regulation—mismatched demands take many forms: endless late-night screen scrolling that hijacks dopamine circuits, academic workloads that assume full impulse control before it exists, peer pressures that exploit heightened reward sensitivity, or unstructured freedom that leaves him navigating high-stakes choices without adequate foresight. When these demands outstrip his developmental readiness, they can reinforce patterns of impulsivity, fragmented attention, or avoidance rather than building the neural pathways needed for sound judgment and long-term planning.

In high-poverty contexts, schools can act as stabilizers, offering meals, counseling, and structured routines to reopen the window. A consistent breakfast program can quiet the hunger that otherwise dominates attention; a caring counselor or mentor can provide a steady presence amid family chaos; clear daily schedules and predictable expectations can create a rare sense of order for a teen whose home life may be unpredictable. These supports do not replace parental guidance, but they can buffer the effects of instability long enough for Marcus's emerging executive functions to strengthen.

Stewardship for Marcus means balancing freedom with guidance: prioritizing meaningful, supported experiences—such as hands-on projects, mentorship, or structured group activities—over unchecked exposure to digital noise or unstructured time. Honor this window, and it forges a capable adult equipped with resilience, self-regulation, and purpose. Neglect it, and the echoes of turbulence may persist, carrying forward habits of distraction, poor judgment, or disengagement into adulthood.

A critical issue for a constitutional republic—and a developmental window concern—is this: at what age should a citizen be vested with full decision-making authority regarding the governing of that republic?

This question is often framed as a matter of fairness or inclusion. But at its core, it is a question of timing. In nearly every other domain of life, we recognize that human capability unfolds in stages, and that certain responsibilities require a level of judgment that matures gradually. The concept of a developmental window captures this reality: there are periods in which individuals are acquiring and consolidating the cognitive capacities necessary for sound decision-making. The question, then, is not whether young people are capable of forming opinions—they clearly are—but whether the full weight of civic responsibility should be placed on individuals who are still within a formative stage of development.

For most of American history, the answer to that question was clear. The age of majority—the point at which one was considered a fully independent adult—was twenty-one. This standard, inherited from English common law, shaped expectations about civic responsibility, contract authority, and independent judgment well into the twentieth century. That understanding began to shift not because of new insights into human development, but because of changing political and military pressures. The most significant milestone came with the Twenty-Sixth Amendment in 1971, which lowered the voting age from twenty-one to eighteen. In the decades since, the trend has continued, with some advocates now proposing that the voting age be lowered further to sixteen. What is striking about this evolution is that it reflects a redefinition of adulthood driven by policy and pressure, rather than by a reconsideration of developmental readiness. From a developmental perspective, proposals to lower the voting age further represent a step away from—rather than toward—alignment between civic responsibility and the capacities required to exercise it well.

The history of the draft makes this pattern even clearer. When the United States entered World War I, the Selective Service Act of 1917 initially applied to men ages twenty-one to thirty, later expanded to eighteen to forty-five as the war intensified. Similarly, when the first peacetime draft was enacted in 1940, it applied to men ages twenty-one to thirty-five, reflecting the long-standing assumption that the obligations of national service fell first on fully mature adults. Only in 1942, under the pressures of global war and urgent manpower needs, was the minimum age lowered to eighteen. This pattern is not unique. In times of total war, societies routinely lower the age threshold for participation in combat. During the American Civil War, both the Union and Confederate armies accepted underage soldiers, sometimes formally, sometimes informally, driven by necessity rather than principle. The pattern is consistent: developmental thresholds tend to be lowered under pressure, not raised in light of new understanding.

The modern justification for voting at eighteen rests heavily on a fairness argument: "old enough to fight, old enough to vote." But fairness arguments are not all the same. Fairness has overwhelming force when a class of people is excluded permanently on the basis of immutable characteristics—such as sex, race, or country of birth. Age is different. Youth is a temporary condition through which individuals pass. A threshold of twenty-one does not permanently exclude the young from participation; it delays participation until a later stage of development. The analogy, therefore, is unstable. The fairness argument resolves a political tension, but it does not answer the developmental question.

Even if one accepts a fairness-based argument for earlier participation, the question becomes more complex when viewed over time. If a portion of the citizenry is granted full decision-making authority before the capacities for judgment, foresight, and long-horizon evaluation are more fully developed, then the consequences of those decisions do not remain confined to the present. They shape the institutions, laws, and conditions that all citizens must live under—including the future selves of those same individuals.

In this sense, the fairness argument begins to turn on itself. Those who vote at eighteen, nineteen, or twenty must later live in a republic shaped in part by decisions made during an earlier stage of development, when their own capacity for judgment was still maturing. If the state knowingly invites consequential civic participation before those capacities are more fully formed, it is not clear that this is fair to anyone—including the very individuals it seeks to include. The question is not simply whether participation is extended, but whether it is extended at a point when it can be exercised with the level of judgment the system depends upon.

Modern developmental science provides a clearer lens. Neuroimaging research shows that the prefrontal cortex— the region responsible for planning, prioritization, impulse control, and long-horizon reasoning—continues to mature structurally and functionally into the mid-twenties (Gogtay et al., 2004; Casey, Jones, & Hare, 2008). At the same time, subcortical systems associated with reward sensitivity and emotional salience are highly active during adolescence and early adulthood, creating a developmental imbalance between control systems and reward systems (Steinberg, 2008). This imbalance has measurable behavioral consequences. Younger individuals exhibit greater sensitivity to peer influence and social evaluation, and show increased responsiveness to immediate rewards relative to delayed outcomes (Chein et al., 2011; Steinberg et al., 2009). Decision-making competence is also context-sensitive: individuals in this developmental stage perform well in structured, low-emotion settings, but their judgment becomes less consistent in emotionally charged or socially framed situations (Fischhoff et al., 2010). These are precisely the conditions under which political decisions are made.

One of the less comfortable implications of this research is an increased susceptibility to persuasive narratives. Younger individuals are often more responsive to messages framed in terms of identity, fairness, and perceived threat. This responsiveness is not a defect of intelligence; it reflects a developmental phase in which social belonging and immediate emotional salience exert stronger influence than long-term coherence. As a result, narratives that are vivid, urgent, or identity-affirming can exert disproportionate influence, even when they are incomplete, exaggerated, or internally inconsistent. The issue is not which narrative prevails, but the conditions under which those narratives are evaluated.

None of this implies that individuals under twenty-one lack the capacity for insight, creativity, or achievement. History provides many examples of extraordinary contributions made at a young age. Blaise Pascal produced foundational work in mathematics as a teenager. Évariste Galois laid the groundwork for group theory before the age of twenty. Louis Braille developed the reading system that bears his name while still a young man. Srinivasa Ramanujan generated profound mathematical insights in his late teens and early twenties.

Among these examples, Mary Shelley stands out, particularly for the depth of insight she demonstrates into questions typically associated with adult judgment. She began writing Frankenstein at eighteen, producing a work that continues to resonate not merely as a piece of fiction, but as a sustained meditation on responsibility. The novel's central question is not how to create life, but what one owes to what one creates. Victor Frankenstein's failure is not technical—it is moral. He brings a being into existence and then abandons it, refusing the responsibility that creation entails. The theme reflects a level of ethical and psychological insight more commonly associated with later stages of maturity. At the same time, Shelley's early life was marked by intense personal experience, including loss and social upheaval, which likely accelerated her engagement with these questions. The result is a work that demonstrates what is possible when exceptional individuals confront serious ideas early in life. It is not merely imaginative power that distinguishes the work, but the presence of judgment applied, unusually, at a very early age.

But a republic cannot be designed around its prodigies. It must be designed around its people. The existence of individuals capable of profound insight at eighteen does not negate the broader developmental reality that, for most, the systems responsible for long-range judgment, impulse control, and consistent evaluation of consequences are still maturing.

The Constitution does not attempt to screen out ideas before they enter the political arena. It protects the right of individuals and organizations to advocate, organize, and seek office—even when their aims include profound changes to law and society. Instead, it relies on a different safeguard: that those who participate in self-government possess the judgment necessary to evaluate competing claims, recognize long-term consequences, and distinguish between persuasion and manipulation.

That assumption raises a more subtle question. If the durability of the republic depends not on restricting ideas but on the quality of civic judgment, then when—and under what conditions—do individuals fully enter that responsibility?

We already recognize that human development unfolds in stages. In nearly every other domain—contracts, military service, alcohol consumption, even insurance risk—we acknowledge that certain forms of judgment mature over time. Yet in the most consequential act of citizenship, the vote, we draw the line at eighteen.

If we take seriously the idea that self-government depends on an informed and fully developed citizenry, then it is reasonable to ask whether that threshold aligns with what we now understand about cognitive and social development. Protecting developmental windows is not about withholding rights indefinitely; it is about ensuring that when those rights are exercised, they are exercised with the level of judgment the system depends upon. In that sense, the voting age is not merely a procedural detail—it is part of the constitutional architecture that determines how well the republic can sustain itself over time. time.

Young Adulthood

Sophia, at twenty-eight, embodies the young adult in full stride—a time when capacities for productivity, intimacy, and self-direction are at their height, yet balanced against emerging awareness of time's limits. Society and the workplace can play pivotal roles in optimizing these strengths while respecting the natural constraints of this stage, drawing from insights in lifespan psychology. For instance, workplaces could foster flexible structures that leverage her peaking fluid intelligence for innovative problem-solving—such as through project-based roles or cross-functional teams—while accommodating the need for work-life integration to support Erikson's intimacy stage (Erikson, 1959). Policies like paid parental leave, mental health days, or sabbaticals after intense projects would honor the fatigue that can accompany ambition, allowing recovery without penalty. Employers might also invest in mentorship programs, pairing young adults like Sophia with seasoned colleagues to accelerate the growth of crystallized intelligence, as Schaie's longitudinal studies show that stimulating environments enhance cognitive reorganization in early adulthood (Schaie, 1994; 2005). On a societal level, accessible lifelong learning resources—such as subsidized online courses or community workshops—could help her navigate the paradox of choice noted by Schwartz and Sharpe (2010), providing tools to prioritize without overwhelming options. Public initiatives promoting affordable housing or childcare would alleviate external pressures, freeing cognitive resources for personal and professional growth rather than survival logistics.

Sophia herself should be mindful of this window's dual nature: her brain's shift toward efficiency means embracing selective focus—choosing depth in a few areas over breadth in many—to avoid burnout. She might cultivate habits like journaling or regular reflection to integrate experiences, building on the prefrontal cortex's maturing ability for long-term planning (Steinberg, 2014). Awareness of emotional undercurrents, such as the drive for meaningful connections amid career demands, could guide her to invest in relationships proactively, reducing isolation risks. Finally, recognizing that fluid abilities won't last forever (Salthouse, 2010), she could prioritize skill-building now, while her adaptability is high, ensuring a resilient foundation for the decades ahead. In honoring these rhythms, Sophia—and those around her—can turn young adulthood into a launchpad for sustained contribution.

Adulthood is often mistaken for cognitive stability—the end of the learning curve. In reality, it is a period of dynamic equilibrium. Fluid intelligence (novel problem-solving) peaks in the late twenties and early thirties, then gradually declines. Crystallized intelligence (accumulated knowledge, vocabulary, expertise) continues to grow well into the sixties and beyond. K. Warner Schaie's Seattle Longitudinal Study (1956 onward) demonstrated that intelligence is multidimensional and plastic. When adults are followed over time, rather than compared cross-sectionally, the pattern is not decline but reorganization. Adults become experts not because they process faster, but because they filter better.

Sophia, at twenty-eight, sits at her laptop long after midnight. The glow softens exhaustion. Slack pings; an online course tab blinks. She feels capable yet stretched thin. Deadlines blur. She recalls when learning felt effortless. Now each new skill demands strategy: chunking, reminders, trade-offs.

She is in young adulthood—the season of building and balancing, where the brain shifts from rapid reorganization to dynamic equilibrium. Fluid intelligence—raw problem-solving speed and the ability to handle novel situations—peaks in the late twenties and early thirties, then begins a gradual decline (Salthouse, 2010; Hartshorne & Germine, 2015). Crystallized intelligence—accumulated knowledge, vocabulary, expertise, and pattern recognition—continues to grow well into the sixties and beyond (Schaie, 1994; 2005; Park & Reuter-Lorenz, 2009). Sophia is not losing ability; she is reallocating it. Her brain has become more economical—pruning distractions, optimizing energy, trading breadth for depth. She builds mental scaffolds: What's the principle? Where does it connect to what I already know? She is not just learning content; she is learning how to learn more efficiently—a distinctly adult adaptation.

Emotionally, Sophia is deep in Erik Erikson's stage of intimacy versus isolation (Erikson, 1959), where the central task is forming deep, committed relationships while maintaining individuality. Success here yields love and connection; failure risks loneliness and self-absorption. At twenty-eight, she is likely navigating career demands, romantic partnerships, perhaps early parenthood or the pressure to "settle down," all while the prefrontal cortex—now nearing full maturity—helps her weigh long-term consequences more reliably than it did in adolescence (Steinberg, 2014; Gogtay et al., 2004). Yet the pace of modern life compresses these choices: career ladders, social media comparisons, economic uncertainty, and the expectation to "have it all" create a paradox of choice that Barry Schwartz and Kenneth Sharpe (2010) describe as paralyzing rather than liberating.

Cognitively, Sophia benefits from what K. Warner Schaie's Seattle Longitudinal Study revealed: intelligence is multidimensional and plastic across adulthood (Schaie, 1956; 1994; 2005). While perceptual speed and working memory narrow slightly, verbal meaning, inductive reasoning, and spatial orientation often plateau or rise through midlife. Sophia compensates for any loss in raw processing power with richer schemas, deeper semantic networks, and selective focus—filtering what matters and applying decades of experience to new problems. She is becoming the expert who sees connections others miss, the strategist who anticipates outcomes, the integrator who turns knowledge into insight.

Yet the weight of time is beginning to register. Every new skill must justify its cost in energy and attention. She feels the tension between ambition and fatigue, freedom and obligation, growth and limits. This is the season when adults often re-evaluate priorities: What do I want to carry forward? What can I let go? Lifelong learning in this phase is less about accumulation and more about refinement—distilling coherence from experience, meaning from change.

Sophia leans back from her glowing screen, exhales, and presses play on the next lesson. She is not declining; she is optimizing. The torch of learning passes not through speed, but through wisdom: the ability to see what endures, to simplify complexity rather than amplify it. In this quiet moment, she embodies the adult brain's greatest strength—not endless novelty, but purposeful depth.

Midlife

William, at fifty-one, steps into his office before sunrise. The quiet hum of the HVAC and coffee aroma greet him. He once chased mastery; now he orchestrates it. He recognizes patterns faster, recalls similar projects instantly, sees pitfalls others miss. But he also feels the weight of time. Every new skill must justify its cost in energy and attention. He closes his laptop, resolving to keep learning—more selectively, more purposefully.

He is in midlife—the season of depth and deliberation, where the brain has become less a processor and more a curator. Processing speed, working memory, and some aspects of fluid reasoning decline steadily after midlife (Salthouse, 2010; Park & Reuter-Lorenz, 2009), but this is not the full story. The older brain trades speed for selectivity, breadth for depth. What adults lose in volume, they often gain in clarity and perspective. Studies in cognitive neuroscience reveal that older adults increasingly recruit both hemispheres of the brain to solve problems that younger adults perform with one, a bilateral activation that suggests a neural strategy of compensation—the brain's way of distributing the cognitive workload as it adapts to aging (Cabeza et al., 2002; Spreng & Turner, 2019).

Emotionally, William is in Erik Erikson's stage of generativity versus stagnation (Erikson, 1959), where the central task is contributing to the next generation through mentoring, creating, or nurturing, while avoiding self-absorption or regret. Success here yields a sense of legacy and fulfillment; with opportunities to guide others, William can channel his accumulated wisdom into meaningful impact. But stagnation—perhaps from unaddressed burnout or rigid routines—can lead to midlife crisis or disengagement.

Cognitively, William benefits from the insights of K. Warner Schaie's Seattle Longitudinal Study (Schaie, 1956; 1994; 2005), which demonstrated that while fluid intelligence wanes, crystallized intelligence—built from experience—continues to rise, enabling superior pattern recognition and integrative judgment. Paul and Margret Baltes' Selective Optimization with Compensation (SOC) model (Baltes & Baltes, 1990) reframes this as strategic adaptation: selecting meaningful goals, optimizing remaining resources, and compensating for declines through tools or delegation. At fifty-one, William is not declining; he is refining—turning knowledge into wisdom, simplifying complexity, and focusing on what endures.

The opportunities in this window are profound: With his prefrontal cortex fully mature and executive functions honed, William can tackle complex, real-world problems that demand insight over speed—mentoring teams, innovating processes, or contributing to community initiatives. Supported experiences, like flexible projects or collaborative roles, leverage his strengths, fostering generativity and sustained engagement.

Yet the risks arise from mismatched expectations: Overloading with novel tasks can exacerbate fatigue, while undervaluing his expertise might lead to disengagement. In high-poverty or unstable contexts, these challenges intensify— midlife adults may juggle elder care, financial strains, or health issues, diverting energy from growth (as echoed in Gibson's 2021 accounts of educators facing similar burdens). Without balance, the echoes of earlier turbulence—unresolved stressors or poor habits—can manifest as burnout or regret.

Without diminishing William's agency—his capacity to direct his own path through intention and choice—society and the workplace can optimize his strengths while respecting his limitations. Workplaces might offer phased workloads, sabbaticals, or role transitions that play to crystallized intelligence, such as advisory positions or mentorship programs, allowing him to contribute deeply without exhaustive demands (Baltes & Smith, 2003). Flexible scheduling, wellness initiatives, or lifelong learning subsidies could accommodate the natural shift toward selectivity, preventing overload while valuing his accumulated expertise. On a societal level, policies like extended family leave, affordable healthcare, or community education hubs would support generativity, enabling midlife adults to mentor youth or pursue encore careers without economic barriers.

William himself should be aware of this equilibrium: His brain's reorganization favors quality over quantity, so embracing selective focus—prioritizing high-impact goals—can sustain productivity and fulfillment. He might cultivate habits like mindfulness or regular reflection to harness generativity, building legacy through relationships and contributions. Recognizing the positivity effect—his tendency to favor meaningful, emotionally satisfying pursuits (Carstensen et al., 2000)—could guide him to invest in what truly endures, turning midlife into a bridge of wisdom rather than a plateau of routine. In honoring these rhythms, William—and those around him—can transform this window into a foundation for enduring purpose.

Older Adulthood

Ellen, at seventy-two, sits at the same oak desk where she once sat to do her engineering job on the rare occasions when she worked remotely at home. The laptop hums quietly; a tablet glows beside it. Scattered across the surface are student papers awaiting her red pen and a growing stack of notes for the book she is writing on electrical engineering—her lifelong passion distilled into chapters that blend theory, practice, and the hard-won lessons of decades in the field. Words come more slowly than they once did, but they arrive layered with meaning. She no longer chases every possibility—she chooses what matters. An email arrives from a former student, now an engineer himself, seeking advice on a design problem. She types deliberately, drawing from memory and experience to offer clarity.

She is in later life—the season of crystallized wisdom and selective mind, where the brain has become less a processor and more a curator. Processing speed and working memory may have slowed (Salthouse, 2010), but crystallized intelligence—accumulated knowledge, expertise, and integrative judgment—remains robust, often enabling superior pattern recognition and reflective synthesis (Schaie, 1994; 2005; Park & Reuter-Lorenz, 2009). Emotionally, Ellen navigates Erik Erikson's stage of integrity versus despair (Erikson, 1959), looking back on a life of contribution—designing systems, mentoring young engineers, raising a family—and finding fulfillment in the legacy she continues to build. The positivity effect, documented by Laura Carstensen and colleagues (Carstensen et al., 2000), draws her toward emotionally satisfying pursuits: guiding students, writing to share what she has learned, and preserving the knowledge she helped create.

The science of lifespan development challenges the artificial notion of retirement in the mid-sixties, a construct rooted in mid-twentieth-century industrial and unionized work patterns rather than biological or cognitive limits. Absent disability or dementia, there is no universal "aging out" of productivity; many in their seventies and beyond maintain high levels of expertise and adaptive reasoning (Baltes & Smith, 2003). Declines in fluid intelligence are offset by gains in wisdom—practical, context-aware insight that Grossmann et al. (2013) found often peaks later in life. Paul and Margret Baltes' Selective Optimization with Compensation model shows that older adults can sustain high-level functioning by selecting high-priority goals, optimizing remaining resources, and compensating for losses through tools, experience, or delegation (Baltes & Baltes, 1990). Ellen's slower word-finding or reduced processing speed are real but minor; they are more than offset by her depth of insight, pattern recognition, and capacity to synthesize decades of technical knowledge into clear, actionable guidance.

At seventy-two, Ellen has transitioned naturally from the full-time demands of an industrial engineering career to a role of teaching, research, and writing. She grades papers from her online courses, mentors students remotely, and writes the book she always intended to write—a synthesis of electrical engineering principles, real-world applications, and the lessons learned from designing systems under pressure. The oak desk remains the same; the work has simply evolved. She could be leading webinars for practicing engineers, consulting on curriculum for technical programs, or advising startups on practical implementation—roles that play to her crystallized intelligence and wisdom without requiring the physical or temporal intensity of her earlier career.

Without diminishing Ellen's agency—her capacity to shape her own path through intention and choice—society and the workplace can optimize her potential by dismantling age-based barriers. Universities and professional organizations might create flexible, part-time roles such as adjunct professorships, online seminar leadership, or emeritus consulting positions that allow experienced professionals to teach, write, and mentor without full-time demands (Baltes & Smith, 2003). Policies such as phased retirement options, stipends for knowledge-sharing activities, or tax incentives for employers who retain older workers in advisory or educational roles would further enable this transition. Community colleges, professional societies, and lifelong learning platforms could formalize "encore careers" for older adults, offering honoraria for lectures, curriculum contributions, or peer mentoring—recognizing that productivity in later life often thrives on purpose, flexibility, and legacy-building rather than rigid hours or physical intensity.

Ellen herself can get the most out of her capabilities by embracing selective optimization. She might prioritize high-impact activities—writing the book, mentoring students, leading occasional workshops—that leverage her crystallized intelligence and wisdom, while using tools (voice-to-text software, research assistants, or digital organization systems) to compensate for slower processing or fatigue. Regular physical activity, social engagement, and cognitive stimulation (reading technical journals, discussing ideas with colleagues) can sustain cognitive reserve (Snowdon et al., 2003). Awareness of the positivity effect—her natural inclination toward emotionally satisfying pursuits (Carstensen et al., 2000)—can guide her to invest in relationships and meaningful work that nourish rather than drain her. By viewing this phase not as decline but as refinement, Ellen can transform the oak desk into a lifelong center of contribution, proving that capability knows no arbitrary age bound.

In honoring these rhythms—society's structures and Ellen's choices—later life becomes not a retreat, but a season of depth, legacy, and continued service to the learning republic.

Conclusion

In the delicate architecture of early childhood development, where Theodore's world is one of boundless curiosity and fragile foundations, stewardship demands a careful balance. Experiences that shape self-concept—those intangible threads of "who I am" woven from family interactions, play, and personal discovery—must unfold naturally, without premature imposition from external authorities. Issues of identity, emerging as they do from a child's innate explorations and peer relationships, are best navigated organically, free from structured interference by educators or institutions. To introduce abstract or prescriptive notions too soon risks distorting the intuitive process, potentially overwhelming the young mind's capacity to integrate them healthfully. As Erik Erikson observed in his 1959 framework, the initiative versus guilt stage thrives on supportive, non-directive guidance that allows children to assert themselves without inducing confusion or shame. Similarly, Piaget's preoperational insights remind us that until logical scaffolding solidifies around age seven, children interpret the world egocentrically, making them suggestible to influences that could prematurely fix or fragment their sense of self. For Theodore, honoring this window means prioritizing environments where identity forms through lived relationships and self-directed play, ensuring his developmental path remains resilient and authentically his own.

For adolescents like Marcus, whose window is one of storm and restructuring, the principle holds even more acutely. With the prefrontal cortex only partially mature—enabling foresight but not yet full impulse control (Steinberg, 2014)—external pressures on identity can amplify turbulence. Peers, family, and personal reflection provide the natural arena for working through these questions, fostering a coherent self without the risk of institutional overreach. Teachers, in this view, serve best as facilitators of knowledge and skills, not architects of personal identity, allowing the adolescent's emerging autonomy to guide the process unencumbered.

From Simcock and Hayne's demonstration that early memories remain locked until language provides the key (2002, 2003), through Piaget's revelation that cognition unfolds in qualitative stages rather than simple accumulation (1952), Erikson's mapping of psychosocial tensions that shape identity across the lifespan (1959), Steinberg's mapping of the neurobiological asynchrony that defines adolescent risk and possibility (2014), Schaie's longitudinal proof that intelligence is multidimensional and plastic into old age (1956; 1994; 2005), and the Baltes' model of selective optimization with compensation that reframes later life as strategic refinement rather than inevitable decline (1990), one truth emerges clearly: learning never stops—it evolves. Each stage reorganizes how we acquire, process, prioritize, and apply knowledge. Protecting developmental windows is not moralism; it is fidelity to biology. It means designing environments—homes, schools, workplaces, digital spaces—that honor the sequence of maturation rather than impose expectations or stimuli that arrive too soon or too late.

Yet protection alone is insufficient. Once the windows of greatest vulnerability close, access becomes the decisive frontier. For adults and older learners, the barriers are less about overexposure and more about opacity: tangled systems, unclear pathways, bureaucratic fog, and outdated assumptions about when contribution ends. The same society that rightly guards the young brain from premature overload must open doors when readiness arrives—ensuring that opportunity is not withheld simply because someone has passed an arbitrary age threshold.

One historical decision illustrates the cost of deferring such questions. When the Twenty-Sixth Amendment lowered the voting age to eighteen in 1971, the moral symmetry was compelling: if young men could be drafted to fight and die, they should have a voice in the policies that sent them (McGovern, 1971; Keyssar, 2000). Yet the developmental readiness of eighteen-year-olds received far less sustained attention. Neuroscience later showed that the prefrontal cortex—central to impulse control, long-term planning, and judgment under uncertainty—continues to mature into the early twenties (Giedd et al., 1999; Casey et al., 2008; Steinberg, 2014). Executive systems, especially under emotional arousal or peer influence, refine well beyond legal adulthood (Somerville & Casey, 2010; Steinberg, 2008). The amendment addressed an immediate injustice without a parallel investment in civic preparation, leaving a quiet tension between biological maturation and democratic expectation (Luna et al., 2010; Casey et al., 2019).

This pattern recurs across the lifespan. Early digital saturation risks wiring circuits toward reaction rather than reflection (Wolf, 2018; Christakis et al., 2018). Adolescent turbulence can entrench distraction if guidance is absent (Blakemore & Mills, 2014). Midlife compression can lead to burnout when choices multiply without structure (Schwartz & Sharpe, 2010). Later life can be misread as decline rather than refinement if society withdraws opportunity (Schaie, 2005; Baltes & Smith, 2003). In each case, the republic pays a price when learning environments fail to align with developmental reality—whether through overexposure, under-support, or premature exclusion.

The first duty of a learning society is protection—not from ideas, but from mistiming. The second duty is access: ensuring that when the brain is ready, the door is open. A republic that stewards developmental windows and then opens pathways for lifelong contribution does not merely educate its citizens; it sustains itself. The next chapter turns to those pathways—how we can remove the opacity and restore opportunity so that readiness meets welcome, and capability serves the common good across every season of life.

Chapter Nine: Barriers to Learning

Structural, Dispositional, and Material Constraints on Opportunity

In the early 2010s, sociologist Sherry Turkle began to notice a pattern. Students sat together in classrooms, in dormitories, in cafés—physically present but mentally elsewhere. Phones lay face-up on the table, intermittently lighting up with notifications. Conversations stalled, resumed, fractured. When discussions grew difficult or emotionally charged, attention drifted toward the screen.

Turkle was not studying distraction in the crude sense. Her subjects were capable, articulate, and earnest. They wanted connection. They wanted to learn. Yet sustained attention—whether to another person, a complex idea, or their own inner thoughts—proved increasingly difficult to maintain.

In interviews, students described a quiet trade-off. Constant connection offered reassurance: no one was ever fully alone. But it came at a cost. Silence felt uncomfortable. Deep focus felt risky. Moments that once invited reflection were now filled automatically.

What troubled Turkle most was not the presence of technology, but its influence on habit. Devices did not forbid thinking; they made it easier to avoid it. Over time, learners began to expect stimulation without effort, response without reflection, engagement without vulnerability.

The barrier to learning was not a lack of access or motivation. It was the erosion of the conditions required for sustained thought. Attention, like memory, depends on the environment. And environments shape what the mind finds possible.

The Lingering Legacy of the Founding Compromise

The legacy of the founding compromises continues to shape educational opportunity in subtler ways. Census categories born in the age of slavery still structure the datasets that inform contemporary policy. School districts and universities routinely collect and report outcomes by race and ethnicity using classifications that evolved from eighteenth- and nineteenth-century political arithmetic—systems originally designed for taxation, apportionment, and control rather than for understanding human learning potential (Hannah-Jones 2019; Anderson 2016). These data are often employed in efforts to remedy disparities, yet they also risk normalizing divisions rooted in inherited traits rather than present capacity or future possibility.

The danger lies not in measuring and ensuring equality of opportunity and equality before the law—which are essential—but in allowing categories designed for governance to harden into civic identities. When learners internalize labels or come to see themselves primarily through the lens of statistical groupings, barriers shift from structural to psychological (Steele 1997; Dweck 2006). When institutions treat those groupings as fixed and natural rather than historical and contingent, barriers become institutional. A learning republic cannot afford to measure its citizens primarily by taxonomies derived from bondage.

At the same time, other barriers operate more quietly but no less powerfully. Attitudinal barriers arise when individuals doubt their own capacity to learn, often as the cumulative result of earlier educational failures. Material barriers include hunger, unstable housing, inadequate healthcare, and lack of reliable internet access (Maslow 1943; Duncan and Murnane 2011). Institutional barriers appear in complex bureaucracies, opaque course catalogs, rigid schedules, and fragmented support services. Informational barriers arise when people cannot easily discover learning opportunities that align with their needs, constraints, and life stages.

These barriers compound one another. Paul Gibson's phenomenological research on teachers working in high-poverty schools documents how students frequently arrive in classrooms hungry, exhausted, or emotionally overwhelmed (Gibson 2018). In such conditions, working memory is already saturated by survival concerns, leaving little capacity for new learning—an effect well documented by cognitive load theory (Sweller 1988). Teachers expend enormous emotional and cognitive effort managing crises before instruction can begin. Over time, chronic guilt, moral distress, and helplessness increase teachers' own cognitive load, reducing their capacity for adaptive and responsive teaching (Hochschild 1983; Jennings and Greenberg 2009).

The movement of education from household to institution assumed that children would arrive at school with certain developmental foundations in place. Families would provide stability, nutrition, rest, language exposure, and emotional security. Schools would build upon those foundations through structured instruction.

In high-poverty contexts, that assumption frequently does not hold.

In his phenomenological study of teachers and students in high-poverty schools, Gibson documented classrooms shaped not only by instructional challenges but by developmental disruption. Teachers described students arriving hungry, exhausted, hypervigilant, or carrying the residue of domestic instability and community violence. Students described learning environments filtered through stress, uncertainty, and interrupted rest.

These are not merely motivational obstacles. They are developmental conditions.

When narrowed exposure to language, limited access to broad cultural knowledge, chronic stress, and diminished expectation of mobility persist during early developmental windows, they can produce real constraints — not merely perceived ones. Reduced language exposure affects vocabulary acquisition and background knowledge. Chronic stress impairs working memory and executive function. Insufficient sleep disrupts memory consolidation. Under such conditions, the construction of durable knowledge structures becomes significantly more difficult.

What appears in the classroom as inattentiveness, low engagement, or weak reasoning often reflects earlier disruption in cognitive scaffolding. The issue is not moral deficiency. It is developmental architecture.

Just as inherited wealth can entrench advantage across generations, persistent deprivation can entrench constraint. Intergenerational poverty is not merely material. It often includes diminished exposure to language and cultural knowledge, accumulated stress physiology, and narrowed opportunity structures. These constraints are not destiny, but they are not trivial. Early developmental environments shape both cognitive architecture and the range of opportunities later learning can realistically leverage.

When families lack the material or social stability necessary to prepare children for learning, responsibility does not evaporate. It shifts unevenly. Schools encounter the consequences. Local institutions confront the aftereffects. Policymakers face the long-term civic implications. The obligations remain specific, even when the causes are complex.

Addressing these realities requires more than federal mandates or test-score accountability. National reforms such as No Child Left Behind and its successors have produced only modest and often temporary gains, in part because they operate far from the daily conditions that shape readiness to learn (Rothstein 2014; Reardon 2011). Gibson's participants proposed a different approach: each school, they argued, should be supported by a Community Resource Officer—a civilian liaison responsible for coordinating assistance from local agencies, civic organizations, and faith communities to address families' material, emotional, and social needs.

Learning, in this view, is inseparable from the conditions that make attention, effort, and persistence possible.

Research on early childhood interventions reinforces the same conclusion. Programs such as the Perry Preschool Project and Head Start demonstrate that well-designed early education for disadvantaged children yields long-term gains in graduation rates, employment, and civic participation, while reducing incarceration and public assistance dependence (Heckman et al. 2010; Schweinhart et al. 2005). Societies that neglect the basic conditions of learning often pay far more later—in criminal justice costs, reduced productivity, and lost human potential—than they would have spent supporting learners at the outset.

Taken together, these patterns point to a deeper structural problem. When learning is detached from consequence—when credentials substitute for capability, when signaling overwhelms substance, and when education unfolds in isolation from productive responsibility—both individuals and institutions lose their bearings. The result is not merely inefficiency or skills mismatch, but a civic vulnerability: citizens trained to speak fluently about ideas without being disciplined by their practical implications.

This is not a new concern. Long before contemporary debates about higher education, American thinkers wrestled with the danger of education severed from work, responsibility, and lived consequence. They understood that democratic societies depend not only on knowledge, but on habits of judgment formed through participation in real economic and civic life. To see what is at stake—and what might be recovered—it is useful to revisit a tradition that treated work itself as a central educational force.

Different Types of Barriers

Learning is often discussed as though it were a property of individuals—something one either does well or poorly, possesses or lacks. From this perspective, failure to learn is frequently attributed to insufficient motivation, ability, or effort. Yet decades of research in cognitive psychology, educational science, and sociology converge on a different conclusion: learning is not merely an internal process, but an interaction between the mind and the conditions under which it operates. When those conditions are poorly aligned with human cognition, learning fails predictably—not because of individual deficiency, but because of environmental design (Sweller, 1988; Bransford, Brown, & Cocking, 2000).

Barriers to learning are therefore best understood not as personal shortcomings, but as constraints—cognitive, dispositional, structural, institutional, technological, and cultural—that interfere with the transformation of experience into durable understanding. These barriers are often invisible to those who are least affected by them, and most punitive to those who encounter several simultaneously. A Learning Republic must take these barriers seriously, because their cumulative effect is not merely educational underperformance, but civic fragility.

Cognitive Barriers: The Limits of Working Memory

At the most fundamental level, learning is constrained by the architecture of the human mind. Working memory—the system responsible for holding and manipulating information in the moment—is sharply limited in both capacity and duration (Miller, 1956; Peterson & Peterson, 1959). When instructional demands exceed those limits, learners experience cognitive overload, a condition in which mental effort is expended without corresponding learning gains (Sweller, 1988; Paas, Renkl, & Sweller, 2003).

Cognitive barriers arise when learners are asked to process too many unfamiliar elements at once, to multitask across competing sources of information, or to engage in complex problem solving before foundational schemas have been established. Under such conditions, working memory becomes saturated, and learning slows or halts altogether. Importantly, this failure is not always experienced consciously as overload. Instead, it often manifests as confusion, frustration, disengagement, or avoidance.

What is commonly interpreted as a lack of motivation may, in fact, be a rational response to repeated cognitive failure. When effort consistently fails to produce understanding, learners conserve resources by withdrawing effort altogether. This adaptive response becomes maladaptive only when environments remain unchanged.

Dispositional Barriers: Learned Avoidance and Self-Protection

Over time, repeated exposure to cognitively overwhelming or emotionally threatening learning environments can produce dispositional barriers—patterns of avoidance, anxiety, or disengagement that persist even when conditions improve. Research on learned helplessness and academic self-efficacy demonstrates that individuals who repeatedly experience failure without adequate support often internalize expectations of incompetence, leading them to disengage preemptively from future learning opportunities (Seligman, 1975; Bandura, 1997).

These barriers are not rooted in an absence of curiosity or desire. On the contrary, many learners experiencing dispositional barriers report strong intrinsic interest alongside a competing need to protect self-worth. Learning becomes emotionally risky. Errors are interpreted not as information, but as evidence of inadequacy. As a result, learners may procrastinate, withdraw, or appear oppositional, behaviors that further reinforce negative judgments by instructors and institutions.

Dispositional barriers illustrate an important principle: motivation cannot be separated from perceived safety. Before learners can invest sustained effort, they must believe that effort will not result in humiliation, exclusion, or futility. Instructional systems that conflate struggle with deficiency inadvertently train learners to avoid struggle altogether.

Structural Barriers: Time, Energy, and Material Constraints

Beyond cognition and disposition lie structural barriers—the external conditions that shape whether learning can occur at all. These include time scarcity, financial pressure, caregiving responsibilities, health concerns, and chronic stress. While such barriers affect learners across the lifespan, they are particularly salient for adults, whose learning must compete with the demands of work, family, and survival.

Cognitive science makes clear that learning is metabolically expensive. Sustained attention, memory consolidation, and conceptual integration require energy and recovery time (Kahneman, 1973). When learners are exhausted, hungry, or chronically stressed, cognitive resources are diverted toward regulation and coping rather than understanding. Under these conditions, even well-designed instruction may fail.

Structural barriers challenge the assumption—still implicit in many educational systems—that learners have discretionary time and uninterrupted attention. When learning environments ignore these realities, they privilege those with surplus resources and penalize those without, all while presenting outcomes as meritocratic.

Institutional Barriers: Systems Optimized for Sorting, Not Learning

Many barriers to learning are embedded not in individual classrooms, but in institutional practices inherited from earlier economic and social contexts. Modern schooling systems were largely designed to sort populations efficiently—by age, by pace, by performance—rather than to support diverse learning trajectories across the lifespan (Tyack, 1974).

Institutional barriers include rigid curricula, punitive grading practices, inflexible scheduling, opaque pathways, and the conflation of credentialing with competence. These structures often reward speed over understanding and compliance over curiosity. Learners who deviate from the assumed norm—whether by age, background, or learning history—encounter friction at every turn.

Crucially, institutions tend to interpret non-participation or attrition as lack of commitment, rather than as feedback about system design. In doing so, they preserve structures that systematically exclude large portions of the population from meaningful learning.

Cultural and Technological Barriers: Belonging and Attention

Finally, learning is shaped by cultural narratives about who belongs in learning spaces and by technologies that mediate attention. Cultural barriers operate through signals—subtle and overt—that communicate who is expected to succeed. When learners feel like outsiders, cognitive resources are diverted toward identity management, reducing capacity for learning (Steele, 1997).

Technological barriers compound this problem when tools fragment attention, reward novelty over depth, or substitute automation for understanding. While technology holds enormous potential to support learning, poorly designed systems often compete with cognition rather than scaffold it.

One of the quiet but powerful barriers to lifelong learning begins long before adulthood: the presence—or absence—of dispositional hope in young people. Hope, in this context, is not vague optimism; it is a practical mindset built on clear goals, the ability to plan pathways toward those goals, and the inner determination to keep moving forward even when obstacles appear (Snyder, 1995; 2002). Research in cognitive neuroscience suggests this mindset is not merely psychological—it is tied to physical brain development. In a study of 231 adolescents aged 16 to 20, higher levels of dispositional hope (measured with Snyder's validated scale) were associated with greater cortical brain volume, even after accounting for age, gender, socioeconomic status, and overall brain size (Wang et al., 2020). In other words, young people who enter late adolescence with stronger hope tend to have more robust neural architecture to support complex thinking and sustained effort later in life.

The implication is sobering. Students who grow up disaffected, discouraged, or without the tools to set goals and pursue them risk entering adulthood with a less developed cognitive foundation. Early experiences of failure, neglect, or lack of encouragement can diminish not only motivation but also the very brain structures needed for lifelong learning. This does not mean hope is destiny, nor that later learning is impossible. But it does mean that the window for building the neural and psychological groundwork for continuous growth is widest in childhood and adolescence. When we under-invest in assumption no longer holds. Older adults, in particular, are acutely selective in how they spend cognitive and temporal resources. A career accountant curious about history, or a psychotherapist interested in finance, is unlikely to sift through every disciplinary silo to discover a single compelling entry point.

The problem is not curiosity; it is design. Course descriptions are typically optimized for compliance, accreditation, and internal classification—not for exploratory learning. They describe content coverage rather than learning outcomes, and they require the learner to infer relevance rather than encounter it directly.

A different model is possible. Imagine a recommender system that surfaces *learning outcomes* rather than courses. Outcomes are categorized by domain—historical reasoning, quantitative literacy, ethical analysis, financial decision-making—and presented in concise, comparable form. Learners could quickly

scan possibilities, select outcomes that align with their interests, and allow the system to recommend the courses from which those outcomes are derived.

Such a system respects the cognitive economy of adult learners. It reduces search costs, minimizes decision fatigue, and supports learning driven by curiosity rather than credential accumulation. The barrier here is not age, motivation, or ability—it is an institutional interface designed for an earlier era.

If lifelong learning is to be more than rhetoric, institutions must treat navigation itself as a pedagogical problem. In a Learning Republic, access means more than availability. It means intelligibility.

Categorization Before Arrival

Long before a child opens a book or meets a teacher, categorization has already begun. In the United States, racial and ethnic classification is commonly recorded at birth as part of standard vital statistics systems, embedding ascribed categories into the earliest administrative story told about a person. The civic rationale for such categorization is familiar—tracking inequities, monitoring compliance, and enforcing civil-rights protections—but the educational danger is just as real. As discussed in Section One, practices adopted with the stated intention of helping society can nonetheless entrench the very conditions they aim to remedy. When racial categories become administratively primary and socially salient, they risk stabilizing group-based expectations, narratives, and institutional responses in ways that perpetuate inequality rather than resolve it.

In education, this dynamic is especially corrosive. Categories designed to diagnose disparity can quietly become explanatory shortcuts, shaping expectations before evidence is available. Over time, the category itself begins to do causal work in the system: influencing placement decisions, interpretations of behavior, and judgments about potential. What begins as a tool for accountability can evolve into a mechanism of prediction—and prediction, when detached from individual evidence, hardens into destiny.

This dynamic also sustains political marketplaces that depend on the persistence of the problem. When social categories are treated as fixed explanatory variables, they generate constituencies, funding streams, institutional roles, and ideological commitments organized around managing disparity rather than eliminating its structural causes. In such systems, the continued visibility of the problem becomes functional. The incentive to resolve it competes with incentives to administer, narrate, and mobilize around it.

When racial categories become the primary lens through which we observe one another, they do not merely describe difference; they actively shape institutional judgment, hardening expectations that can perpetuate inequality under the guise of measurement—and, at times, under the language of equity itself. Over time, practices introduced to address injustice can become embedded in administrative routines, producing systems more adept at managing disparity than eliminating its root causes.

A Learning Republic must therefore confront an uncomfortable possibility: that some practices intended to advance justice may, through their long-term cognitive and institutional effects, slow the very progress they seek to achieve. This does not require denying historical injustice or abandoning civil-rights enforcement. It requires recognizing that durable learning—individual and civic—depends on environments that foreground evidence, growth, and personhood over inherited classification. When categories precede encounter, they constrain not only learners, but the imagination of the institutions that serve them.

This form of barrier operates before instruction and often beneath conscious awareness. Teachers may sincerely endorse equal treatment while still carrying culturally absorbed associations that shape day-to-day judgments—who is called on, who receives elaborated feedback, who is presumed "bright," and whose errors are treated as evidence of limits rather than of a moment in learning. A large empirical literature shows that teacher expectations are not neutral: they vary systematically, and differences in background between teachers and students can shape expectations—even when the same student is evaluated by different teachers. Parallel research shows that implicit bias can influence how behaviors are interpreted and disciplined, with downstream effects on classroom belonging and opportunity to learn. Peers quickly learn these cues as well: they infer who is "supposed" to excel and who is "supposed" to struggle, and those expectations harden into classroom social reality.

The cognitive consequences are subtle but severe. When identity is under evaluation, attention is diverted; working memory is spent monitoring risk, managing impressions, and protecting self-worth. Social psychology has repeatedly demonstrated that when students fear confirming a negative group stereotype in a high-stakes academic setting, their performance can drop—not because of lower ability, but because the situation imposes an extra cognitive and affective load. Du Bois (1903) described the internal experience of living under such evaluation as a "double consciousness"—a condition of seeing oneself through the eyes of a society that devalues one's group. Read educationally, this is not merely a poetic metaphor. It is a description of how identity management becomes a constant secondary task, siphoning resources from the primary task of learning.

Woodson (1933) pressed the critique further by arguing that schooling can become a vehicle for transmitting the dominant society's assumptions—so that even well-intentioned instruction carries "bias" and "prejudices" in content, framing, and expectations. While Woodson's *Mis-Education* was aimed at the systemic deformation of Black education, its relevance here is broader: when students are treated as representatives of a category before they are known as persons, the environment risks becoming less a site of discovery than of social sorting. In modern terms, the label becomes a filter through which evidence is interpreted. The child is "read" before the child is understood.

Jarvis gives this phenomenon a complementary language. His concept of *disjuncture*—the felt mismatch between lived experience and one's existing meaning structures—helps explain why pre-categorization can become educationally corrosive. If a learner's experience of school is repeatedly shaped by signals of diminished expectation or conditional belonging, the disjuncture is not simply academic ("I don't understand this yet") but existential ("this may not be for someone like me"). When that happens, avoidance can become an adaptive self-protection strategy rather than a sign of indifference—precisely the sort of barrier that is misdiagnosed as "motivation." (Jarvis, 1987; 1992; 2006).

Even voices that disagree sharply about the causes of group differences tend to converge on a practical warning: institutions should not treat racial categories as destiny. Thomas Sowell, for example, has argued—often controversially—that explanations rooted in culture, incentives, and institutional performance are more useful than explanations that naturalize group outcomes. His advocacy for evaluating what schools *do* (and what designs work) rather than treating disparities as fixed is consistent with the narrower thesis here: categorical stories can become excuses—either to stigmatize learners or to absolve institutions of responsibility. Booker T. Washington, in his time, insisted on the dignity and agency of learners in the face of prejudice, repeatedly emphasizing the destructive effects of racial animus and the necessity of building conditions where capability can be demonstrated rather than presumed absent. His point is clear: a just learning environment is one in which individuals are given room to become visible as individuals.

The tragedy is that these labels precede evidence. Before the teacher knows the child's curiosity, persistence, humor, or kindness—before classmates know anything at all—the learning environment has already been shaped. The barrier is not located in the child. It is embedded in our society—within the democratic institutions, norms, and practices through which schooling is organized and governed. Expectation effects, interpretive bias, stereotype threat, and differential discipline operate not as individual moral failures, but as structural mechanisms by which an ascribed category can become an academic constraint. Because these mechanisms are socially produced, they are also socially alterable.

In a Learning Republic, this distinction matters. Barriers that are treated as natural or personal invite resignation; barriers that are recognized as institutional invite responsibility. Pre-categorization is therefore not merely unjust; it is inefficient. It wastes human potential by imposing cognitive taxes on some learners that others never have to pay, reducing the total learning capacity of the citizenry. A democracy that depends on informed, adaptive citizens cannot afford to squander learning through avoidable design choices.

To recognize that these barriers are embedded in democratic practice is also to acknowledge democratic agency. What has been built can be rebuilt. If learning is the operating system of self-government, then removing such barriers is not an act of charity—it is an act of civic maintenance.

Removing this barrier requires more than goodwill. It requires institutional awareness, structural redesign, and deliberate countersignals that restore the learner's right to be known before being judged. That does not mean pretending race is irrelevant or abandoning civil-rights data. It means refusing to let administrative categories become pedagogical destiny— designing classrooms, routines, and decision processes so that expectation, evaluation, and belonging are anchored in evidence of learning rather than inherited scripts.

The Cognitive Reality of High-Poverty Classrooms

Paul Gibson's work with teachers in high-poverty schools forces an uncomfortable but essential recognition: for many children, the classroom is not the primary site of cognitive demand they face each day. It is merely one demand layered atop many others.

In *Thanking Teachers Working in High-Poverty Schools*, Gibson does not frame the challenge as one of inadequate pedagogy or insufficient effort. Instead, he situates learning within the lived cognitive ecology of the child. Hunger, fatigue, fear, and instability are not peripheral distractions; they are dominant loads on working memory. A child who arrives at school after a night of disrupted sleep, who has not eaten breakfast, or who

is still processing the arrest of a parent hours earlier is already operating near—or beyond—the limits of cognitive capacity before the lesson begins.

This reality was understood long before modern cognitive science provided its vocabulary. W. E. B. Du Bois wrote extensively about the psychic and attentional toll imposed by poverty and social marginalization, arguing that material deprivation and social stress distort not only opportunity but consciousness itself (Du Bois, 1903). His concept of *double consciousness* captures an early recognition that sustained environmental pressure fragments attention and diverts cognitive energy toward survival and self-monitoring—conditions fundamentally hostile to learning.

From the outside, such a child may appear inattentive, unmotivated, or defiant. From the inside, the experience is very different. Cognitive bandwidth is finite. When survival concerns dominate attention, there is little capacity left for abstraction, symbolic manipulation, or sustained concentration. What the teacher experiences as disengagement is, in many cases, a rational triage decision by the mind.

Booker T. Washington, often mischaracterized as dismissive of academic learning, was in fact acutely aware of this constraint. His insistence on addressing material stability—food, shelter, routine, and work—was grounded in the belief that intellectual development requires a foundation of security (Washington, 1901). Whatever one makes of his broader program, Washington recognized a principle now confirmed by cognitive science: learning presupposes conditions that allow attention to be spared from survival.

Carter Woodson sharpened this critique by arguing that schools serving impoverished communities frequently mistake the effects of deprivation for evidence of intellectual deficiency. In *The Mis-Education of the Negro*, Woodson warned that when schools ignore students' lived realities, they risk interpreting cognitive overload as incapacity and disengagement as indifference (Woodson, 1933). In modern terms, Woodson anticipated what Gibson documents empirically: the misdiagnosis of context as character.

Peter Jarvis's theory of *disjuncture* provides a powerful explanatory bridge between these historical insights and contemporary cognitive theory. When children experience a persistent mismatch between the demands of schooling and the realities of their lives, learning is no longer merely difficult—it becomes threatening. Disengagement, in Jarvis's framework, is not a lack of motivation but an adaptive response to repeated disruption without sufficient support (Jarvis, 1987; 1992; 2006). In high-poverty classrooms, disjuncture is not episodic; it is chronic.

Thomas Sowell, though writing from a very different intellectual tradition, reinforces a complementary warning. Sowell has repeatedly argued that institutions err when they treat outcomes divorced from context, mistaking environmental constraints for evidence of innate limitation (Sowell, 1981; 1994). His critique of "cosmic justice" is not a denial of inequality, but a caution against analytic shortcuts that obscure causation. Applied here, the lesson is straightforward: educational systems that ignore cognitive load imposed by poverty risk building policies on false diagnoses.

George F. Will has similarly warned against moralizing structural conditions. While often critical of bureaucratic solutions, Will has emphasized that responsibility and agency cannot be meaningfully exercised where institutions ignore the realities shaping human behavior (Will, 1983; 2019). In education, this means that exhortations to effort ring hollow when learners are cognitively depleted before instruction begins.

Gibson's contribution is therefore not merely descriptive; it is moral. By thanking teachers who persist in these environments, he reframes teaching as cognitive caregiving. These teachers are not merely transmitting content—they are attempting to create temporary islands of psychological safety in which learning can occur at all. The barrier here is not intelligence. It is not effort. It is context.

This has profound implications for how societies interpret educational outcomes. When standardized assessments or classroom behaviors are used to infer ability or potential, they often measure exposure to adversity more than aptitude. A Learning Republic must therefore reject narratives that pathologize children for conditions they did not choose and cannot control. If learning is to be possible, cognitive load must be reduced before instruction can be effective.

At the same time, learning is not something that can be engineered from a distance. However, sophisticated our measurements, children are not abstractions, and learning remains grounded in the lived conditions of daily life—hunger, sleep, safety, stability, and belonging (Maslow, 1943; Mani et al., 2013). Federal policy can set broad protections and incentives, but it cannot ensure that a child arrives at school rested, fed, and emotionally supported (Dee & Jacob, 2011; NCES, 2023). These themes—categorization, civic trust, and the limits of centralized solutions—will be treated in fuller historical and institutional detail in Chapter One as part of the broader argument that a learning republic depends on how communities recognize learners as individuals and cultivate the civic conditions under which learning can take root.

Research on teachers in high-poverty schools underscores a basic reality: children cannot learn when hunger, exhaustion, and instability overwhelm their capacity to attend, reflect, and engage (Gibson, 2024; Maslach & Leiter, 2016; Jensen, 2009). These conditions are shaped by families, neighborhoods, congregations, employers, and local institutions long before a student enters the classroom. However sophisticated policy becomes, learning remains grounded in the lived circumstances of daily life.

For this reason, the work of preparing children to learn cannot be accomplished through federal programs alone. Partnerships among schools, civic groups, and faith-based organizations—institutions embedded in local communities— are uniquely positioned to recognize and respond to basic human needs in ways no centralized system can replicate. National policy can establish protections, incentives, and large-scale investments, but it cannot ensure that a child arrives at school fed, rested, safe, and supported. That work belongs primarily to families, and secondarily to the communities and community organizations that surround and support them.

Recognizing the limits of centralized authority does not diminish the vital role of the national government. Some of the most consequential expansions of learning opportunity in American history—the Northwest Ordinance, vocational education legislation, and the G.I. Bill—required federal action to mobilize resources at scale. Yet even these successes depended on local institutions to translate national investment into lived educational outcomes. A healthy republic relies on this division of labor: national government sets conditions for opportunity, while citizens and communities do most of the work of sustaining learning.

Across American history, major shifts in educational *need* have followed technological revolutions rather than political cycles, requiring repeated reinvestment in the learning capacity of ordinary citizens (Goldin & Katz, 2008; Labaree, 2010). The technologies change, but the civic purpose of education does not. A learning republic must continually cultivate character, competence, and common purpose across all ages and abilities.

Barriers to learning—whether cognitive, dispositional, structural, material, institutional, or cultural—represent more than individual hurdles; they are systemic vulnerabilities that undermine the foundational promise of a learning republic. As this chapter has explored, these constraints often stem from environments misaligned with human cognition, legacies of historical compromises like the census categories rooted in slavery, and modern disruptions such as technology's erosion of sustained attention. From Sherry Turkle's observations of fragmented focus in digital spaces to Paul Gibson's insights into the cognitive overload faced by students and teachers in high-poverty schools, the evidence is clear: learning falters not due to inherent deficiencies in individuals, but because of designs that saturate working memory, perpetuate stereotypes, or neglect basic human needs like stability, nutrition, and safety.

The implications extend far beyond the classroom. In a constitutional self-governing society, where informed judgment and adaptive capacity sustain democracy, unaddressed barriers erode civic resilience. W. E. B. Du Bois's double consciousness, Booker T. Washington's emphasis on material foundations, Carter G. Woodson's critique of mis-education, and contemporary voices like Thomas Sowell and George F. Will remind us that ignoring these dynamics risks misdiagnosing context as character, perpetuating cycles of exclusion and inefficiency. When racial or socioeconomic labels precede evidence of potential, or when chronic stress diverts attention from growth, the republic loses not just talent but trust—weakening the shared commitment to self-government.

Yet these barriers are not immutable. They are alterable through deliberate redesign: reducing cognitive load with supportive environments, fostering local partnerships among schools, communities, and faith-based organizations to address material needs, and prioritizing evidence-based interventions like early childhood programs that yield long-term civic and economic returns. Peter Jarvis's theory of disjuncture underscores the need for learning systems that bridge life realities with educational demands, while cognitive science offers practical tools—such as schema-building and overload mitigation—to make instruction more accessible.

Ultimately, a learning republic thrives when barriers are dismantled not through centralized mandates alone, but through a balanced division of labor: national investments in equity and access complemented by community-driven efforts to cultivate attention, agency, and belonging. By recognizing learning as an interaction between mind and context, we affirm its role in sustaining individuals and democracy. As technological and social changes accelerate, overcoming these constraints is not optional—it is essential to renewing the republic's capacity for adaptation, justice, and civic vitality. The work begins with seeing barriers not as fate, but as invitations to build better.

Case Study: Overcoming Barriers to Learning

Few examples in American history demonstrate the power of learning to overcome barriers more clearly than the experience of African Americans from slavery through the twentieth century. Denied education by law, excluded by custom, and often opposed by violence, they nevertheless built traditions of learning that sustained communities, nurtured civic responsibility, and carried forward across generations.

Faith and Meaning Under Slavery

The enslaved Africans who encountered Christianity in America were rarely persuaded by the example of the slaveholder. The conduct of the "master's religion" often stood in stark contradiction to the teachings it professed. Yet within the biblical story they encountered something different. As writer Joe Carter has observed, many enslaved people were drawn not to the behavior of those who claimed the faith, but to the figure at its center. The story of Jesus Christ—a man unjustly persecuted, beaten, humiliated, and executed—spoke directly to their own experience of suffering.

If this man truly was the Son of the Most High God, they reasoned, then he understood their suffering. And if he understood their suffering, perhaps he would hear their prayers.

They believed. They prayed. Help came—Lincoln, Emancipation, Citizenship.

History unfolded slowly, but events moved in ways that eventually transformed their circumstances. The crisis of the Civil War brought the nation to a reckoning with slavery. Under the leadership of Abraham Lincoln, the Union government issued the Emancipation Proclamation, and in the years that followed the Thirteenth Amendment to the United States Constitution abolished slavery while the Fourteenth Amendment to the United States Constitution affirmed citizenship.

Freedom did not bring equality, security, or acceptance. But it brought something profoundly important: agency. The responsibility for rebuilding life now rested largely in the hands of those who had once been denied even the right to read.

They rose to challenge.

Literacy as the Path to Opportunity

Among those who articulated the connection between learning and freedom most powerfully was Frederick Douglass. Born into slavery and largely self-educated, Douglass described literacy as the turning point in his life. Once he learned to read, he later wrote, he had discovered "the pathway from slavery to freedom."

For Douglass and many others, education was not merely a means of personal advancement. It was the cultivation of intellectual independence, moral judgment, and the capacity to participate fully in civic life. Literacy opened access to ideas, laws, history, and the language of citizenship. It allowed individuals not only to navigate the world around them but also to question and reshape it.

The pursuit of learning therefore became one of the most powerful acts of resistance available to those emerging from slavery. Across the South, newly freed people sought education with remarkable determination, establishing schools and teaching one another whenever formal institutions were absent.

Building Institutions of Learning

The commitment to learning quickly translated into institution-building. Churches became centers of education as well as worship. Congregations raised funds to hire teachers and construct schoolhouses. Mutual aid societies provided support for students and families. Colleges founded during the Reconstruction era would later educate generations of leaders.

Among the most influential figures in this movement was Booker T. Washington, founder of Tuskegee Institute. Washington emphasized the integration of education with practical skill, discipline, and character formation. In his view, learning should equip individuals not only for employment but also for responsible citizenship and community leadership.

Churches, schools, and fraternal organizations reinforced these values. Together they created networks of support that helped families navigate a society that frequently denied them opportunity. Despite segregation, discrimination, and periodic violence, these institutions cultivated traditions of dignity, work, and mutual responsibility that would shape communities for generations.

Migration and Urban Community

Beginning in the early twentieth century, millions of African Americans left the rural South in search of opportunity in northern and midwestern cities. This movement, known as the Great Migration, transformed the demographic and cultural landscape of the United States.

Migrants carried more than their labor with them. They brought churches, social organizations, educational aspirations, and deeply rooted expectations about personal conduct and community responsibility. In cities such as Chicago, Detroit, and Cleveland, these traditions helped shape new urban neighborhoods.

Many of these neighborhoods were formed not by voluntary separation but by exclusion. Housing discrimination and restrictive covenants confined Black families to specific districts. The term "ghetto," originally used in Europe to describe the quarters where Jews were required to live, came to be applied to these American neighborhoods as well. Yet, as in the original European ghettos, the residents did not create the boundaries that confined them.

Within those boundaries, however, communities developed institutions, norms, and networks of support that sustained social life. Within those boundaries, communities flourished in ways that outsiders often failed to see.

Respectability and Mentorship

A vivid portrait of this moral world appears in Slim's Table: Race, Respectability, and Masculinity, the ethnographic study by sociologist Mitchell Duneier. Spending several years observing a group of working-class Black men who gathered regularly at a cafeteria on Chicago's South Side, Duneier documented a community sustained by shared expectations of responsibility and respect.

At what the regulars informally called "Slim's table," older men advised younger ones, disputes were quietly mediated, and community standards were reinforced through everyday conversation. The men valued work, self-respect, and proper conduct. They expected younger men to behave with dignity, to treat women respectfully, and to contribute positively to the neighborhood.

Equally important was the sense of obligation toward elders. Younger men often checked on older residents who had no remaining family, ensuring that they had food, companionship, and assistance when needed. These acts of care were rarely formalized, and rarely visible to outsiders, but were widely understood as part of the moral fabric of the community.

Residents who remembered earlier decades often contrasted that earlier neighborhood life with later changes that began to unfold in the second half of the twentieth century. Factories closed. Industrial jobs disappeared. At the same time, the policy environment surrounding poverty shifted dramatically during the era of the 1960s. Economic restructuring and government programs alike altered the conditions under which families and communities attempted to sustain the moral and social traditions that had long guided them.

The resulting changes were complex and are still debated today. Deindustrialization alone cannot explain the transformation of many urban neighborhoods, yet the disappearance of stable employment undeniably weakened one of the central pillars of community life. At the same time, some observers—including older residents themselves—worried that systems of assistance sometimes unintentionally discouraged the very habits of work and responsibility that earlier generations had struggled so hard to build.

What remains unmistakable in Duneier's account, however, is the strength of the moral vision that preceded these disruptions. The men at Slim's table were heirs to a long tradition shaped by faith, hardship, and perseverance—a tradition in which learning, work, and mutual responsibility were understood not merely as personal virtues but as essential foundations for the health of the community.

When viewed across generations, a clear continuity emerges. The insistence by Frederick Douglass that learning opened the path to freedom, the emphasis by Booker T. Washington on work and education, and the everyday expectations of responsibility observed decades later at Slim's table are not isolated historical episodes. They represent successive expressions of a cultural inheritance rooted in faith, learning, and the conviction that personal dignity and community responsibility must be cultivated deliberately if freedom is to endure.

The story of these communities illustrates a central lesson for any learning society: even in the presence of formidable barriers, traditions of learning and responsibility can survive—carried forward not only through formal institutions but also through the daily practices of ordinary people who understand that the health of a community depends on the character of its members.

Conclusion

This chapter has laid bare a hard truth: learning does not fail because people are broken or unwilling. It fails because the environments we build around it too often ignore the realities of human minds, bodies, and lives. From the quiet erosion of sustained attention in a world of constant notifications (Turkle), to the crushing cognitive load carried by hungry, exhausted children in under-resourced classrooms (Gibson), to the lingering weight of administrative categories born in an era of slavery, the barriers are real—and they compound. When working memory is already saturated by survival, when early hope is starved and neural foundations left underdeveloped (Wang et al., 2020), when institutions sort rather than scaffold, and when technology fragments rather than focuses, learning becomes harder than it needs to be. The result is not just individual struggle; it is civic fragility—a republic less able to renew itself through informed, adaptive citizens.

Yet none of these barriers is inevitable. They are not fate. They are design choices—some inherited, some accidental, many simply unexamined. The same cognitive science that reveals the limits of working memory also shows us how to reduce unnecessary load: clearer goals, fewer distractions, positive incentives, time for recovery, and feedback that builds rather than shames. The same historical record that exposes the damage of rigid categorization also points toward redesign: stop measuring citizens primarily as group members and start seeing them as individuals with unique potential. The same research that links early hope to stronger brain architecture also reminds us that investment in childhood—stability, encouragement, agency, and possibility—pays dividends across a lifetime.

A learning republic does not pretend barriers do not exist. It refuses to accept them as permanent. It recognizes that schools alone cannot solve hunger, trauma, or fractured attention— but that schools, families, congregations, civic groups, and local leaders working together can. National policy can set the guardrails and provide resources, but the daily work of removing obstacles belongs to communities that know their people by name. When we treat access as more than availability—when we make it intelligible, recoverable, and human-centered—we do not merely help individuals learn. We strengthen the shared capacity that keeps a self-governing society alive.

The barriers described here are serious, but they are alterable. The invitation is clear: see them not as proof of human limitation, but as evidence of where we have room to build better. A republic that learns how to lower unnecessary burdens, restore hope early, and design for real human lives is not a utopia. It is a practical, achievable renewal—one worthy of the name we claim.

Chapter Ten: Lifelong Learning as a Civic Duty

Sustaining Competence, Judgment, and Self-Government

It is 1817 in Virginia. The Revolutionary War lies decades in the past, yet Thomas Jefferson—now an aging statesman—walks the grounds of Monticello not in celebration of victory, but in quiet concern for the future. Independence, he believed, was never secured once and for all by muskets or declarations. It had to be renewed by every generation through learning and sustained vigilance.

The experiment in self-government rested on a fragile premise: that the people themselves—who together constituted the sovereign authority of the nation—would remain capable of disciplined judgment.

In 1816, writing to Charles Yancey, Jefferson warned plainly, "If a nation expects to be ignorant and free, in a state of civilization, it expects what never was and never will be." Liberty, in his view, was not sustained by sentiment but by knowledge. Ignorance, to Jefferson, was not merely a personal shortcoming; it was a political danger.

Three decades earlier, in a letter to Edward Carrington, he had expressed the same conviction in sharper contrast: "Were it left to me to decide whether we should have a government without newspapers, or newspapers without a government, I should not hesitate a moment to prefer the latter." The statement was not a rejection of government, but a declaration of priority. The basis of republican government, he insisted, was "the opinion

of the people." Without informed opinion, institutional design could not endure.

Jefferson's reasoning echoes the earlier distinction drawn by Thomas Paine in *Common Sense*. For both thinkers, the vitality of society precedes the legitimacy of political authority. Government exists to secure order and protect rights, but it derives its authority from the judgment of the people. An informed citizenry is therefore not a luxury; it is the condition that makes self-government possible. Jefferson's preference for "newspapers without a government" underscores a priority claim: public opinion, formed through access to information, is the foundation upon which republican institutions rest. Without that foundation, even a well-constructed government becomes unstable.

Years earlier, Jefferson had drafted *A Bill for the More General Diffusion of Knowledge*, proposing a system of publicly supported primary schools in every county, open to all free children regardless of wealth or status (Jefferson, 1779). The Virginia legislature rejected the plan. But Jefferson never abandoned the principle behind it.

This vision marked a decisive shift from the informal learning circles of Franklin's Philadelphia toward a more systematic conception of civic education. Where Franklin's Junto cultivated self-improvement among engaged adults, Jefferson sought to embed learning into the republic's very structure. Education, in his view, was neither a private luxury nor a charitable endeavor. It was a public necessity. A self-governing people could remain free only if they possessed the knowledge required to judge leaders, laws, and events for themselves.

Schooling in the early republic remained fragmented—dependent on churches, tutors, and family resources—but Jefferson's insistence that the state bore responsibility for educating its citizens planted a durable seed. That seed would not fully flower in his lifetime. Still, it shaped the trajectory of American education in lasting ways. Jefferson regarded the founding of the University of Virginia in 1819 as one of his greatest achievements, not because it served elites, but because it embodied his belief that knowledge should be organized, secular, and oriented toward public life (Peterson, 1960).

Standing on the hills of Virginia, Jefferson envisioned a republic sustained not by inherited authority or aristocratic habit, but by informed citizens capable of renewing freedom through reasoned judgment. Learning, for Jefferson, was not merely preparation for life in a republic. It was the condition that made republican life possible at all.

The Recurring Logic of a Learning Republic

Across these eras runs a continuous thread. Whenever America has invested seriously in the learning capacity of ordinary people—through settlement houses, land-grant colleges, the G.I. Bill, community colleges, online programs, or early childhood initiatives—the nation has expanded its economic resilience and civic vitality. When it has withheld education—through slavery, caste, underfunded schools, or rigid bureaucratic systems—it has paid a high price in stagnation, conflict, and wasted talent.

Today, we possess technologies that can make learning opportunities available to anyone with an internet-connected device and the determination to use it. We also possess a growing body of scientific knowledge about how learning unfolds across the lifespan and how cognitive load can be managed. But tools and theories are not enough. The deeper challenge is whether we will design educational systems—formal and informal—that respect the realities of human development, remove unnecessary barriers, and extend meaningful opportunities for growth to people at every stage of life.

The story of American education is not simply a record of schools and policies. It is a centuries-long attempt to keep pace with the speed of our own inventions and to extend the fruits of knowledge to each new generation. Understanding that story is the first step toward building a society in which lifelong learning is not a slogan but a lived reality.

American history offers many examples of learning that unfolded not through formal schooling, but through disciplined adult practice embedded in work and community. Figures as different as Samuel Gompers, who defended skill and worker education against *industrial deskilling*—the breakdown of skilled labor into simplified, machine-directed tasks that transferred judgment from workers to managers and machines, weakening apprenticeship, autonomy, and economic leverage; Andrew Carnegie, whose public libraries reflected both the promise and the limits of self-improvement through access to knowledge alone; James Naismith, who designed learning environments that emphasized restraint, cooperation, and character formation rather than mere competition; Vince Lombardi, who framed excellence not as innate talent but as continual refinement through disciplined practice; and Frank Lloyd Wright, who treated architecture as a lifelong craft rather than a completed credential—*across paths that ranged from formal higher education to apprenticeship and self-directed mastery*—all illustrate a common truth: meaningful learning in adulthood is sustained by standards, purpose, and practice. These examples matter not because of fame, but because they reveal how learning persists when it is tied to identity, work, and shared norms.

Learning as the Operating System of Self-Government

Imagine a republic not as a static structure secured once and for all by constitutions or courts, but as a living system—one that depends on the continuous exchange of knowledge, reflection, and adaptation among its citizens. Laws may define the framework of governance, but they cannot govern themselves. What sustains democratic life is the ongoing capacity of citizens to understand new conditions, revise beliefs, and act with discernment. Each individual, through self-directed inquiry, becomes a node of thought and agency within this civic network. When learning stagnates, the network weakens. When learning thrives, democracy renews itself.

This chapter argues that learning—not schooling, not credentials, not mere access to education—is the operating system of self-government. Education can be provided; learning must be claimed. In the industrial age, a fixed credential such as a high school diploma could plausibly support a lifetime of work and civic participation, in part because technology, institutions, and social roles changed at a comparatively slow and predictable pace. That stability has vanished. What sustains a democratic society today is not the transmission of information alone, but the ability of citizens to transform information into understanding under conditions of change.

This insight was anticipated long before the digital age. Alfred North Whitehead warned in 1929 that "the cycle of new knowledge now outpaces the span of human life." His concern was not merely pedagogical, but civic. In a world where facts age and paradigms shift, the health of a republic depends on citizens who can update their own mental models—who can learn, unlearn, and relearn as conditions evolve. Learning, in this sense, is not preparation for civic life; it is the mechanism by which civic life remains possible.

For this reason, lifelong learning cannot be treated as a private virtue or an optional enrichment. It is a civic necessity. Thomas Jefferson understood this when he warned that a nation could not be both ignorant and free. John Dewey extended the argument, insisting that democracy "has to be born anew every generation," with education as its midwife. In the twenty-first century, learning no longer merely assists that birth; it sustains the entire system. It is the operating logic by which democratic self-government continues to function under pressure.

This reframing also clarifies the limits of schooling alone. Formal education plays an indispensable role in establishing foundations, but it cannot carry the full burden of civic competence. A learning republic depends first on the strength of its childhood education, which lays the cognitive, moral, and civic foundations upon which all later learning is built. However, it does not depend solely on early schooling. Its long-term vitality rests on whether citizens continue to learn—deliberately, humbly, and persistently—across the lifespan. When learning becomes episodic or is deferred entirely to institutions, self-government weakens. When it becomes continuous, distributed, and self-directed, democratic capacity expands.

In a networked world where information and complexity routinely overwhelm judgment, citizens no longer encounter politics episodically, but continuously. Each individual now navigates a persistent referendum on what to believe, whom to trust, and how to act—often without the stabilizing presence of intermediaries. Under these conditions, learning is not optional or ornamental; it is the ongoing work that keeps civic judgment functional. The question facing our republic is therefore not whether education matters, but whether the capacity to learn, revise, and recalibrate understanding is being actively sustained—or steadily eroded.

If self-government is to endure under conditions of constant change, learning cannot be episodic. It must be continuous.

Childhood is the Foundation—Adulthood is the Load-Bearing Structure

A learning republic depends deeply on how well it cares for and educates its children—not because childhood determines destiny, but because it establishes the initial conditions under which learning becomes possible or prohibitively costly. Early childhood and K–12 schooling shape far more than academic skills. They calibrate expectations about effort, trust, authority, and the emotional safety of thinking itself. As Gibson's work with teachers serving children in extreme poverty makes clear, many learning difficulties observed later in life are not failures of intelligence or motivation, but adaptive responses to environments in which cognitive effort was repeatedly punished, interrupted, or rendered futile. In such contexts, avoidance is not apathy; it is protection.

Children raised amid chronic stress—hunger, instability, exposure to violence, or persistent uncertainty—enter classrooms with severely constrained cognitive bandwidth. Gibson documents how teachers in these environments routinely confront students whose working memory is already saturated before instruction begins. Hunger, sleep deprivation, fear, and unresolved trauma function as a continuous background load, leaving little capacity for abstraction, sustained attention, or error-tolerant exploration. When instruction proceeds as if this load does not exist, difficulty is misinterpreted as defiance, slowness as laziness, and withdrawal as lack of interest. Over time, students learn a powerful lesson: that intellectual engagement carries emotional risk with little prospect of reward.

The most enduring consequence of such early experiences is not gaps in content knowledge, but the formation of dispositional expectations about learning itself. Repeated exposure to cognitive overload without recovery trains the mind to disengage preemptively. Gibson's observations align with cognitive load theory's central insight: when working memory is overwhelmed too often, learners do not simply fail—they adapt by avoiding effortful cognition altogether. This adaptation may preserve self-worth in the short term, but it exacts a long-term civic cost. A citizen who has learned, implicitly, that thinking is unsafe or humiliating will approach later learning opportunities—no matter how well intentioned—with suspicion or quiet resistance.

Yet childhood, however formative, is not fate. A learning republic does not assume that early disadvantage permanently disqualifies individuals from civic competence. Rather, it recognizes that adults who were denied stable learning conditions in childhood will require learning environments explicitly designed for recovery. This is where the civic obligation shifts decisively from schooling children to sustaining adults. Adult education, workforce training, community colleges, libraries, and online learning platforms become not remedial afterthoughts, but structural supports that restore learning capacity over time. They offer what early environments often could not: predictable structure, psychological safety, respect for prior experience, and opportunities to rebuild confidence through manageable success.

In this sense, childhood education lays the foundation, but adulthood bears the load. The survival of a republic depends not only on how well it prepares children, but on whether it provides adults with repeated, dignified chances to relearn how to learn. When societies neglect this responsibility, early inequities calcify into permanent civic stratification. When they embrace it, learning becomes a lifelong process of recovery and renewal—one that allows citizens to reenter the shared work of self-government regardless of where they began.

Beyond the Myth of Completion

Industrial modernity introduced a powerful organizing convenience: the segmentation of life into stages. Childhood became preparation. Midlife became productivity. Later life became retirement. These divisions brought administrative clarity and economic efficiency. They enabled pension systems, workforce planning, and institutional stability.

But they also fostered a subtle misconception: that learning belongs primarily to youth and productivity to midlife.

Just as mass schooling linked education to childhood in the public imagination, industrialization linked contribution to a bounded span of working years. The result has been a cultural narrative of completion. One finishes school. One finishes a career. One enters retirement.

Biology does not recognize this script.

Cognitive development research demonstrates that while certain forms of fluid processing may gradually decline with age, crystallized intelligence—the accumulated structure of knowledge, pattern recognition, and judgment—often strengthens across decades. Neuroplasticity does not vanish in later life. Expertise deepens. Perspective widens. Schemas become more richly interconnected. For many domains of civic life—mentorship, governance, institutional memory, ethical reasoning—these capacities are not incidental. They are central.

A republic that treats later adulthood as civic dormancy discards one of its most valuable resources: accumulated judgment.

Lifelong learning, therefore, is not merely remedial or recreational. It is the continued refinement of sovereignty. It is the maintenance of competence in a world that changes faster than any initial education can anticipate. It is the refusal to allow earlier achievement to fossilize into complacency.

Retirement from paid employment need not mean retirement from intellectual growth, mentorship, or civic engagement. Contribution evolves. Its forms change. But its necessity does not diminish. A learning republic requires not only prepared youth but engaged elders. The continuity of judgment across generations depends upon it.

The founders did not conceive of citizenship as a phase of life. They conceived of it as a permanent condition.

From Knowledge Worker to Knowledge Citizen

In 1959, Peter Drucker coined the term *knowledge worker* to describe a new kind of laborer whose primary capital was not physical strength or mechanical skill, but information, judgment, and the capacity to learn. For Drucker, learning was never merely an economic asset. It was a civic obligation. "The educated person," he wrote, "is the one who has learned how to learn—and to keep learning." Productivity in a modern society, he argued, would depend less on obedience to procedure than on the ability to adapt, collaborate, and think critically in the face of change (Drucker, 1959).

As automation and organizational complexity reshaped the workforce, Drucker warned that societies that failed to educate continuously would face not only economic stagnation but moral decline. His model of *management by objectives* assumed workers were capable of understanding goals, exercising judgment, and coordinating their efforts with others. These were not narrow technical skills; they were civic virtues. A workforce incapable of self-direction, Drucker understood, would ultimately require coercion or paternalism. In this sense, the knowledge worker was always a political figure as well as an economic one.

The twenty-first century, however, has exposed the limits of that original formulation. Knowledge work has not disappeared, but it has become inseparable from citizenship itself. Modern democracies now require *knowledge citizens*—individuals capable not only of performing cognitively demanding labor, but of evaluating claims, discerning reliable information from noise, and participating in reasoning about public problems. Citizens are asked to weigh competing interpretations of scientific data, economic tradeoffs, and policy outcomes in environments saturated with information and increasingly shaped by algorithmic mediation. What confronts them is not merely complexity, but deliberate misinformation crafted to fracture trust and weaken self-governance.

This shift marks a critical escalation of responsibility. Where the knowledge worker applied judgment primarily within organizational contexts, the knowledge citizen must apply judgment continuously in civic life. Voting, jury service, professional practice, parenting, and community participation now demand interpretive skills once reserved for specialists. Without widespread lifelong learning, these capacities concentrate in elites—technical, bureaucratic, or ideological—and democracy decays into technocracy on one side and resentment on the other. Self-government cannot survive such asymmetry for long.

In this environment, the most urgent form of knowledge work is civic work: learning how to live responsibly with complexity. Citizens must interpret data dashboards, evaluate probabilistic claims about climate or medicine, recognize manipulation in media ecosystems, and revise beliefs in light of new evidence. These tasks cannot be automated away without surrendering judgment itself. Artificial intelligence may assist by extending perception and analysis, but it cannot replace the moral work of deciding what ought to be done. That work remains irreducibly human.

A learning republic, therefore, requires more than public investment in accessible education, essential as that is. It also requires cultural investment in curiosity, humility, and open discourse—the dispositions that allow learning to continue under conditions of disagreement. Karl Popper argued that a free society depends on citizens capable of critical judgment—able to test claims against reality, recognize error, and revise their understanding over time. That capacity cannot be delegated to institutions, credentials, or algorithms. It must be cultivated—again and again—by learners at every stage of life.

Seen in this light, the transition from knowledge worker to knowledge citizen represents not a departure from Drucker's vision, but its fulfillment. The challenge of the present moment is not simply to train workers for a changing economy, but to sustain citizens capable of governing themselves amid accelerating change. Lifelong learning is the bridge between those two tasks. Without it, productivity may persist for a time—but self-government will not.

Learning as Public Infrastructure

Like clean water, public roads, or electrical grids, learning must be understood as shared infrastructure—accessible, maintained, and equitably distributed—not because it guarantees equal outcomes, but because it sustains equal participation. A republic cannot rely on the private accumulation of learning any more than it can rely on private roads to support commerce or private wells to protect public health. When access to learning becomes fragmented, sporadic, or contingent on personal circumstance alone, the civic system itself becomes brittle. The result is not merely inequality of opportunity, but inequality of voice, judgment, and agency.

Seen in this light, policies that support libraries, open educational resources, community colleges, adult education, apprenticeships, and digital access are not ancillary social programs. They are investments in civic continuity. A population capable of renewing its understanding over time is more resilient than one dependent on static credentials or inherited knowledge. Just as infrastructure requires upkeep, learning systems require sustained attention to access, quality, and recovery. Neglect does not announce itself immediately; it accumulates quietly until failure becomes systemic.

From Jefferson's insistence on an educated citizenry to Whitehead's warning that the pace of new knowledge now outstrips the human lifespan, the central thread is continuity through change. Jefferson understood education as the foundation of liberty, essential for enabling citizens to judge laws and leaders for themselves. Whitehead recognized that in a world of accelerating discovery, learning could no longer be treated as a phase of life, but as a permanent condition. Both grasped the same civic truth: freedom demands mental vigilance. What changed was the scale of the demand. Where vigilance once required literacy and basic reasoning, it now requires the ability to evaluate competing claims, interpret data, and resist manipulation in environments saturated with information.

This expanded demand makes learning infrastructure more— not less—important. Individual motivation, however admirable, cannot compensate for systems that exhaust cognitive bandwidth or deny opportunities for recovery. A learning republic must therefore provide spaces where citizens can reengage learning after interruption, failure, or long absence. Libraries that serve as community learning hubs, online programs designed for working adults, and public institutions that respect prior experience while scaffolding new knowledge all contribute to this restorative function. They do not merely transmit information; they rebuild confidence, capacity, and trust in one's own ability to think.

The rise of online and hybrid learning should be understood in this same infrastructural frame. These models do not merely represent technological alternatives to campus-based education; they expand the republic's learning bandwidth. By decoupling learning from physical location and rigid schedules, scalable digital platforms make it possible for citizens to remain embedded in families, workplaces, and communities while continuing to learn. For working adults, caregivers, veterans, and mid-career professionals, this flexibility is not a convenience—it is the condition under which learning remains possible at all. When designed with attention to cognitive load, pacing, and support, online and hybrid environments can function as civic utilities: always available, adaptable to changing needs, and capable of supporting recovery after interruption.

At the same time, treating learning as infrastructure clarifies the responsibilities that accompany scale. Infrastructure that merely delivers content without regard to usability, reliability, or maintenance fails in its purpose. The same is true of learning systems. Platforms that overwhelm learners with information, fragment attention, or substitute automation for pedagogy risk reproducing the very failures they are meant to solve. The promise of scalable learning lies not in efficiency alone, but in the deliberate design of environments that respect human cognitive limits while extending opportunity across the lifespan. When learning is integrated into ongoing adult life rather than isolated within a brief residential interval, it becomes less susceptible to ideological capture and more tightly coupled to real-world accountability.

Recoverable Learning

Seen from this perspective, the policy question is not whether governments should "provide" lifelong learning in the abstract, but whether public institutions are aligning incentives to sustain learning capacity where it actually resides. Investment in broadband access, support for libraries and community colleges, recognition of prior learning, and partnerships that allow adults to combine work with study are best understood as measures that preserve civic competence rather than redistribute advantage. Such policies do not dictate what citizens must learn; they ensure that citizens retain the practical ability to learn at all. A republic that neglects these conditions risks creating formal freedoms without functional access to the means of judgment.

This infrastructural view also prepares the ground for a necessary comparison. Different learning environments shape civic development in different ways—not only through what they teach, but through how they situate learners within social life. To understand the future of a learning republic, it is therefore necessary to examine how scale, immersion, and identity interact across educational models, and how those interactions can either strengthen or strain the habits of self-government.

Crucially, scalable online and hybrid learning environments align directly with what this book has described as the Principle of Recoverable Learning. Recovery is not rest alone; it is the opportunity to reengage learning after overload, interruption, or failure under conditions that reduce unnecessary cognitive burden. Traditional, time-bound educational models often assume uninterrupted participation and penalize deviation, treating withdrawal as attrition rather than as a predictable feature of adult life. By contrast, well-designed online learning infrastructures allow learners to pause, return, recalibrate pace, and rebuild schemas over time. This capacity for reentry is not a secondary benefit—it is the core civic advantage of scalable learning systems. In a learning republic, recovery is not remediation for the few but a structural feature for the many, ensuring that citizens can resume learning as conditions change rather than being permanently excluded by earlier disruption.

The American experiment depends not only on the right to speak, but on the ability to think. That ability—critical, adaptive, and self-correcting—does not emerge spontaneously, nor is it sustained automatically. It arises within cultures that treat learning as a public good rather than a private luxury, and within institutions that recognize learning as a lifelong process rather than a youthful rite of passage. Each generation must therefore renew its educational covenant with the next, not only by teaching the skills of a trade, but by cultivating the habits of inquiry, skepticism, and self-education that allow citizens to revise beliefs, absorb change, and govern themselves under conditions of uncertainty.

In this sense, learning infrastructure is civic infrastructure. It is how a republic preserves continuity without stagnation, adaptability without chaos, and freedom without fragility. When learning is broadly accessible and recoverable across the lifespan, democracy retains the capacity to correct itself. When it is not, the republic becomes vulnerable—not first to external enemies, but to its own inability to understand the world it must govern.

When Learning Fails: Misinformation and Civic Breakdown

What confronts citizens of a modern republic is no longer merely the presence of competing opinions, but an informational environment in which error, distortion, and partial truths circulate with unprecedented speed and reach. A self-governing republic is a rare and historically fragile achievement, and it has always existed amid pressures—both external and internal—that test social trust and civic cohesion. When citizens who should regard one another as co-equals instead withdraw into antagonistic camps, they weaken the shared frameworks of understanding upon which self-government depends. Division, in this sense, is not simply a social inconvenience; it is a condition that leaves democratic institutions less resilient.

As Whittaker Chambers observed in Witness, the contest between truth and deception is never abstract. It unfolds within individual minds, across families, and through the institutions that bind a society together. From this perspective, learning is not merely a private pursuit of self-improvement, but a civic responsibility. The habits that sustain learning—questioning sources, tracing evidence, tolerating uncertainty, and revising beliefs in light of new information—are the same habits that sustain civic life. Citizens practiced in these disciplines are less susceptible to simplification and less dependent on ideological certainty. In this way, learning functions not as a guarantee against error, but as a source of resilience within a free and self-governing society.

This challenge is intensified by the accelerating pace of knowledge change. In the industrial era, a single credential could plausibly sustain a lifetime of work and civic competence. In today's knowledge economy, that stability has vanished. In many fields, the half-life of usable knowledge is now measured in years rather than decades (González, 2020). At the same time, digital media environments amplify confirmation bias at unprecedented speed, feeding individuals a steady stream of information calibrated to reinforce existing beliefs rather than challenge them (Vosoughi et al., 2018). As shared factual ground erodes, trust in expertise declines, and the conditions necessary for democratic dialogue—disagreement grounded in common reality—begin to collapse (Putnam, 2020).

The consequences of learning stagnation follow a grim but predictable progression. When learning stops, misunderstanding grows. When misunderstanding grows, cooperation fails. And when cooperation fails, the self-government becomes strained. Continuous learning is therefore not a luxury reserved for the curious or ambitious; it is a civic duty—the primary mechanism through which societies renew their shared understanding of reality. The danger facing modern democracies is not ignorance alone, but engineered misunderstanding designed to exploit ignorance: a condition in which citizens are overwhelmed with information yet lacking in the capacity to evaluate it. Against that threat, lifelong learning and civic responsibility remain the republic's most reliable line of defense.

If the threat to civic life were simply a deficit of information, the remedy would be straightforward: provide more content. The deeper problem, however, is not informational scarcity but cognitive overload without recovery. Citizens are exposed to claims, data, and narratives at a pace faster than they can evaluate, integrate, or reconcile. Under such conditions, disengagement is not irrational—it is adaptive. The Principle of Recoverable Learning reminds us that learning fails not because difficulty arises, but because individuals are denied the time, structure, and support needed to reorganize experience into usable knowledge. If lifelong learning is to function as the immune system of democracy, it cannot rest on individual willpower alone; it must be deliberately supported by institutions, policies, and technologies designed to restore cognitive capacity rather than exhaust it.

The vulnerability of self-government to misinformation is intensified when citizens lack not only shared facts, but the independent standing from which to judge them. For the thinkers who most clearly articulated the logic of republican self-rule, learning and material independence were inseparable. John Locke argued that property was not merely a social convention, but the extension of individual labor and judgment into the world—a concrete expression of personal agency. In this sense, property created a domain of action beyond arbitrary authority, enabling individuals to test ideas against reality, learn from consequences, and resist coercion without forfeiting survival. When that domain erodes, a crucial foundation for independent reasoning erodes with it.

Thomas Jefferson extended this logic into explicitly civic terms. His insistence that a nation could not be both ignorant and free rested on the assumption that citizens must be able to think—and live—without constant dependence on centralized power. Widespread ownership, for Jefferson, was not an economic preference but a political safeguard: a way of distributing power so that no authority could easily monopolize truth, livelihood, or loyalty. A population wholly dependent on state allocation, however benevolent its intentions, would find dissent increasingly costly and learning increasingly constrained. Under such conditions, misinformation does not merely mislead; it disciplines. Citizens learn not to inquire, but to comply.

Alexis de Tocqueville, observing American democracy in practice, warned that the gravest threat to liberty would not arrive through overt tyranny, but through a form of *soft despotism* in which citizens gradually relinquish judgment and agency in exchange for comfort and security. When individuals no longer manage property, work, or local affairs for themselves, they lose—often imperceptibly—the habits of responsibility and discernment that self-government requires. Centralized provision may promise equality, but it also risks narrowing the range of acceptable judgment and weakening the incentives for independent thought. In such a landscape, misinformation gains traction not because citizens are incapable of understanding truth, but because the social conditions that support independent judgment have thinned.

Seen through this lens, the danger posed when understanding is overwhelmed by a flood of ambiguous or misleading information is compounded as material independence erodes. A citizen who lacks independent standing must rely on institutions for access to work, learning, and security; under such dependence, the costs of questioning prevailing accounts rise, even in the absence of overt coercion. Lifelong learning cannot function as a civic defense under conditions of total reliance. The capacity to question sources, revise beliefs, and resist simplification presupposes not only cognitive skill, but a degree of independence from the structures being evaluated. When that independence diminishes, self-government gives way—quietly—to administration.

From James Madison, who warned that popular government depends on citizens capable of governing themselves rather than surrendering judgment to faction, to Abraham Lincoln, who insisted that a free people must think and act for themselves if self-government is to endure, the American tradition has treated civic judgment as a learned discipline. Theodore Roosevelt sharpened this claim by arguing that loyalty without criticism corrodes public life. Richard Nixon, reflecting on the burdens of office, emphasized that citizenship ultimately requires placing the public's interests above faction, passion, or power. Across these figures, the throughline is clear: a republic survives not by unanimity or obedience, but by citizens capable of learning, revising judgment, and acting with restraint under conditions of disagreement.

The Illusion of Collective Freedom

Self-government presupposes a population of citizens who possess not only formal political rights, but meaningful spheres of independent action. Private property has historically functioned as one such sphere—not merely as an economic arrangement, but as a structural safeguard for civic autonomy. When individuals control resources outside direct state allocation, they retain the capacity to act, associate, dissent, and experiment without first seeking permission. The abolition of private property would therefore have consequences extending far beyond markets; it would alter the balance of power between citizen and state in ways that bear directly on the viability of self-government.

From a civic standpoint, the most immediate consequence is the erosion of independence. In systems where productive assets are collectively owned and centrally administered, access to housing, employment, and material security becomes contingent on administrative allocation. Even when introduced with egalitarian intent, such arrangements concentrate discretionary power upward. Citizens who depend on the state for livelihood become structurally disincentivized from sustained dissent—not because dissent is formally prohibited, but because its personal costs increase. Over time, political participation risks narrowing from active self-government to cautious accommodation.

The loss of private property also weakens the informational foundations of democratic decision-making. Markets, for all their imperfections, generate decentralized feedback about scarcity, preference, and innovation through countless independent choices. When ownership is abolished, those signals must be replaced by administrative judgment. As Friedrich Hayek argued, the resulting knowledge problem is not merely technical but epistemic: no central authority can fully replicate the distributed information embedded in individual decision-making. When errors occur—as they inevitably do—citizens lack independent bases from which to identify, contest, and correct them.

Equally important are the consequences for learning and civic development. Ownership encourages responsibility, long-term planning, and experiential learning. Individuals who manage property—whether land, tools, businesses, or homes—encounter real constraints, tradeoffs, and feedback. These encounters cultivate judgment rather than compliance. When property is abolished, learning increasingly occurs within administratively defined roles rather than through self-directed engagement with consequences. Civic competence shifts from problem-solving to rule-following, from adaptation to conformity. Over time, the population's capacity for independent reasoning—the essential capacity self-government requires—atrophies.

Finally, the abolition of private property alters the moral relationship between citizen and state. In a republic, the state is a delegated authority, entrusted with limited powers by citizens who retain ultimate sovereignty. When all productive resources are held in common and administered by the state, that delegation subtly reverses. Citizens become stewards of state-managed resources rather than owners of their own labor and lives. Political legitimacy increasingly rests on allocation rather than consent, and citizenship is redefined less by participation than by entitlement. Under such conditions, the outward forms of self-government, to the extent that they persist, risk becoming procedural rather than substantive.

None of this implies that unregulated markets or extreme inequality are compatible with a learning republic. Concentrations of private power can undermine self-government just as surely as concentrations of state power. The civic danger arises not from the regulation of property, but from its abolition. A republic requires a pluralistic distribution of power—economic, social, and intellectual—so that no single institution monopolizes the conditions of survival. Private property, properly constrained by law and oriented toward the common good, remains one of the mechanisms by which that pluralism is sustained.

In the context of lifelong learning, the stakes are especially high. A citizen who lacks independent standing must rely on institutions for access to work, learning, and security. If those institutions fail—or if inquiry becomes inconvenient—there is little recourse. A learning republic, therefore, depends not only on public investment in education but on preserving the material independence that allows citizens to learn freely, question authority, and revise beliefs without fear. Self-government survives only where citizens retain both the capacity *and the freedom* to think for themselves.

The United States has long stood as a refuge for those fleeing systems that denied individuals ownership of their lives and labor—whether under Marxist regimes or other forms of coercive rule. Again and again, those who arrived carried with them firsthand knowledge of what it meant to live without the freedom to choose one's work, to speak without permission, or to plan a future beyond the reach of political favor. Notably, such regimes have rarely permitted members of their permanent laboring classes to travel freely abroad, particularly to societies where independent ownership and voluntary association might reveal alternative possibilities of life and citizenship.

There is a quiet irony, then, in the contemporary moment. Ideas that once drove people to seek refuge in the United States now reappear—often abstracted from their historical consequences—as attractive solutions to civic frustration. In many large cities, these ideas gain traction among younger citizens who have known neither material deprivation nor political dependency, and who understandably seek fairness, security, and meaning, but who have not experienced the conditions such systems impose once power is consolidated.

A learning republic does not respond to this irony with condemnation, but with memory. It recognizes that freedom is rarely lost through malice alone, but through forgetting—forgetting what earlier generations fled, what independence enables, and why self-government requires citizens capable of judging not only intentions, but outcomes. For many who found refuge in the United States after living through political campaigns of humiliation, forced conformity, and denied opportunity, this knowledge was not theoretical but lived. The task of lifelong learning, at its highest civic level, is to preserve that memory and to transmit it before choice hardens into consequence.

Impact of Cognitive Load on Adult Learning

For adult learners, especially in workplace training, "distraction" is often not environmental noise but psychosocial intrusion: stress related to finances, family responsibilities, health, job security, time pressure, identity threat, or the cognitive residue of prior demands. Cognitive Load Theory predicts that such pressures function as extraneous cognitive load, consuming scarce working-memory resources needed for comprehension, integration, and schema construction—that is, the learner's conscious workspace (Sweller, 1988; Sweller, Ayres, & Kalyuga, 2011; Plass & Kalyuga, 2019).

This prediction is strongly supported by cognitive research demonstrating that stress and anxiety impair the executive control processes most central to working memory, including inhibition, attentional shifting, and updating. When these processes are compromised, cognitive efficiency declines even when effort and motivation remain high (Eysenck et al., 2007; Schmeichel, 2007).

A large theoretical and empirical literature formalizes this mechanism through Attentional Control Theory, which proposes that anxiety weakens goal-directed attentional control while increasing stimulus-driven, threat-oriented capture (Eysenck et al., 2007). The result is not merely a subjective feeling of distraction, but a measurable reduction in performance efficiency on complex tasks that depend on working memory and executive control—precisely the kinds of tasks adult learners encounter in certification, compliance training, and reskilling contexts.

Experimental stress research makes these working-memory costs concrete. In a widely cited study using the Trier Social Stress Test, psychosocial stress produced significant impairments in working-memory performance on n-back tasks—tests in which participants monitor a sequence of stimuli and must indicate when the current item matches one presented n steps earlier in the sequence—demonstrating that acute stress can directly reduce working-memory capacity during demanding cognitive activity (Schoofs, Preuß, & Wolf, 2008). Related work using cold-pressor stress paradigms has shown similar impairments on executive-function and working-memory tasks (Duncko et al., 2009). In Cognitive Load Theory terms, stress adds a persistent form of background extraneous load, shrinking the effective workspace available for learning.

Evidence from workplace-based learning further confirms that cognitive load is not an abstract classroom construct but a measurable factor in real-world settings where novices must reason and decide under time pressure. Studies in clinical and professional training contexts explicitly apply Cognitive Load Theory—distinguishing intrinsic and extraneous load and examining their effects on memory and decision making—demonstrating that learning breakdowns often reflect load mismanagement rather than lack of effort or aptitude (van Merriënboer & Sweller, 2010; recent clinical workplace learning studies, 2024).

Taken together, these findings support a central claim of Cognitive Load Theory: adult learning is constrained not only by task complexity, but by the lived cognitive context in which learning occurs. Stress, anxiety, and psychosocial strain compete directly with learning for limited working-memory resources, shaping what can be understood, retained, and transferred.

Impact of Extraneous Cognitive Load on the Education of Children and Adolescents

In K–12 education—particularly in schools serving communities of extreme poverty—the distractions that impair learning are rarely incidental or temporary. They are chronic features of lived experience, shaping attention, emotion regulation, and the effective capacity of working memory for both students and teachers. Cognitive Load Theory provides the architectural explanation for why learning degrades under these conditions: when the workspace of consciousness is persistently occupied by stress, vigilance, and moral concern, there is less capacity available for biologically secondary learning (Sweller, 1988; Sweller, Ayres, & Kalyuga, 2011; Plass & Kalyuga, 2019).

For students living in poverty, psychosocial stressors such as food insecurity, housing instability, unsafe neighborhoods, and family crisis impose a continuous cognitive tax. Neuroscience and developmental research show that chronic stress heightens threat monitoring and emotion-regulation demands, recruiting prefrontal executive systems that are also required for comprehension, problem solving, and schema construction (Evans & Schamberg, 2009; Blair & Raver, 2012). Attentional Control Theory predicts this outcome precisely: anxiety weakens goal-directed attentional control and increases stimulus-driven, threat-oriented vigilance, thereby reducing the efficiency of working-memory–dependent processing (Eysenck et al., 2007). In Cognitive Load Theory terms, poverty does not merely coexist with learning difficulties; it manufactures extraneous cognitive load, shrinking the effective bandwidth of working memory before instruction even begins (Sweller et al., 2011; Plass & Kalyuga, 2019).

Dr. Gibson's work, particularly Thanking Teachers Working in High-Poverty Schools, shifts attention to a complementary but often overlooked dimension of this problem: the cognitive and moral burden carried by teachers themselves (Gibson, 2020). Gibson documents how educators in high-poverty contexts routinely confront students' unmet basic needs while lacking the institutional authority, resources, or community support to address them fully. The result is not only fatigue or burnout, but a persistent state of moral tension—a mixture of anxiety, guilt, and grief arising from the knowledge that more could be done, even when the system does not permit it.

From a cognitive perspective, this moral strain functions as an internal distraction analogous to stress, rumination, or emotion suppression. Research in cognitive psychology and neuroscience demonstrates that emotion regulation, suppression of distress, and self-monitoring consume executive resources and reduce working-memory capacity (Gross, 1998; Richards & Gross, 2000; Schmeichel, 2007; Ochsner & Gross, 2005). Teachers operating under conditions of chronic moral conflict must continuously regulate emotion, suppress frustration, and reconcile professional commitment with structural constraint. Each of these processes competes directly with instructional planning, attentional clarity, and adaptive scaffolding for limited working-memory resources.

This represents a crucial extension of Cognitive Load Theory: extraneous load does not originate solely in instructional design or student characteristics; it can also be produced by ethical conflict and social awareness. While traditional CLT analyses focus on task structure and presentation, recent theoretical integrations explicitly recognize affective and emotional demands as contributors to cognitive load through their depletion of executive and working-memory resources (Plass & Kalyuga, 2019). Gibson's work makes visible a form of cognitive load that is rarely measured but deeply consequential—the load imposed by caring in systems that ration care.

Equally important, Gibson emphasizes gratitude not as sentimentality, but as recognition of cognitive and moral labor (Gibson, 2020). To "thank" teachers in high-poverty schools, in his framing, is to acknowledge that they are operating under conditions that systematically deplete attention, emotional regulation capacity, and reflective bandwidth. Gratitude becomes a corrective to invisibility, but it does not substitute for structural change. When communities possess the resources to help but lack the incentive structures or leadership to mobilize them, the resulting inertia becomes yet another source of cognitive strain for those closest to the problem.

Seen through the lens of Cognitive Load Theory, the implications are stark. Students under chronic stress and teachers under chronic moral strain are both being asked to perform complex cognitive work with diminished working-memory capacity. Learning difficulties, classroom-management challenges, and instructional breakdowns that follow are often misattributed to motivation, discipline, or individual deficiency, when they are more accurately understood as predictable outcomes of architectural overload (Sweller et al., 2011; Eysenck et al., 2007).

Paul Gibson's work occupies a distinctive place in this discussion of cognitive load theory, and reflects a rare combination of intellectual discipline and moral seriousness. Trained as an educational leader and writing from sustained engagement with schools serving communities of extreme poverty, Gibson brings a form of evidence that is often absent from cognitive theory: careful, phenomenological attention to the lived experience of educators. His accounts document, with clarity and restraint, what sustained cognitive and moral strain feels like in real classrooms— how anxiety, guilt, and responsibility compete with attention and reflection when structural support is insufficient. In doing so, Gibson provides both phenomenological evidence and ethical illumination, complementing cognitive load theory by revealing the human cost of educational systems that presume surplus attention where none is available.

Together, phenomenological accounts and cognitive theory form a convergent explanation: what teachers describe as exhaustion, guilt, and divided attention corresponds precisely to what cognitive science predicts under sustained extraneous load.

Scale, Access, and the New Learning Ecology

Traditional, campus-based higher education has played a vital role in American learning, but it is inherently limited in scale. Physical campuses depend on classrooms, housing, faculty availability, geographic proximity, and fixed academic calendars. These constraints make face-to-face education intensive, immersive, and often transformative—but also costly and difficult to expand rapidly (Trow, 1973). For much of American history, this model effectively restricted advanced learning to those who could relocate, afford tuition and living expenses, and step away from work or family responsibilities for extended periods. As a result, access to sustained learning was often concentrated among those already positioned to absorb its risks (Goldin & Katz, 2008).

By contrast, the emergence of large-scale online learning—through MOOCs and fully online degree programs—represents a structural shift in the republic's learning ecology. Online platforms decouple instruction from physical space, allowing institutions to reach learners regardless of geography, age, or employment status (Allen & Seaman, 2017). Universities such as Southern New Hampshire University have demonstrated that degree programs can be delivered to tens of thousands of students simultaneously while maintaining structured curricula, faculty oversight, and assessment standards (SNHU, 2022). This does not diminish the value of campus-based education; it widens the distribution of learning opportunities across the population.

From the perspective of a learning republic, the significance of this shift lies not in replacing traditional campuses, but in expanding the nation's learning bandwidth. Online programs make it possible for working adults, caregivers, veterans, and mid-career professionals to engage in sustained learning without withdrawing from civic and economic life (OECD, 2021). Learning becomes embedded rather than immersive; Layered onto existing responsibilities rather than requiring temporary separation from them. This embeddedness aligns closely with the Principle of Recoverable Learning developed earlier: learners can pause, return, and rebuild momentum as life intervenes, rather than being permanently excluded by interruption (Sweller, 1988; Paas & van Merriënboer, 1994).

MOOCs further extend this ecology by enabling targeted, exploratory, or refresher learning at low or no cost, often on demand (Hollands & Tirthali, 2014). While such offerings vary widely in quality and completion rates, their civic value lies less in credentialing than in permeability. They lower the threshold for reentry into learning, allowing citizens to test new domains, refresh dormant knowledge, or respond to changing conditions without committing to full degree pathways. In this way, they function less as replacements for formal education than as on-ramps into it.

At the same time, scale introduces new challenges. Learning at scale requires careful attention to instructional design, learner support, assessment integrity, and community formation (Means et al., 2014). Not all learning experiences translate equally well to online formats, and not all learners thrive without in-person structure. Poorly designed digital environments can exhaust attention, fragment understanding, and replicate the very cognitive overload that recoverable learning seeks to avoid (Sweller, Ayres, & Kalyuga, 2011). The most promising developments, therefore, are not purely digital solutions, but hybrid and adaptive models that combine the depth of traditional education with the reach and flexibility of networked learning.

The central question is no longer whether online education is legitimate, but how societies can use scalable learning models responsibly—to broaden access, support lifelong learning, and strengthen civic competence—without reducing education to content delivery alone. In an era of rapid technological change, the ability to scale learning while preserving judgment, recovery, and accountability may prove as consequential to the future of the republic as the common school movement was in the nineteenth century (Dewey, 1916; OECD, 2021).

Scale vs Immersion

The immersive character of residential, face-to-face education has long been regarded as one of its greatest strengths. John Henry Newman argued in *The Idea of a University* (1852) that education unfolds not only through formal instruction but through sustained participation in an intellectual community, where habits of thought are shaped by proximity, conversation, and shared life. From a sociological perspective, Émile Durkheim likewise understood educational institutions as moral communities, contending that immersion accelerates the internalization of norms, responsibilities, and civic roles that cannot be transmitted through instruction alone (1922).

Modern higher-education research has reinforced these claims empirically. Alexander Astin's work on student involvement demonstrated that residential environments—by increasing time on task, peer interaction, and institutional engagement—are associated with stronger educational outcomes (1993). Vincent

Tinto similarly emphasized the importance of academic and social integration, noting that immersion within campus life strengthens persistence and commitment by embedding learners within networks of shared purpose and expectation (1975). For critics of the modern university such as Allan Bloom, residential immersion served an additional function: it insulated serious intellectual inquiry from distraction and fragmentation, creating a total environment in which enduring questions could be confronted with depth and discipline (1987).

Taken together, these accounts help explain why residential education has been so persistently defended—not merely as a delivery mechanism for content, but as a formative environment capable of shaping judgment, identity, and civic orientation. The argument that follows does not deny these strengths. Rather, it asks how immersion functions under contemporary conditions of scale, varied life circumstances, and lifelong learning—and whether the same features that once supported formation may, under different conditions, introduce new risks alongside their well-documented benefits.

By placing learners within a shared physical and social environment organized around study, discussion, and community life, traditional campuses foster deep intellectual engagement and rapid personal growth. Students are not merely exposed to ideas; they live among them, debate them, and incorporate them into emerging identities. Developmental and educational research consistently shows that such immersion can accelerate intellectual maturation, moral reasoning, and a sense of belonging within a broader intellectual tradition (Perry, 1970; Baxter Magolda, 2001). At its best, residential education initiates learners into the norms of disciplined inquiry, civil disagreement, and shared pursuit of truth.

Yet the same conditions that make identity immersion powerful also make it fragile. When a learning environment becomes the primary—or exclusive—source of social belonging, moral affirmation, and identity formation, it can amplify not only curiosity and growth, but also conformity, polarization, and susceptibility to moral absolutism. Social identity theory and decades of group-dynamics research demonstrate that tightly bound communities, especially those organized around shared moral narratives, are prone to in-group reinforcement and out-group derogation under conditions of perceived threat (Tajfel & Turner, 1979; Sunstein, 2009). Phenomenological studies of student experience further suggest that when academic communities become the dominant locus of identity, intellectual disagreement is often experienced affectively—as personal invalidation rather than epistemic challenge (Brookfield, 2012).

History suggests that developing minds—especially when separated from family, work, and broader civic life—can, under certain conditions, become unusually receptive to movements that frame disagreement as moral transgression and complexity as betrayal. Longitudinal and qualitative studies of ideological radicalization indicate that periods of identity consolidation, when combined with social isolation from moderating influences, increase vulnerability to absolutist belief systems (Hogg, 2014; Della Porta, 2018). In such environments, learning can shift subtly from inquiry to affiliation, and intellectual virtue may give way to moral signaling.

None of these dynamics is inherent to residential education itself, nor do they characterize most campus environments. Under ordinary conditions, immersive academic communities support intellectual risk-taking, pluralism, and disciplined disagreement.

Such risk-taking is valuable when it strengthens the habits of inquiry that responsible work and citizenship require. The concern arises only when immersion becomes socially totalizing—when separation from work, family, and broader civic roles removes stabilizing sources of identity, and academic belonging begins to substitute for them rather than complement them.

Recent episodes of campus unrest, including violent protests and targeted acts against controversial speakers, have underscored this vulnerability. These events are not the product of higher education alone, nor are they representative of most students or institutions. They do, however, reveal how immersive learning environments can become susceptible to mobilization by actors who thrive on emotional intensity, moral compression, and the narrowing of acceptable thought. Empirical studies of political intolerance on campuses show that high affective polarization correlates strongly with support for speech suppression when beliefs are framed as threats to identity or safety (Haidt & Lukianoff, 2018; Crawford & Pilanski, 2014). First-person accounts from students involved in such conflicts consistently report a perception of heightened stakes—where dissent is experienced less as disagreement to be examined than as harm to be prevented (Hunter & Smith, 2021).

From the perspective of a learning republic, this raises a difficult but necessary question: under what conditions does identity immersion support civic development, and under what conditions does it undermine it? Education aimed at self-government must cultivate not only conviction, but restraint; not only engagement, but tolerance for disagreement; not only passion, but judgment. Civic learning research suggests that these capacities require exposure to plural social roles and competing loyalties—conditions that prevent any single moral framework from monopolizing identity (Gutmann, 1999; Galston, 2001). Immersion that lacks such counterweights risks producing not thoughtful citizens capable of self-rule, but mobilized partisans skilled in rhetoric yet brittle in judgment.

In this respect, large-scale online learning offers an instructive contrast. Online programs typically integrate learning into the ongoing lives of adults who remain embedded in families, workplaces, and local communities. Rather than replacing existing identities, online learning often layers new intellectual capacities onto established roles. Qualitative studies of adult online learners consistently emphasize this additive character: learning is described not as a transformation of identity, but as an expansion of competence within existing social commitments (Kahu & Nelson, 2018; Stone & Springer, 2019). The result is a different form of development— slower, less theatrical, but often more stable and civically grounded.

This is not an argument for abandoning residential education, nor for insulating students from challenging or unsettling ideas. It is an argument for recognizing that identity immersion is a powerful educational force that must be deliberately shaped, not simply assumed to be benign. Political theory has long warned that concentrated sources of meaning, even when well-intentioned, can weaken civic pluralism (Tocqueville, 1835). In a learning republic, diversity of learning environments—including scalable, hybrid, and online models—may therefore serve not only access and efficiency, but civic resilience by diffusing the concentration of identity formation. When no single institution monopolizes belonging, education is less easily captured by movements that reward intensity over judgment.

One critical stabilizing force is often missing from the lives of students immersed exclusively in residential academic environments: meaningful work. Study is itself a form of work, requiring discipline and sustained effort, but paid, consequential labor introduces a different and indispensable grounding. Sociological and phenomenological research on work-based learning shows that engagement with real constraints—deadlines, budgets, safety requirements, customers, and colleagues— reinforces accountability, humility, and practical judgment (Sennett, 1998; Billett, 2001). When learning is integrated with real work—through apprenticeships, cooperative education, military service, or professional practice—it becomes harder for ideological commitments to drift free of reality. Such integration does not diminish education; it anchors it.

In a learning republic, pathways that combine study with meaningful work may therefore play a quiet but essential role in cultivating citizens capable of disagreement without dehumanization and conviction without absolutism. They reinforce a central civic lesson: ideas matter most when they must answer not only to peers, but to the world they seek to govern.

The Ethical Imperative of Lifelong Learning

By this point in the twenty-first century, lifelong learning can no longer be understood as a policy preference, an economic strategy, or a personal virtue alone. It has become a moral imperative. In a self-governing constitutional republic, every voter, every professional, and every parent functions as a node in a shared civic knowledge network. The quality of that network depends not on the brilliance of its elites, but on the distributed capacity of ordinary citizens to interpret information, revise beliefs, and act with judgment. When individuals continue to learn, they strengthen not only themselves but the epistemic fabric that allows a free people to reason together through institutions of law and representation. When learning stagnates, that fabric frays—first quietly, then catastrophically.

This ethical obligation does not arise from abstract idealism, but from the practical requirements of republican self-government. A constitutional republic presumes that citizens can evaluate claims, weigh evidence, and tolerate disagreement without retreating into cynicism, tribalism, or fanaticism. It further presumes that citizens can assess those who seek to govern on their behalf—not merely reacting to slogans, spectacle, or financial dominance, but examining records, arguments, incentives, and character. Because representatives act as proxy lawmakers, errors of judgment at the ballot box are amplified through law, policy, and administration. Learning, therefore, is not optional preparation for civic life; it is the ongoing work that makes responsible delegation of authority possible.

Political theorists from Thomas Jefferson to John Dewey recognized that the capacities required for self-rule are learned, not innate, and that they must be renewed across generations (Jefferson, 1816/1999; Dewey, 1916). Contemporary empirical research reinforces this insight: civic reasoning, media literacy, and resistance to misinformation correlate strongly with ongoing engagement in learning, particularly among adults whose formal schooling has long since ended (Nyhan & Reifler, 2010; Guess et al., 2020). Lifelong learning is therefore not merely supportive of republican government; it is constitutive of it.

To learn across the lifespan is, in this sense, an act of patriotism—not a performative allegiance to symbols, but a substantive commitment to the conditions that make liberty durable. It renews Jefferson's faith in reasoned judgment as the foundation of freedom, Alfred North Whitehead's insistence that adaptability is the only defense against obsolescence, and Whittaker Chambers's warning that truth decays when citizens surrender the discipline of thought (Whitehead, 1929; Chambers,

1952). These figures differed profoundly in temperament and ideology, yet converged on a single conviction: that freedom cannot survive where citizens abandon the effort to understand the world they inhabit and the power exercised in their name.

When many citizens disengage from learning, those who remain informed do not gain greater political power. Votes remain equal, and informed judgment can still lose to emotional appeal. What changes instead is how decisions are made and justified. As large numbers of citizens disengage from learning, institutions often respond by insulating complex decisions from public reasoning—placing them in expert bodies, administrative processes, or procedural safeguards. In the short term, this can appear to be a practical adjustment, intended to preserve stability when shared understanding weakens.

The danger arises when political actors who owe their power not to reasoned consent but to emotional appeal, grievance, or spectacle gain control of these insulated systems. Processes designed to protect good judgment can then be repurposed to shield bad judgment from scrutiny. What began as a compensating mechanism becomes an instrument of consolidation, allowing authority to be exercised without explanation and power to be maintained without accountability.

The result is not rule by the knowledgeable, but the erosion of the shared reasoning on which self-government depends. In a constitutional republic, equal suffrage does not guarantee equal effort. While every citizen holds the same vote, that vote carries a moral responsibility: to be cast with care, reflection, and an honest attempt to understand what is being decided and who is being entrusted with authority. When voting is treated as an act of identity, impulse, or protest rather than judgment, the safeguards of the republic are weakened from both directions—by manipulation from above and disengagement from below.

This dynamic clarifies a deeper civic risk long identified by Alexis de Tocqueville. Liberty, he warned, is often lost not through overt tyranny, but through a soft despotism in which citizens relinquish judgment in exchange for comfort and security. When individuals no longer manage property, work, or local affairs for themselves, they gradually lose the habits of responsibility that self-government requires. Centralized provision may promise equality, but it also risks narrowing thought and normalizing dependence. In such conditions, misinformation flourishes not because citizens are incapable of understanding truth, but because the social rewards for independent judgment have eroded.

Against this drift, lifelong learning emerges not as enrichment, but as civic maintenance. Jefferson insisted that freedom requires an educated citizenry. Dewey showed how learning and self-government reinforce one another through lived experience. Whitehead warned that knowledge now advances faster than any single lifetime can absorb. Drucker anticipated a society in which learning would no longer end with schooling but would define productive and civic life itself. Together, they form a lineage that treats education not as preparation for liberty, but as its ongoing condition.

The path forward does not lie in nostalgia for earlier institutions, nor in the hope that technology or administration will relieve citizens of responsibility. A learning republic must be deliberately designed. It must treat learning as public infrastructure—accessible, maintained, and recoverable across the lifespan. It must scale opportunity without exhausting learners, integrate education with meaningful work, preserve diverse learning environments, and cultivate judgment alongside skill. Most of all, it must sustain the moral expectation that citizens remain intellectually awake: willing to consult, to revise, and to learn again when the world changes.

In a constitutional republic, equal suffrage does not imply equal effort. While every citizen holds the same vote, that vote carries a moral responsibility: to be cast with care, reflection, and an honest attempt to understand what is being decided and who is being entrusted with authority. When voting is treated as an act of identity, impulse, or protest rather than judgment, the safeguards of self-government weaken—from manipulation above and disengagement below.

There may be no legal requirement to cast a well-reasoned vote, but there is a civic one. A republic cannot compel judgment, yet it cannot endure without it. Lifelong learning is therefore not a policy to be imposed, but a responsibility to be accepted—the unlegislated price of participation in self-government.

Self-government, therefore, rests on an unspoken but essential condition: that citizens accept learning as part of the price of participation. There may be no legal requirement to cast a well-reasoned vote, but there is a civic one. A republic cannot compel judgment, yet it cannot endure without it. Lifelong learning is therefore not a policy to be imposed, but a responsibility to be accepted—the un-legislated price of participation in self-government.

These questions point to a tension that no constitutional republic can escape. If informed judgment is essential to self-government, why not require it? If disengagement carries such consequences, why not restrict participation to those who demonstrate learning, competence, or economic contribution? The answer is that a republic cannot impose such conditions without destroying the very legitimacy it seeks to preserve. Equal political standing cannot be contingent on certification of virtue, knowledge, or productivity without replacing consent with authorization by power. Any attempt to enforce judgment by law would collapse into exclusion, arbitrariness, or control by incumbents. Yet the absence of legal requirements does not erase responsibility; it relocates it. In a free society, voting is not an act of self-expression, but an act of delegated authority exercised on behalf of others. A republic cannot compel citizens to think well, but it cannot endure if they refuse to try. Lifelong learning is therefore not a policy solution to be imposed, but a civic obligation to be accepted—the unlegislated price of participation in self-government.

Importantly, this obligation does not demand omniscience, nor does it privilege formal education over lived experience. Lifelong learning takes many forms: reading critically, listening charitably, acquiring new skills, revisiting assumptions, and remaining open to correction. It includes the discipline of evaluating sources, distinguishing argument from advertising, and resisting appeals designed to bypass judgment rather than inform it. Philosophical and phenomenological studies of adult learning emphasize that the moral core of learning lies not in the accumulation of facts, but in the cultivation of epistemic humility—the willingness to acknowledge error and revise belief in light of new evidence (Mezirow, 1991; Brookfield, 2017). Such humility is not weakness; it is the psychological precondition of responsible self-government.

In a learning republic, lifelong learning is best understood as a form of civic maintenance. Just as infrastructure requires ongoing repair to remain functional, republican culture requires continual reinforcement of the habits that sustain it. These habits—curiosity, skepticism, patience, and self-correction—do not persist automatically. They must be practiced, modeled, and supported across the lifespan. When they are neglected, freedom does not collapse overnight. It decays through misunderstanding, polarization, and the gradual normalization of unreason.

A free people sustain liberty not by clinging to certainty, but by remaining capable of learning under conditions of change. Lifelong learning is how a constitutional republic remembers how to govern itself.

Learning Isolated from Work and Consequence

As earlier chapters have shown, for much of American history, learning for young people—particularly males in their teens and early twenties—was embedded directly in productive work. Apprenticeships, farm labor, shop work, and early professional practice combined skill acquisition with adult responsibility, social contribution, and accountability (Kett, 1994; Jacoby, 1999). Learning occurred under real constraints, and identity formation was tightly coupled to contribution.

During the late nineteenth and twentieth centuries, this arrangement shifted dramatically. Industrialization, child labor laws, credential inflation, and the expansion of secondary and postsecondary schooling progressively removed young people from productive roles for longer periods of time (Goldin & Katz, 2008). By the mid-twentieth century, formal education had become the dominant pathway for skill acquisition, even as apprenticeship systems declined sharply in both scale and cultural prestige (Lerman, 2014).

Importantly, this shift did not reflect reduced learning demand. On the contrary, technological complexity increased learning requirements. What changed was where learning occurred—in classrooms rather than in accountable participation in adult work.

Developmental Timing and the Expectation–Agency Gap

Developmental research helps explain why this shift matters. Erikson's theory of psychosocial development identified adolescence and early adulthood as the period in which individuals must resolve questions of identity, competence, and social role (Erikson, 1950; 1968). Subsequent research has shown that identity formation stabilizes most effectively when young people engage in roles that involve responsibility, feedback, and meaningful contribution.

Early adulthood is a period of maximal cognitive capacity paired with incomplete structural control. Fluid intelligence is high, working memory is robust, and individuals are capable of absorbing complex abstractions rapidly. At the same time, authority, economic security, and institutional voice are still forming. This creates a distinctive cognitive condition: high expectations carried under sustained cognitive load.

Rising Expectations: Awareness Before Capacity

A century ago, media theorists like Harold Innis noted that changes in communication technology do more than speed information— they transform how people see their potential and what they expect of their societies. Drawing on this lineage, John T. A. Koumoulides (1977) described a "revolution of rising expectations" driven by expanding communications and the awareness it produces.

Today, MOOCs and open digital learning environments concretize that revolution: when millions anywhere can see what peers are learning elsewhere, aspirations expand, and access becomes a civic imperative. Research on MOOCs shows they can significantly enhance educational outcomes and skill development precisely because they meet these rising expectations with new pathways to engagement and mastery.

Rising expectations, however, do not depend solely on improvements in material conditions. A large body of social and political research shows that expectations also rise simply through exposure to knowledge of how others live. Individuals assess their prospects not in isolation, but relative to visible reference groups; when new standards of possibility become cognitively available, aspirations expand—even if local conditions remain unchanged (Stouffer et al., 1949; Runciman, 1966; Gurr, 1970).

Advances in communication, travel, and media have repeatedly produced what scholars describe as a "revolution of rising expectations," in which awareness precedes capacity (Davies, 1962; Appadurai, 2004). This dynamic helps explain why authoritarian systems have historically restricted education, travel, and information flows: not because citizens would immediately become wealthier, but because knowledge itself alters what people believe is possible.

In a learning republic, this tension is resolved not by suppressing expectations, but by expanding learning pathways—ensuring that as awareness grows, citizens are equipped to translate aspiration into competence, participation, and self-government rather than frustration or instability.

Overloaded Agency and Political Substitution

When learning environments emphasize symbolic mastery—ideological fluency, critique, moral reasoning—without simultaneously providing responsibility-bearing practice, working memory becomes occupied not only with tasks, but with unresolved comparisons: what I know is possible versus what I can yet do.

Research on decision fatigue and chronic cognitive load shows that when effort does not reliably convert into agency, individuals increasingly seek external simplification—structures that promise to resolve complexity on their behalf (Baumeister et al., 1998; Inzlicht et al., 2014; Mullainathan & Shafir, 2013).

This does not reflect diminished intelligence or civic disengagement. It reflects overloaded agency—a condition in which the mind is capable of reasoning about systems but lacks stable pathways to act within them. In such conditions, political frameworks that promise immediate coordination, redistribution, or centralized resolution become cognitively attractive, not because they are better aligned with freedom, but because they reduce the burden of unresolved choice.

Alternative Learning Pathways as Expectation Regulators

Massive Open Online Courses, competency-based credentials, apprenticeships, and project-centered learning environments play a distinctive role in a Learning Republic precisely because they short-circuit the expectation–agency gap.

Unlike traditional institutions that front-load abstraction and defer consequence, these environments:

- link learning directly to use,
- reward persistence with visible capability,
- and allow individuals to convert cognitive effort into agency without waiting for institutional permission.

From a cognitive load perspective, these pathways reduce extraneous load by embedding knowledge in scripts and schemas that are immediately actionable. From a civic perspective, they cultivate self-directed learners who experience learning not as credential accumulation, but as capacity expansion.

Research on adult learning and self-determination consistently shows that perceived autonomy, competence, and relatedness are decisive in sustaining long-term engagement (Deci & Ryan, 2000; Knowles et al., 2015).

In this sense, alternative learning pathways are not supplements to higher education; they are expectation regulators in the best possible way. They do not lower aspirations. They raise the learner's ability to meet them—thereby stabilizing both individual psychology and civic life.

Institutional Warnings, Historical Recurrence, and Social Strain

A final caution is warranted—quietly, but clearly. History shows that authoritarian systems have often sought to *manage expectations* by restricting education, travel, and information—not because citizens would immediately defect, but because awareness itself reshapes what people believe is possible. In such systems, limiting knowledge is a tool for maintaining social equilibrium.

The irony, then, is subtle but real: when citizens in a free society—where learning opportunities are abundant and self-directed advancement is possible—transfer responsibility for fulfilling their aspirations to governing philosophies built on expectation management, the result is not empowerment but dependency.

This is not a moral failure on the part of citizens. It is an institutional warning. When learning environments fail to convert rising expectations into lived agency, political substitutes rush in to fill the gap.

A Learning Republic avoids this outcome not by discouraging ambition, nor by promising outcomes without effort, but by ensuring that pathways from learning to capability remain open, visible, and recoverable throughout adulthood. In doing so, it preserves the essential bargain of self-government: that citizens are not managed, but prepared—free to aspire, free to learn, and equipped to act on both.

This is not a moral failure on the part of citizens. It is an institutional warning. When learning environments fail to convert rising expectations into lived agency, political substitutes rush in to fill the gap.

This warning is not new. John Dewey cautioned repeatedly that education detached from experience—learning isolated from work, consequence, and social responsibility—would produce individuals fluent in symbols yet uncertain in action. In *Democracy and Education* and later in *Experience and Education*, Dewey argued that learning divorced from participation undermines the very habits required for self-government: judgment, responsibility, and the ability to connect means to ends (Dewey, 1916; 1938).

Earlier American reformers anticipated the same danger. Seth Luther warned that education that elevated awareness without expanding practical competence risked generating frustration rather than empowerment. Fanny Wright, advocating for learning embedded in productive labor and civic participation, feared that instruction separated from lived responsibility would cultivate expectations that institutions could not honor. In different vocabularies and political moments, they converged on the same concern: learning must prepare individuals not merely to know more, but to act effectively within the social order they inhabit.

What they intuited, cognitive science now helps explain. Awareness expands faster than agency when learning is symbolic but not situated. Expectations rise; working memory fills with abstract possibility; yet without pathways to apply knowledge under real constraints, individuals experience overload rather than mastery. In such conditions, it is not surprising that citizens seek external structures—political, bureaucratic, or ideological—that promise to reconcile aspiration with outcome on their behalf.

A Learning Republic avoids this fate not by managing expectations, but by honoring them—by ensuring that learning remains embedded in work, accountability, and consequence across the lifespan. When citizens can reliably translate effort into capability, knowledge into agency, and aspiration into action, the pressure for political substitutes diminishes. Self-government becomes not an abstract ideal, but a practiced competence.

The tension we now confront—between rising expectations and uneven agency—is not a failure of character or civic virtue. It is a failure of design. From the earliest days of the republic, American thinkers warned that learning severed from work, responsibility, and consequence would weaken both individuals and self-government.

Benjamin Franklin understood this instinctively. The Junto was not a debating society for abstract refinement; it was a working fraternity of tradesmen, printers, artisans, and merchants who treated learning as a practical civic tool. Knowledge was valuable because it improved judgment, workmanship, and public life—because it could be *used*.

John Dewey later gave this intuition its philosophical foundation, insisting that democracy depends not on schooling alone but on participation in meaningful activity. Seth Luther and Fanny Wright echoed the same warning from different directions: awareness without agency breeds instability, not empowerment.

Across centuries and disciplines, the message has remained consistent. A republic that expands knowledge without expanding pathways for competent action invites frustration to replace responsibility—and politics to substitute for learning. A learning republic endures only when education remains embedded in work, lived experience, and accountability.

The United States has encountered this pattern before. In the decades following World War II, higher education expanded rapidly through the GI Bill and subsequent federal investments. While this expansion democratized access to credentials, it also accelerated the separation of learning from productive responsibility. Degrees increasingly functioned as signals rather than confirmations of applied competence (Collins, 1979; Labaree, 1997).

By the late twentieth century, this divergence had become pronounced. Large numbers of young adults accumulated educational debt and credentials without commensurate opportunities to exercise agency in meaningful work. Sociologists described the resulting condition as *credential inflation*, while economists noted declining returns for non-specialized degrees (Brown, Lauder, & Ashton, 2011).

The result was not ignorance, but dislocation: citizens aware of what *should* be possible, yet uncertain how to realize it. Periods of heightened social unrest, ideological polarization, and declining institutional trust have repeatedly coincided with such gaps between expectation and lived agency—confirming the earlier warnings of Franklin, Dewey, and their successors.

From Franklin's Junto to Dewey's laboratory schools to modern cognitive science, a single principle emerges: learning flourishes when it is anchored in action. Human beings do not become capable of self-government merely by accumulating information, nor by mastering symbols in isolation. They become capable by repeatedly translating knowledge into judgment under real conditions—by learning in contexts where effort has consequence and understanding has purpose.

When learning is embedded in work, biologically secondary knowledge is gradually organized into durable schemas, reducing cognitive load and expanding agency. When it is abstracted from experience, learning becomes fragile, effortful, and politically volatile. A Learning Republic succeeds not by managing expectations downward, but by designing environments in which rising expectations can be met with growing competence—so that awareness leads to agency, agency to responsibility, and responsibility to self-government.

A related consequence of credential inflation is the growing disconnect between formal educational attainment and labor-market demand. Employers across advanced manufacturing, infrastructure, energy, and technical services report persistent difficulty filling well-compensated roles that require applied skills, systems thinking, and hands-on competence—but not necessarily traditional academic credentials. Industry leaders have repeatedly noted that thousands of such positions remain open despite offering wages that would historically have been associated with professional or managerial careers.

At the same time, many graduates with broadly defined or non-specialized degrees enter the labor market with expectations shaped by years of formal education but with limited opportunities to translate that education into immediate, productive responsibility. The issue here is not the legitimacy of any field of study, nor the value of intellectual exploration. It is a structural misalignment between how learning is organized, how credentials are signaled, and how competence is developed and recognized in practice.

From the perspective of a learning republic, this misalignment is consequential. When educational pathways emphasize symbolic mastery while underemphasizing application, accountability, and skill formation, graduates may possess awareness without agency. Rising expectations collide with constrained opportunity—not because opportunity is scarce, but because pathways from learning to contribution are poorly designed. The resulting frustration is not a moral failing of individuals or institutions; it is a signal that learning has become detached from the environments in which it can mature into capability.

Work, Dignity, and the Misrecognition of Competence

One of the most striking parallels between the present moment and the antebellum South lies not in economics alone, but in attitudes toward work.

In the slaveholding South, manual labor was systematically degraded—not because it lacked skill, value, or necessity, but because it was associated with bondage. Enslaved people performed the overwhelming share of agricultural, mechanical, and domestic labor. As a result, free white non-elites, even those with limited education and few prospects, came to view such work as demeaning precisely because it had been defined as "slave work." This stigma outlived slavery itself. After emancipation, Southern societies struggled to build robust systems of technical education, apprenticeship, and skilled trades, in part because the cultural meaning of manual labor had been poisoned. Work that required physical effort but offered no credentialed status was avoided when possible, even at great personal cost. Educational opportunity was scarce—but so, too, was the willingness to dignify the kinds of work that could have supported broader learning and mobility.

What is striking is how similar patterns can re-emerge under very different conditions.

Today, educational opportunity—at least formally—is far more abundant. Yet many individuals with non-specialized degrees express strong reluctance to take work outside their field of study, even when such work offers higher wages, stability, and pathways to advancement. A labor or technical role paying far more than a clerical or contingent professional job may be dismissed as "beneath" one's education, not because it lacks skill or responsibility, but because it does not align with a credentialed identity. In this sense, work once again becomes stigmatized—not by coercion, but by cultural signaling.

The parallel is not exact, but the mechanism rhymes. In both cases, learning has been separated from work in a way that distorts judgment. When education is framed primarily as identity formation rather than capacity building, and when dignity is attached to credentials rather than competence, certain forms of work become symbolically degraded—even when they are economically vital and cognitively demanding. The result is a mismatch between aspiration and opportunity: individuals wait for work that "fits" their education, while industries with real learning ladders go understaffed.

This raises a difficult but necessary question for a learning republic: how did a society that once valorized upward mobility through work, adaptation, and skill acquisition drift back toward an attitude in which whole categories of productive labor are quietly treated as unworthy of educated citizens?

The answer is unlikely to lie in individual failure. It lies instead in the cumulative effects of institutional design—how schooling, credentials, cultural narratives, and economic signaling have once again allowed learning to float free of responsibility, consequence, and contribution. History suggests that when this separation persists, both learning and work suffer—and social frustration fills the gap.

When learning is extended but responsibility is deferred, young adults may experience what sociologists later described as "roleless roles"—settings that demand effort without granting agency or consequence. This mismatch can produce anxiety, disengagement, and prolonged identity diffusion, even among cognitively capable individuals (Arnett, 2004; Côté, 2000).

Historical studies of strikes, riots, youth movements, and political instability show that periods of rapid structural change—especially when institutions fail to integrate large populations into meaningful roles—are often accompanied by increased social strain (Tilly, 1978; Hobsbawm, 1962). While education expansion is often a response to such change, it does not automatically resolve the problem if learning remains disconnected from agency and contribution.

From a cognitive perspective, research on motivation, cognitive load, and self-regulation reinforces these findings. Learning that lacks clear purpose, feedback, or consequence imposes higher extraneous cognitive load and is more difficult to sustain (Sweller, 1988; Paas & van Merriënboer, 2020).

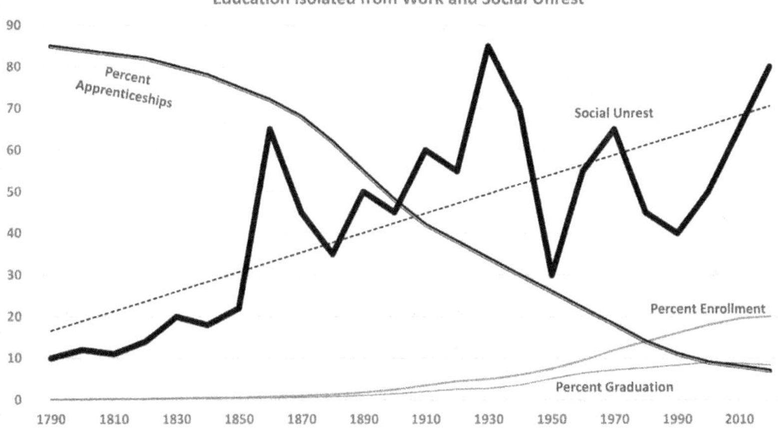

is necessarily composite and normalized, drawing on multiple well-established historical sources. Its purpose is comparative and illustrative: to show *directional alignment over time*, not exact magnitudes.

The Social Unrest Index employed here aligns closely with Peter Turchin's (ref) structural-demographic theory, which links periods of heightened instability to the convergence of popular immiseration, elite overproduction, and institutional strain. Where this work extends Turchin's framework is in identifying learning environments—particularly the balance between credentialed education and productive, responsibility-bearing learning—as a central mechanism through which these pressures intensify or abate.

The Historical Role of Universities

The tension modern universities face is not accidental. It is structural—and it is inherited.

When John Henry Newman articulated *The Idea of a University* (1852), he argued forcefully that the university's purpose was not professional training, technical skill, or even discovery. Its aim was the cultivation of intellect—what he called *liberal knowledge*: the disciplined capacity to reason, judge, and see relationships among ideas. Knowledge, for Newman, was valuable precisely because it was *not* subordinated to utility. The university trained minds, not workers.

Similarly, the modern research university took shape under the influence of Wilhelm von Humboldt, whose early nineteenth-century reforms in Prussia emphasized *Bildung*: the formation of the individual through engagement with knowledge pursued for its own sake. Humboldt's university united teaching and research, but not work and accountability. Learning was to be autonomous, reflective, and protected from immediate practical demands.

Both models were coherent. Both were noble. And both were designed for a small elite operating in relatively stable social systems, where learning prepared individuals for interpretive, clerical, or administrative roles—not for rapid adaptation under technological pressure.

What neither Newman nor Humboldt envisioned was a university system educating half the population, for continuously evolving forms of work, in a society where biologically secondary learning must be sustained across an entire lifetime.

The modern university, then, is not failing because it has abandoned its mission—but because it has *outgrown it*.

The Modern Role of Universities

Modern universities are not broken institutions; they are inherited ones. Designed to cultivate a narrow class of symbolic thinkers, they now bear responsibility for educating entire populations for adaptive, consequential work—often without having fully rearchitected the processes by which learning occurs.

The classical university, as articulated by John Henry Newman, prioritized intellectual formation over utility. The research university, shaped by Wilhelm von Humboldt, elevated autonomous inquiry and theoretical depth. These models were coherent responses to the societies they served. They are less well matched to a world in which technological change continuously raises the cognitive demands of work and citizenship.

A learning republic does not abandon universities. It situates them correctly.

Universities remain essential for deep theory, conceptual integration, ethical reasoning, and the preservation of knowledge. But they cannot serve as the sole or even primary engine of mass learning in a technologically dynamic society. That role belongs to a broader ecosystem in which learning emerges first through practice, responsibility, and consequence—and is later consolidated, refined, and credentialed by formal institutions.

The future of higher education is therefore not expansion alone, but differentiation: universities doing fewer things better, while learning itself is distributed across work, civic life, and self-directed inquiry. In such a system, education is no longer confined to a phase of life or a set of buildings. It becomes a durable civic capacity.

Naught Without Labor

As we have mentioned in the earlier chapters, extreme multi-generational inherited wealth has often corroded societies by fostering detachment from earned labor, breeding entitlement, and enabling ideologies that challenge the foundations of self-government. When fortunes pass unearned from one generation to the next, heirs may grow unmoored from the practical realities that ground virtue and civic responsibility, sometimes channeling their resources into radical visions that seek to dismantle the very systems that enriched them (Toynbee, 2023).

A stark example is Friedrich Engels, born in 1820 into a prosperous German industrial family that owned textile mills in Prussia and England (Hunt, 2009). Engels inherited a significant share of the family business, which he managed briefly in Manchester before using its profits to live a life largely free from daily toil. This unearned wealth allowed him to fund the work of his collaborator, Karl Marx, for decades—covering Marx's living expenses, research, and publications while Engels co-authored texts like The Communist Manifesto (1848) and edited Marx's posthumous volumes (Sperber, 2013; Stedman Jones, 2016).

Marx himself came from a comfortable middle-class background: born in 1818 in Trier, Prussia, to a father who was a successful lawyer (though the family faced financial strains after converting from Judaism to Lutheranism for professional reasons). Marx studied law and philosophy at university but never pursued a steady career in either. He worked briefly as a journalist and editor for radical newspapers in the 1840s, but spent much of his life in exile, poverty, and intellectual pursuit—often unemployed and reliant on Engels' support, occasional freelance writing, and small family inheritances that he quickly depleted (Sperber, 2013; Stedman Jones, 2016). Marx did not engage in traditional "honest work" like manual labor or professional practice; his days were devoted to theory, activism, and writing that critiqued capitalism and advocated revolutionary change.

The partnership of Engels and Marx stands as a worst-case scenario: inherited wealth enabling the development and dissemination of ideas that sought to upend societies built on individual effort, property, and self-reliance. In the American Republic, where the founders deliberately abolished mechanisms like primogeniture and entail to prevent such corrosive concentrations (Jefferson, 1776–1785; Madison, Federalist No. 10), this example serves as a cautionary reminder. Unearned fortunes, detached from the discipline of productive labor, can fuel visions that erode the civic virtues essential to sustaining self-government—underscoring the need to preserve a broad middle ground of responsible, capable citizens grounded in earned contribution.

Conclusion

This book began by advancing a hypothesis rather than a program: that learning fails whenever it is reduced to the narrow acquisition of knowledge or skill, divorced from responsibility, judgment, and character formation. Moreover, learning is intrinsically more difficult when reduced to symbology and abstractions rather than woven into lived experience.

It situated that claim within the historical development of American educational institutions, tracing how education came to be understood as both a personal opportunity and a civic obligation. The discussion then examined how learning actually occurs across the lifespan—drawing on research into cognition, development, memory, and experience to show how different phases of life present distinct opportunities and constraints for learning, and how developmental timing shapes not only what can be learned, but how it is understood and applied. It also explored the material, social, and institutional barriers that complicate learning at different stages of life. The book returned to learning as a civic responsibility, revisiting the hypothesis in light of these findings and considering its implications for institutions, credentials, and the formation of individuals capable of sustaining a free society.

As Thomas S. Kuhn observed, institutions rarely abandon prevailing arrangements simply because better explanations are available. Paradigms persist because they organize identity, authority, and legitimacy. Universities, credentialing systems, and workplaces alike are shaped by inherited assumptions about what learning is for, whom it serves, and how success is measured. The separation of knowledge from responsibility, and of skill from formation, did not arise by accident; it emerged from systems that functioned well within their own internal logic.

Yet as Karl Popper insisted, the growth of knowledge depends on a willingness to submit even our most settled assumptions to criticism. This book does not claim certainty, only responsibility: the responsibility to ask whether our educational and training systems are producing individuals capable not merely of performing tasks, but of exercising judgment; not merely of earning credentials, but of sustaining trust.

The American republic was founded on a radical idea: that the sovereignty of a nation need not reside in a monarch or ruling class but could instead be divided among the citizens themselves. This vision, however, has long been contested by two major factions—one favoring a conservative representative republic that prioritizes stability and elite oversight, and the other advocating for a more complete democracy that empowers the broader populace. The framers of the Constitution designed it with deliberate safeguards against unchecked democracy, such as federalism, separation of powers, and indirect mechanisms like the Electoral College, to prevent the potential tyranny of the majority while balancing popular will with structured governance.

In *The Age of Jackson*, Arthur Schlesinger, Jr. observed that as democratic ideals gained strength within the republic during that era—through expanded suffrage and populist movements—the opposing Whig party, although rooted in more conservative republican principles, began reframing the nation as a democracy to appeal to the masses and compete politically. The Whig Party itself collapsed in the mid-1850s, largely due to irreconcilable sectional divisions over slavery's expansion. The decisive trigger was the Kansas-Nebraska Act of 1854, a bill introduced by Democratic Senator Stephen Douglas of Illinois. This legislation organized new western territories and repealed the Missouri Compromise by introducing "popular sovereignty," allowing residents to decide on slavery—thereby opening the door to its potential spread into areas previously designated as free.

Northern Whigs (especially anti-slavery "Conscience Whigs") viewed Southern Whig support for the bill as a betrayal, shattering the party's fragile national coalition. This fracture led anti-slavery Northern Whigs, along with Free Soilers, some anti-slavery Democrats, and abolitionists, to form a new coalition: the Republican Party, founded in 1854 explicitly to oppose the extension of slavery into the territories. Although suffrage has been expanded universally to the adult citizenry, and although we have democratic processes, we are still a constitutional republic.

This American tradition, from Benjamin Franklin onward, treated learning as inseparable from agency and consequence. Knowledge mattered because it enabled action, and action mattered because it bound individuals to the world they helped shape. That understanding did not privilege universities over apprenticeships, or theory over practice. It assumed, instead, that a free society depends on people who can be entrusted with tools, with authority, and with one another—individuals whose learning is rooted in lived experience rather than isolated abstractions, fostering the judgment and responsibility essential to civic life.

In an era defined by rapid technological change, credential inflation, and fragmented pathways of learning, lifelong education increasingly unfolds in association with work. This reality does not diminish the importance of early formal education; it heightens it. The habits formed there—how learners relate knowledge to responsibility, how institutions relate credentials to trust—carry forward into every later stage of learning and work.

The hypothesis advanced here, therefore, resolves not into a policy prescription, but into a standard: that universities, career-technical systems, and workplaces alike should be judged not only by what they teach, but by whom they form. When learning cultivates judgment, responsibility, and character alongside knowledge and skill—integrating lived experience rather than reducing it to mere symbols and abstractions—it strengthens both individual lives and the civic order they sustain. When it does not, the costs are borne not only by learners, but by the republic itself.

Whether this hypothesis ultimately holds will depend, as Popper would remind us, on what comes next—on the willingness of institutions and individuals alike to test it against experience, to revise it where it fails, and to act on it where it proves true.

Epilogue

In *A Christmas Carol* (1843), Charles Dickens offers one of the most enduring moral warnings in Western literature. When the Spirit of Christmas Present reveals the two wretched children concealed beneath its robe—Ignorance and Want—the spirit issues a grave admonition:

"This boy is Ignorance. This girl is Want. Beware them both, and all of their degree, but most of all beware this boy, for on his brow I see that written which is Doom, unless the writing be erased."
—Dickens, *A Christmas Carol* (1843)

Dickens's judgment is unequivocal. Want is tragic, but ignorance is catastrophic. A society may survive poverty, but it cannot long survive citizens who lack the knowledge, judgment, and moral discernment required for self-government. This was not merely a Victorian moral lesson but a civic diagnosis. Dickens understood that ignorance corrodes freedom not through force, but through incapacity—by leaving people unable to understand their circumstances, evaluate competing claims, or resist manipulation.

Dickens also understood the power of imagery in shaping public understanding. The original publication of *A Christmas Carol* was inseparable from its illustrations by John Leech, whose engravings gave visual form to abstract social dangers. Securing those images was neither easy nor inexpensive. Illustrated books in the mid-nineteenth century required skilled labor, time-consuming engraving processes, and substantial financial commitment. Dickens personally oversaw the production and bore much of the cost at a moment when his own finances were far from secure. His collaboration with Leech was not ornamental; it was essential to making moral and civic truths visible to a broad public.

The contrast with our own moment is instructive. Today, authors and educators possess tools that dramatically lower the barriers to explanation, illustration, and revision. We can experiment, adapt, and refine in ways that would have been prohibitively expensive or impossible in Dickens's time. This abundance of capability, however, does not guarantee clarity or wisdom. It raises the standard of responsibility. When better tools are available, the ethical obligation is not to impress, but to illuminate.

What follows from this responsibility is a change not merely in tools, but in expectations. As avoidable errors become easier to prevent, grammar, spelling, clarity of formatting, and basic polish are rightly held to higher standards. Access to better tools has never diminished intellectual responsibility; it has clarified it.

Artificial intelligence belongs to this same lineage of cognitive augmentation—but it raises the standard at a deeper level. When tools exist that can surface competing arguments, recall historical precedent, expose internal inconsistencies, and challenge unexamined assumptions, the expectation rises not merely for polish but for judgment. Argumentation must be more coherent, evidence handling more careful, and reasoning more explicit. In such a moment, citizens who continue to decide while refusing to consult available intelligence are not preserving independence; they are choosing to reason below the level of care their time demands.

This moment therefore demands a more mature relationship with intelligence itself. In *Star Trek: The Next Generation*, Commander Data once observed—without pride or irony—that he possessed "the sum of human knowledge." The significance of that remark lies not in authority, but in availability. Data does not govern; he is consulted. He extends perception, memory, and analysis, while judgment remains human. To possess access to such intelligence and refuse to consult it would not be independence, but negligence.

Our own age has reached a comparable threshold. Tools now exist that can support memory, surface disagreement, and challenge unexamined assumptions at a scale no individual could manage alone. In a learning republic, such tools are not threats to self-government; they are tests of it. The danger lies not in consulting intelligence—artificial or otherwise—but in surrendering judgment, or worse, declining to learn while continuing to decide.

Whether such tools strengthen or weaken a republic depends not on their power, but on the habits of restraint, interpretation, and judgment with which they are used.

Richard B. Birrer's *Peace: A Compendium* offers a crucial corrective to naïve conceptions of peace as mere absence of conflict. Birrer frames peace as an active condition sustained by institutions, norms, and educated restraint—not a natural equilibrium that emerges spontaneously. Peace, in his formulation, is learned behavior at scale: a social achievement requiring continual renewal through understanding, empathy, and disciplined judgment.

This insight dovetails with the central argument of *A Learning Republic*. If conflict emerges where expectations rise faster than capacity, then peace depends not on suppressing expectations, but on expanding learning fast enough to meet them. Peace is fragile when populations feel cognitively, economically, or civically disempowered—when individuals perceive themselves as acted upon rather than acting. Societies that give citizens tools to interpret complexity, manage cognitive load, and revise beliefs without humiliation are societies that reduce the probability of violent rupture. In this sense, peace is not opposed to conflict— but to unmanaged complexity.

The lesson Dickens offered remains unchanged, even as the tools evolve. Ignorance is still the condition most to be feared—not because information is scarce, but because discernment is fragile. A learning republic depends on citizens who continue to learn, who remain willing to revise their understanding, and who share accumulated insight across generations. The purpose of learning, and of the tools and images that support it, is not novelty but continuity: the preservation of judgment, memory, and civic capacity in a world that constantly tempts us to surrender them.

One Final Word

An often-overlooked corollary of lifelong learning—essential to informed participation in a self-governing republic and to remaining capable of supporting one's family—is the obligation to preserve one's own capacities. The late Tony Bennett expressed this simply and without moralism: Do not sin against your talent.

To enjoy life, to take satisfaction in work, and to remain present to the people who depend on you requires more than opportunity; it requires care. Excess and harmful substances or behaviors do not merely damage the individual—they dull judgment, narrow possibilities, and quietly erode the very capacities that freedom presumes. Avoiding them is not an act of asceticism, but of stewardship.

In a learning republic, maintaining one's ability to think clearly, learn continuously, and act responsibly is a personal good. It is also a civic responsibility.

John Adams once wrote:

"Our Constitution was made only for a moral and religious people. It is wholly inadequate to the government of any other."

Adams did not mean that citizens must share identical beliefs, but that self-government presumes a people capable of governing themselves. Discipline, responsibility, and the cultivation of one's faculties cannot be delegated to institutions without consequence. When government assumes more responsibility for the individual, the individual often assumes less responsibility for himself. Over time, this quiet transfer erodes the habits of character on which constitutional self-government depends.

A learning republic, therefore, requires more than schools, technologies, or policies. It requires citizens who take responsibility for their own development—intellectually, morally, and practically.

The work of sustaining those capacities cannot be outsourced. It belongs to each of us.

References

Aamodt, A., & Plaza, E. (1994). Case-based reasoning: Foundational issues, methodological variations, and system approaches. *AI Communications*, 7(1), 39–59.

Acemoglu, D., Laibson, D., & List, J. A. (2014). Equalizing superstars: The internet and the democratization of education. American Economic Review, 104(5), 523–27. https://doi.org/gghw94

Addams, J. (1902). *Democracy and social ethics*. Macmillan.

Adichie, C. N. (2009). The danger of a single story [Video]. TED Conferences. https://www.ted.com/talks/chimamanda_ngozi_adichie_the_danger_of_a_single_story

Ajzen, I., & Fishbein, M. (1977). Attitude-behavior relations: A theoretical analysis and review of empirical research. *Psychological Bulletin, 84*(5), 888. https://doi.org/d6tbgc

Al-Badarenah, A., & Alsakran, J. (2016). An automated recommender system for course selection. *International Journal of Advanced Computer Science and Applications*, 7(3), 166-175. https://doi.org/hm8j

Alexander, W. H., & Brown, J. W. (2010). Computational models of performance monitoring and cognitive control. *Topics in Cognitive Science, 2*(4), 658–677. https://doi.org/fk2rvx

Allen, I. E., & Seaman, J. (2017). *Digital learning compass: Distance education enrollment report 2017*. Babson Survey Research Group. https://onlinelearningsurvey.com/reports/digtiallearningcompass2017.pdf

Alone, K. (2017). Adoption of e-learning technologies in education institutions/organizations: A literature review. *Asian Journal of Educational Research Vol, 5*(4), 63–71.

Altieri, M., Trojano, L., Gallo, A., & Santangelo, G. (2020). The relationships between cognitive reserve and psychological symptoms: A cross-sectional study in healthy individuals. *The American Journal of Geriatric Psychiatry, 28*(4), 404–409. https://doi.org/gh3gkm

Alvina, J., Bunt, A., Chilana, P. K., Malacria, S., & McGrenere, J. (2020, July). Where is that feature? Designing for cross-device software learnability. In *Proceedings of the 2020 ACM Designing Interactive Systems Conference* (pp. 1103–1115). https://doi.org/hm8k

Ambrose, S. H., & Krigbaum, J. (2003). Bone chemistry and bioarcheology. *Journal of Anthropological Archaeology, 22*(3), 193–199. https://doi.org/fnmgn4

Amin, R. W., Rivera-Muñiz, B., & Guttmann, R. P. (2021). A spatial study of quality of life in the USA. *SN Social Sciences, 1*(5), 1–19. https://doi.org/hm8m

Anderberg, P., Eivazzadeh, S., & Berglund, J. S. (2019). A novel instrument for measuring older people's attitudes toward technology (TechPH): development and validation. *Journal of Medical Internet Research, 21*(5), e13951. https://doi.org/ghtdtq

Anderson, M., & Perrin, A. (2017). Technology use among seniors. *Washington, DC: Pew Research Center for Internet & Technology.*

Angelidis, A., Solis, E., Lautenbach, F., van der Does, W., & Putman, P. (2019). I'm going to fail! Acute cognitive performance anxiety increases threat-interference and impairs WM performance. *PLoS One, 14*(2), e0210824. https://doi.org/gjkh49

Appleton-Knapp, S. L., & Krentler, K. A. (2006). Measuring student expectations and their effects on satisfaction: The importance of managing student expectations. *Journal of marketing education, 28*(3), 254-264. https://doi.org/df63fr

Arnett, J. J. (2004). Emerging adulthood: The winding road from the late teens through the twenties. Oxford University Press.

Arsenault, N., Anderson, G., & Swedburg, R. (1998). Understanding older adults in education: Decision-making and Elderhostel. *Educational Gerontology: An International Quarterly, 24*(2), 101-114. https://doi.org/c5xzvqAtkinson, R. C., & Shiffrin, R. M. (1968). Human memory: A proposed system and its control processes. In *Psychology of learning and motivation* (Vol. 2, pp. 89–195). Academic Press. https://doi.org/dnbb7v

Autor, D. H., Levy, F., & Murnane, R. J. (2003). The skill content of recent technological change: An empirical exploration. *Quarterly Journal of Economics*, 118(4), 1279–1333. https://doi.org/10.1162/003355303322552801

Aydin, N., Krueger, J. I., Frey, D., Kastenmüller, A., & Fischer, P. (2014). Social exclusion and xenophobia: Intolerant attitudes toward ethnic and religious minorities. *Group Processes & Intergroup Relations, 17*(3), 371–387. https://doi.org/f52m78

Ayres, P., & Sweller, J. (2005). The split-attention principle in multimedia learning. *The Cambridge handbook of multimedia learning, 2*, 135-146.

Baddeley, A. (1992). Working memory. *Science, 255*(5044), 556-559. https://doi.org/brjntb

Baddeley, A. D. (2000). The episodic buffer: A new component of working memory? *Trends in Cognitive Sciences*, 4(11), 417–423. https://doi.org/10.1016/S1364-6613(00)01538-2

Baddeley, A. D., & Hitch, G. (1974). Working memory. In G. H. Bower (Ed.), *Psychology of learning and motivation* (Vol. 8, pp. 47–89). Academic Press. https://doi.org/10.1016/S0079-7421(08)60452-1

Baddeley, A. D., Thomson, N., & Buchanan, M. (1975). Word length and the structure of short-term memory. *Journal of Verbal Learning and Verbal Behavior*, 14(6), 575–589. https://doi.org/10.1016/S0022-5371(75)80045-4

Baker, J. (2012). The technology–organization–environment framework. *Information Systems Theory*, 231–245. https://doi.org/d6d3wd

Baker, S. (2011). *Final Jeopardy: The story of Watson, the computer that will transform our world*. HMH.

Balagtas-Fernandez, F., & Hussmann, H. (2009, November). A methodology and framework to simplify usability analysis of mobile applications. In *2009 IEEE/ACM international conference on automated software engineering* (pp. 520-524). IEEE.

Baldissera, T. A., Camarinha-Matos, L. M., & De Faveri, C. (2017, May). Service personalization requirements for elderly care in a collaborative environment. In *Doctoral conference on computing, electrical and industrial systems* (pp. 20–28). Springer. https://doi.org/hm8n

Baltes, M. M. (1995). Dependency in old age: Gains and losses. *Current directions in psychological science, 4*(1), 14–19. https://doi.org/btk57p

Baltes, P. B. (1987). Theoretical propositions of life-span developmental psychology: On the dynamics between growth and decline. *Developmental Psychology, 23*(5), 611. https://doi.org/c5wkr6

Baltes, P. B. (1987). Theoretical propositions of life-span developmental psychology: On the dynamics between growth and decline. *Developmental Psychology*, 23(5), 611–626. https://doi.org/10.1037/0012-1649.23.5.611

Baltes, P. B. (1987). Theoretical propositions of life-span developmental psychology: On the dynamics between growth and decline. *Developmental Psychology*, 23(5), 611–626. https://doi.org/10.1037/0012-1649.23.5.611

Baltes, P. B., & Baltes, M. M. (1990). Psychological perspectives on successful aging: the model of selective optimization with compensation. In P. Baltes & M. Baltes (Eds.), Successful aging: perspectives from the behavioral sciences (pp 1–34). Cambridge University Press. https://doi.org/fvbdkn

Baltes, P. B., & Baltes, M. M. (1990). Psychological perspectives on successful aging: The model of selective optimization with compensation. In P. B. Baltes & M. M. Baltes (Eds.), *Successful aging: Perspectives from the behavioral sciences* (pp. 1–34). Cambridge University Press. https://doi.org/10.1017/CBO9780511664298.003

Baltes, P. B., & Baltes, M. M. (1990). Psychological perspectives on successful aging: The model of selective optimization with compensation. In P. B. Baltes & M. M. Baltes (Eds.), *Successful aging: Perspectives from the behavioral sciences* (pp. 1–34). Cambridge University Press. https://doi.org/10.1017/CBO9780511664298.003

Bandura, A. (1984). Recycling misconceptions of perceived self-efficacy. *Cognitive Therapy and Research, 8*(3), 231–255. https://doi.org/bbkbsx

Bandura, A. (1986). The explanatory and predictive scope of self-efficacy theory. *Journal of Social and Clinical Psychology, 4*(3), 359–373. https://doi.org/d4t6h2

Bangor, A., Kortum, P., & Miller, J. (2009). Determining what individual SUS scores mean: Adding an adjective rating scale. *Journal of Usability Studies, 4*(3), 114–123.

Baraka, A., Salem, R. M., & Joseph, N. J. (1998). The origin of the "algorithm." *The Journal of the American Society of Anesthesiologists, 89*(1), 277–277. https://doi.org/bzshm6

Barifah, M., Landoni, M., & Eddakrouri, A. (2020). Evaluating the user experience in a digital library. *Proceedings of the Association for Information Science and Technology, 57*(1), e280. https://doi.org/hm8p

Barrett, B. P. (2018). Computer anxiety, computer self-efficacy, and computer experience: prediction of performance and engagement in online college students. (Publication No.

2228632482) [Doctoral dissertation, Capella University]. ProQuest Social Sciences Premium Collection.

Barrick, M. R., Stewart, G. L., & Piotrowski, M. (2002). Personality and job performance: test of the mediating effects of motivation among sales representatives. *Journal of Applied Psychology, 87*(1), 43. https://doi.org/ftsh3v

Basavaraj, P., & Garibay, I. (2018, January). A Personalized "Course Navigator" Based on Students' Goal Orientation. In *Proceedings of the 2018 ACM Conference on Supporting Groupwork* (pp. 98-101). https://doi.org/hkr7

Baumeister, R. F., Bratslavsky, E., Muraven, M., & Tice, D. M. (1998). Ego depletion: Is the active self a limited resource? *Journal of Personality and Social Psychology*, 74(5), 1252–1265. https://doi.org/10.1037/0022-3514.74.5.1252

Bell, C., Lee, G., Pazzani, L., & Vuk, M. (2021). If looks could kill: Do characteristics of female offenders influence death penalty sentencing decisions? *Women & Criminal Justice, 31*(2), 87-107. https://doi.org/ggpqvv

Berger, N., Richards, A., & Davelaar, E. J. (2019). Preserved proactive control in ageing: A stroop study with emotional faces vs. words. *Frontiers in Psychology, 10*, 1906. https://doi.org/ggqk3z

Berners-Lee, T., Cailliau, R., Groff, J. F., & Pollermann, B. (1992). World-wide web: The information universe. *Internet Research.* https://doi.org/c8qg8h

Bhardwaj, P. (2019). Types of sampling in research. *Journal of the Practice of Cardiovascular Sciences*, 5(3), 157. https://doi.org/hsc2

Bialystok, E., Abutalebi, J., Bak, T. H., Burke, D. M., & Kroll, J. F. (2016). Aging in two languages: Implications for public health. *Ageing Research Reviews, 27*, 56–60. https://doi.org/ggqc37

Billett, S. (2001). Learning in the workplace: Strategies for effective practice. Allen & Unwin.

Bloesch, E. K., Davoli, C. C., & Abrams, R. A. (2013). Age-related changes in attentional reference frames for peripersonal space. *Psychological Science, 24*(4), 557–561. https://doi.org/f4xtzk

Bloesch, E. K., Davoli, C. C., & Abrams, R. A. (2013). Age-related changes in attentional reference frames for peripersonal space. *Psychological Science*, 24(4), 557–563. https://doi.org/10.1177/0956797612457385

Bloesch, E. K., Davoli, C. C., Roth, N., Brockmole, J. R., & Abrams, R. A. (2012). Watch this! Observed tool use affects perceived distance. *Psychonomic Bulletin & Review*, 19(2), 177–183. https://doi.org/10.3758/s13423-011-0200-z

Bloom, B. S. (1956). *Taxonomy of educational objectives: The classification of educational goals: Cognitive Domain*. Longman.

Bloomfield, J., & Fisher, M. J. (2019). Quantitative research design. *Journal of the Australasian Rehabilitation Nurses Association, 22*(2), 27-30.

Blyth, A. (1981). From individuality to character: The Herbartian sociology applied to education. *British Journal of Educational Studies, 29*(1), 69-79. https://doi.org/cswxvc

Boateng, G. O., Neilands, T. B., Frongillo, E. A., Melgar-Quiñonez, H. R., & Young, S. L. (2018). Best practices for developing and validating scales for health, social, and behavioral research: A primer. *Frontiers in Public Health, 6*, 149. https://doi.org/gfsqzs

Boone, H. N., & Boone, D. A. (2012). Analyzing Likert data. *Journal of extension, 50*(2), 1-5.

Booth, M. (1999). *Opium: A history*. Macmillan.

Box, G. E. (1976). Science and statistics. *Journal of the American Statistical Association, 71*(356), 791-799. https://doi.org/gdm28w

Breeuwsma, M., De Jongh, M., Klaver, C., Van Der Knijff, R., & Roeloffs, M. (2007). Forensic data recovery from flash memory. *Small Scale Digital Device Forensics Journal, 1*(1), 1–17.

Brooke, J. (1986). System usability scale (SUS): A quick-and-dirty method of system evaluation user information. *Reading, UK: Digital Equipment Co Ltd, 43*, 1–7.

Brookfield, S. D. (2017). *Becoming a critically reflective teacher* (2nd ed.). Jossey-Bass.

Brown, P., Lauder, H., & Ashton, D. (2011). *The global auction: The broken promises of education, jobs, and incomes.* Oxford University Press.

Burns, R. (1785). To a mouse, on turning her up in her nest with the plough. *reprinted in WE Henley, & TF Henderson (Eds), The poetry of Robert Burns, 1*, 152–154.

Büssing, A., & Glaser, J. (2002). Work analysis instrument for hospitals—self-report version (TAA-KH-S). *Göttingen: Hogrefe.*

Büssing, A., & Perrar, K. M. (1992). Die messung von burnout. Untersuchung einer deutschen fassung des maslach burnout inventory (MBI-D). *Diagnostica.*

Cacioppo, J. T., & Hawkley, L. C. (2009). Perceived social isolation and cognition. *Trends in Cognitive Sciences, 13*(10), 447–454. https://doi.org/cpghkc

Calvert, M. A. (1967). *The mechanical engineer in America, 1830–1910: Professional cultures in conflict.* Johns Hopkins University Press.

Campbell, D. T., & Stanley, J. C. (1963). *Experimental and quasi-experimental designs for research.* Cengage learning.

Campbell, K. L., & Hasher, L. (2018). Hyper-binding only apparent under fully implicit test conditions. *Psychology and Aging, 33*(1), 176. https://doi.org/hm88

Campbell, K. L., & Hasher, L. (2018). Hyper-binding: A unique age effect. *Psychological Science*, 19(8), 816–821. https://doi. org/10.1111/j.1467-9280.2008.02163.x

Cardwell, D. S. L. (1971). *From Watt to Clausius: The rise of thermodynamics in the early industrial age*. Cornell University Press.

Carnevale, A. P., Smith, N., & Strohl, J. (2010). *Help wanted: Projections of jobs and education requirements through 2018*. Georgetown University Center on Education and the Workforce. https://cew.georgetown.edu/cew-reports/help-wanted/

Carnot, S. (1824). *Réflexions sur la puissance motrice du feu et sur les machines propres à développer cette puissance* [Reflections on the motive power of fire and on machines fitted to develop that power]. Bachelier.

Caro, R. A. (1982). *The years of Lyndon Johnson: Volume I: The Path to Power.* Vintage Books.

Caro, R. A. (2002). *The years of Lyndon Johnson: Master of the senate.*

Caro, R. A. (2011). *Means of ascent: The years of Lyndon Johnson II* (Vol. 2). Vintage.

Caro, R. A. (2012). *The passage of power: The years of Lyndon Johnson* (Vol. 4). Knopf.

Carstensen, L. L. (2014). Our aging population—it may just save us all. *The upside of aging: How long life is changing the world of health, work, innovation, policy, and purpose*, 1–18. https://doi.org/hm8q

Carstensen, L. L., Isaacowitz, D. M., & Charles, S. T. (1999). Taking time seriously: A theory of socioemotional selectivity. *American Psychologist*, 54(3), 165–181. https://doi. org/10.1037/0003-066X.54.3.165

Carstensen, L. L., Isaacowitz, D. M., & Charles, S. T. (1999). Taking time seriously: A theory of socioemotional selectivity.

American Psychologist, 54(3), 165–181. https://doi.
org/10.1037/0003-066X.54.3.165

Carstensen, L. L., Isaacowitz, D. M., & Charles, S. T. (1999).
Taking time seriously: A theory of socioemotional selectivity.
American Psychologist, 54(3), 165–181. https://doi.
org/10.1037/0003-066X.54.3.165

Cartwright, M. A. (1945). The history of adult education in the
United States. *The Journal of Negro Education*, *14*(3), 283-
292. https://doi.org/bjxr3c

Castro-Alonso, J. C., & Sweller, J. (2019, July). The modality effect
of cognitive load theory. In *International Conference on
Applied Human Factors and Ergonomics* (pp. 75-84). Springer,
Cham. https://doi.org/hm8s

Castro-Alonso, J. C., Ayres, P., & Sweller, J. (2019). Instructional
visualizations, cognitive load theory, and visuospatial
processing. In *Visuospatial processing for education in health
and natural sciences* (pp. 111-143). Springer, Cham. https://
doi.org/hm8r

Castro-Alonso, J. C., Wong, R. M., Adesope, O. O., & Paas, F.
(2021). Effectiveness of Multimedia Pedagogical Agents
Predicted by Diverse Theories: A Meta-Analysis. *Educational
Psychology Review*, 1-27. https://doi.org/gkr7c8

Chad Rogers et al. (2018). [Title not provided in draft; likely EEG
evoked potentials and aging selectivity in auditory tasks].
[Publication details not provided].

Chambers, W. (1952). *Witness*. Random House.

Chandler, P., & Sweller, J. (1991). Cognitive load theory and the
format of instruction. *Cognition and instruction*, 8(4), 293-332.
https://doi.org/cfpj7t

Charles, S. T., Mather, M., & Carstensen, L. L. (2003). Aging
and emotional memory: The forgettable nature of negative
images for older adults. *Journal of Experimental Psychology:
General*, *132*(2), 310. https://doi.org/c39mbm

Chase, W. G., & Simon, H. A. (1973). Perception in chess. *Cognitive psychology, 4*(1), 55-81. https://doi.org/c226rf

Chen, I., & Chang, C. C. (2009). Cognitive load theory: An empirical study of anxiety and task performance in language learning. *Electronic Journal of Research in Educational Psychology, 7*(2), 729–746.

Chen, K., & Chan, A. H. S. (2014). Gerontechnology acceptance by elderly Hong Kong Chinese: A senior technology acceptance model (STAM). *Ergonomics, 57*(5), 635-652. https://doi.org/ghmcw2

Chen, K., & Lou, V. W. Q. (2020). Measuring senior technology acceptance: Development of a brief, 14-item scale. *Innovation in Aging, 4*(3), igaa016.

Chen, L. K., & Wang, S. T. (2016). Seniors' demographic correlates for motivations to enroll in degree-conferring programs in universities. *Educational Gerontology, 42*(6), 431–442. https://doi.org/hm8t

Chen, O., Castro-Alonso, J. C., Paas, F., & Sweller, J. (2018). Extending cognitive load theory to incorporate working memory resource depletion: Evidence from the spacing effect. *Educational Psychology Review, 30*(2), 483–501. https://doi.org/gf2qvk

Chen, O., Kalyuga, S., & Sweller, J. (2017). The expertise reversal effect is a variant of the more general element interactivity effect. *Educational Psychology Review, 29*(2), 393-405. https://doi.org/jgdg

Chen, X. (2013). *STEM attrition: College students' paths into and out of STEM fields*. National Center for Education Statistics. https://nces.ed.gov/pubs2014/2014001rev.pdf

Chevalier, A., & Kicka, M. (2006). Web designers and web users: Influence of the ergonomic quality of the web site on the information search. *International Journal of Human-Computer Studies, 64*(10), 1031–1048. https://doi.org/bqkvv9

Chi, M. T., Bassok, M., Lewis, M. W., Reimann, P., & Glaser, R. (1989). Self-explanations: How students study and use examples in learning to solve problems. *Cognitive Science, 13*(2), 145–182. https://doi.org/b5sctj

Chmelar, C., Jörres, R. A., Kronseder, A., Müller, A., Nowak, D., & Weigl, M. (2017). Associations between age, psychosocial work conditions, occupational well-being, and telomere length in geriatric care professionals. *Journal of Occupational and Environmental Medicine*, 59(10), 949–955. https://doi.org/ggwg87

Chu, W. S., De la Torre, F., & Cohn, J. F. (2013). Selective transfer machine for personalized facial action unit detection. In *Proceedings of the IEEE Conference on Computer Vision and Pattern Recognition* (pp. 3515–3522).

Chung, S., & Cheon, J. (2020). Emotional design of multimedia learning using background images with motivational cues. *Journal of Computer Assisted Learning, 36*(6), 922-932. https://doi.org/hm9b

Cicconi, S., & Marchese, M. (2019). Augmented learning: An e-learning environment in augmented reality for older adults. *INTED 2019 Proceedings*, 3652–3662. https://doi.org/hm9c

Clark, J. M., & Paivio, A. (1991). Dual coding theory and education. *Educational psychology review, 3*(3), 149-210. https://doi.org/c9gpvp

Clinton, B., & Gore, A. (1996). Excerpts from transcribed remarks by the president and the vice president to the people of Knoxville on internet for schools. *Speech. Knoxville: White House.* https://govinfo.library.unt.edu/npr/library/speeches/101096.html

Clinton, W. J. (2000). *My life.* Alfred A. Knopf.

Cochran, W. G. (1946). Relative accuracy of systematic and stratified random samples for a certain class of populations. *The Annals of Mathematical Statistics*, 164–177. https://doi.org/fn99p7

Cohen, S., & Williamson, G. M. (1991). Stress and infectious disease in humans. *Psychological bulletin, 109*(1), 5.

Cohen, S., Kamarck, T., & Mermelstein, R. (1983). A global measure of perceived stress. *Journal of Health and Social Behavior, 24*(4), 385. https://doi.org/d2wgms

Collins, R. (1979). *The credential society: An historical sociology of education and stratification.* Academic Press.

Compeau, D. R., & Higgins, C. A. (1995). Computer self-efficacy: development of a measure and initial test. *MIS Quarterly, 19*(2). 189. https://doi.org/cj6p9n

Coombs, P. H. (1969). The world educational crisis: A systems analysis. *British Journal of Educational Studies, 17*(3).

Cooper-Gaiter, E. D. (2015). *Computer anxiety and computer self-efficacy of older adults.* [Doctoral Dissertation, Walden University]. https://scholarworks.waldenu.edu/dissertations/349

Cooper, G. (1998). Research into cognitive load theory and instructional design at UNSW. The University of New South Wales.

Cooper, G., & Sweller, J. (1987). Effects of schema acquisition and rule automation on mathematical problem-solving transfer. *Journal of educational psychology, 79*(4), 347.

Côté, J. E. (2000). *Arrested adulthood: The changing nature of maturity and identity.* New York University Press.

Counts, G. S. (1932). Dare progressive education be progressive. *Progressive Education, 9*(4), 257–263. https://talkcurriculum.files.wordpress.com/2014/09/counts-g-1932-dare-progressive-education-be-progressive.pdf

Cox, K. M., Aizenstein, H. J., & Fiez, J. A. (2008). Striatal outcome processing in healthy aging. *Cognitive, Affective, & Behavioral Neuroscience, 8*(3), 304–317. https://doi.org/bgtk8w

Cruce, T. M., & Hillman, N. W. (2012). Preparing for the silver tsunami: The demand for higher education among older adults. *Research in Higher Education, 53*(6), 593–613.

Cubanski, J., Orgera, K., Damico, A., & Neuman, T. (2018). How many seniors are living in poverty? National and state estimates under the official and supplemental poverty measures in 2016. *Kaiser Family Foundation report, November, 19*. https://www.kff.org/medicare/issue-brief/how-many-seniors-live-in-poverty/

Curtis, A. E., Smith, T. A., Ziganshin, B. A., & Elefteriades, J. A. (2016). The mystery of the Z-score. *Aorta, 4*(04), 124-130. https://doi.org/hrvd

Darkenwald, G. G., & Merriam, S. B. (1982). Adult Education: Foundations of Practice.

Dattilo, A. E. L., Ewart, A., & Dattilo, J. (2012). Learning as leisure: Motivation and outcome in adult free time learning. *Journal of Park and Recreation Administration, 30*(1).

Davies, G., et al. (2018). [Title not provided in draft; likely education and cognitive reserve/health across the lifespan]. [Publication details not provided].

Davies, N. M., Dickson, M., Smith, G. D., Van Den Berg, G. J., & Windmeijer, F. (2018). The causal effects of education on health outcomes in the UK Biobank. *Nature Human Behaviour, 2*(2), 117–125.

Davis, F. D. (1989). Perceived usefulness, perceived ease of use, and user acceptance of information technology. *MIS Quarterly*, 319–340. https://doi.org/cc6

Davis, F. D., Bagozzi, R. P., & Warshaw, P. R. (1989). User acceptance of computer technology: A comparison of two theoretical models. *Management science, 35*(8), 982-1003. https://doi.org/cc7

De Groot, A. D. (1966). Perception and memory versus thought: Some old ideas and recent findings. In Kleinmuntz, B. (ed), *Problem solving; research, methods, and theory.*, 19-50.

De Jong, T. (2010). Cognitive load theory, educational research, and instructional design: Some food for thought. *Instructional science, 38*(2), 105-134. https://doi.org/fq6b8x

De Koning, B. B., Rop, G., & Paas, F. (2020). Effects of spatial distance on the effectiveness of mental and physical integration strategies in learning from split-attention examples. *Computers in Human Behavior, 110*, 106379. https://doi.org/hm9d

Deci, E. L., & Ryan, R. M. (2000). The "what" and "why" of goal pursuits: Human needs and the self-determination of behavior. *Psychological Inquiry*, 11(4), 227–268. https://doi. org/10.1207/S15327965PLI1104_01

Dede, C. J., & Richards, J. (Eds.). (2020). *The 60-year curriculum: New models for lifelong learning in the digital economy.* Routledge.

Delors, J. (1998). *Learning: the treasure within.* Unesco.

Densen, P. (2011). Challenges and opportunities facing medical education. *Transactions of the American Clinical and Climatological Association, 122*, 48. https://www.ncbi.nlm.nih. gov/pmc/articles/PMC3116346/

Densen, P. (2011). Challenges and opportunities facing medical education. *Transactions of the American Clinical and Climatological Association*, 122, 48–58.

Dewey, J. (1916). *Democracy and education: An introduction to the philosophy of education.* Macmillan.

Dewey, J. (1916). *Democracy and education: An introduction to the philosophy of education.* Macmillan.

Dewey, J. (1923). *Democracy and education: An introduction to the philosophy of education.* Macmillan.

Dewey, J. (1927). *The public and its problems.* Henry Holt and Company.

Dewey, J. (1937). Education and social change. *The Social Frontier*, 3(5), 165–168.

Dewey, J. (1938). *Experience and education.* Kappa Delta Pi.

Dewey, J. (1938). *Experience and education.* Kappa Delta Pi.

Dillman, D. A., & Bowker, D. K. (2001). The web questionnaire challenge to survey methodologists. *Online social sciences, 7,* 53-71.

Divine, R. A. (1993). *The Sputnik challenge.* Oxford University Press.

Dixon, P. (1991). From research to theory to practice: Commentary on Chandler and Sweller. *Cognition and Instruction, 8*(4), 343-350. https://doi.org/bwm6v3

Douglas, S. K., & Roberts, R. A. (2020). Older and more engaged: The influence of an employee's age on work engagement. *The Journal of Business Diversity, 20*(4), 73–84.

Dragland, A. (2013). Big data, for better or worse: 90% of world's data generated over last two years. *Science Daily.* 22. https://www.sciencedaily.com/releases/2013/05/130522085217.htm

Drucker, P. F. (1959). *The landmarks of tomorrow.* Harper & Row.

Drucker, P. F. (2011). *Landmarks of tomorrow: A report on the new.* Transaction Publishers. (Original work published 1957).

Duneier, M. (2015). *Slim's table: Race, respectability, and masculinity.* University of Chicago Press.

Eisenstein, J. (2019). *Introduction to natural language processing.* MIT press.

Elfert, M. (2015). UNESCO, the Faure report, the Delors report, and the political utopia of lifelong learning. *European Journal of Education, 50*(1), 88-100.

Elfert, M. (2019). Revisiting the Faure Report and the Delors Report: Why Was UNESCO's Utopian Vision of Lifelong Learning an "Unfailure"? In *Power and Possibility* (pp. 17-25). Brill Sense. https://doi.org/hm9f

Emch, J., et al. (2019). [Title not provided in draft; likely meta-analysis of frontoparietal involvement in aging]. [Publication details not provided].

Erikson, E. H. (1950). *Childhood and society*. W. W. Norton & Company.

Erikson, E. H. (1968). *Identity: Youth and crisis*. W. W. Norton & Company.

Eysenck, M. W., Derakshan, N., Santos, R., & Calvo, M. G. (2007). Anxiety and cognitive performance: Attentional control theory. *Emotion*, 7(2), 336–353. https://doi.org/10.1037/1528-3542.7.2.336

Fan, J. P., Geng, H. Z., Ji, Y. W., Jia, T., Treweek, J. B., Li, A. A., Zhou, C., Gradinaru, V., & Xiao, C. (2021). Age-dependent alterations in key components of the nigrostriatal dopaminergic system and distinct motor phenotypes. *Acta Pharmacologica Sinica*, 1–14. https://doi.org/hm9g

Fan, J., et al. (2021). [Title not provided in draft; likely dopamine modulation in aging]. [Publication details not provided]

Fancourt, D., & Steptoe, A. (2019). Television viewing and cognitive decline in older age: Findings from the English longitudinal study of aging. *Scientific Reports*, 9(1), 1–8. https://doi.org/c26r

Fanon, F. (1963). *The wretched of the earth*. Grove Press.

Farley, J. (2022). [Title not provided in draft; likely public statements on skilled worker shortages]. [Publication details not provided; e.g., interviews or Ford Motor Company reports].

Farley, J. (2023). [Title not provided in draft; likely public statements on skilled worker shortages]. [Publication details not provided; e.g., interviews or Ford Motor Company reports].

Farrell, J. A. (2018). *Richard Nixon: The Life*. Vintage.

Faure, E. (1972). *Learning to be: The world of education today and tomorrow*. Unesco.

Fenerci, E., et al. (2024). [Title not provided in draft; likely schemas facilitating memory reinstatement]. [Publication details not provided].

Ferdinand, N. K., & Czernochowski, D. (2018). Motivational influences on performance monitoring and cognitive control across the adult lifespan. *Frontiers in Psychology, 9*, 1018. https://doi.org/gds4w7

Ferreira, D., MacLean, G., & Center, G. E. (2018). Andragogy in the 21st century: Applying the assumptions of adult learning online. *Language Research Bulletin, 32*(11), 10-19.

Finstad, K. (2006). The system usability scale and non-native English speakers. *Journal of Usability Studies, 1*(4), 185–188.

Firth, A. (2019). Low vision and colour blindness. In *Practical Web Inclusion and Accessibility* (pp. 55–92). Apress.

Fogel, R. W. (1964). *Railroads and American economic growth: Essays in econometric history*. Johns Hopkins University Press.

Freeman, S., Marston, H. R., Olynick, J., Musselwhite, C., Kulczycki, C., Genoe, R., & Xiong, B. (2020). Intergenerational effects on the impacts of technology use in later life: Insights from an international, multi-site study. *International Journal of Environmental Research and Public Health, 17*(16), 5711. https://doi.org/ghmc36

Fujii, T., Fukatsu, R., Yamadori, A., & Kimura, I. (1995). Effect of age on the line bisection test. *Journal of Clinical and Experimental Neuropsychology, 17*(6), 941-944. https://doi.org/cqqnjt

Galustyan, O. V., Borovikova, Y. V., Polivaeva, N. P., Kodirov, B. R., & Zhirkova, G. P. (2019). E-learning within the field of andragogy. *International Journal of Emerging Technologies in Learning, 14*(9). https://doi.org/gmk8fq

García-Peñalvo, F. J., Conde, M. Á., & Matellán-Olivera, V. (2014, June). Mobile apps for older users–The development of a mobile apps repository for older people. In *International Conference on Learning and Collaboration Technologies* (pp. 117–126). Springer, Cham. http://repositorio.grial.eu/handle/grial/575

Gardner, B. S. (2011). Responsive web design: Enriching the user experience. *Sigma Journal: Inside the Digital Ecosystem, 11*(1), 13–19.

Gardner, H. (1983). *Frames of mind: The theory of multiple intelligences.* Basic Books.

Gardner, H. (1999). *Intelligence reframed: Multiple intelligences for the 21st century.* Basic Books.

Garrow, D. J. (2015). *Bearing the cross: Martin Luther King, Jr., and the southern Christian leadership conference.* Open Road Media.

Gatterer, G. (1988). The Geriatric Concentration Test and correlations with intelligence, memory ability, orientation and professional assessment in geriatric patients between 60 and 85 years of age in a nursing home. *Zeitschrift fur Gerontologie, 21*(1), 32-37.

Geary, D. C. (2008). An evolutionarily informed education science. *Educational Psychologist, 43*(4), 179–195. https://doi.org/fvz2h3

Geiger, R. L. (1997). *Research and relevant knowledge: American research universities since World War II.* Oxford University Press.

Gelbard-Sagiv, H., et al. (2008). [Title not provided in draft; likely fMRI of episodic memory retrieval]. [Publication details not provided].

Geoffrey, M., DeMatteo, D., & Festinger, D. (2019). Essentials of Research design and methodology. John Wiley & Sons, Inc.

George, G., & Lal, A. M. (2019). Review of ontology-based recommender systems in e-learning. *Computers & Education, 142*, 103642. https://doi.org/ghjm7q

Gerjets, P., Scheiter, K., & Cierniak, G. (2009). The scientific value of cognitive load theory: A research agenda based on the structuralist view of theories. *Educational Psychology Review, 21*(1), 43-54. https://doi.org/bxw3rv

Ginns, P. (2005). Imagining instructions: Mental practice in highly cognitive domains. *Australian Journal of Education*, *49*(2), 128–140. https://doi.org/hksw

Glass, C. R., Shiokawa-Baklan, M. S., & Saltarelli, A. J. (2016). Who takes MOOCs? *New Directions for Institutional Research*, *2015*(167), 41–55.

Glass, J. C., Jr. (1996). Factors affecting learning in older adults. *Educational Gerontology: An International Quarterly*, *22*(4), 359-372. https://doi.org/cnzbnz

Goldin, C., & Katz, L. F. (2008). *The race between education and technology*. Harvard University Press.

Goldman, S. R. (1991). On the derivation of instructional applications from cognitive theories: Commentary on Chandler and Sweller. *Cognition and Instruction*, *8*(4), 333-342. https://doi.org/dg7dgb

Golubev, A. G. (2022). Carving the senescent phenotype by the chemical reactivity of catecholamines: An integrative review. *Ageing Research Reviews*, 101570. https://doi.org/hm9h

González, C. (2020). [Title not provided in draft; likely half-life of knowledge analysis]. [Publication details not provided].

Gopher, D., & Braune, R. (1984). On the psychophysics of workload: Why bother with subjective measures? *Human Factors*, *26*(5), 519–532. https://doi.org/ghkpg9

Graesser, A. C. (1982). [Title not provided in draft; likely schema theory and inferences in comprehension]. [Publication details not provided].

Green, A. (2002). The many faces of lifelong learning: Recent education policy trends in Europe. *Journal of education policy*, *17*(6), 611–626. https://doi.org/fpqc3g

Gross, J. J. (1998). The emerging field of emotion regulation: An integrative review. *Review of General Psychology*, *2*(3), 271–299. https://doi.org/10.1037/1089-2680.2.3.271

Guess, A. M., Nyhan, B., & Reifler, J. (2020). Exposure to untrustworthy websites in the 2016 US election. *Nature Human Behaviour*, 4(5), 472–480. https://doi.org/10.1038/s41562-020-0833-x

Guha, M. (2014). APA dictionary of statistics and research methods. *Reference Reviews*. https://doi.org/hm9j

Guitart Hormigo, M. I., Conesa Caralt, J., Bañeres Besora, D., Moré López, J., Duran Cals, J., & Gañán Jiménez, D. (2016). Extraction of relevant terms and learning outcomes from online courses. *International Journal of Emerging Technologies in Learning, 2016, 11 (10)*. https://doi.org/hm9k

Gulzar, Z., Leema, A. A., & Deepak, G. (2018). Pcrs: Personalized course recommender system based on hybrid approach. *Procedia Computer Science, 125*, 518-524. https://doi.org/gnjgqg

Guruge, D. B., Kadel, R., & Halder, S. J. (2021). The state of the art in methodologies of course recommender systems—a review of recent research. *Data, 6*(2), 18. https://doi.org/hm9m

Gutmann, A. (1999). *Democratic education* (rev. ed.). Princeton University Press.

Haapalainen, E., Kim, S., Forlizzi, J. F., & Dey, A. K. (2010, September). Psycho-physiological measures for assessing cognitive load. In *Proceedings of the 12th ACM International Conference on Ubiquitous Computing* (pp. 301–310). https://doi.org/btkv9r

Hagel, J. (2021). *The journey beyond fear: Leverage the three pillars of positivity to build your success*. McGraw Hill.

Hagel, J., Seely Brown, J., & Davison, L. (2009). The big shift: Measuring the forces of change. *Harvard Business Review, 87*(7/8), 86–89. https://leadlocal.global/wp-content/uploads/2016/12/The-Big-Shift-Measuring-the-Forces-of-Change.pdf

Haidt, J., & Lukianoff, G. (2018). *The coddling of the American mind: How good intentions and bad ideas are setting up a generation for failure.* Penguin Press.

Halberstam, D. (1972). *The best and the brightest.* Random House.

Hansen, R. J., Thaxton, S. P., Connaughton, K. M., Talmage, C., & Knopf, R. C. (2020). Report on the 2018 national survey of the Osher Lifelong Learning Institutes' membership. *Technical Report.* National Resource Center for Osher Lifelong Learning Institutes.

Hari, R., Baillet, S., Barnes, G., Burgess, R., Forss, N., Gross, J., Hämäläinen, M., Jensen, O., Kakigi, R., Mauguière, F., Nakasato, N., Puce, A., Romani, G., Schnitzler, A., & Taulu, S. (2018). IFCN-endorsed practical guidelines for clinical magnetoencephalography (MEG). *Clinical Neurophysiology, 129*(8), 1720-1747. https://doi.org/gdw2vs

Harwell, M. R., & Gatti, G. G. (2001). Rescaling ordinal data to interval data in educational research. *Review of Educational Research, 71*(1), 105-131.

Heckhausen, J., & Schulz, R. (1995). A life-span theory of control. *Psychological Review, 102*(2), 284. https://doi.org/cgn6nc

Hefter, M. H., ten Hagen, I., Krense, C., Berthold, K., & Renkl, A. (2019). Effective and efficient acquisition of argumentation knowledge by self-explaining examples: Videos, texts, or graphic novels? *Journal of Educational Psychology, 111*(8), 1396. https://doi.org/gjgcn3

Heilbron, J. L. (1979). *Electricity in the 17th and 18th centuries: A study of early modern physics.* University of California Press.

Henry, H., Zacher, H., & Desmette, D. (2017). Future time perspective in the work context: A systematic review of quantitative studies. *Frontiers in Psychology, 8,* 413. https://doi.org/f92tpx

Hermann, K. S. (2005). *The influence of social self-efficacy, self-esteem, and personality differences on loneliness and depression.* [Doctoral dissertation, The Ohio State University]. http://rave.ohiolink.edu/etdc/view?acc_num=osu1112104621

Hertel, G., & Zacher, H. (2018). Managing the aging workforce. *The SAGE Handbook of Industrial, Work, & Organizational Psychology, 3*, 396–428.

Hilbert, D. M., & Redmiles, D. F. (2000). Extracting usability information from user interface events. *ACM Computing Surveys (CSUR), 32*(4), 384-421. https://doi.org/dwv97k

Hoffman, R. R., Marx, M., Amin, R., & McDermott, P. L. (2010). Measurement for evaluating the learnability and resilience of methods of cognitive work. *Theoretical Issues in Ergonomics Science, 11*(6), 561–575. https://doi.org/fjwgbr

Hollands, F. M., & Tirthali, D. (2014). *MOOCs: Expectations and reality.* Columbia University, Teachers College, Center for Benefit-Cost Studies in Education.

Hollands, F., & Kazi, A. (2019). Benefits and costs of MOOC-based alternative credentials: 2018–2019 results from end-of-program surveys. *Center for Benefit-Cost Studies of Education, Teachers College, Columbia University.*

Holt-Lunstad, J., Smith, T. B., & Layton, J. B. (2010). Social relationships and mortality risk: a meta-analytic review. *PLoS Medicine, 7*(7), e1000316. https://doi.org/c3f27d

Holzinger, A. (2005). Usability engineering methods for software developers. *Communications of the ACM, 48*(1), 71-74.

Horrigan, J. B. (2016). Lifelong learning and technology. *Pew Research Center, 22*.

Hoy, W. K., & Adams, C. M. (2015). *Quantitative research in education: A primer.* Sage Publications.

Hudomiet, P., & Willis, R. J. (2021). Computerization, Obsolescence and the Length of Working Life. *Labour Economics*, 102005. https://doi.org/hm9p

Hughes, T. P. (1983). *Networks of power: Electrification in Western society, 1880–1930*. Johns Hopkins University Press.

Hurlbut, B. J., Lubar, J. F., & Satterfield, S. M. (1987). Auditory elicitation of the P300 event-related evoked potential in the rat. *Physiology & behavior, 39*(4), 483-487. https://doi.org/dgj79r

Hutchins, R. M. (1969). *The learning society*. F. A. Praeger, Publishers.

Ibili, E., & Billinghurst, M. (2019). Assessing the relationship between cognitive load and the usability of a mobile augmented reality tutorial system: A study of gender effects. *International Journal of Assessment Tools in Education, 6*(3), 378–395. https://doi.org/ghq7v7

International Organization for Standardization (ISO). (2018). Ergonomics of human-system interaction – Part 11: Usability: Definitions and concepts. (ISO Standard No. 9241-11:2018). https://www.iso.org/obp/ui/#iso:std:iso:9241:-11:ed-2:v1:en

Inzlicht, M., Schmeichel, B. J., & Macrae, C. N. (2014). Why self-control seems (but may not be) limited. *Trends in Cognitive Sciences*, 18(3), 127–133. https://doi.org/10.1016/j.tics.2013.12.009

Irish, M. (2020). [Title not provided in draft; likely semanticization of episodic memories in aging]. [Publication details not provided].

Israel, P. (1998). *Edison: A life of invention*. John Wiley & Sons.

Ivanović, M., Milicević, A. K., Ganzha, M., Bâdicâ, A., Paprzycki, M., & Bâdicâ, C. (2018). Usability and quality parameters for e-learning environments and systems. In *CEUR Workshop Proceedings*. CEUR.

James, W., Burkhardt, F., Bowers, F., & Skrupskelis, I. K. (1890). *The principles of psychology* (Vol. 1, No. 2). Macmillan.

Jefferson, T. (1816, January 6). *Letter to Charles Yancey*. In *The papers of Thomas Jefferson*. Library of Congress. (Original work published 1816)

Jefferson, T. (1816, January 6). *Letter to Charles Yancey*. In *The papers of Thomas Jefferson*. Library of Congress. (Original work published 1816)

Jefferson, T. (1816). Letter to Charles Yancey, January 6, 1816. In *The papers of Thomas Jefferson*. Library of Congress. (Original work published 1816)

Jefferson, T. (1816). Letter to Colonel Charles Yancey. *January, 6, 1816.* https://founders.archives.gov/documents/Jefferson/03-09-02-0209

Jeong, J., Kim, N., & In, H. P. (2020). Detecting usability problems in mobile applications on the basis of dissimilarity in user behavior. *International Journal of Human-Computer Studies, 139*, 102364.

Jünemann, K., et al. (2020). [Title not provided in draft; likely music learning and hippocampal volume in aging]. [Publication details not provided].

Jünemann, K., Worschech, F., Sinke, C., Marie, D., Scholz, D., Kliegel, M., Van De Ville, D., James, C., Krüger, T., Tillmann, H. C., Altenmüller, E., & Sinke, C. (2020). Train the brain with music: Six months of piano playing leads to neuroplastic changes in a healthy elderly population. In *13th Graduate School Days: 20/21 November 2020/Stiftung Tierärztliche Hochschule Hannover* (p. 20). https://doi.org/hm9q

Kahneman, D. (1973). *Attention and effort*. Prentice-Hall.

Kapp, A. (1833). *Platon's Erziehungslehre, als Pädagogik für die Einzelnen und als Staatspädagogik. Oder dessen praktische Philosophie aus den Quellen dargestellt von Alexander Kapp.* F. Essmann.

Karim, J., Weisz, R., & Rehman, S. U. (2011). International positive and negative affect schedule short-form (I-PANAS-SF):

Testing for factorial invariance across cultures. *Procedia-Social and Behavioral Sciences*, *15*, 2016–2022. https://doi.org/d2xtj4

Karpinska, K., Henkens, K., & Schippers, J. (2013). Retention of older workers: Impact of managers' age norms and stereotypes. *European sociological review*, *29*(6), 1323-1335. https://doi.org/f5mb4x

Katz, S. (1983). Assessing self-maintenance: Activities of daily living, mobility, and instrumental activities of daily living. *Journal of the American Geriatrics Society*, *31*(12), 721–727. https://doi.org/ggx738

Keena, A., Latner, M., McGann, A. J. M., & Smith, C. A. (2021). *Gerrymandering the states: Partisanship, race, and the transformation of American federalism*. Cambridge University Press.

Kennedy, B. L., & Mather, M. (2019). Neural mechanisms underlying age-related changes in attentional selectivity. In G. R. Samanez-Larken (Ed.), *The aging brain: Functional adaptation across adulthood* (pp. 45–72). American Psychological Association. https://doi.org/hm9r

Kett, J. F. (1994). *The pursuit of knowledge under difficulties: From self-improvement to adult education in America, 1750–1990*. Stanford University Press.

Kirschner, F., Paas, F., & Kirschner, P. A. (2011). Task complexity as a driver for collaborative learning efficiency: The collective working-memory effect. *Applied Cognitive Psychology*, *25*(4), 615–624. https://doi.org/ds3tt9

Kirschner, P. A. (2002). Cognitive load theory: Implications of cognitive load theory on the design of learning. *Learning and Instruction*, *12*(1), 1–10. https://doi.org/d8vv8w

Knowles, M. (1973). *The adult learner: a neglected species*. Gulf Publishing Company. https://files.eric.ed.gov/fulltext/ED084368.pdf

Knowles, M. S. (1970). *The modern practice of adult education: Andragogy versus pedagogy.* Association Press.

Knowles, M. S. (1972). Toward a Model of Lifelong Education. UNESCO Institute for Education. http://files.eric.ed.gov/fulltext/ED066632.pdf

Knowles, M. S., Holton, E. F., III, & Swanson, R. A. (2015). *The adult learner: The definitive classic in adult education and human resource development* (8th ed.). Routledge.

Köhncke, Y., et al. (2018). [Title not provided in draft; likely dopamine modulation via exercise in aging]. [Publication details not provided].

Köhncke, Y., Papenberg, G., Jonasson, L., Karalija, N., Wåhlin, A., Salami, A., Andersson, M., Axelsson, J. E., Nyberg, L., Riklund, K., Backman, L., Lindenberger, U., & Lövdén, M. (2018). Self-rated intensity of habitual physical activities is positively associated with dopamine D2/3 receptor availability and cognition. *NeuroImage, 181,* 605–616. https://doi.org/gd4ss5

Kooij, D., & Van De Voorde, K. (2011). How changes in subjective general health predict future time perspective, and development and generativity motives over the lifespan. *Journal of Occupational and Organizational Psychology, 84*(2), 228–247. https://doi.org/bbz5sk

Kornaropoulos, E. M., Papamanthou, C., & Tamassia, R. (2019, May). Data recovery on encrypted databases with k-nearest neighbor query leakage. In *2019 IEEE Symposium on Security and Privacy (SP)* (pp. 1033-1050). IEEE.

Kortum, P., & Sorber, M. (2015). Measuring the usability of mobile applications for phones and tablets. *International Journal of Human-Computer Interaction, 31*(8), 518–529. https://doi.org/ggxssk

Krathwohl, D. R. (2002). A revision of Bloom's taxonomy: An overview. *Theory into Practice, 41*(4), 212–218. https://doi.org/c6z6ht

Krell, M. (2017). Evaluating an instrument to measure mental load and mental effort considering different sources of validity evidence. *Cogent Education, 4*(1), 1280256.

Laal, M. (2011). Barriers to lifelong learning. *Procedia-Social and Behavioral Sciences, 28,* 612–615. https://doi.org/dbfxjc

Laal, M., & Laal, A. (2012). Challenges for lifelong learning. *Procedia-Social and Behavioral Sciences, 47,* 1539–1544. https://doi.org/ghpp3v

Laanan, F. S. (2003). Older adults in community colleges: choices, attitudes, and goals. *Educational Gerontology, 29*(9), 757–776. https://doi.org/cqr6q2

Labaree, D. F. (1997). How to succeed in school without really trying: The credentials race in American education. *Yale University Press.*

Labaree, D. F. (1997). *How to succeed in school without really trying: The credentials race in American education.* Yale University Press.

Lai, A. F., Chen, C. H., & Lee, G. Y. (2019). An augmented reality-based learning approach to enhancing students' science reading performances from the perspective of the cognitive load theory. *British Journal of Educational Technology, 50*(1), 232–247. https://doi.org/ghq8rm

Lara, E., Caballero, F. F., Rico-Uribe, L. A., Olaya, B., Haro, J. M., Ayuso-Mateos, J. L., & Miret, M. (2019). Are loneliness and social isolation associated with cognitive decline? *International Journal of Geriatric Psychiatry, 34*(11), 1613–1622. https://doi.org/gjrm8v

Larson, E. (2017). Tracking criminals with internet protocol addresses: Is law enforcement correctly identifying perpetrators? *North Carolina Journal of Law & Technology, 18*(5), 316. https://scholarship.law.unc.edu/ncjolt/vol18/iss5/10

Lee, Y. H., Hsieh, Y. C., & Hsu, C. N. (2011). Adding innovation diffusion theory to the technology acceptance model: Supporting employees' intentions to use e-learning systems. *Journal of Educational Technology & Society, 14*(4), 124–137.

Leenders, M. P., Lozano-Soldevilla, D., Roberts, M. J., Jensen, O., & De Weerd, P. (2018). Diminished alpha lateralization during working memory but not during attentional cueing in older adults. *Cerebral Cortex, 28*(1), 21-32. https://doi.org/gc3x7w

Leenders, M., et al. (2018). [Title not provided in draft; likely MEG alpha waves and aging attention]. [Publication details not provided].

LeFevre, J. A., & Dixon, P. (1986). Do written instructions need examples? *Cognition and Instruction, 3*(1), 1-30. https://doi.org/ckcw59

Lemoine, P. A., & Richardson, M. D. (2019). Creative disruption in higher education: Society, technology, and globalization. In *Educational and social dimensions of digital transformation in organizations* (pp. 275-293). IGI Global.

Lerman, R. I. (2014). Do we face a slowdown in the rate of skill-biased technological change? Evidence from U.S. occupational data. *IZA Discussion Paper No. 8250.* Institute of Labor Economics.

Lester, D., Yang, B., & James, S. (2005). A short computer anxiety scale. *Perceptual and Motor Skills, 100*(3_suppl), 964–968.

Levine, D. M., Lipsitz, S. R., & Linder, J. A. (2018). Changes in everyday and digital health technology use among seniors in declining health. *The Journals of Gerontology: Series A, 73*(4), 552–559. https://doi.org/gf5s99

Li, Y. (2017, July). Massive open online courses (MOOCs) in The United States, China, and India. In *2017 2nd International Conference on Modern Management, Education Technology, and Social Science (MMETSS 2017)*. Atlantis Press. https://doi.org/hm9s

Likert, R. (1932). A technique for the measurement of attitudes. *Archives of psychology, 22 140*, 55.

Lipnic, V. A. (2018). The state of age discrimination and older workers in the US 50 years after the Age Discrimination in Employment Act (ADEA). *Washington, DC: US Equal Employment Opportunity Commission.*

Liskin, V., Serdobolskiy, E., Sopilko, I., & Okhrimenko, T. (2020). Two-factor User Authentication Using Biometrics. In *CEUR Workshop Proceedings, 2654.* CEUR.

Lister, J. P., & Barnes, C. A. (2009). [Title not provided in draft; likely hippocampal volume decline in aging]. [Publication details not provided].

Livne, A., Tov, E. S., Solomon, A., Elyasaf, A., Shapira, B., & Rokach, L. (2022). Evolving context-aware recommender systems with users in mind. *Expert Systems with Applications, 189*, 116042. https://doi.org/jhr3

Liyanagunawardena, T. R., & Williams, S. A. (2016). Elderly learners and massive open online courses: A review. *Interactive Journal of Medical Research, 5*(1), e4937. https://doi.org/ghbrp8

Loeng, S. (2017). Alexander Kapp–the first known user of the andragogy concept. *International Journal of Lifelong Education, 36*(6), 629–643. https://doi.org/hm9t

Loeng, S. (2018). Various ways of understanding the concept of andragogy. *Cogent Education, 5*(1), 1496643. https://doi.org/hm9v

Lövdén, M., et al. (2020). [Title not provided in draft; likely early education and cognitive reserve]. [Publication details not provided].

Lövdén, M., Fratiglioni, L., Glymour, M. M., Lindenberger, U., & Tucker-Drob, E. M. (2020). Education and cognitive functioning across the life span. *Psychological Science in the Public Interest, 21*(1), 6–41.

Luck, S. J., & Vogel, E. K. (1997). The capacity of visual working memory for features and conjunctions. *Nature*, 390(6657), 279–281. https://doi.org/10.1038/36846

Lynn, N. D., & Emanuel, A. W. R. (2021, March). A review on recommender systems for course selection in higher education. In *IOP Conference Series: Materials Science and Engineering* (Vol. 1098, No. 3, p. 032039). IOP Publishing.

Machado, E., Singh, D., Cruciani, F., Chen, L., Hanke, S., Salvago, F., Kropf, J., & Holzinger, A. (2018, March). A conceptual framework for adaptive user interfaces for older adults. In *2018 IEEE International Conference on Pervasive Computing and Communications Workshops (PerCom Workshops)* (pp. 782–787). IEEE.

Magsamen-Conrad, K., & Dillon, J. M. (2020). Mobile technology adoption across the lifespan: A mixed methods investigation to clarify adoption stages, and the influence of diffusion attributes. *Computers in Human Behavior*, *112*, 106456. https://doi.org/ghfqz9

Maguire, E. A., et al. (2006). [Title not provided in draft; likely hippocampal enlargement in cab drivers]. [Publication details not provided].

Maguire, E. A., Woollett, K., & Spiers, H. J. (2006). London taxi drivers and bus drivers: a structural MRI and neuropsychological analysis. *Hippocampus*, *16*(12), 1091–1101. https://doi.org/b5g734

Maher, N. M. (2017). *Apollo in the Age of Aquarius.* Harvard University Press.

Mahmud, S., Alvina, J., Chilana, P. K., Bunt, A., & McGrenere, J. (2020, April). Learning through exploration: How children, adults, and older adults interact with a new feature-rich application. In *Proceedings of the 2020 CHI Conference on Human Factors in Computing Systems* (pp. 1–14). https://doi.org/hm9w

Masís-Obando, R., et al. (2022). [Title not provided in draft; likely mPFC activation and schema scaffolding]. [Publication details not provided].

Maslach, C., Jackson, S. E., & Leiter, M. P. (1996). *MBI: Maslach burnout inventory*. CPP, Incorporated.

Mather, M., & Carstensen, L. L. (2005). Aging and motivated cognition: The positivity effect in attention and memory. *Trends in Cognitive Sciences*, *9*(10), 496–502. https://doi.org/bs8x8w

Mayer, R. E. (2019). Thirty years of research on online learning. *Applied Cognitive Psychology*, *33*(2), 152-159. https://doi.org/gfgn5h

Mayer, R. E., & Anderson, R. B. (1992). The instructive animation: Helping students build connections between words and pictures in multimedia learning. *Journal of educational Psychology*, *84*(4), 444. https://doi.org/cw7zbq

Mayer, R. E., & Moreno, R. (1998). A cognitive theory of multimedia learning: Implications for design principles. *Journal of Educational Psychology*, *91*(2), 358–368. https://esoluk.co.uk/calling/pdf/chi.pdf

McCrae, J. (1919). *In Flanders Fields: And Other Poems, by John McCrae*. William Biggs.

McGee, P. (2020). [Title not provided in draft; likely computing power comparison to Apollo guidance computer]. [Publication details not provided].

McKay, T. H., Teimouri, Y., Sağdıç, A., Salen, B., Reagan, D., & Malone, M. E. (2021). The cagey C-test construct: Some evidence from a meta-analysis of correlation coefficients. *System*, *99*, 102526. https://doi.org/f8t9

McKendrick, A. M., Chan, Y. M., & Nguyen, B. N. (2018). Spatial vision in older adults: Perceptual changes and neural bases. *Ophthalmic and Physiological Optics*, *38*(4), 363–375. https://doi.org/hm9x

McKillop, M., & Boucher, A. (2018). Aging prison populations drive up costs. Pew Charitable Trusts. https://www.pewtrusts.org/en/research-and-analysis/articles/2018/02/20/aging-prison-populations-drive-up-costs

McWilliams, S. C., & Barrett, A. E. (2018). "I hope I go out of this world still wanting to learn more": Identity work in a lifelong learning institute. *The Journals of Gerontology: Series B, 73*(2), 292-301. https://doi.org/hm9z

Mena, M., Corral, A., Iribarne, L., & Criado, J. (2019). A progressive Web application based on microservices combining geospatial data and the internet of things. *IEEE Access, 7*, 104577–104590. https://doi.org/hm92

Mews, J. (2020). Leading through andragogy. *College and University, 95*(1), 65–68. https://www.proquest.com/scholarly-journals/leading-through-andragogy/docview/2369314548/se-2?accountid=201395

Mezirow, J. (1991). *Transformative dimensions of adult learning.* Jossey-Bass.

Mickley, K. S., & Kensinger, E. A. (2009). [Title not provided in draft; likely vivid positive low-arousal memories in aging]. [Publication details not provided].

Millard, A. J. (1990). *Edison and the business of innovation.* Johns Hopkins University Press.

Miller, G. A. (1956). The magical number seven, plus or minus two: Some limits on our capacity for processing information. *Psychological Review, 63*(2), 81–97. https://doi.org/d5gq57

Miller, G. A. (1995). WordNet: a lexical database for English. *Communications of the ACM, 38*(11), 39-41.

Mok, L. W., et al. (2019). [Title not provided in draft; likely fMRI of selective attention in aging]. [Publication details not provided].

Mok, R. M., O'Donoghue, M. C., Myers, N. E., Drazich, E. H., & Nobre, A. C. (2019). Neural markers of category-based selective working memory in aging. *Neuroimage, 194*, 163-173. https://doi.org/hksp

Moody, H. R., & Tulle, E. (2004). Structure and agency in late-life learning. *Old Age and Agency. Nova Science Publishers: New York*, 29-4.

Moravec, H. (1999). Rise of the robots. *Scientific American, 281*(6), 124–135. https://www.jstor.org/stable/26058531

Moreno, R. (2010). Cognitive load theory: More food for thought. *Instructional science, 38*(2), 135-141. https://doi.org/brnmz7

Moreno, R., & Mayer, R. (2007). Interactive multimodal learning environments. *Educational psychology review, 19*(3), 309-326. https://doi.org/fkmph5

Moroney, L. (2017). The firebase realtime database. In *The Definitive Guide to Firebase* (pp. 51-71). Apress, Berkeley, CA.

Morrison, D., & McCutheon, J. (2019). Empowering older adults' informal, self-directed learning: Harnessing the potential of online personal learning networks. *Research and Practice in Technology Enhanced Learning, 14*(1), 1–16. https://doi.org/hm94

Mullainathan, S., & Shafir, E. (2013). *Scarcity: Why having too little means so much*. Times Books.

Munn, Z., Peters, M. D., Stern, C., Tufanaru, C., McArthur, A., & Aromataris, E. (2018). Systematic review or scoping review? Guidance for authors when choosing between a systematic or scoping review approach. *BMC Medical Research Methodology, 18*(1), 1–7.

Murphy, C. A., Coover, D., & Owen, S. V. (1989). Development and validation of the computer self-efficacy scale. *Educational and Psychological Measurement, 49*(4), 893–899. https://doi.org/bwdp6f

Na, K., & Jeong, Y. (2020). Exploring older adults' views on health information seeking: A cognitive load perspective and qualitative approach. *Journal of the Korean Society for Information Management, 37*(3), 177–202. https://doi.org/hm96

Nan-Zhao, Z. (2005). Four "pillars of learning" for the reorientation and reorganization of curriculum: Reflections and discussions. *International Bureau of Education-UNESCO.*

Nardone, A., Chiang, J., & Corburn, J. (2020). Historic redlining and urban health today in US cities. *Environmental Justice, 13*(4), 109–119. https://doi.org/gk5v4v

Narushima, M., et al. (2018). [Title not provided in draft; likely phenomenological rewards of lifelong learning]. [Publication details not provided].

Narushima, M., Liu, J., & Diestelkamp, N. (2018). I learn, therefore I am: A phenomenological analysis of meanings of lifelong learning for vulnerable older adults. *The Gerontologist.* 58(4). 696–705.

NASA. (2019). [Title not provided in draft; likely Apollo guidance computer specifications]. [Publication details not provided].

National Academies of Sciences, Engineering, and Medicine. (2017). *Building America's skilled technical workforce.* The National Academies Press. https://doi.org/10.17226/23452

National Commission for the Protection of Human Subjects of Biomedical and Behavioral Research. (1979). *The Belmont report: Ethical principles and guidelines for the protection of human subjects of research.* U.S. Department of Health and Human Services. https://www.hhs.gov/ohrp/regulations-and-policy/belmont-report/read-the-belmont-report/index.html

Navarro, E., & Calero, M. D. (2018). Cognitive plasticity in young-old adults and old-old adults and its relationship with successful aging. *Geriatrics, 3*(4), 76. https://doi.org/hm97

Nesselroade, J. R., Stigler, S. M., & Baltes, P. B. (1980). Regression toward the mean and the study of change. *Psychological Bulletin, 88*(3), 622. https://doi.org/dncpnx

Neubert, M. J., Kacmar, K. M., Carlson, D. S., Chonko, L. B., & Roberts, J. A. (2008). Regulatory focus as a mediator of the influence of initiating structure and servant leadership on employee behavior. *Journal of Applied Psychology, 93*(6), 1220. https://doi.org/b9s3s7

Newcomen, T. (1712). [Patent and historical description of atmospheric steam engine]. [Publication details not provided; historical patent record].

Nichols, M. (2003). A theory for eLearning. *Journal of Educational Technology & Society, 6*(2), 1–10. https://www.jstor.org/stable/jeductechsoci.6.2.1

Nielsen, J. (1994). *Usability engineering*. Morgan Kaufmann.

Nimrod, G. (2020). Aging well in the digital age: Technology in processes of selective optimization with compensation. *The Journals of Gerontology: Series B, 75*(9), 2008–2017. https://doi.org/dhqr

Nixon, R. (2013). *RN: the memoirs of Richard Nixon*. Simon and Schuster.

Nixon, R. M. (1990). *Richard Nixon in the arena: A memoir of victory, defeat and renewal*. Pocket Books.

Noble, D. F. (1977). *America by design: Science, technology, and the rise of corporate capitalism*. Oxford University Press.

Nye, D. E. (1990). *Electrifying America: Social meanings of a new technology, 1880–1940*. MIT Press.

Nyhan, B., & Reifler, J. (2010). When corrections fail: The persistence of political misperceptions. *Political Behavior, 32*(2), 303–330. https://doi.org/10.1007/s11109-010-9112-2

O'Doherty, J. P. (2004). Reward representations and reward-related learning in the human brain: Insights from neuroimaging. *Current opinion in neurobiology, 14*(6), 769-776. https://doi.org/chxv5b

Oberschall, A. R. (1969). Rising expectations and political turmoil. *The Journal of Development Studies, 6*(1), 5-22.

Obhi, H. K., Hardy, A., & Margrett, J. A. (2021). Values of lifelong learners and their pursuits of happiness and whole-person wellness. *Aging & Mental Health, 25*(4), 672–678.

Obhi, S. S., et al. (2021). [Title not provided in draft; likely phenomenological rewards of learning in older adults]. [Publication details not provided].

Ohland, M. W., Sheppard, S. D., Lichtenstein, G., Eris, O., Chachra, D., & Layton, R. A. (2008). Persistence, engagement, and migration in engineering programs. *Journal of Engineering Education*, 97(3), 259–278. https://doi. org/10.1002/j.2168-9830.2008.tb00978.x

Old, S. R., & Naveh-Benjamin, M. (2008). Memory for people and their actions: Further evidence for an age-related associative deficit. *Psychology and Aging*, 23(2), 467–472. https://doi. org/10.1037/0882-7974.23.2.467

Orleck, A. (2017). *Common sense and a little fire: Women and working-class politics in the United States, 1900-1965*. UNC Press Books.

Orth, U., Trzesniewski, K. H., & Robins, R. W. (2010). Self-esteem development from young adulthood to old age: a cohort-sequential longitudinal study. *Journal of Personality and Social Psychology*, 98(4), 645. https://doi.org/dn9dz9

Özer, D., Tansan, M., Özer, E. E., Malykhina, K., Chatterjee, A., & Göksun, T. (2017, July). The effects of gesture restriction on spatial language in young and elderly adults. In *Proceedings of the 39th Annual Meeting of the Cognitive Science Society*.

Paas, F. G. (1992). Training strategies for attaining transfer of problem-solving skill in statistics: A cognitive-load approach. *Journal of Educational Psychology*, 84(4), 429. https://doi.org/c74hkc

Paas, F. G. W. C., Ayres, P., & Pachman, M. (2008). Assessment of cognitive load in multimedia learning. *Recent Innovations in Educational Technology That Facilitate Student Learning, Information Age Publishing Inc.*, 11–35.

Paas, F. G., Van Merriënboer, J. J., & Adam, J. J. (1994). Measurement of cognitive load in instructional research. *Perceptual and motor skills, 79*(1), 419-430.

Paas, F., & Sweller, J. (2012). An evolutionary upgrade of cognitive load theory: Using the human motor system and collaboration to support the learning of complex cognitive tasks. *Educational Psychology Review, 24*(1), 27–45. https://doi.org/btrd4h

Paas, F., & Van Gog, T. (2006). Optimising worked example instruction: Different ways to increase germane cognitive load. *Learning and instruction, 16*(2), 87-91. https://doi.org/bg2wtc

Paas, F., & Van Merriënboer, J. J. (2020). Cognitive-load theory: Methods to manage working memory load in the learning of complex tasks. *Current Directions in Psychological Science, 29*(4), 394–398. https://doi.org/gg745f

Paas, F., & van Merriënboer, J. J. G. (1994). Instructional control of cognitive load in the training of complex cognitive tasks. *Educational Psychology Review*, 6(4), 351–371. https://doi.org/10.1007/BF02213420

Paas, F., Renkl, A., & Sweller, J. (2003). Cognitive load theory and instructional design: Recent developments. *Educational Psychologist*, 38(1), 1–4. https://doi.org/10.1207/S15326985EP3801_1

Paas, F., Renkl, A., & Sweller, J. (2004). Cognitive load theory: Instructional implications of the interaction between information structures and cognitive architecture. *Instructional Science, 32*(1/2), 1-8.

Paine, T. (1776). *Common sense: 1776.* Infomotions, Incorporated.

Payne, L., Rogers, C. S., Wingfield, A., & Sekuler, R. (2017). A right-ear bias of auditory selective attention is evident in alpha oscillations. *Psychophysiology, 54*(4), 528-535. https://doi.org/f9kfkb

Pearson, C. (2021). The single usability metric (SUM) — A completion rate conundrum. *UX Collective.* https://uxdesign. cc/the-single-usability-metric-a-completion-rate-conundrum-c6fd0e5a54ca

Pearson, S. W., & Bailey, J. E. (1980). Measurement of computer user satisfaction. *ACM SIGMETRICS Performance Evaluation Review, 9*(1), 59-68.

Pekrun, R. (2006). The control-value theory of achievement emotions: Assumptions, corollaries, and implications for educational research and practice. *Educational Psychology Review, 18*(4), 315–341. https://doi.org/d6rrq9

Perera, N., Dehmer, M., & Emmert-Streib, F. (2020). Named entity recognition and relation detection for biomedical information extraction. *Frontiers in cell and developmental biology,* 673. https://doi.org/gj7dvh

Pergher, V., Tournoy, J., Schoenmakers, B., & Van Hulle, M. M. (2019). P300, gray matter volume and individual characteristics correlates in healthy elderly. *Frontiers in Aging Neuroscience, 11, 104.* https://doi.org/gj2p3h

Perrin, D., et al. (2020). [Title not provided in draft; likely epistemic feelings of pastness]. [Publication details not provided].

Perry, W. G., Jr. (1970). *Forms of intellectual and ethical development in the college years: A scheme.* Holt, Rinehart and Winston.

Persson, E., Barrafrem, K., Meunier, A., & Tinghög, G. (2019). The effect of decision fatigue on surgeons' clinical decision making. *Health Economics, 28*(10), 1194–1203. https://doi. org/gjbnp5

Peterson, L. R., & Peterson, M. J. (1959). Short-term retention of individual verbal items. *Journal of Experimental Psychology,* 58(3), 193–198. https://doi.org/10.1037/h0049234

Peterson, L., & Peterson, M. J. (1959). Short-term retention of individual verbal items. *Journal of Experimental Psychology, 58*(3), 193. https://doi.org/bmvr95

Pfenninger, K. H., & Polz, D. (2018). [Title not provided in draft; likely language acquisition and hippocampal volume]. [Publication details not provided].

Pfenninger, S. E., & Polz, S. (2018). Foreign language learning in the third age: A pilot feasibility study on cognitive, socio-affective and linguistic drivers and benefits in relation to previous bilingualism of the learner. *Journal of the European Second Language Association, 2*(1). https://doi.org/hm98

Plass, J. L., & Kalyuga, S. (2019). Four ways of considering emotion in cognitive load theory. *Educational Psychology Review, 31*(2), 339–359. https://link.springer.com/article/10.1007/s10648-019-09473-5

Plass, J. L., & Kalyuga, S. (2019). Four ways of considering emotion in cognitive load theory. *Educational Psychology Review, 31*(1), 1–21. https://doi.org/10.1007/s10648-019-09473-8

Pollock, E., Chandler, P., & Sweller, J. (2002). Assimilating complex information. *Learning and Instruction, 12*(1), 61–86. https://doi.org/ffngp4

Pool, I. D. S. (1965). *Mass communication and political science.* Center for International Studies, Massachusetts Institute of Technology, [1965].

Popper, K. (1945). *The open society and its enemies.* Routledge.

Portenhauser, A. A., Terhorst, Y., Schultchen, D., Sander, L. B., Denkinger, M. D., Stach, M., Waldherr, N., Dallmeier, D., Baumeister, H., & Messner, E. M. (2021). Mobile apps for older adults: Systematic search and evaluation within online stores. *JMIR Aging, 4*(1), e23313. https://doi.org/gm38wc

Pouw, W., Van Gog, T., Zwaan, R. A., Agostinho, S., & Paas, F. (2018). Co-thought gestures in children's mental problem solving: Prevalence and effects on subsequent performance. *Applied Cognitive Psychology, 32*(1), 66–80. https://doi.org/gcwwst

Prensky, M. (2001). Digital natives, digital immigrants—part 1. *On the Horizon, 9*(5), 1–6. https://doi.org/cxwdzq

Prewitt, K. (2005). Racial classification in America: where do we go from here? *Daedalus, 134*(1), 5–17. https://doi.org/dq5769

Putnam, R. D. (2020). *The upswing: How America came together a century ago and how we can do it again.* Simon & Schuster.

Quade, D. (1967). Rank analysis of covariance. *Journal of the American Statistical Association, 62*(320), 1187-1200.

Ramesh, R., Sasikumar, M., & Iyer, S. (2016, July). Integrating the learning objectives and syllabus into a domain ontology for data structures course. In *Proceedings of the 2016 ACM Conference on Innovation and Technology in Computer Science Education* (pp. 266–271). https://doi.org/hm99

Raza, S., & Ding, C. (2019). Progress in context-aware recommender systems—An overview. *Computer Science Review, 31*, 84-97. https://doi.org/jhrz

Renkl, A. (2002). Worked-out examples: Instructional explanations support learning by self-explanations. *Learning and instruction, 12*(5), 529-556. https://doi.org/cpbdhv

Reyneke, R. (2019). *Improving interactive user experience with microinteractions: An application of biometric and affect detection systems on landing pages.* (Publication No. 28275840) [Doctoral dissertation, Harvard University]. ProQuest Dissertations Publishing.

Rice, S., Winter, S. R., Doherty, S., & Milner, M. (2017). Advantages and disadvantages of using internet-based survey methods in aviation-related research. *Journal of Aviation Technology and Engineering, 7*(1), 5. https://doi.org/gpb2kv

Richards, J. M., & Gross, J. J. (2000). Emotion regulation and memory: The cognitive costs of keeping one's cool. *Journal of Personality and Social Psychology*, 79(3), 410–424. https://doi.org/10.1037/0022-3514.79.3.410

Road Scholar. (2018). Road scholar lifelong learning resource network. Administrator survey, 2017–2018. (Released: June 20, 2018). https://www.roadscholar.org/globalassets/llis/2018-summary-road-scholar-lli-resource-network-administrator-survey.pdf

Roberti, J. W., Harrington, L. N., & Storch, E. A. (2006). Further psychometric support for the 10-item version of the perceived stress scale. *Journal of College Counseling, 9*(2), 135–147. https://doi.org/fztkv4

Robins, L. N., Helzer, J. E., & Davis, D. H. (1975). Narcotic use in Southeast Asia and afterward: An interview study of 898 Vietnam returnees. *Archives of General Psychiatry*, 32(8), 955-961.

Robinson, O. J., Vytal, K., Cornwell, B. R., & Grillon, C. (2013). The impact of anxiety upon cognition: Perspectives from human threat of shock studies. *Frontiers in Human Neuroscience, 7*, 203. https://doi.org/fk9v

Rogers, C. S., Payne, L., Maharjan, S., Wingfield, A., & Sekuler, R. (2018). Older adults show impaired modulation of attentional alpha oscillations: Evidence from dichotic listening. *Psychology and aging, 33*(2), 246. https://doi.org/gppspq

Rogers, E. M. (2010). *Diffusion of innovations*. Simon and Schuster.

Rosenbaum, M. S., Russell-Bennett, R., & Contreras-Ramírez, G. (2021). business education in profound disruption. *Journal of Services Marketing*.

Rubínová, E., et al. (2021). [Title not provided in draft; likely schema formation and narrative recall]. [Publication details not provided].

Rudolph, J. L. (2002). *Scientists in the classroom: The cold war reconstruction of American science education*. Palgrave Macmillan.

Saadé, R. G., & Otrakji, C. A. (2007). First impressions last a lifetime: Effect of interface type on disorientation and cognitive load. *Computers in Human Behavior, 23*(1), 525–535. https://doi.org/fw685q

Sablonnière, R. (2017). Toward a psychology of social change: A typology of social change. *Frontiers in psychology, 8*, 397. https://doi.org/f9w9mz

Saladin, M., Saper, Z., & Breen, L. (1988). Perceived attractiveness and attributions of criminality: What is beautiful is not criminal. *Canadian Journal of Criminology, 30*(3), 251-259.

Salthouse, T. A. (2019). [Title not provided in draft; likely fluid intelligence declines in aging]. [Publication details not provided].

Salthouse, T. A. (2019). Trajectories of normal cognitive aging. *Psychology and Aging, 34*(1), 17. https://doi.org/gfvzzs

Samanez-Larkin, G. R., Levens, S. M., Perry, L. M., Dougherty, R. F., & Knutson, B. (2012). Frontostriatal white matter integrity mediates adult age differences in probabilistic reward learning. *Journal of Neuroscience, 32*(15), 5333–5337. https://doi.org/10.1523/JNEUROSCI.5756–11.2012

Satterfield, S., Reichherzer, T., Coffey, J., & El-Sheikh, E. (2012, December). Application of structural case-based reasoning to activity recognition in smart home environments. In *2012 11th International Conference on Machine Learning and Applications* (Vol. 1, pp. 1-6). IEEE.

Satterfield, S., Reichherzer, T., Coffey, J., & El-Sheikh, E. (2012). Application of structural case-based reasoning to activity recognition in smart home environments. *2012 11th International Conference on Machine Learning and Applications*, 391–396. https://doi.org/10.1109/ICMLA.2012.10

Sauer, J., Sonderegger, A., & Schmutz, S. (2020). Usability, user experience and accessibility: Towards an integrative model. *Ergonomics, 63*(10), 1207-1220. https://doi.org/gn2vjb

Sauro, J., & Kindlund, E. (2005, April). A method to standardize usability metrics into a single score. In *Proceedings of the SIGCHI conference on Human factors in computing systems* (pp. 401-409). https://doi.org/c3bp76

Schaie, K. W., & Willis, S. L. (2010). [Title not provided in draft; likely quasi-longitudinal cognitive aging data]. [Publication details not provided].

Schaie, K. W., & Willis, S. L. (2010). The Seattle longitudinal study of adult cognitive development. *ISSBD Bulletin, 57*(1), 24.

Schank, R. C. (1999). *Dynamic memory revisited*. Cambridge University Press.

Schank, R. C., & Abelson, R. P. (1977). *Scripts, plans, goals, and understanding: An inquiry into human knowledge structures*. Lawrence Erlbaum Associates.

Schleiffer, R. (2005). An intelligent agent model. *European Journal of Operational Research, 166*(3), 666-693. https://doi.org/bbmqvw

Schmeichel, B. J. (2007). Attention control, memory updating, and emotion regulation temporarily reduce the capacity for executive control. *Journal of Experimental Psychology: General*, 136(2), 241–255. https://doi.org/10.1037/0096-3445.136.2.241

Schnotz, W., & Kürschner, C. (2007). A reconsideration of cognitive load theory. *Educational psychology review, 19*(4), 469-508. https://doi.org/bnh23t

Schunk, D. H. (1989). Self-efficacy and cognitive achievement: Implications for students with learning problems. *Journal of learning disabilities, 22*(1), 14-22. https://doi.org/c54b7k

Schwartz, P. M., & Solove, D. J. (2011). The PII problem: Privacy and a new concept of personally identifiable information. *New York University Law Review., 86*, 1814.

Seligman, M. E. P. (1975). *Helplessness: On depression, development, and death*. W. H. Freeman.

Sennett, R. (1998). *The corrosion of character: The personal consequences of work in the new capitalism*. W. W. Norton & Company.

Sepp, S., Howard, S. J., Tindall-Ford, S., Agostinho, S., & Paas, F. (2019). Cognitive load theory and human movement: Towards an integrated model of working memory. *Educational Psychology Review, 31(2)*, 293–317. https://doi.org/ggjgpq

Seyhan, A. A. (2019). Lost in translation: The valley of death across preclinical and clinical divide–identification of problems and overcoming obstacles. *Translational Medicine Communications, 4*(1), 1-19. https://doi.org/hnbf

Seymour, E., & Hewitt, N. M. (1997). *Talking about leaving: Why undergraduates leave the sciences*. Westview Press.

Shallice, T., & Burgess, P. (1991). Deficits in strategy application following frontal lobe damage in man. *Brain*, 114(2), 727–741. https://doi.org/10.1093/brain/114.2.727

Shannon, C. E., & Weaver, W. (1948). *The mathematical theory of communication*. Nokia Bell Labs. https://doi.org/b39t

Sheppard, B. H., Hartwick, J., & Warshaw, P. R. (1988). The theory of reasoned action: A meta-analysis of past research with recommendations for modifications and future research. *Journal of consumer research, 15*(3), 325-343.

Simcock, G., & Hayne, H. (2002). Breaking the barrier? Children fail to translate their preverbal memories into language. *Psychological Science, 13*(3), 225–231. https://doi.org/cwr9cr

Simon, H. A., & Newell, A. (1971). Human problem solving: The state of the theory in 1970. *American Psychologist, 26*(2), 145. https://doi.org/ckmsq7

Simon, M. K. (2011). *Dissertation and scholarly research: Recipes for success*. Dissertation Success, LLC.

Sklar, K. K. (1985). Hull House in the 1890s: A community of women reformers. *Signs: Journal of Women in Culture and Society, 10*(4), 658-677.

Slack, M. K., & Draugalis, J. R., Jr. (2001). Establishing the internal and external validity of experimental studies. *American Journal of Health-System Pharmacy, 58*(22), 2173–2181. https://doi.org/hnbg

Smith, G. S. (2013). Aging and neuroplasticity. *Dialogues in Clinical Neuroscience, 15*(1), 3. https://doi.org/hnbh

Snyder, C. R. (1995). Conceptualizing, measuring, and nurturing hope. *Journal of Counseling & Development, 73*(3), 355–360. https://doi.org/fz2pbj

Snyder, C. R. (2002). Hope theory: Rainbows in the mind. *Psychological inquiry, 13*(4), 249–275. https://doi.org/c2vdm8

Sowell, T. (1981). *Ethnic America: A history*. Basic Books.

Sowell, T. (1994). *Race and culture: A world view*. Basic Books.

Spence, M. (1973). Job market signaling. *Quarterly Journal of Economics,* 87(3), 355–374. https://doi.org/10.2307/1882010

Spreng, R. N., & Turner, G. R. (2019). [Title not provided in draft; likely brain networks and cognitive aging]. [Publication details not provided].

Spreng, R. N., & Turner, G. R. (2019). The shifting architecture of cognition and brain function in older adulthood. *Perspectives on Psychological Science, 14*(4), 523-542. https://doi.org/gf4x64

Steele, C. M. (1997). A threat in the air: How stereotypes shape intellectual identity and performance. *American Psychologist,* 52(6), 613–629. https://doi.org/10.1037/0003-066X.52.6.613

Steffener, J., & Stern, Y. (2012). Exploring the neural basis of cognitive reserve in aging. *Biochimica et Biophysica Acta (BBA)-Molecular Basis of Disease, 1822*(3), 467-473. https://doi.org/b8nchp

Sternberg, R. J. (1997). *Successful intelligence*. Plume.

Stiller, K. D., & Bachmaier, R. (2018, June). Cognitive loads in a distance training for trainee teachers. In *Frontiers in Education, 3*, 44. https://doi.org/hnbj

Stojanovska, M., Tingle, G., Tan, L., Ulrey, L., Simonson-Shick, S., Mlakar, J., Eastman, H., Gotschall, R., Boscia, A., Enterline, R., Henninger, E., Herrmann, K. A., Simpson, S. W., Groswold, M. A., & Wish-Baratz, S. (2019). Mixed reality anatomy using Microsoft HoloLens and cadaveric dissection: A comparative effectiveness study. *Medical Science Educator*, 1–6.

Stover, J. F. (1977). *American railroads*. University of Chicago Press.

Stroop, J. R. (1935). Studies of interference in serial verbal reactions. *Journal of experimental psychology, 18*(6), 643. https://doi.org/b77m95

Sturtevant, D. (2019). [Title not provided in draft; likely technical capability crisis analysis]. [Publication details not provided].

Sturtevant, D. (2019). [Title not provided in draft; likely technical capability crisis analysis]. [Publication details not provided].

Sun, H., & Zhang, P. (2006). The role of moderating factors in user technology acceptance. *International Journal of Human-Computer Studies, 64*(2), 53–78. https://doi.org/fs9tftSweller, J. (1988). Cognitive load during problem solving: Effects on learning. *Cognitive Science, 12*(2), 257–285. https://doi.org/cmgsv8

Sweller, J. (1988). Cognitive load during problem solving: Effects on learning. *Cognitive Science*, 12(2), 257–285. https://doi. org/10.1207/s15516709cog1202_4

Sweller, J. (1993). Some cognitive processes and their consequences for the organization and presentation of information. *Australian Journal of Psychology, 45*(1), 1-8.

Sweller, J. (1994). Cognitive load theory, learning difficulty, and instructional design. *Learning and Instruction, 4*(4), 295–312. https://doi.org/dhh7hs

Sweller, J. (2005). The redundancy principle in multimedia learning. *The Cambridge handbook of multimedia learning*, 159-167.

Sweller, J. (2010). Element interactivity and intrinsic, extraneous, and germane cognitive load. *Educational Psychology Review, 22*(2), 123–138.

Sweller, J. (2012). Human cognitive architecture: Why some instructional procedures work and others do not. In K. R. Harris, S. Graham, T. Urdan, C.B. McCormick, G. M. Sinatra, & J. Sweller (Eds.), *APA Educational Psychology Handbook, Vol. 1. Theories, Constructs, and Critical Issues*, 295–325. American Psychological Association. https://doi.org/fsj345

Sweller, J., & Chandler, P. (1991). Evidence for cognitive load theory. *Cognition and instruction, 8*(4), 351-362.

Sweller, J., Ayres, P., & Kalyuga, S. (2011). *Cognitive load theory.* Springer.

Sweller, J., Van Merriënboer, J. J., & Paas, F. (2019). Cognitive architecture and instructional design: 20 years later. *Educational Psychology Review, 31*(2), 261–292. https://link.springer.com/article/10.1007/s10648-019-09465-5

Sweller, J., Van Merrienboer, J. J., & Paas, F. G. (1998). Cognitive architecture and instructional design. *Educational psychology review, 10*(3), 251-296.

Swirsky, L. T., & Spaniol, J. (2019). Cognitive and motivational selectivity in healthy aging. *Wiley Interdisciplinary Reviews: Cognitive Science, 10*(6), e1512. https://doi.org/hnbk

Symonds, W. C., Schwartz, R. B., & Ferguson, R. (2011). *Pathways to prosperity: Meeting the challenge of preparing young Americans for the 21st century.* Harvard Graduate School of Education. https://www.gse.harvard.edu/news/11/02/pathways-prosperity-meeting-challenge-preparing-young-americans-21st-century

Szulewski, A., Gegenfurtner, A., Howes, D. W., Sivilotti, M. L., & Van Merriënboer, J. J. (2017). Measuring physician cognitive load: Validity evidence for a physiologic and a psychometric tool. *Advances in Health Sciences Education, 22*(4), 951–968. https://link.springer.com/article/10.1007/s10459-016-9725-2

Tajfel, H., & Turner, J. C. (1979). An integrative theory of intergroup conflict. In W. G. Austin & S. Worchel (Eds.), *The social psychology of intergroup relations* (pp. 33–47). Brooks/Cole.

Tamm, L., Menon, V., & Reiss, A. L. (2002). Maturation of brain function associated with response inhibition. *Journal of the American Academy of Child & Adolescent Psychiatry, 41*(10), 1231–1238. https://doi.org/d7bj8q

Taylor, S., & Todd, P. (1995). Decomposition and crossover effects in the theory of planned behavior: A study of consumer adoption intentions. *International Journal of Research in Marketing, 12*(2), 137-155.

Thompson, E. R. (2007). Development and validation of an internationally reliable short-form of the positive and negative affect schedule (PANAS). *Journal of Cross-Cultural Psychology, 38*(2), 227–242. https://doi.org/dv68xh

Thrasher, G. R., Zabel, K. L., Bramble, R. J., & Baltes, B. B. (2018). Who is aging successfully at work? A latent profile analysis of successful agers and their work motives. *Work, Aging and Retirement, 4*(2), 175–188. https://doi.org/ggwptc

Thurstone, L. L. (1928). Attitudes can be measured. *American Journal of Sociology, 33*(4), 529–554. https://doi.org/bg4kw3

Tocqueville, A. de. (1835). *Democracy in America* (Vol. 1). (H. Reeve, Trans.). Saunders and Otley. (Original work published 1835)

Toepoel, V., Vermeeren, B., & Metin, B. (2019). Smileys, stars, hearts, buttons, tiles or grids: Influence of response format on substantive response, questionnaire experience and response time. *Bulletin of Sociological Methodology/Bulletin de Méthodologie Sociologique, 142*(1), 57–74. https://doi.org/hnbm

Tomić, I., et al. (2024). [Title not provided in draft; likely Dynamic Neural Resource model]. [Publication details not provided].

Toossi, M., & Torpey, E. (2017). Older workers: Labor force trends and career options. *Career outlook, 4*(1), 45-64.

Torricelli, E. (1644). [Historical description of vacuum experiments]. [Publication details not provided; historical scientific record].

Tran, K. N., Lau, J. H., Contractor, D., Gupta, U., Sengupta, B., Butler, C. J., & Mohania, M. (2018). Document chunking and learning objective generation for instruction design. *arXiv preprint arXiv:1806.01351.* https://doi.org/jsjw

Trelle, A. N., et al. (2020). [Title not provided in draft; likely pattern completion impairment in aging]. [Publication details not provided].

Trow, M. (1973). *Problems in the transition from elite to mass higher education.* Carnegie Commission on Higher Education.

Tse, I. A. (1998). National Workplace Literacy Program (NWLP) at Chinatown Manpower Project, Inc. Final Performance Report. ERIC.

Tulving, E. (1972). Episodic and semantic memory. In E. Tulving & W. Donaldson (Eds.), *Organization of memory* (pp. 381–403). Academic Press.

Tulving, E. (1983). *Elements of episodic memory.* Oxford University Press.

Turchin, P. (2006). *War and peace and war: The rise and fall of empires.* Pi Press.

U.S. Bureau of Labor Statistics. (2000). [Title not provided in draft; likely occupational structure data]. [Publication details not provided].

U.S. Census Bureau. (1900). [Title not provided in draft; likely occupational census data]. [Publication details not provided].

U.S. Census Bureau. (2018). The population 65 years and older in the United States: 2016. https://www.census.gov/content/dam/Census/library/publications/2018/acs/ACS-38.pdf.

U.S. Census Bureau. (2020). County Population Totals: 2010–2019. https://www.census.gov/data/tables/time-series/demo/popest/2010s-counties-total.html

UNESCO. (1970). 1970: Education at the crossroads. https://en.unesco.org/courier/january-1970

UNESCO. (2019). UNESCO in brief - mission and mandate. https://en.unesco.org/about-us/introducing-unesco

United Nations Department of Economic and Social Affairs. (2002). *World population ageing, 1950–2050*. United Nations Publications. http://globalag.igc.org/ruralaging/world/ageingo.htm

University of West Florida. (2020). Facts & figures: 2018–2019 academic year. https://uwf.edu/about/facts-and-figures/.

van Merriënboer, J. J. G., & Sweller, J. (2010). Cognitive load theory in health professional education: Design principles and strategies. *Medical Education*, 44(1), 85–93. https://doi.org/10.1111/j.1365-2923.2009.03498.x

Van Merriënboer, J. J., Kester, L., & Paas, F. (2006). Teaching complex rather than simple tasks: Balancing intrinsic and germane load to enhance transfer of learning. *Applied Cognitive Psychology: The Official Journal of the Society for Applied Research in Memory and Cognition*, 20(3), 343–352. https://doi.org/b743x3

Van Nuland, S. E., Eagleson, R., & Rogers, K. A. (2017). Educational software usability: Artifact or design? *Anatomical Sciences Education*, 10(2), 190–199. https://doi.org/hnbn

Veríssimo, J., et al. (2022). [Title not provided in draft; likely cognitive aging trends]. [Publication details not provided].

Veríssimo, J., Verhaeghen, P., Goldman, N., Weinstein, M., & Ullman, M. T. (2022). Evidence that ageing yields improvements as well as declines across attention and executive functions. *Nature Human Behaviour*, 6(1), 97-110. https://doi.org/gmh3bj

Vosoughi, S., Roy, D., & Aral, S. (2018). The spread of true and false news online. *Science, 359*(6380), 1146–1151. https://doi.org/10.1126/science.aap9559

Wang, D., Liang, Y., Xu, D., Feng, X., & Guan, R. (2018). A content-based recommender system for computer science publications. *Knowledge-Based Systems, 157*, 1–9. https://doi.org/gh3prs

Wang, S., Zhao, Y., Li, J., Lai, H., Qiu, C., Pan, N., & Gong, Q. (2020). Neurostructural correlates of hope: dispositional hope mediates the impact of the SMA gray matter volume on subjective well-being in late adolescence. *Social Cognitive and Affective Neuroscience, 15*(4), 395–404. https://doi.org/hnbp

Warner, R. M. (2012). *Applied statistics: From bivariate through multivariate techniques.* Sage Publications.

Waterman, A. S., & Archer, S. L. (1990). A life-span perspective on identity formation: Developments in form, function, and process. In Baltes, P. B., Featherman, D. L., & Lerner, R. M. (Eds.), *Life-span Development and Behavior: volume 10.* (pp. 29–57). Psychology Press. https://doi.org/hnbq

Watson, D. (1988). The vicissitudes of mood measurement: Effects of varying descriptors, time frames, and response formats on measures of positive and negative affect. *Journal of Personality and Social Psychology, 55*(1), 128. https://doi.org/bvrjsh

Watt, J. (1769). [Patent and historical description of separate condenser improvement]. [Publication details not provided; historical patent record].

Weber, J., Jörres, R., Kronseder, A., Müller, A., Weigl, M., & Chmelar, C. (2019). Learning on the job, the use of selection, optimization, and compensation strategies, and their association with telomere length as an indicator of biological aging. *International Archives of Occupational and Environmental Health, 92*(3), 361–370. https://doi.org/hkss

Weikum, G., Dong, X. L., Razniewski, S., & Suchanek, F. (2021). Machine knowledge: Creation and curation of comprehensive knowledge bases. *Foundations and Trends® in Databases, 10*(2-4), 108-490. https://doi.org/hksr

Whitehead, A. N. (1929). *The aims of education and other essays*. Macmillan

Whitehead, A. N. (1931). Introduction: On foresight. In Donham, W. B., Business adrift. (pp. xi-xxix) McGraw-Hill Book Company, Inc.

Whitehead, A. N. (1931). *The aims of education and other essays*. Macmillan.

Wildenbos, G. A., Peute, L., & Jaspers, M. (2018). Aging barriers influencing mobile health usability for older adults: A literature based framework (MOLD-US). *International Journal of Medical Informatics, 114*, 66–75. https://doi.org/gdgj2k

Wolf, T., Chaumond, J., Debut, L., Sanh, V., Delangue, C., Moi, A., Cistac, P., Rault, T., Louf, R., Funtowica, M., Davison, J., Shleifer, S., Von Platen, P., Ma, C., Jernite, Y., Plu, J., Xu, C., Le Scao, T., Gugger, S., ... Rush, A. M. (2020, October). Transformers: State-of-the-art natural language processing. In *Proceedings of the 2020 Conference on Empirical Methods in Natural Language Processing: System Demonstrations* (pp. 38–45). https://doi.org/ghs3bd

Wong, A., Leahy, W., Marcus, N., & Sweller, J. (2012). Cognitive load theory, the transient information effect and e-learning. *Learning and Instruction, 22*(6), 449–457. https://doi.org/f4bcg6

Woodson, C. G. (1933). The Mis-education of the Negro. Winston.

Wright, G. (1986). *Old South, new South: Revolutions in the southern economy since the Civil War*. Basic Books.

Wroblewski, L. (2011). *Mobile first*. A Book Apart.

Zacher, H., & Frese, M. (2011). Maintaining a focus on opportunities at work: The interplay between age, job complexity, and the use of selection, optimization, and compensation strategies. *Journal of Organizational Behavior, 32*(2), 291–318. https://doi.org/cb9h54

Zervas, T. G. (2017). Finding a Balance in Education: Immigration, Diversity, and Schooling in Urban America, 1880-1900. *Athens Journal of Education, 4*(1), 77-84.

Zhao, X., & Chui, E. (2019). The development and characteristics of universities of the third Age in mainland China. In *The University of the Third Age and Active Ageing* (pp. 157–168). Springer. https://doi.org/hnbr

Appendices

Appendix A — Founders: Learning and the Republic

This appendix introduces civic founders whose ideas established learning as a prerequisite for self-government rather than a private or technical concern. These figures were not educational theorists in the modern sense; they were architects of a political vision that assumed citizens must continually develop judgment, knowledge, and moral agency if a republic is to endure. Their writings frame education as a public responsibility tied to liberty, accountability, and resistance to tyranny.

The figures included here reflect a range of philosophical dispositions—liberal, republican, and conservative—united by the shared conviction that self-government presupposes an educated citizenry.

In *A Learning Republic*, these founders provide the normative foundation: the answer to why learning matters at the level of civic survival.

Benjamin Franklin (1706–1790)

Self-Directed Learning and Civic Utility

Benjamin Franklin embodied the ideal of lifelong, self-directed learning long before the term existed. Largely self-educated, Franklin treated learning as a practical enterprise—something to be pursued continuously, opportunistically, and in service of both personal improvement and the common good. He read widely, experimented relentlessly, and moved fluidly among trades, sciences, and civic roles.

Franklin rejected the notion that education was confined to youth or formal institutions. Through initiatives such as the Junto—a mutual-improvement society—he demonstrated that learning thrives in peer networks, discussion, and collaborative inquiry. His founding of libraries, academies, and civic institutions reflected a belief that access to knowledge should be distributed, not hoarded.

In *A Learning Republic*, Franklin represents the learning citizen rather than the learning system. Where Jefferson articulated education as a safeguard of the republic, Franklin lived it as a daily practice. His emphasis on utility, experimentation, and moral self-regulation aligns closely with modern concepts of competence-based learning, intrinsic motivation, and recoverable failure.

Franklin also anticipated later insights from signaling theory. He understood reputation, demonstrated competence, and visible effort as forms of social currency—but unlike credential-based signaling, his proof of capability was grounded in observable contribution. In this sense, Franklin offers an alternative model of signaling rooted in practice rather than formal certification.

His legacy reinforces a core thesis of *A Learning Republic*: a free society depends not only on schools and credentials, but on citizens who take personal responsibility for their own intellectual growth—and who view learning as inseparable from civic duty.

Edmund Burke (1729–1797)

Tradition as Cognitive Inheritance

Edmund Burke understood learning as the slow formation of judgment through inherited cultural, moral, and institutional knowledge. He rejected the idea that societies—or learners—could be reconstructed from abstract principles alone without incurring catastrophic loss. Knowledge, Burke argued, accumulates through tradition, habit, and lived practice, forming a cognitive inheritance that no single generation can reproduce from scratch.

For Burke, tradition was not the enemy of reason but its precondition. Inherited frameworks compress experience across time, allowing individuals to reason without bearing the full cognitive burden of first-principles reconstruction. When these frameworks are discarded, individuals are forced to deliberate continuously under excessive cognitive load, mistaking novelty for insight and abstraction for understanding. Reform detached from historical continuity, Burke warned, risks destroying the very capacities—judgment, restraint, and practical wisdom—it seeks to improve.

In *A Learning Republic*, Burke anchors the insight that learning depends on accumulated schemas transmitted across generations. His work reinforces skepticism toward decontextualized reform and complements cognitive load theory by revealing tradition as a form of cognitive scaffolding rather than mere conservatism. Burke thus supports the book's central claim that durable learning systems must respect cognitive inheritance as much as innovation. When inherited knowledge is treated as disposable, societies do not become freer or more rational—they become cognitively overburdened and fragile.

John Adams (1735–1826)

Education, Virtue, and the Limits of Law

John Adams believed that no constitution could preserve liberty without an educated and morally formed citizenry. His oft-quoted assertion that the Constitution was made for a "moral and religious people" is best understood not as sectarian doctrine, but as an educational claim: self-government requires judgment, restraint, and the capacity to govern one's own passions before attempting to govern others. Law, in Adams's view, presupposes character.

Adams emphasized local institutions—schools, churches, families, and civic associations—as the primary means by which judgment and restraint are cultivated. These institutions did not merely transmit information; they formed habits of responsibility, deliberation, and self-command. Knowledge without virtue, Adams warned, does not liberate—it amplifies ambition, cleverness, and the capacity for harm. Where internalized restraint is absent, legal systems become increasingly coercive and fragile.

In *A Learning Republic*, Adams represents the founding recognition that learning is formative as well as cognitive. Civic failure, in his account, is ultimately educational failure: when citizens lack the habits of judgment and restraint, no constitutional design can compensate. Adams reinforces the book's central claim that sustainable self-government depends not only on institutions and laws, but on citizens shaped by learning long before they encounter either.

Thomas Jefferson (1743–1826)

Education as the Safeguard of Liberty

Thomas Jefferson argued that a republic can survive only if its citizens are educated well enough to govern themselves. He viewed education not as a private good or a tool of economic advancement, but as a public necessity, essential to resisting tyranny and preserving liberty across generations. Concentrated ignorance, he believed, inevitably produces concentrated power; only a broadly educated populace can prevent authority from collapsing into domination.

Jefferson's proposals for public education were grounded in this civic logic. He believed citizens must possess sufficient knowledge to evaluate leaders, laws, and claims made in the public sphere. Without that capacity, formal rights become hollow, and democratic institutions persist in name while failing in function. Education, in Jefferson's account, is preventive: it guards against corruption, manipulation, and the gradual erosion of self-government.

Although Jefferson's vision was constrained by the exclusions and contradictions of his era, his structural insight endures. Ignorance is incompatible with self-rule, regardless of who is excluded or included. Liberty cannot be sustained by sentiment, tradition, or institutional form alone; it requires an informed citizenry capable of judgment and restraint.

In *A Learning Republic*, Jefferson anchors the book's normative claim that learning is not optional in a democracy. Education is not merely preparation for citizenship—it is the condition that makes citizenship possible. Where learning falters, self-government decays quietly, leaving behind the appearance of freedom without its substance.

James Madison (1751–1836)

Knowledge, Faction, and Informed Judgment

James Madison's constitutional thought reflects a keen understanding of cognitive vulnerability in mass politics. In *The Federalist Papers*, he warned that faction, misinformation, and unexamined passion posed persistent threats to republican government. His concern was not merely political instability, but the tendency of human judgment to be distorted by partial information, short time horizons, and emotionally charged appeals.

Madison's response to faction was not enforced uniformity or elite rule, but the diffusion of knowledge within a large and pluralistic republic. By expanding the sphere of debate and encouraging an informed public, Madison believed competing interests would check one another and reduce the influence of demagogues. Liberty, in his account, depended not on the absence of conflict, but on citizens' capacity to evaluate arguments, weigh evidence, and deliberate across difference.

In *A Learning Republic*, Madison represents the cognitive dimension of constitutional design. His work anticipates modern concerns about information overload, incentive distortion, and fragmented attention by recognizing that freedom requires more than access to information—it requires the ability to reason under complexity. Madison thus reinforces the book's central claim: learning systems must prepare citizens not simply to consume information, but to exercise informed judgment amid competing claims if self-government is to endure.

Gouverneur Morris (1752–1816)

The Cognitive Burden of "We the People"

Gouverneur Morris, principal author of the Constitution's Preamble, understood that republican government imposes extraordinary cognitive demands on ordinary citizens. The phrase *"We the People"* is not merely rhetorical; it presumes a populace capable of abstraction, civic reasoning, delayed gratification, and judgment extended across time. Self-government, in Morris's view, is not sustained by sentiment alone but by the mental capacities required to evaluate arguments, resist manipulation, and act with foresight rather than impulse.

Morris worried openly that ignorance, volatility, and susceptibility to demagoguery could undermine self-rule as surely as external tyranny. His skepticism toward unprepared democracy has often been labeled elitist, but it rested on a sober cognitive assessment rather than disdain for the public. Morris recognized that political equality does not erase differences in preparation, attention, or knowledge—and that constitutional design quietly assumes a minimum threshold of learning capacity among citizens.

In *A Learning Republic*, Morris gives voice to a foundational but often unspoken truth: democracy presupposes learning capacity. The Constitution does not merely authorize self-government; it embeds an educational demand at its core. When that demand is unmet—when citizens lack the cognitive resources to deliberate, contextualize, and judge—the mechanisms of republican government continue to operate in form while eroding in substance. Morris thus anticipates the book's central claim: the survival of a republic depends not only on institutions, but on the sustained learning capacity of the people who animate them.

Appendix B — Theorists: How Learning Works

The theorists in this appendix explain the mechanisms that govern learning—its limits, efficiencies, failures, and distortions. Drawing from cognitive psychology, educational science, and economics, they illuminate how working memory, schema formation, mental effort, and incentive structures shape learning outcomes independently of motivation or intent. Their work clarifies why well-meaning educational systems often overload learners, misinterpret avoidance as apathy, or reward credentials over competence.

These theorists represent diverse intellectual traditions, including progressive, conservative, and empirically pragmatic perspectives, unified by a commitment to explanatory clarity rather than ideological alignment.

This appendix provides the scientific and analytical backbone for the book's claims about recoverable learning and instructional responsibility.

George A. Miller (1920–2012)

Limits of Working Memory

George A. Miller's seminal paper, *"The Magical Number Seven, Plus or Minus Two,"* marked a decisive shift in cognitive science by identifying hard limits on working-memory capacity. His central insight—that humans can hold only a small number of discrete elements in conscious awareness—challenged assumptions that learning failure resulted primarily from lack of effort or intelligence. Cognitive limitation, Miller showed, is a universal human condition.

Crucially, Miller did not argue that humans are limited in what they can know, but in how much unstructured information they can process at once. His work introduced the concept of *chunking*, demonstrating that information organized into meaningful structures dramatically reduces cognitive burden. This distinction between information quantity and information structure laid the groundwork for later theories of schema formation, cognitive load, and instructional design.

In *A Learning Republic*, Miller's contribution underpins the book's core claim that difficulty is not merely a function of volume, but of organization. Instruction that ignores working-memory limits overwhelms learners regardless of motivation, while well-structured learning allows complexity to be mastered incrementally. Miller thus provides the foundational insight upon which all later discussions of cognitive load, recoverable learning, and instructional responsibility depend. His work makes clear that learning environments must be designed for human cognition as it actually exists—not as educators might wish it to be.

E. D. Hirsch Jr.

Background Knowledge and Cultural Literacy

E. D. Hirsch Jr. argued that educational failure often stems not from deficits in skill or intelligence, but from gaps in shared background knowledge. Through empirical work on reading comprehension, he demonstrated that understanding is domain-specific and heavily dependent on prior information stored in long-term memory. Skills such as "critical thinking" or "reading strategies" cannot compensate when learners lack the contextual knowledge required to make sense of a text.

Hirsch's work aligns closely with schema theory. When background knowledge is absent, learners must expend scarce working-memory resources deciphering context, leaving little capacity for meaning-making or integration. Instruction that emphasizes generic skills while neglecting content inadvertently increases cognitive load and widens achievement gaps, particularly for learners who lack access to knowledge-rich environments outside school.

Hirsch challenged prevailing progressive assumptions that skills could be taught independently of content, insisting instead that knowledge is not the enemy of thinking but its precondition. Shared cultural literacy, in his account, is not about conformity or canon enforcement, but about providing learners with the common reference points that make communication, comprehension, and participation possible.

In *A Learning Republic*, Hirsch provides a crucial conservative complement to cognitive load theory. His work reinforces the claim that learning capacity depends on cultural inheritance as well as instructional design, and that motivation alone cannot overcome missing knowledge structures. By reframing educational equity as a problem of access to shared knowledge rather than abstract skill, Hirsch strengthens the book's argument that sustainable learning requires both cognitive realism and civic continuity.

Allan Bloom (1930–1992)

Depth, Seriousness, and Intellectual Formation

Allan Bloom critiqued modern education for abandoning seriousness in favor of relativism, immediacy, and cultural mirroring. He argued that education should initiate learners into enduring questions, texts, and intellectual traditions that resist easy consumption, rather than reducing learning to the affirmation of contemporary attitudes or preferences. For Bloom, education was not meant to flatter students, but to *form* them.

Bloom emphasized disciplined reading, sustained attention, and reverence for ideas that demand patience and effort. These practices, he believed, were not antiquarian habits but cognitive necessities: deep engagement with difficult texts trains attention, judgment, and the capacity to hold complex ideas in mind over time. When education substitutes breadth for depth or exposure for mastery, it weakens these capacities even as it expands content.

Although often polemical in tone, Bloom's underlying concern was neither nostalgia nor ideology, but the erosion of intellectual formation. Shallow engagement, he warned, produces shallow thought—not because learners lack intelligence, but because educational environments no longer require sustained cognitive investment.

In *A Learning Republic*, Bloom represents the conservative warning that breadth without depth erodes intellectual capacity. His critique complements the book's analysis of overload and fragmented attention by highlighting a different but related failure mode: learning environments that avoid difficulty in the name of accessibility ultimately deprive learners—especially adults—of the very rigor required for independent judgment and self-government.

Thomas Sowell

Tradeoffs, Incentives, and Educational Outcomes

Thomas Sowell approached education through the lens of incentives, constraints, and unintended consequences, consistently challenging reforms that treated outcomes as matters of intention rather than structure. He argued that educational systems are shaped less by stated goals than by the incentives they create and the behavioral realities they must operate within. Policies that ignore these dynamics, Sowell warned, often produce results opposite to those intended.

Sowell emphasized that disparities in educational outcomes cannot be understood apart from culture, preparation, and accumulated knowledge. While acknowledging the existence of structural barriers, he rejected explanations that reduce educational failure to discrimination or funding alone, noting that such accounts often obscure more actionable causes. For Sowell, refusing to examine preparation gaps or incentive distortions does not advance equity; it merely prevents learning systems from correcting themselves.

In *A Learning Republic*, Sowell contributes a disciplined insistence on causal humility. His work reinforces the book's resistance to moralized explanations of failure and complements signaling theory by showing how credentials, mandates, and reforms can function as symbolic gestures rather than capacity-building mechanisms. Most importantly, Sowell reminds readers that learning systems fail predictably when they promise outcomes without accounting for incentives, preparation, and cognitive limits—an error that no amount of goodwill can overcome.

Allan Baddeley

The Architecture of Working Memory

Allan Baddeley extended George A. Miller's work on capacity limits by proposing a multi-component model of working memory, consisting of the phonological loop, the visuospatial sketchpad, and a central executive that coordinates attention and control. This framework replaced the notion of working memory as a single bottleneck with a more accurate account of how different types of information are processed in parallel yet remain jointly constrained.

Baddeley's model explains why learners can be overloaded in one channel while unused capacity remains in another—and why instructional designs that appear information-rich can still fail. When verbal explanations, visual representations, and task demands are poorly aligned, the central executive becomes overtaxed, producing confusion, fatigue, and disengagement. Conversely, when information is distributed coherently across channels, learning efficiency improves rather than deteriorates.

In *A Learning Republic*, Baddeley's framework is essential for understanding instructional overload, split attention, and decision fatigue, particularly in modern multimedia and digitally saturated environments. His work clarifies why adding resources, choices, or modalities does not automatically support learning and often undermines it. By revealing how attentional control collapses under excessive coordination demands, Baddeley provides a critical foundation for ethical instructional design—one that respects not just how much information learners receive, but how their limited executive capacity must manage it over time.

Peter Jarvis (1937 – 2018)

Learning, Disjuncture, and the Lived Experience of the Adult Learner

One of the most influential theorists of adult learning in the late twentieth and early twenty-first centuries, Peter Jarvis's enduring insight is that learning is not preparation for life; it is something people do *while living* (Jarvis, 2006). A society that depends on lifelong learning must therefore design environments that acknowledge disruption, support reflection, and treat struggle not as deficiency but as the normal condition of learning in a changing world. Whether learning occurs depends not simply on motivation, but on the learner's cognitive, emotional, and situational capacity to engage with disruption rather than avoid it (Jarvis, 1992; Jarvis, Holford, & Griffin, 2003).

Jarvis insisted that learning cannot be separated from biography, emotion, and social context. In contrast to models that frame learning as the linear acquisition of knowledge or skills, he conceptualized learning as a response to *disjuncture*—a felt mismatch between an individual's existing understanding and lived experience (Jarvis, 1987; 2006).

A central contribution of Jarvis's work is his rejection of the idea that adult learners enter educational settings as blank slates. Adults bring accumulated identities, responsibilities, memories of schooling, and histories of success and failure. These biographical factors shape how disjuncture is interpreted— either as an opportunity for meaning-making or as a threat to self-worth. In this way, Jarvis directly challenges deficit-based explanations of disengagement, reframing avoidance not as apathy or lack of ability, but as an adaptive response to prior experience (Jarvis, 2006).

In the context of *A Learning Republic*, Jarvis's perspective is particularly important for understanding barriers to learning across the lifespan. Cognitive overload, social categorization, institutional rigidity, and chronic stress all intensify disjuncture while simultaneously reducing the learner's capacity to work through it. In such contexts, disengagement should not be interpreted as indifference; it is often a protective strategy aimed at preserving identity and psychological equilibrium (Jarvis,

2012). Learning cannot be mandated, accelerated, or automated without regard for the learner's lived reality. When institutions fail to recognize disjuncture—or treat it as error rather than as the starting point of meaning-making—they transform learning environments into mechanisms of exclusion rather than growth.

John Sweller

Cognitive Load Theory

John Sweller formalized the distinction between intrinsic, extraneous, and germane cognitive load, providing a precise account of how instructional demands interact with the limits of working memory. Intrinsic load reflects the inherent complexity of the material; extraneous load arises from poor instructional design; germane load supports schema construction. Learning succeeds when instructional design minimizes extraneous load while supporting the transformation of intrinsic complexity into durable knowledge structures.

Sweller's experimental work demonstrated that unguided problem solving often impedes learning for novices—not because effort is undesirable, but because working memory is consumed by inefficient search rather than schema acquisition. In such cases, learners may appear engaged while learning little. What feels like "productive struggle" can, in fact, be cognitively unproductive when guidance is withheld prematurely.

In *A Learning Republic*, Sweller's theory anchors the book's critique of struggle romanticized without regard to cognitive limits. His work reframes instructional failure as a design problem rather than a motivational one and establishes a clear standard of responsibility: when learners disengage or fail to retain, the first question must concern how instruction was structured, not how much effort learners were willing to exert.

Cognitive Load Theory thus grounds an ethical claim—effective instruction must respect human cognitive architecture if learning is to remain recoverable across the lifespan.

Michael Spence

Signaling, Credentials, and the Cost of Proof

Michael Spence's theory of signaling reframed education not primarily as a mechanism for skill formation, but as a costly signal used to convey otherwise unobservable traits—such as perseverance, reliability, and cognitive endurance—to employers. In his seminal paper, *"Job Market Signaling,"* Spence demonstrated that even when education adds little direct productivity, it can still function as a sorting mechanism because it is *hard to fake*. Those who complete demanding credentials reveal information about themselves simply by having endured the process.

In *A Learning Republic*, signaling theory explains why formal credentials persist even when alternative learning pathways exist—and why individuals may rationally avoid learning opportunities that *would* increase competence but *would not* improve their signal. This distinction clarifies a common misinterpretation: avoidance of certain educational pathways may reflect signal optimization, not laziness or lack of motivation.

Spence's work also exposes a tension at the heart of modern education systems. When credentials become increasingly decoupled from genuine learning—either through credential inflation or overly narrow certification regimes—the signal degrades. The result is an arms race of ever-higher formal requirements that increase cognitive and economic load without commensurate gains in human capital.

This insight supports the book's broader claim that a healthy Learning Republic must cultivate credible, flexible signals of competence—signals that reward real learning and sustained effort without unnecessarily excluding capable individuals who learn through nontraditional or self-directed means.

Roger Schank (1946–2023)

Scripts, Stories, and Meaning-Making

Roger Schank rejected the view of learning as the accumulation of abstract facts, arguing instead that human understanding is organized around stories, scripts, and expectations derived from experience. In his model, memory is not a passive storehouse but an active interpretive system that encodes events as narratives used to predict and explain future situations.

Schank's work demonstrated that transfer occurs not through general rules, but through recognition of structurally similar stories. When learners fail to apply knowledge, the problem is often the absence of a relevant narrative schema to retrieve and adapt.

In *A Learning Republic*, Schank provides the missing cognitive explanation for why context-rich learning endures while decontextualized instruction evaporates. His emphasis on explanation, failure, and narrative aligns directly with the book's arguments about schema consolidation, reflective disengagement, and the centrality of meaning. Schank shows that learning is not optimized by exposure alone, but by experiences that can be remembered, interpreted, and retold.

Paul Gibson

Basic Needs, Cognitive Capacity, and Community Involvement

Paul Gibson's work advanced a theory of teaching and learning under conditions of chronic stress, cognitive overload, and depleted executive control. Drawing on extensive qualitative research with K–12 educators, Gibson identified a recurring pattern: instructional failure often occurs not because learners lack ability or motivation, but because they arrive cognitively exhausted by forces outside the classroom.

Gibson conceptualized teaching in such contexts as a form of *ministry*—not in a narrowly religious sense, but as a sustained, relational practice aimed at restoring learners' capacity to engage. In this framework, effective teaching begins not with content delivery, but with stabilizing attention, rebuilding trust, and reducing extraneous cognitive load so that learning can occur at all.

Gibson also documents the often-overlooked burden placed on teachers themselves, who must navigate the space between what communities *could* do to restore learning capacity and what is actually done. He recounts cases in which well-intentioned community groups offered assistance in ways that publicly marked students as recipients, increasing shame and cognitive threat rather than reducing it. In such moments, teachers are forced to choose between accepting symbolic support and protecting the dignity necessary for learning. This tension produces chronic stress and moral injury, further degrading the instructional environment. Gibson's account makes clear that teaching under overload is not only a cognitive challenge, but an ethical one.

In *A Learning Republic*, Gibson's work provides a theoretical bridge between cognitive load theory and lived educational reality. He explains how stress, instability, and unmet needs systematically erode working memory and executive function, producing behaviors frequently misdiagnosed as apathy or defiance. By reframing teaching as capacity restoration under load, Gibson extends learning theory beyond instructional design into the moral and relational conditions that make learning possible at all.

Harlene Hayne

Memory, Transfer, and Learning Without Language

Harlene Hayne's work on infant and early childhood memory demonstrates that learning and memory are robust long before verbal recall is possible. Through careful experimental design, she showed that infants can retain, retrieve, and transfer learning across contexts—provided the new situation matches key features of the original experience.

Hayne's research revealed that transfer is cue-dependent, relying on structural similarity rather than abstract generalization. When cues change too drastically, apparent forgetting may occur even though underlying memory remains intact.

In *A Learning Republic*, Hayne's findings illuminate why learners often fail to apply prior knowledge in new contexts: not because learning never occurred, but because instructional environments fail to provide recognizable cues. Her work complements schema theory and cognitive load theory by showing that transfer is fragile and context-sensitive from the very beginning of life. This insight reinforces the book's emphasis on recoverable learning and thoughtful instructional continuity.

Fred Paas

Measuring Mental Effort

Fred Paas made a decisive contribution to learning science by developing reliable methods for measuring perceived mental effort, allowing instructional effectiveness to be evaluated not only by outcomes, but by the cognitive cost imposed on learners. This work transformed cognitive load theory from a descriptive framework into an empirically testable and practically actionable discipline.

By demonstrating that two instructional approaches can produce similar performance while imposing vastly different levels of mental effort, Paas revealed why outcome-based evaluation alone is insufficient. Instruction that "works" in the short term may still exhaust learners, accelerate disengagement, or undermine transfer if it consumes excessive cognitive resources. Mental effort, in this sense, becomes a diagnostic signal rather than a subjective complaint.

In *A Learning Republic*, Paas provides the empirical foundation for the concept of recoverable learning. His work supports instructional designs that allow learners to reorganize information into schemas without overload, making temporary difficulty productive rather than destructive. Most importantly, Paas introduces a standard of instructional accountability: when learning fails, the burden of explanation shifts from learner motivation to design quality. By measuring effort directly, his research makes it possible to distinguish necessary challenge from preventable exhaustion—an essential distinction for sustaining adult learning across the lifespan.

David C. Geary

Biologically Primary and Secondary Learning

David Geary distinguished between *biologically primary* learning—skills humans acquire naturally through evolution, such as language, social cognition, and basic tool use—and *biologically secondary* learning, which includes reading, mathematics, and formal scientific reasoning. Primary learning emerges effortlessly in supportive environments; secondary learning requires deliberate instruction, sustained effort, and cultural scaffolding.

Geary's framework explains why much of schooling feels cognitively taxing in ways that play, conversation, or imitation do not. Secondary learning competes directly for limited working-memory resources and is therefore vulnerable to overload, stress, and avoidance. When learners disengage, Geary argues, the cause is often evolutionary mismatch rather than lack of motivation.

In *A Learning Republic*, Geary's work clarifies why adult learning requires intentional design and why avoidance can be an adaptive response to poorly structured demands. His distinction supports the book's central claim that effortful learning must be made *recoverable* if adults are to sustain it across the lifespan.

Raymond B. Cattell (1905 – 1998) and John L. Horn (1928 - 2006)

Fluid and Crystallized Intelligence Across the Lifespan

Raymond Cattell and John Horn advanced the distinction between *fluid intelligence*—the capacity for novel problem solving and rapid processing—and *crystallized intelligence*, which reflects accumulated knowledge, experience, and expertise. While fluid abilities tend to peak earlier in life, crystallized intelligence often continues to grow well into adulthood.

This framework challenges deficit-based views of adult learning. Cognitive change across the lifespan is not simple decline, but reorganization. As processing speed slows, knowledge structures deepen, enabling judgment, pattern recognition, and transfer at higher levels of abstraction.

In *A Learning Republic*, Cattell and Horn provide a scientific basis for lifelong learning without nostalgia or alarmism. Their work reinforces the argument that adult education should leverage accumulated knowledge rather than mimic youth-oriented instructional models. Learning remains possible—and essential—when it aligns with how cognition actually evolves over time.

K. Warner Schaie (1928 – 2020)

Cognitive Trajectories Across the Lifespan

K. Warner Schaie's Seattle Longitudinal Study transformed understanding of adult cognition by showing that many intellectual abilities remain stable—or even improve—well into midlife and beyond, depending on education, occupation, health, and engagement. Decline, where it occurs, is neither uniform nor inevitable.

Schaie demonstrated that cognitive change is profoundly context-dependent. Adults who continue to learn, solve problems, and participate in intellectually demanding environments maintain higher levels of functioning than those who disengage. Learning, in this sense, is both a cause and a consequence of sustained capacity.

In *A Learning Republic*, Schaie's work supports the book's rejection of age-based deficit narratives. Cognitive trajectories are shaped by opportunity, expectation, and use. A republic that withdraws learning opportunities from adults accelerates decline; one that sustains them preserves both individual agency and civic competence.

Timothy Salthouse

Processing Speed, Compensation, and Adult Learning

Timothy Salthouse documented age-related changes in processing speed and working-memory efficiency, providing a precise account of why some cognitive tasks become more effortful with age. His work showed that declines in speed place greater demands on attentional coordination and temporary storage, increasing the cost of poorly structured tasks. Importantly, Salthouse also demonstrated that adults routinely compensate for these changes through accumulated knowledge, strategy selection, and experience.

Salthouse reframed cognitive aging not as a collapse of capacity, but as a shift in balance. As speed decreases, reliance on crystallized knowledge, pattern recognition, and strategic control increases. Learning remains robust when instruction aligns with these strengths, but falters when designs assume youthful processing rates or overload the coordination demands of working memory. Slower processing does not eliminate learning; it changes the conditions under which learning is efficient and sustainable.

Crucially, Salthouse's findings expose how age-neutral instructional norms can become age-biased in practice. Materials that rush pacing, fragment attention, or require rapid switching impose *extraneous cognitive load* that disproportionately harms adult learners—producing disengagement that is often misattributed to motivation or ability.

In *A Learning Republic*, Salthouse provides empirical grounding for age-aware instructional design. His research reinforces the claim that adult learning environments must respect pacing, reduce unnecessary coordination demands, and leverage prior knowledge if they are to remain viable across the lifespan. Learning failure, here again, is frequently a design failure rather than a personal one—a conclusion that aligns with the book's broader insistence on cognitive realism and instructional responsibility.

Alfred North Whitehead (1861 – 1947)

Inert Ideas, Lifelong Learning, and Institutional Re-Examination

Alfred North Whitehead warned that education fails when it produces *inert ideas*—knowledge received but not used, tested, or connected to life. Learning, he argued, must remain active, applied, and meaningful, or it decays into ritual without understanding. Ideas that do not enter experience cease to function as resources for judgment and instead become cognitive burdens.

Whitehead's critique was not anti-intellectual but anti-abstraction divorced from purpose. He insisted that ideas must shape action, guide interpretation, and be continually re-engaged in new contexts. Knowledge that cannot be used does not accumulate power; it exhausts attention. In this sense, inert learning is not merely ineffective—it actively undermines intellectual vitality.

Crucially, Whitehead also articulated what would later be called lifelong learning—and did so decades before the term entered policy discourse. In his 1939 Harvard commencement address, and again in the foreword to *Business Adrift* (1939),

Whitehead argued that the historical assumption underlying traditional education—that one generation could prepare the next for a largely unchanged world—had collapsed. In an era of accelerating scientific, technological, and social change, education could no longer be confined to youth. Learning, he insisted, must extend across the lifespan, with institutions continually re-examined in light of changing conditions.

Educational systems rooted in generational stability, Whitehead warned, risk producing graduates equipped for a world that no longer exists. When change becomes the norm rather than the exception, all institutions rooted in generational continuity without revision must be re-examined. Lifelong learning, in this formulation, is not enrichment or remediation—it is a structural necessity.

In *A Learning Republic*, Whitehead provides the philosophical foundation for the book's central claim: learning survives only when it remains alive, adaptive, and continuous. His work establishes lifelong learning not as a modern policy innovation, but as a logical response to modernity itself—one that places permanent responsibility on educational, civic, and professional institutions to evolve alongside the world they serve.

Malcolm Knowles (1913 – 1997)

Andragogy and Self-Directed Adult Learning

Malcolm Knowles extended Whitehead's insight into a theory of adult learning. Distinguishing *andragogy* from pedagogy, Knowles argued that adults learn most effectively when treated as self-directed agents rather than dependent recipients. Adult learners bring prior experience, established identity, and clear expectations of relevance.

Knowles emphasized facilitation over transmission. Learning succeeds when adults understand why something matters, retain control over pace and direction, and see their experience respected rather than overridden. Traditional pedagogic teaching methods, by contrast, often produces resistance or withdrawal.

In *A Learning Republic*, Knowles provides the adult-facing counterpart to childhood education models. His theory explains why lifelong learning cannot rely on compliance-based structures and why democratic societies depend on voluntary, self-directed intellectual engagement. Adult learning is not remediation—it is the normal condition of civic life.

Gabrielle Simcock

Early Experience and the Formation of Expectations

Gabrielle Simcock's research demonstrates that learning begins well before language or explicit memory, and that early experiences shape how infants interpret and respond to the world. Her work shows that even very young learners form expectations based on prior exposure, influencing attention, anticipation, and later learning behavior.

Simcock's findings challenge the assumption that learning readiness emerges only with formal instruction. Instead, she reveals that infants encode patterns of interaction—what to expect from caregivers, environments, and tasks—long before they can articulate those expectations. These early schemas influence whether novelty is approached with curiosity or avoidance.

In *A Learning Republic*, Simcock's work supports the claim that what later appears as disengagement or low motivation may reflect learned expectations about effort, reward, and safety, not conscious choice. Her research strengthens the book's argument that instructional design must account for developmental history, and that educational systems inherit cognitive conditions shaped long before schooling begins.

Appendix C — Public Interpreters of Learning

This appendix highlights public figures who confronted learning not as an abstraction, but as a lived civic challenge shaped by time, labor, inequality, culture, and community. These individuals interpreted the conditions of learning for the broader society—designing schools, settlements, movements, and institutions, or shaping public understanding through leadership and critique. In doing so, they often discovered that learning succeeds or fails less because of curriculum than because of the conditions under which it is attempted.

The figures included here span reformist, conservative, religious, secular, and labor traditions, reflecting the reality that champions of effective learning have emerged across ideological boundaries when human limits are taken seriously. Their work makes visible the gap between access and capacity, and between formal opportunity and meaningful participation.

Together, they demonstrate how learning systems, when interpreted and structured for public life, can either expand human potential or quietly exhaust it.

Robert Owen (1771–1858)

Education, Environment, and the Malleability of Human Capacity

Robert Owen was among the first modern thinkers to argue—empirically and unapologetically—that human character is shaped by environment, not fixed by nature. As a mill owner and social reformer, Owen rejected punitive discipline and instead redesigned working and learning conditions to cultivate cooperation, curiosity, and moral development.

At New Lanark in Scotland, Owen implemented reduced working hours, banned child labor for the very young, and established schools that emphasized play, observation, and moral education rather than rote memorization. He believed that learning could flourish only when fear and exhaustion were removed from daily life.

In *A Learning Republic*, Owen represents a foundational systems insight: learning outcomes cannot be separated from social design. His work anticipates modern findings in cognitive load theory, stress research, and developmental psychology—demonstrating that capacity expands when environments are structured to support it.

Although some of Owen's later utopian ventures failed economically, their educational core proved enduring: learning is not a reward for virtue, but a precondition for it.

Frances Wright (1795–1852)

Radical Education and Intellectual Autonomy

Frances "Fanny" Wright was one of the most radical educational thinkers of the early nineteenth century, advocating for universal, secular, and emancipatory education at a time when such views were widely condemned. She believed education should cultivate independent judgment rather than obedience—to church, state, or tradition.

Wright championed adult education, public lectures, and the dissemination of controversial ideas precisely because she viewed ignorance as a tool of social control. Her educational philosophy emphasized reason, science, and open inquiry, particularly for groups excluded from formal schooling, including women and the working poor.

In *A Learning Republic*, Wright represents the argument that learning is inseparable from intellectual freedom. Instruction that transmits skills without encouraging critical thought may increase productivity, but it does not produce citizens capable of self-government.

Wright's work also foreshadows later insights from signaling theory and civic education: when access to learning is restricted or stigmatized, credentials become markers of conformity rather than competence. Her insistence on open, public learning spaces aligns with the book's call for distributed, self-directed learning ecosystems beyond institutional walls.

Seth Luther (1795–1833)

Education, Time, and the Working Mind

Seth Luther was among the earliest American voices to argue that education could not be separated from working conditions or from workers' control over their time. A carpenter by trade and a labor activist by conviction, Luther observed that long hours, physical exhaustion, and economic precarity systematically deprived working people of the cognitive and temporal resources required for learning.

In his *Address to the Working Men of New England* (1832), Luther contended that formal education reforms were insufficient unless accompanied by reductions in labor hours. Learning, he argued, requires mental bandwidth, not merely access to schools. A twelve- or fourteen-hour workday left workers cognitively depleted, rendering education nominal rather than real.

In *A Learning Republic*, Luther's insight anticipates modern understandings of cognitive load, stress, and decision fatigue. His work underscores a central thesis of the book: when observers label adults as "unmotivated," they often overlook the structural conditions that have already consumed the learner's capacity to engage.

Luther thus represents an early recognition that learning opportunity without recoverability is illusion—a theme that resonates directly with contemporary adult education, workforce retraining, and lifelong learning policy.

Robert Dale Owen (1801–1877)

Public Education, Civic Equality, and Adult Learning

Robert Dale Owen carried his father's educational philosophy into the American civic and political arena. More pragmatic than his father, he worked to embed learning into the institutions of democracy rather than isolate it in experimental communities.

As a reformer, legislator, and intellectual, Robert Dale Owen championed free public education, women's rights, public libraries, and broader access to scientific and secular knowledge. He viewed education as essential not only for children, but for adults navigating rapid social and technological change.

In *A Learning Republic*, Robert Dale Owen exemplifies the translation of educational ideals into civic infrastructure. Where his father redesigned environments at the community level, the son sought to scale learning through public institutions capable of sustaining a democratic society.

His work reinforces a core theme of the book: a republic must invest not only in schools, but in lifelong learning systems that recognize adults as ongoing learners rather than finished products.

Horace Mann (1796–1859)

Common Schools and the Architecture of Civic Learning

Horace Mann championed the creation of free, universal public education as a means of social stability, economic mobility, and civic cohesion. He believed common schools could serve as the "great equalizer," preparing citizens not only for productive work but for participation in democratic life. Education, in Mann's view, was preventive infrastructure—reducing crime, disorder, and inequality by cultivating shared knowledge, habits, and moral sensibility.

Mann emphasized professional teacher training, standardized curricula, and moral education grounded in broadly shared civic values. These design choices reflected an urgent practical challenge: how to educate large populations rapidly and consistently in a young, diverse republic. Common schools succeeded precisely because they imposed order, predictability, and uniform standards where none had previously existed. In doing so, they dramatically expanded access to literacy and basic civic competence.

In *A Learning Republic*, Mann's legacy illustrates both the promise and the limits of institutional schooling. The very features that made common schools scalable—standardization, age-grading, and centralized curricula—also planted the seeds of later rigidity. Systems optimized for uniformity struggle to adapt to cognitive diversity, technological change, and lifelong learning beyond childhood.

Mann thus represents a foundational tension that runs throughout the book: institutions that expand access to learning can, over time, constrain learning if they fail to evolve. His work underscores the necessity of revisiting educational structures as conditions change, reminding readers that civic learning requires not only access and order, but adaptability across the lifespan.

Abraham Lincoln (1809–1865)
Restoring the Possibility of Learning

Abraham Lincoln's preservation of the Union and the abolition of slavery restored the civic possibility of learning in the United States. Emancipation did not merely remove a legal constraint; it reopened the conditions under which learning could occur as a right rather than a transgression. Without that restoration, later educational efforts—especially those directed toward formerly enslaved populations—would have been inconceivable.

Largely self-educated, Lincoln practiced lifelong learning under conditions of extreme cognitive, emotional, and moral load. He read continuously, returning to foundational texts in law, history, science, mathematics, and literature not for display but for clarification of judgment. Lincoln relied heavily on narrative, analogy, and parable as cognitive tools—means of compressing complexity, testing ideas, and communicating under uncertainty. He also made deliberate use of withdrawal and reflection, recognizing that disengagement was sometimes necessary for consolidation rather than avoidance.

In *A Learning Republic*, Lincoln represents learning as something leadership itself requires, not something completed in preparation for authority. His life demonstrates that adult learning remains possible under extraordinary strain when it is self-directed, purposeful, and tied to responsibility. Most importantly, Lincoln's actions made subsequent educational progress possible by reestablishing learning as a civic right rather than a conditional privilege.

Booker T. Washington (1856–1915)

Skill, Dignity, and Learning Under Constraint

Booker T. Washington emphasized practical education, vocational training, and economic self-sufficiency as pathways to dignity and social advancement for formerly enslaved people living under severe social and political constraints. Through the founding and leadership of the Tuskegee Institute, Washington demonstrated how disciplined skill development—agriculture, trades, industry, and applied science—could translate directly into individual agency and community resilience.

Washington's educational philosophy was grounded in realism. He understood that learning systems operate within existing power structures and that strategies for advancement must account for constraints as they exist, not as they are wished away. Competence-based learning, in his view, provided tangible proof of capability, reduced vulnerability, and created leverage in environments hostile to abstract claims of equality. Skill mastery was not merely economic preparation; it was a means of restoring self-respect and social standing through visible contribution.

Critics have often framed Washington's emphasis on vocational education as accommodationist, but such readings miss the strategic dimension of his approach. Washington did not deny the value of intellectual cultivation; he prioritized forms of learning that could survive immediate scrutiny, generate material stability, and sustain institutions under pressure. His work raises enduring questions about signaling: which forms of learning are legible, trusted, and rewarded under unequal conditions.

In *A Learning Republic*, Washington highlights the enduring value of competence-based learning—education that directly expands agency and improves material conditions. His approach complements, rather than contradicts, Du Bois's emphasis on intellectual leadership by illuminating a different problem: how learning functions when social recognition is scarce and failure carries disproportionate risk. Washington's legacy reinforces the book's broader claim that effective learning systems must be designed not only for ideal conditions, but for the realities learners actually face.

Theodore Roosevelt (1858–1919)

Strenuous Learning and the Discipline of Citizenship

Theodore Roosevelt understood learning as an active, lifelong process of self-formation tied directly to civic responsibility. Physically fragile as a child, Roosevelt deliberately cultivated strength of body and mind through disciplined effort, wide reading, and sustained engagement with history, natural science, literature, and public affairs. Learning, for Roosevelt, was not passive acquisition but strenuous practice.

Throughout his adult life, Roosevelt read voraciously and wrote extensively, producing serious historical and political works while serving in demanding public roles. He treated intellectual development as inseparable from character, believing that democratic citizenship required individuals capable of sustained attention, judgment, and moral courage. Ease, complacency, and comfort were, in his view, corrosive to both learning and self-government.

In *A Learning Republic*, Roosevelt represents the idea that adult learning must be chosen and exercised, not merely enabled. His emphasis on effort and discipline complements Franklin's self-directed curiosity and Lincoln's reflective judgment, illustrating a different but compatible mode of lifelong learning. Roosevelt's life demonstrates that learning capacity is strengthened through purposeful challenge—and that a republic depends on citizens willing to undertake that discipline rather than evade it.

John Dewey (1859–1952)

Learning by Doing

John Dewey reconceptualized education as an active, experiential process rather than the passive transmission of knowledge. Learning, he argued, occurs through inquiry—when individuals engage real problems, test ideas through action, reflect on consequences, and revise their understanding. Knowledge is not something possessed in advance of experience, but something constructed through it.

For Dewey, schools should function as miniature democracies: environments in which learners practice cooperation, deliberation, and shared problem-solving. Education was inseparable from civic life, because the habits required for learning—curiosity, reflection, tolerance of uncertainty—are the same habits required for democratic participation. Instruction divorced from lived experience, he warned, produces inert knowledge rather than judgment.

Dewey was attentive to the pace of social change. He recognized that industrialization, technological advancement, and shifting social roles continually reshape the problems citizens must confront. Education, therefore, could not be confined to childhood preparation; it had to cultivate adaptive intelligence capable of lifelong revision and learning. Fixed curricula and rote methods were ill-suited to societies defined by change.

In *A Learning Republic*, Dewey bridges cognitive theory and civic philosophy. His insistence that education prepare individuals for participation in an evolving society resonates directly with modern challenges of technological acceleration and adult learning under uncertainty. Dewey reinforces the book's central claim that learning is not merely preparation for democracy—it is democracy's ongoing practice.

Jane Addams (1860–1935)

Learning Embedded in Community

Jane Addams rejected the notion that education occurs only in classrooms or through formal instruction. Through Hull House and the broader settlement movement, she demonstrated that learning emerges from social participation, civic engagement, and shared problem-solving. For Addams, education was not a discrete activity separated from life, but a process embedded in work, family, culture, and community—especially for immigrants and working-class populations navigating the disruptions of industrialization.

Addams understood that learning capacity is shaped by material and social conditions. Poverty, insecurity, isolation, and humiliation narrow attention and suppress initiative, while safety, dignity, and belonging expand the cognitive space required for reflection and growth. Hull House functioned not merely as a service center, but as a learning environment in which individuals acquired language, civic understanding, and practical judgment through participation in civic life.

Her approach anticipated later insights from cognitive science and adult learning theory: learning fails not solely because of poor instruction, but because learners lack the bandwidth to engage. Addams did not romanticize struggle; she sought to reduce unnecessary burdens so that learning could occur organically through engagement with real problems.

In *A Learning Republic*, Addams exemplifies the principle that restoring learning capacity often requires restoring the conditions of life that make learning possible. Her work reinforces the book's claim that education policy cannot be separated from housing, labor, health, and civic inclusion. Learning, in Addams's account, is not transmitted—it is cultivated by creating environments in which people are able to participate, contribute, and be taken seriously as members of a shared civic project.

W. E. B. Du Bois (1868–1963)

Intellectual Leadership and the Life of the Mind

W. E. B. Du Bois insisted that full citizenship requires access not only to practical skills but to intellectual cultivation and leadership development. Education, in his view, was not merely a means of economic survival but a pathway to judgment, moral imagination, and civic agency. A democracy that limits learning to utility, Du Bois argued, risks producing compliance without vision.

His concept of the *"Talented Tenth"* has often been misunderstood as elitist, but it reflected a structural claim about democratic societies: complex social problems require thinkers, scholars, and cultural leaders capable of articulating shared aspirations, interpreting injustice, and challenging prevailing assumptions. Advanced intellectual development was not a privilege to be withheld, but a public good whose absence impoverishes civic life.

Du Bois rejected the false dichotomy between mass education and elite formation. He believed societies must cultivate broad competence and sustain pathways for advanced intellectual growth. When either dimension is neglected, the result is stagnation or stratification—populations trained for labor but excluded from leadership, or elites detached from the conditions of the many.

In *A Learning Republic*, Du Bois underscores a central tension that learning systems must navigate across the lifespan: how to expand access without flattening aspiration, and how to pursue inclusion without abandoning excellence. His work reinforces the book's claim that democratic learning requires not only inclusion, but the sustained cultivation of intellectual depth capable of renewing civic life.

Carter G. Woodson (1875–1950)

Historical Truth and Agency

Carter G. Woodson argued that education which ignores, distorts, or erases a people's history inflicts profound psychological and civic harm. When learners are taught a version of the past that denies their ancestors' agency, achievement, or complexity, education becomes alienating rather than empowering. Such instruction, Woodson warned, produces disengagement not because learners lack ability or motivation, but because learning itself is stripped of meaning.

Through his scholarship and the founding of what became Black History Month, Woodson sought to restore historical truth as a foundation for self-respect and agency. His work was not merely corrective but structural: he understood that accurate historical knowledge provides the cognitive and moral scaffolding necessary for learners to situate themselves within a shared civic narrative. Without that grounding, learners are asked to reason, aspire, and participate while standing on erased or falsified foundations.

Woodson's critique extended beyond curriculum to the deeper function of education. He argued that schooling divorced from truthful history trains compliance rather than judgment and habituates learners to accept diminished expectations of themselves and their role in society. In this sense, miseducation is not neutral error—it is a systematic constraint on learning capacity.

In *A Learning Republic*, Woodson reinforces the central claim that learning is inseparable from identity and meaning. Education that denies learners an honest account of their place in history undermines motivation, erodes trust, and weakens democratic participation. By insisting that historical truth is a prerequisite for agency, Woodson stands alongside Lincoln and Jefferson as a figure who understood that civic learning depends not only on access and instruction, but on the dignity conferred by truthful inclusion in the nation's story.

Peter Drucker (1909–2005)

The Knowledge Worker as Citizen

Peter Drucker interpreted learning as the defining condition of modern economic and civic life. In 1959, he coined the term *knowledge worker* to describe a new class of laborer whose primary capital was not physical strength or machinery, but information, judgment, and the capacity to learn continuously. For Drucker, learning was not merely a means to employment; it was the organizing principle of a society increasingly shaped by complexity and change.

Drucker insisted that the educated person is "the one who has learned how to learn—and to keep learning." As automation and specialization reshaped work, he warned that societies failing to educate their citizens continuously would face not only economic stagnation but moral and institutional decay. Knowledge work, in his view, demanded autonomy, responsibility, and the ability to integrate information into action—capacities indistinguishable from those required for democratic citizenship.

His concept of *management by objectives* depended on workers capable of self-direction, collaboration, and critical judgment. Authority could no longer rest solely on hierarchy or command; it required individuals who could understand goals, assess tradeoffs, and adapt intelligently. Learning thus became a shared responsibility across organizations, professions, and the lifespan.

In *A Learning Republic*, Drucker represents the transition from industrial education to lifelong civic learning. He reinforces the book's claim that adult learning is not optional enrichment but social infrastructure. When learning is confined to youth, both work and democracy deteriorate; when learning is sustained across adulthood, citizens remain capable of judgment, contribution, and renewal in a rapidly changing world.

George F. Will

Historical Context, Rigor, and the Misuse of Education

George F. Will has argued that education fails when it substitutes presentist moralization for historical context, or when it prioritizes therapeutic comfort over intellectual rigor. He contends that serious learning requires disciplined engagement with ideas, texts, and events on their own terms, rather than filtering them through contemporary moral frameworks that reward affirmation over understanding. When history is reduced to a vehicle for moral signaling, learning collapses into performance.

Will has further observed that the danger of conflating affirmation with education has been intensified by political and cultural frameworks that sort individuals into fixed categories based on traits beyond their control. These frameworks encourage validation in place of inquiry, discouraging the discomfort that genuine learning often entails. In such environments, disagreement is treated as harm, and intellectual challenge is reframed as exclusion.

For Will, education worthy of the name demands sustained attention, historical imagination, and respect for complexity. Intellectual rigor is not cruelty, and discomfort is not injustice; they are often the conditions under which judgment is formed. By shielding learners from difficulty in the name of care, institutions risk producing graduates fluent in moral posture but ill-prepared for reasoning across difference or uncertainty.

In *A Learning Republic*, Will represents public civic criticism as educational practice. His work reinforces the book's resistance to moralized explanations of failure and complements its critique of overload by highlighting a parallel danger: learning environments that avoid rigor in favor of affirmation erode the very capacities—historical judgment, empathy grounded in context, and intellectual resilience—that self-government requires.

Richard B. Birrer

Peace, Practice, and the Polymath Ideal

Richard Birrer, M.D., the author of Peace: A Compendium, exemplifies the kind of integrated, lifelong learner that *A Learning Republic* argues is essential to a durable democracy. Trained and practiced as a physician, Birrer has worked across emergency medicine, sports medicine, and academic clinical education, contributing extensively to the medical literature. His peer-reviewed research addresses themes such as injury prevention, clinical outcomes, physician education, and evidence-based practice, reflecting a sustained commitment to empirical rigor and patient-centered care.

In *Peace: A Compendium*, he undertakes an interdisciplinary examination of peace that draws from philosophy, ethics, psychology, history, and social science. Peace, in Birrer's formulation, is not merely the absence of conflict but an active condition requiring discernment, justice, and relational responsibility. For A Learning Republic, relational and structural peace must be woven into our learning systems and civic institutions. His work in writing children's literature reflects an appreciation for imagination, moral development, and the early formation of meaning. These works underscore an implicit developmental insight echoed throughout this book: that learning unfolds across stages, and that the capacities required for mature judgment must be carefully cultivated rather than prematurely imposed.

Beyond scholarship and writing, Birrer is a serious alpinist who has climbed the Seven Summits and more, a pursuit that reinforces a recurring theme across his life's work—the integration of physical discipline, long-term commitment, humility before complexity, and resilience under uncertainty. This experiential dimension illustrates learning that is not solely cognitive but embodied and sustained across the lifespan.

Richard Birrer is noteworthy not only for his individual works, but for the coherence of a scholarly and vigorous life lived across domains. In an age that increasingly rewards narrow specialization, his career offers a living counterexample: that breadth and depth can reinforce one another, and that a republic capable of sustaining peace may depend on citizens who can move fluently between practice, reflection, and care for the next generation.

Catherine Beecher (1800–1878)

Schools, Character, and the Moral Foundations of the Republic

Catherine Beecher was one of the most influential advocates for education in nineteenth-century America. At a time when educational opportunities for women were limited, Beecher argued that women should be educated not merely for personal refinement but for meaningful participation in the intellectual and moral formation of society. Through her writing, lecturing, and institutional work, she helped expand opportunities for women to become teachers and educational leaders.

Beecher believed that the health of the American republic depended upon the character and judgment of its citizens, and she saw education as the primary means of cultivating those qualities. In works such as A Treatise on Domestic Economy and The Duty of American Women to Their Country, she emphasized the role of the household and the classroom as foundational environments where habits of discipline, responsibility, and civic virtue could take root.

Although she worked within the cultural expectations of her era, Beecher helped transform teaching into a respected profession for women and encouraged the establishment of schools and training institutions to prepare them for that role. Her efforts contributed to the rapid expansion of teaching as a vocation for women during the nineteenth century, strengthening the educational infrastructure that supported a growing republic.

Tony Bennett (1926–2023)

Talent, Conviction, and the Voice of Conscience

Before he became one of the most enduring voices in American music, Tony Bennett—born Anthony Dominick Benedetto in New York City—served as an infantryman in the U.S. Army during the final months of World War II. As part of the 63rd Infantry Division, he fought in the Rhineland campaign and witnessed both the devastation of combat and the liberation of a Nazi concentration camp. Those experiences left a lasting impression, shaping his lifelong opposition to war and strengthening his conviction that human dignity must be defended wherever it is threatened.

One episode during his Army service would remain particularly formative. While stationed in occupied Germany after the war, Bennett encountered a friend from his New York neighborhood who was Black. Bennett invited him to share a holiday meal with his unit. In the segregated military culture of the time, the gesture angered his commanding officer, who publicly stripped Bennett of his corporal's rank. Soon afterward, Bennett was reassigned to Special Services, where soldiers organized musical performances for the troops. There, singing for fellow servicemen, Bennett began the performing career that would later make him famous.

Bennett never forgot the lessons of those years. The war's brutality and the injustice he witnessed reinforced his belief that prejudice and hatred ultimately destroy the very societies that tolerate them. In the 1960s he supported the civil-rights movement and marched with Dr. Martin Luther King Jr. in Selma, Alabama, joining many Americans who believed the country must live more fully up to its founding ideals.

Over a career spanning more than seven decades, Bennett became one of the great interpreters of the American songbook. Fellow singer Frank Sinatra once remarked, "For my money, Tony Bennett is the best singer in the business. He excites me when I watch him. He moves me." The praise reflected what audiences had long recognized: Bennett possessed not only technical mastery but the rare ability to communicate the emotional core of a song.

Bennett's life offers a reminder that some of the most important lessons in a free society are not learned in classrooms alone. They emerge from experience—through hardship, conscience, and the courage to act on what one knows to be right. In that sense, the young soldier who quietly defied prejudice by inviting a friend to dinner exemplified a principle at the heart of a learning republic: that the formation of character is as essential to self-government as the acquisition of knowledge.

Appendix D — U.S. Colleges and Universities Founded by 1830

Institution	Founded	Location	Original Orientation
Harvard University	1636	MA	Clerical, classical
College of William & Mary	1693	VA	Clerical, civic elite
St. John's College	1696	MD	Classical liberal arts
Yale University	1701	CT	Clerical
University of Pennsylvania	1740	PA	Classical, civic
Moravian College	1742	PA	Religious
University of Delaware	1743	DE	Classical
Princeton University	1746	NJ	Clerical
Washington & Lee University	1749	VA	Classical
Columbia University	1754	NY	Clerical, royal charter
Brown University	1764	RI	Classical
Rutgers University	1766	NJ	Religious
Dartmouth College	1769	NH	Clerical
College of Charleston	1770	SC	Classical
Salem College	1772	NC	Religious
Dickinson College	1773	PA	Classical
Hampden–Sydney College	1775	VA	Clerical
Transylvania University	1780	KY	Classical
Vincennes University	1801	IN	Frontier classical
Indiana University	1820	IN	Classical (early state)
McKendree University	1828	IL	Religious
LaGrange College (UNA)	1830	AL	Classical
Capital University	1830	OH	Religious

Sources: Institutional founding dates and original missions compiled from Geiger (2015), Rudolph (1962), Thelin (2011), and institutional archival records.

Appendix E — College Participation and Technological Drivers in the U.S.

The Print & Early Industrial Era / Elite College Era (1790–1850)

Decade	Enroll-ment	Gradu-ation	Delta	Driver	Reference Category
1790	<1%	<1%	~0	Printing press culture; literacy in early republic	Colonial college records; early Census
1800	<1%	<1%	~0	Newspaper expansion; postal networks	University archives; Rothblatt
1810	<1%	<1%	~0	Growth in civic information flow	State academy reports; Herbst
1820	~1%	<1%	~1%	Market Revolution begins; clerical needs rise	Census 1820; Goldin
1830	~1%	<1%	~1%	Early mechanical innovation; proto-engineering	Tyack; college catalogs
1840	1–2%	<1%	~1–2%	Telegraph revolution (1844) increases technical demand	Census 1840; engineering school rosters
1850	~2%	~1%	~1%	Railroad expansion; surveying & engineering	Census 1850; education abstracts

(Enrollment/attainment percentages are approximate and represent the share of young adults around college age.)

Appendix E — College Participation and Technological Drivers in the U.S.

Industrial & Technological Acceleration (1860–1910)

Decade	Enroll-ment	Gradu-ation	Delta	Driver	Reference Category
1860	2–3%	~1%	~1–2%	Land-grant colleges; steam industrialization	Morrill Act records; Commissioner reports
1870	~3%	~1%	~2%	Railroads; mechanized agriculture	Census 1870; Goldin & Katz
1880	3–4%	~1–2%	~2%	Electrification begins; telephone invention	Census 1880; enrollment ledgers
1890	4–5%	~2%	~2–3%	Corporate office systems; typewriter, adding machine	Commissioner of Education reports
1900	3–5%	2–3%	~1–2%	Early automobile industry; business administration emerges	NCES; Census 1900
1910	5–7%	~3%	~2–4%	Scientific management; early radio technology	NCES Table 105; Goldin reconstructions

(Enrollment/attainment percentages are approximate and represent the share of young adults around college age.)

Appendix E — College Participation and Technological Drivers in the U.S.

The Early 20th-Century Transition (1920–1940)

Decade	Enroll-ment	Gradu-ation	Delta	Driver	Reference Category
1920	~8%	3–4%	~4–5%	Electrification; telephone networks; automotive economy	Goldin & Katz (2008)
1930	10–12%	4–5%	~6–7%	Corporate complexity; radio broadcast engineering	NCES historical; Census 1930
1940	12–15%	~5%	~7–10%	Pre-war industrial science; aviation	Census 1940; NCES 1993 Table 193

(Enrollment/attainment percentages are approximate and represent the share of young adults around college age.)

Appendix E — College Participation and Technological Drivers in the U.S.

The War & Postwar Mass Education Era (1950–1980)

Decade	Enroll-ment	Gradua-tion	Delta	Driver	Reference Category
1950	~20%	~6%	~14%	WWII technologies; GI Bill; early computing	GI Bill records; NCES Table 104
1960	~25%	~7%	~18%	Space race; Cold War engineering	Census 1960; NCES 120 Years
1970	30–32%	11%	~19–21%	Mainframes; global corporate systems	Census 1970; Goldin & Katz
1980	~35%	22%	~13%	Personal computers; early software economy	NCES Digest; Census 1980

(Enrollment/attainment percentages are approximate and represent the share of young adults around college age.)

Appendix E — College Participation and Technological Drivers in the U.S.

The Digital & Early Internet Era (1990–2010)

Decade	Enroll-ment	Gradu-ation	Delta	Driver	Reference Category
1990	~40%	24%	~16%	Internet emergence; PC dominance	NCES 1940–1990 trends
2000	~50%	29%	~21%	Knowledge economy; IT and globalization	Census 2000; NCES 2000–10
2010	55–60%	32%	~23–28%	Smartphones; cloud computing; data economy	ACS 2010; NCES 2012 Digest
2020	60%+	38–40%	~20–22%	AI, automation, remote work infrastructure	ACS 2020; Lumina attainment reports

(Enrollment/attainment percentages are approximate and represent the share of young adults around college age.)

Appendix E — College Participation and Technological Drivers in the U.S.

The AI & Networked Era (2020–2030)

Decade	Enroll-ment	Gradu-ation	Delta	Driver	Reference Category
2020–2030 (pro-jected)	~55–60%	~35–40%	+20–25 pts	Ubiquitous broad-band; large-scale online degree pro-grams; MOOCs; AI-assisted instruction; employer-integrated learning; unbundled credentials	NCES trend data; OECD lifelong learning reports; online higher-education literature

(Enrollment/attainment percentages are approximate and represent the share of young adults around college age.)

Appendix F — U.S. College Enrollment by Field Group, 1790–1940

Year	%	Field Group	% Enrollment	% Population
1790	~0.8%	Classical Fields	~90%	~0.72%
		Education	~5%	~0.04%
		STEM & Technical	~3%	~0.02%
		Business & Professional	~1%	~0.01%
		Health & Applied	~1%	~0.01%
1870	~2%	Classical Fields	~80%	~1.6%
		Education	~10%	~0.2%
		STEM & Technical	~5%	~0.1%
		Business & Professional	~3%	~0.06%
		Health & Applied	~2%	~0.04%
1900	~5%	Classical Fields	~65%	~3.25%
		Education	~15%	~0.75%
		STEM & Technical	~10%	~0.5%
		Business & Professional	~7%	~0.35%
		Health & Applied	~3%	~0.15%
1920	~8%	Classical Fields	~55%	~4.4%
		Education	~18%	~1.4%
		STEM & Technical	~12%	~1.0%
		Business & Professional	~10%	~0.8%
		Health & Applied	~5%	~0.4%

Appendix F (*Continued*)

Year	%	Field Group	% Enroll-ment	% Population
1940	~15%	Classical Fields	~45%	~6.8%
		Education	~20%	~3.0%
		STEM & Technical	~15%	~2.3%
		Business & Professional	~12%	~1.8%
		Health & Applied	~8%	~1.2%

Appendix G — U.S. College Enrollment by Field Group, 1950–2020

Year	%	Field Group	% Enrollment	% Population
1950	~20%	Classical Fields	~45%	~9.0%
		Education	~20%	~4.0%
		STEM & Technical	~15%	~3.0%
		Business & Professional	~10%	~2.0%
		Health & Applied	~10%	~2.0%
1970	~30%	Classical Fields	~35%	~10.5%
		Education	~18%	~5.4%
		STEM & Technical	~20%	~6.0%
		Business & Professional	~17%	~5.1%
		Health & Applied	~10%	~3.0%
1990	~45%	Classical Fields	~28%	~12.6%
		Education	~14%	~6.3%
		STEM & Technical	~25%	~11.3%
		Business & Professional	~23%	~10.4%
		Health & Applied	~10%	~4.5%
2020	~60%	Classical Fields	~20%	~12.0%
		Education	~9%	~5.4%
		STEM & Technical	~32%	~19.2%
		Business & Professional	~27%	~16.2%
		Health & Applied	~12%	~7.2%

Appendix H — Major Non-College Learning Pathways, 1790–1945

Era	Pathways	Partici-pation	Skills	Driver	Reference
1790–1820 Early Republic	Appren-ticeships; self-study; guild-like training	High	Craft skills; literacy; numeracy	Agrarian economy; early mechani-zation	Labor history; early U.S. education
1820–1870 Industrial Expansion	Appren-ticeships; mechanics' institutes; military acad-emies	High	Mechani-cal skills; surveying; engineering basics	Steam power; railroads; telegraph	Industrial education history
1870–1920 Second Industrial Revolution	Trade schools; nor-mal schools; corporate training	Growing	Engineering; accounting; management	Electrifica-tion; mass produc-tion	Progressive Era education
1920–1945 Corporate & Bureau-cratic Era	Vocational schools; corporate training; cor-respondence courses	High	Clerical; technical; administra-tive	Electri-fication; corporate bureau-cracy	Business history

Appendix I — Major Non-College Learning Pathways, 1945 – 2030

Era	Pathways	Partici-pation	Skills	Driver	Reference
1945–1970 Postwar Expansion	GI Bill training; community colleges; union apprenticeships	Very high	Technical trades; applied science	Cold War; industrial science	Federal education policy
1970–1990 Computerization	Corporate IT training; certifications	Moderate–high	Programming; systems operation	Mainframes; PCs	Workforce development
1990–2010 Internet Era	Online certifications; bootcamps; vendor training	High	IT; networking; software	Internet; globalization	Digital learning
2010–2020 Platform Era	Bootcamps; MOOCs; employer training	Very high	Data; software; analytics	Cloud computing	Online learning research
2020–2030 AI & Networked Era	Microcredentials; AI-assisted training; lifelong learning	Expanding	AI literacy; adaptive skills	AI; automation	OECD / WEF

Appendix J — Evolution of College Curricula by Technological Era

Era	Curriculum	Technology Integration Level	New Degree Types Introduced	Lag vs. Technology
1790–1850 Classical Elite Era	Classical liberal arts	Minimal	None	Very high
1850–1870 Early Industrial	Classical + moral philosophy	Low	Civil engineering (limited)	High
1870–1900 Land-Grant Era	Liberal arts + applied science	Moderate	Engineering; agriculture	Moderate
1900–1940 Progressive Era	Expanded sciences; professional schools	Growing	Business; education	Moderate
1945–1970 Postwar Science	STEM expansion	High	Physics; engineering; CS (early)	Lower
1970–1990 Computing Era	STEM + electives	High	Computer science	Low
1990–2010 Digital Economy	Interdisciplinary tech	High	IT; IS; digital media	Low
2010–2020 Platform Era	Online & hybrid programs	Very high	Data science; cybersecurity	Low
2020–2030 AI Era	Modular, adaptive curricula	Emerging	AI; ML; analytics	TBD

About the Author

Steve Satterfield is an educator and software engineer, and a U.S. Air Force veteran whose work draws on cognitive science, technology, and adult education. He is an adjunct faculty member at Southern New Hampshire University and teaches computer science and software development, working primarily with adult learners who balance education with professional, military, and family responsibilities. His teaching emphasizes clarity, durable understanding, and the development of learning habits that extend beyond any single course or credential.

Dr. Satterfield holds advanced degrees in neuropsychology and computer science, along with specialist and doctoral degrees in education. His academic preparation spans cognitive science, software engineering, and instructional design, and his professional experience includes developing and maintaining complex technical systems in high-consequence environments such as nuclear engineering and electronic warfare, as well as teaching in applied, skills-focused programs.

A Learning Republic represents his first sustained exploration of civic education. In this work, he brings together insights from cognitive science and technology to examine how individuals learn, adapt, and update their understanding over time—and why that capacity is foundational to democratic life under conditions of rapid change. In an era marked by large-scale migration and an expanding civic body shaped by diverse cultural and ethical traditions, Dr. Satterfield emphasizes the importance of shared civic understanding and the learning capacities that allow democratic principles to be understood, transmitted, and sustained across generations.

A republic does not sustain itself.

It depends upon citizens capable of disciplined thought, skilled work, and moral seriousness. From the artisan workshops of the early American republic to the collaborative technologies of the present, learning has always been the invisible infrastructure of self-government.

Freud suggested that psychological health rests on the capacity to love and to work. Constitutional health rests on a third pillar: the capacity to reason. A republic endures only when its citizens can work productively, love generously, and reason clearly about the common good.

In *A Learning Republic*, Steve Satterfield traces how learning—formal and informal, scholarly and practical—forms the character required for constitutional liberty. Drawing from history, cognitive science, and lived technical experience, he argues that education is not merely preparation for employment. It is the sustaining architecture of freedom.

A free society cannot be inherited passively. It must be learned.